D0910130

THE FIRST AND SECOND UNITED STATES EMPIRES

The First and Second United States Empires *Governors and Territorial Government, 1784–1912*

Jack Ericson Eblen

University of Pittsburgh Press

Library of Congress Catalog Card Number: 68-21623

Manufactured in the United States of America

For Trudi
and Jennifer

Acknowledgments

MOST of the research for this study was done at the Wisconsin Historical Society Library, the University of Wisconsin Library, the Library of Congress, and the National Archives. Their staffs deserve special thanks, but the people at every library and depository visited in the course of preparing this book were exceptionally kind and helpful. Vernon Carstensen and the Graduate School of the University of Wisconsin provided the fellowships that largely supported the first years of work on the study. Subsequently, I have received a University Faculty Fellowship, a Research Foundation Grant, and other financial and material assistance from the University of Connecticut that enabled me to do additional research and prepare the manuscript for publication.

I am indebted to the following people for ideas, encouragement, and constructive criticism: Robert Calhoun of the University of North Carolina at Greensboro; David A. Baerreis, Allan G. Bogue, Paul Buhle, Merle Curti, Philip D. Curtin, and Eric Lampard of the University of Wisconsin; James D. Norris of the University of Missouri at St. Louis; Van Beck Hall of the University of Pittsburgh; John Bloom, editor of the *Territorial Papers*, at the National Archives; and to my colleagues in the History Department at the University of Connecticut, particularly Richard Orr Curry, R. Kent Newmyer, Thomas G. Paterson, and Robert F. Smith. Richard Boyer, Hope

Becker, and Sharon Mullins, also of the University of Connecticut, offered additional criticisms as well as material assistance; Raymond Blanchette, of the University of Connecticut Publications Department, prepared the map and chart for publication; and David P. Henige of Toledo, Ohio, provided the data on the tenure of state governors for Chapter IX. I owe my largest debts, however, to Vernon Carstensen of the University of Washington, with whom I worked for four years as a graduate student at the University of Wisconsin, to the Goodnight-Loving Institute, and to my wife Trudi, who helped immeasurably during every phase of research and writing.

Contents

Tables, Diagram, Map

THE FIRST AND SECOND UNITED STATES EMPIRES

Introduction

FROM the turn of the century to the present, a diverse group of scholars, which includes Frederick Jackson Turner as well as Richard W. Van Alstyne, has pointed to imperialism as a primary determinant or cardinal feature of United States history. Van Alstyne and Alpheus H. Snow, among others, have traced the evolution of the idea of an American empire and demonstrated that the founders of the republic intended the United States to be an imperial state in the sense both that it would possess territories and that it would exercise preponderant influence over far-flung areas. To this end, in 1787 the Confederation Congress adopted a system of colonial government for its possessions Northwest of the Ohio River, while the Philadelphia Convention drafted a new Constitution that vested imperial powers in a stronger central government. Early leaders could not always agree on the proper territorial limits of the incorporated empire, as opposed to the American sphere of influence, but they were as one in the conviction that the United States should extend its hegemony to comprehend, and "reform," much if not all of the world.[1] Their conviction has persisted to the present.

Van Alstyne concentrates on the unrelenting passion for both continental and overseas expansion and on the tenacity of the notion

1. Richard W. Van Alstyne, *The Rising American Empire* (Oxford, 1960); Alpheus H. Snow, *The Administration of Dependencies. A Study of the Evolution of the Federal Empire, with Special Reference to American Colonial Problems* (New York, 1902).

that the United States had a "mission" and was "destined" to become a "moral leader" in an immoral world. However, in documenting the fundamental continuity of an expansionist ideology throughout United States history, he does not deny the presence of change. On the contrary, he also shows that as the industrial state matured late in the nineteenth century, America's quest for markets and influence abroad superseded in overall importance the march across the continent, and that the advocates of expansion adapted their rhetoric to the shifting focus of empire without altering the underlying rationale of imperialism. Thus, by implication, Van Alstyne divides United States expansion into the two eras commonly accepted by modern historians.

If special attention is given to the progressive enlargements of the empire, in terms both of the changing character and of the primary focus of American imperialism since the founding of the republic, a more refined periodization, consisting of four general phases, becomes discernible. These phases necessarily overlap significantly in some respects; nonetheless, each is distinct enough to warrant the four being treated as separate empires. The First Empire, covering the sixty-year period between 1787 and 1848, extended from the Appalachian Mountains through the first tier of states west of the Mississippi River. The Second, dating from 1848 to the 1890s, consisted of the Great Plains, the Rocky Mountain region, and the Pacific Slope. The Third, embracing the generation from the 1890s to about 1920, included Alaska and a number of islands and concessions in the Pacific and the Caribbean. We are currently somewhere in the era of the Fourth Empire, which emerged as a distinctive period in the 1920s and which encompasses most of the world. Since the basic geographic scope of the empires differs, they may also be given descriptive names and identified as the Mississippi Valley, Trans-Continental, Oceanic, and Global Empires respectively.

Aside from the geographic differences, there were distinct levels of technology and industrialization associated with each empire. For example, there is a rough parallel between W. W. Rostow's stages of economic growth[2] and the four phases of United States imperialism.

2. *The Stages of Economic Growth. A Non-Communist Manifesto* (London, 1960).

The First Empire was essentially pre-industrial, although it includes the period of incipient industrialization. Westward expansion in this period was not characterized by capitalistic forms of organization, except in land speculation. In contrast, the Second Empire (which corresponds to Rostow's "Take-off" and "Drive to Maturity") was an era of rapid capital accumulation and industrialization, along the continental frontiers as well as in the East. The Third Empire was one of flux—of economic reorientation and consolidation on the American continent, accompanied by increasing capitalist expansion abroad—manifesting traits of the too-brief period that Rostow inappropriately calls "Phase One" of "The Age of High Mass-Consumption." With some changes in tactics, overseas expansion has continued unabated in the Fourth Empire—that is, during the remaining phases of Rostow's "Age of High Mass-Consumption." As the United States realizes its ambition of global empire, it finds itself simultaneously in the terminal period of Rostow's universal schema of economic development.

The First and Second Empires encompass the era of overland expansion during which the Anglo-Americans expropriated, segregated, and relentlessly strove to exterminate the American Indians, occupied their lands in ever-growing numbers, and, under the direction of the federal government, formed the true colonies ordinarily referred to, in euphemistic terms, as "territories." The Confederation Congress organized the Mississippi Valley Empire in 1787, following its enactment of the Northwest Ordinance. Within the succeeding sixty years, Congress subdivided the Old Northwest—the five-state region north of the Ohio River, and extended the provisions of the Ordinance to the public domain south of the Ohio River and to the Louisiana Purchase west of the Mississippi, organizing new colonies in each region when it deemed expedient. As it turned out, Congress organized colonies and admitted them to statehood with some regularity; overall, the organization and absorption of possessions occurred concurrently as the Anglo-Americans moved out from the population centers. This casual expansion and liquidation of the First Empire ended with Wisconsin's admission to statehood in May 1848. At that time, and for the only time since 1787, the United States had no organized possessions. All of the territories east of the Mississippi

River and the first tier of states west of it, with the exception of Minnesota, had become fully incorporated members of the imperial state. The remainder of the Louisiana Purchase—that is, the Great Plains, which was still popularly known as the Great American Desert and officially labeled the Permanent Indian Frontier—was closed to settlement and, like the Oregon Country and Mexican Cession, was unorganized.

The system of colonial government to be used for the administration of the succeeding two empires was modified as it matured during the first fifty years of the Mississippi Valley Empire, and refined during the last decade (1838–1848). In the meantime, American expansionists reassessed the imperial capacities of the nation and reoriented federal policies accordingly. During the Revolutionary and Confederation periods, the mood of the country may not have been pessimistic, but aside from the positive economic impetus for imperialism engendered by the potential and real wealth of the trans-Appalachian West, the attitude toward empire was certainly defensive. Specifically, American leaders placed a high strategic value on having a colonial empire in the interior of the continent, largely because they thought western settlements would guard the fledgling nation against foreign interference and assure its independence. Initially, Jefferson, among others, questioned the wisdom of attempting to bring the transmontane West into the new Union and talked about creating a separate yet closely allied confederation of states between the Appalachian Mountains and the Mississippi River. By 1780, however, Congress settled the issue by resolving to make the colonies of the trans-Appalachian West into states—equal members of the Union—when they were mature. Early in the nineteenth century there was similar questioning of the efficacy of incorporating first the Louisiana Purchase and then the Pacific Slope. As late as 1825, the ardent expansionist, Thomas Hart Benton, still called the Continental Divide the "natural and everlasting boundary" of the United States and agitated for the creation of a friendly, Anglo-American republic west of the Rocky Mountains under American tutelage.[3]

Between 1825 and 1848, however, the country underwent a trans-

3. Frederick Merk, *Albert Gallatin and the Oregon Problem* (Cambridge, Mass., 1950), 13; quoted in Van Alstyne, 94.

formation in thinking. As John Quincy Adams' continental vision gained currency, the classical idea of natural limits gave way to voracious expansionism. By 1840, if not sooner, the idea of forming a transcontinental empire became popular even though the Great Plains and Rocky Mountains remained formidable barriers to the settlement and retention of the Far West. But on the eve of the Mexican War it was clear that the United States could vault the geographic obstacles and, equally important, that at least the eastern Plains could be brought under cultivation or used for grazing. During the Mexican War, as the feasibility of a transcontinental empire was firmly established, the somewhat circumspect attitude of previous generations gave way to one of boundless optimism and far-reaching imperial ambitions. By 1848, the United States also began again to cast covetous eyes on Canada and was ready to consider making new thrusts into Latin America. As Van Alstyne suggests, it was probably only the rapidly developing sectional crisis that kept the United States from forging an insular empire in the Caribbean between 1848 and the end of the Civil War.

The United States began collecting real estate for a Second Empire before the end of the First. The Adams-Onís Treaty, ratified in 1821, settled the Louisiana Purchase boundary and established an American claim to the Pacific Slope north of the 42nd parallel. The United States, however, did not acquire a definitive title to the Oregon Country until 1846, when the British ceded their claim south of the 49th parallel. During the preceding year the republic of Texas had been annexed, and during the ensuing war with Mexico the United States seized and annexed the 650,000 square miles of northern Mexico lying between Texas and the Pacific Ocean north of the Gila River. Thus, with the exception of the small area south of the Gila that was purchased in 1853, the United States reached the present boundaries of its contiguous territories between 1845 and 1848. Nevertheless, it is symbolic that Mexico and the United States did not formally exchange ratifications of the Guadelupe-Hidalgo Treaty confirming the cession of northern Mexico until May 30, 1848, a day after Wisconsin's statehood brought the First Empire to an end, and three months before Congress provided for the organization of Oregon, the first colony of the Second Empire.

The Trans-Continental Empire can be divided into two phases of approximately equal length. During the first phase, Congress organized thirteen settlement territories in addition to Oregon, and established an administrative imperium over the future state of Oklahoma—the remnant of the Permanent Indian Frontier—thereby extending some form of colonial government to all of its contiguous possessions. Between 1858 and 1868 five territories—Minnesota, Oregon, Kansas, Nevada, and Nebraska—also became states, so the pattern of organization and liquidation was not dissimilar to that of the First Empire. In contrast, the second phase of the Second Empire, beginning with General Grant's ascendance to the Presidency, was one of stability. Except for the admission of Colorado in 1876, the Empire remained unchanged for twenty years. During this time Congress created no new territories, and its members gave up their efforts to secure the enactment of an Organic Act extending the standard form of territorial government to Indian Territory. Instead, toward the end of the period, the government began removing and concentrating the Indians in order to provide additional land for Anglo-American settlement. In 1889 the area cleared of Indian titles was thrown open to settlement, and the following year it was organized as Oklahoma Territory.

Although Oklahoma did not become a state until 1907, largely because the federal government had difficulty deciding on how to dispose of the ever-shrinking Indian Territory, the commitment implicit in creating it as a white man's country suggests that its very organization was an integral part of the final liquidation of the Second Empire. The timing of the organization of Oklahoma supports this view, for in 1889 and 1890 five of the territories that had existed when Grant became President were transformed into six states: Washington, Idaho, Montana, Wyoming, and North and South Dakota. As with Oklahoma, however, narrow cultural attitudes helped to delay inordinately the statehood of the three remaining contiguous territories. Congress did not seriously consider admitting Utah until after 1890, when the Mormons began to show signs of willingness to conform to "Gentile" norms and the Church hierarchy officially abandoned polygamy. In addition, by 1896 the federal government had gained about as much as it ever would through its long-drawn-out campaign to break the political power of the Mormon Church, and Congress made Utah a state. A majority of Arizona's population—Indians excluded—was Anglo-American, but the number of settlers was deemed to be too small to warrant statehood. On the other hand, the Latin-Americans far outnumbered Anglo-Americans in the more populous New Mexico, and given the atmosphere of "scientific racism" that prevailed toward the turn of the century, which reinforced the already strong Anglo-American ethnocentrism, it is not surprising that New Mexico was not regarded as worthy of statehood. When, in 1905, Congress attempted to overcome the problems that these two territories presented by passing an enabling act to combine them and make one state, the Arizonans balked—in part because of the basic impracticality of joining such widely separated settlements into a single state, but perhaps more because of their fear of Latin-American domination—and the territories were not admitted separately until 1912. Thus, while the Second Empire as such may be said to have ended effectively early in the 1890s, it had a rather prolonged afterlife, or perhaps more appropriately, aftermath.

In the meantime, the United States had set out to organize an Oceanic Empire stretching from Puerto Rico to Asia. As in the case of the Trans-Continental Empire, the acquisition of territory for a Third Empire preceded both the general public concern for new areas of expansion and the dissolution of the Second Empire. The first successful annexation of noncontiguous lands occurred in 1867, when the United States purchased Alaska and occupied Midway. In the same year it almost bought the Virgin Islands, and during the succeeding thirty years, the United States unsuccessfully sought to procure a number of other islands, in both the Caribbean and the Pacific, and exclusive control over the right of way for an interocean canal in Central America. Congress took the first tentative step toward organizing an Oceanic Empire in 1884, when it passed the Alaska Organic Act, but the government did little to implement the Act. Consequently, it was not until the Spanish-American War that the United States seized and annexed the principal islands around which the Third Empire was built, and set up the administrative machinery to govern them. At the time that the Third Empire came into existence, the government had completed the primary liquidation of the Second Empire, the continental frontier had "come to an end," industrial capitalism had reached maturity, and the presumed need for large overseas markets had gained widespread acceptance.

During the first two empires, the Indian population of the United States was replaced primarily by Anglo-Americans, who carried with them the institutions and traditions of the older territories and states. As a result of this change in the character of the population, federal officials were either unwilling or unable to reverse the trend toward territorial autonomy, which developed during the First Empire and persisted throughout the Second. Even in the case of Utah, the federal government objected primarily to the tenets and power of the Mormon Church rather than to the existence of territorial autonomy.

In contrast, the territories of the Third Empire, besides Alaska, were not sparsely inhabited by people who could easily be pushed aside. The government could expect Alaska's mining population to be largely transient and unruly—that is, to require strong government. Similarly the principal islands, although they were densely populated, did not share an Anglo-American culture. Since they were not considered likely to become Anglo-American settlement areas, the United States government would not entrust the native peoples with republican institutions, except under close supervision. Consequently, although Congress used the time-honored model of the Mississippi Valley Empire in organizing the Oceanic Empire, it made minor changes that significantly altered the character of administration, and the federal government exercised its full powers to assure tight imperial control. In so doing, the United States created a true administrative empire, much like those of the European nations in the era of the "white man's burden." It did not deliberately destroy or remove the indigenous populations as it had on the mainland; rather, they were governed and exploited by an elite cadre of the imperial government backed by the military.

The Third Empire did not end abruptly. On the contrary, some parts have yet to escape their inferior status. The seat of the Empire is among them, for the District of Columbia is still governed as despotically as any colonial area in American history. Following the First World War, however, the governments of the major colonies began to conform more closely to the pattern of the mainland empires as the inhabitants adapted, as substantial Anglo-American settlements took root in the colonies, and as more positive attitudes toward the capacity of indigenous groups to run their own affairs developed. Subsequently the Empire was partially liquidated: the Philippines won "independence," Alaska and Hawaii attained statehood, and Congress extended home rule to Puerto Rico and the Virgin Islands.

Judging from these considerations, it would seem that the dividing line between the Third and Fourth Empires is purely arbitrary; nonetheless, important changes in the tactics and scope of American imperialism as well as in the status of the United States make the two distinct entities. For one thing, the transition from Oceanic to Global Empire corresponds with America's emergence as the preeminent world power. This can be reasonably dated about 1920, when the United States became the undisputed creditor nation of the world. By that time it was also a giant among the mature industrial exporting nations. In addition, after World War I somewhat more subtle forms of indirect or informal political and economic imperialism—or, to use the current euphemism, penetration—clearly superseded the direct forms that were by then thoroughly discredited. Finally, by 1920 the idea of forging a Global Empire had ceased to be an abstraction.

Ideological expansion, based on the twin notions of the superiority of American institutions and the "Manifest Destiny" or "mission" of the white Anglo-Americans, is a prime feature of the Global Empire. These ideas have roots deep in the Puritan past, but until well into the nineteenth century ideological imperialism was essentially defensive, restrictive, and tentative in character. It was not until 1823, when President Monroe proclaimed an hegemony over the entire Western Hemisphere, that the United States formally declared imperial goals. Whether or not the Monroe Doctrine was defensive in conception, it became a tool for aggressive overseas expansion around midcentury. Nevertheless, it did not really come into its own until the end of the century as John Hay, Theodore Roosevelt, and others began extending it to include Eastern Asia and amplified its meaning.

Similarly, at the dawn of the twentieth century, informal economic imperialism assumed its characteristic pattern. As the United States economy matured, American industrial and finance capitalists went abroad to meddle in the economies of other countries. This new imperialism first supplemented the much older maritime commerce, which for several centuries had been expansive, and since the end of the eighteenth century had been worldwide in scope, and then surpassed it in importance. Capitalistic expansion gave rise to informal empire as varying degrees of economic and political control emanated from American investments. The United States government did not intend to administer these new colonial areas directly, but in the twentieth century it has increasingly intervened militarily and in other ways, both overtly and covertly, in the affairs of its economic dependencies "to protect" its own and its citizens' "interests."

The pattern of informal empire was well developed before World War I, yet its scope was not global. Government and business still looked primarily to the Western Hemisphere and East Asia for markets and investments, in spite of the fact that the Europeans continued to be their largest customers. After World War I, however, both government and business began to appreciate fully the existing potential for economic expansion across the Atlantic. At about the same time, Africa assumed new importance. Thus, around 1920, informal expansion on a worldwide scale came to typify American imperialism, and the United States moved into the period of Global Empire.

Though all the different kinds of expansion were present in each phase, in terms of predominance there has been a rather regular progression from the First to the Fourth Empire, paralleling the nation's growth in wealth and power, which may be reduced to the rhetoric of the "Cold War." After independence, the United States adopted a defensive "containment" policy, ostensibly to protect itself from European interference, and proceeded to implement it by creating the First Empire and enlarging its territorial possessions. Toward the middle of the nineteenth century, however, the defensive posture gave way to an offensive one, as is illustrated by the aggression against Mexico and the Oregon settlement. During the last half of the century the United States redefined its policy to include the Pacific, consolidated its overseas gains, and by formally extending the Monroe Doctrine to East Asia at the end of the century, brought over half of the world within its ring of containment. Since then, the ring has been contracting, more or less constantly, around America's competitors and foes—currently the "Communist World." The modern, aggressive containment policy is buttressed by elaborate alliance systems, but its enforcement is primarily dependent upon the global application of the Monroe Doctrine through United States interventions, which in recent years increasingly suggest a return to the direct administrative imperialism of the Third Empire.

This modern imperialism in many respects parallels the development of nineteenth-century Indian policy. After gaining their independence, the Americans established an hegemony over the "domestic dependent nations" of the Indians within the boundaries claimed by the United States. The fur trade epitomized this hegemony in economic terms. In the mid-1780s, Congress began creating an informal imperium like that exercised by the English prior to the Revolution. It enacted laws systematizing its relations with the Indians and regulating the Indian trade, but made no effort to govern the Indians directly. Instead, the federal government officially regarded the Indian tribes as sovereign nations within the American sphere of influence, and dealt with them through pseudo-diplomatic channels. Until the 1870s, it continued to maintain the façade of Indian sovereignty and acted as if Indian treaties, for example, were equivalent to any international agreements between peers. In the meantime, however, the federal government intervened increasingly in Indian affairs, both militarily and through political and economic intrigue—in ways not dissimilar to those currently used by the United States overseas. The American hegemony over the Indians, of course, expanded with territorial acquisitions and the growth of national power. By the 1860s, moreover, indirect controls gave way fully to direct management of Indian nations, and in the early 1870s Congress formally declared them to be "wards" of the State; that is, true administrative imperial possessions or colonies.

Within the next fifteen years another trend reached maturity. In 1887 Congress adopted the Dawes Severalty Act, whose purpose was to "Americanize" the American Indians—a goal not alien to modern American expansion and "foreign aid" programs. With the Dawes Act various governmental and "humanitarian" movements, some of them nearly a century old, realized their desire for a comprehensive plan by which to destroy Indian cultures and convert the "savages" to the blessed trinity of agrarianism, Christianity, and republicanism.

They never succeeded, but the Anglo-Americans have not yet given up their efforts to remake the Indians. In terms of ideological objectives, the Third Empire can be viewed as a logical outgrowth and extension of American Indian policies. It was also a logical combination of the administrative forms used for the Indian "reservations" and the Anglo-American settlement colonies of the Second Empire. The Fourth Empire, in this context, approximates an implicit reversion to the earliest Indian policies of the United States, with respect both to its informal structure and to its goal of "Americanizing" other peoples. Moreover, in both cases of informal imperialism there has been a marked correspondence between the greater use of force to induce conformity and the growth of United States power.

Once stated, the division of United States expansion into four empires is obvious enough, but it is an altogether different matter to go beyond the outline to a detailed general history. This study deals with only a portion of that history, the government of the First and Second Empires. It is a logical prerequisite for the larger undertaking, designed to meet the long-standing need for a comprehensive analysis of territorial government on the continent that is divorced from the narrow ideological confines of the debate over the Turner thesis.

Max Farrand[4] outlined the structural development of the governmental system in federal law but did not examine its operation. More recently, Earl Pomeroy[5] did a fairly extensive analysis of federal-territorial relations from 1861 to 1890, but he did not deal with territorial law in depth and only touched on the local power structures and their significance. Howard Lamar[6] and a few other scholars have since written intensive studies on politics in one or more territories, but have paid little attention to local government.[7] Moreover, like Pomeroy, those people who have dealt with the trans-Mississippi

4. *The Legislation of Congress for the Government of the Organized Territories of the United States, 1789–1895* (Newark, 1896).

5. *The Territories and the United States, 1861–1890. Studies in Colonial Administration* (Philadelphia, 1947).

6. *Dakota Territory, 1861–1889. A Study of Frontier Politics* (New Haven, 1956, 1966); *The Far Southwest, 1846–1912. A Territorial History* (New Haven, 1966).

7. Francis Philbrick's Introduction to *The Laws of Indiana Territory, 1801–1809* (Springfield, Ill., 1930), is the major exception to this generalization.

West have tended to base their studies on the unwarranted assumption that the government of their areas, primarily after 1860, differed fundamentally from that of the earlier, more eastern territories. There has, of course, also been a flood of writing on the validity of the Turner thesis during the past seventy-five years, but, as John Barnhart pointed out fifteen years ago, the particularistic debate on Turner's central theme—that American democracy is a product of the frontier—"has become [and remains in 1968] largely an exchange of opinions which has generated more heat than light."[8] Thus, in short, surprisingly little work of major importance has been done on the origins, evolution and operation of territorial government, and none of it has been comprehensive.

Any analysis or interpretation is necessarily selective, and in the case of the territorial system it is neither feasible nor desirable to give equal attention to the governments in each of the twenty-eight contiguous territories, whose cumulative existence from 1784 to 1912 was 544 years. This study is built on an intensive examination of the First Empire partially because of its transcendent importance. As Howard Lamar has noted, the early "governing officers . . . encountered every major problem that faced administrators of all territories established subsequently . . . [and] set many important precedents and patterns" that "virtually determined territorial policy."[9] Consequently, a thorough understanding of the evolution of government during the First Empire is essential to any interpretation of the Second Empire. Since much of the scholarship on the First Empire is weak and none of it is comprehensive, concentration on the period prior to 1848 was dictated in part by necessity. On the other hand, there are some excellent studies of government in the period after 1860 which could be used to supplement a detailed analysis of the First Empire to permit generalization over the whole period of continental expansion.

An understanding of the Ordinance of 1787, the cornerstone of American colonialism, is clearly central to a viable analysis of the First Empire, not to mention the Second, but heretofore its origins and

8. *Valley of Democracy. The Frontier versus the Plantation in the Ohio Valley, 1775–1818* (Bloomington, Ind., 1953), viii.
9. Lamar, *Dakota Territory*, 6.

political significance have not been adequately explained. Consequently the evolution of the Ordinance is examined in the first chapter. Succeeding chapters deal with the governmental system in operation giving special attention to the territories of the Old Northwest where the primary development and standardization largely occurred. In analyzing the colonial system it is not sufficient to study only the general territorial governments and their relationship with the federal government as most historians have done. Pomeroy, for example, has implied that neither played a commanding role in territorial development and Philbrick has shown that local governments wielded immense power and strongly influenced territorial government. Therefore, any determination of the extent to which form and content corresponded in the territories is fundamental to a balanced appraisal of the colonial system, and presupposes some consideration of the nature and significance of government at every level, from the township on up. This, in effect, boils down to a problem of status quo versus change—of tracing the statutory evolution of the colonial system and evaluating it in terms of the presence or absence of substantive changes in practice.

Because of their unique position in government, the governors were the ideal subjects through which to analyze the structural development and operation of the colonial system without restricting either the scope or depth of the study. In law they held the key positions of power in every essential respect. As federal officials, they were the liaisons between the federal and territorial governments. As territorial executives, they were also intermediaries between territorial and local governments, both of which they theoretically controlled. Thus, by examining their relations with the federal, territorial, and local governments, and with the Indians, it is possible to determine the governors' functional role and the extent of their real power. Moreover, through them, the substantive attitudes of the federal government, as opposed to the official policies, and the sources of power and power relationships within the territories can be discerned. Finally, inasmuch as the governors were central figures, they provide a starting point for analysis; thus it is important to know who they were and how they acted, and to attempt to explain why they behaved as they did and to measure their effectiveness. Their activities with respect to the Indians are treated separately, primarily for the sake of clarity.

In conclusion, it must be emphasized that this study does *not* pretend to offer a definitive analysis of the territorial governments of the continental empires. It deals with only the most fundamental themes and is intended to do no more than provide a general overview which will hopefully serve as a useful frame of reference for further research.

I

Origins of the United States Colonial System: The Ordinance of 1787

THE month of July 1787 was an important one in American history. In that month the Philadelphia Convention and the Confederation Congress simultaneously resolved fundamental problems of government and paved the way for the formation of the First United States Empire. The Philadelphia Convention labored over the basic provisions for a new Constitution, which would establish a stronger central government. In developing its plan to replace the Articles of Confederation, the Convention worked out the ideas and mechanics of federalism between the states, and formulated the concept of a federal empire. Controversy over the exact form of the empire resulted in the unanimous adoption, in August, of Gouverneur Morris' vague proposal, which simply granted the new Congress imperial powers without delineating or limiting them, rather than James Madison's more detailed plan.[1]

In the meantime, the Confederation Congress, sitting in New York City, had been moving along a parallel line. On July 13, 1787, after more than a year of sporadic debate, it enacted a relatively precise plan of colonial government for the public domain north of the Ohio River. One of the most significant laws in American history, the Northwest Ordinance prescribed the philosophical and structural framework

1. See Alpheus H. Snow, *The Administration of Dependencies. A Study of the Evolution of the Federal Empire, with Special Reference to American Colonial Problems* (New York, 1902), 454-73, 538-39, hereafter cited as Snow, *Dependencies*.

of western colonies in the existing union had gained public favor. Maryland's persistent refusal to ratify the Articles of Confederation had centered on the western land problem, and on September 6, 1780, the Virginia delegates finally introduced a "recommendation" in Congress intended to meet Maryland's objections. Jefferson, who was then governor of Virginia, undoubtedly had a hand in drafting the recommendation, which clearly reflects his new attitude toward the West and marks his emergence as an imperialist. Assuming that a peace treaty ending the war would assure United States sovereignty over all lands north of Florida and east of the Mississippi River, the recommendation urged states claiming western lands to cede them to Congress on the grounds that "the back lands, . . . secured by the blood and treasure of all, ought, in reason, justice, and policy, to be considered a common stock, to be parcelled out by Congress." As passed on October 10, the Congressional resolution further stipulated that, under Congress, "the unappropriated lands shall be . . . formed into distinct republican states, which shall become members of the federal union, and have the same rights of sovereignty, freedom and independence, as the other states: . . . each state shall . . . contain a suitable extent of territory, not less than one hundred nor more than one hundred and fifty miles square."[3] This resolution represents the first general statement of a national colonial policy, the first stone laid in the construction of a federal empire.

States claiming western land promptly acted on the Congressional resolution. Before the end of 1781, Congress received cessions of the principal claims to land north of the Ohio River, but the Virginia General Assembly attached unacceptable conditions to its act of cession and did not alter them to the satisfaction of Congress for another two years. Congress, therefore, did not obtain sole title to the Northwest Territory until it accepted the Virginia deed of cession on March 1, 1784—more than a year after the Treaty of Paris had ended the Revolution and Britain had recognized United States claims to a Great Lakes-Mississippi River boundary.[4] A national plan for empire was now

3. *Journals of the Continental Congress, 1774–1789* (34 vols., Washington, D.C., 1904–37), XVII:806–08; XVIII:915–16, hereafter cited as *JCC*.

4. *JCC*, XXV:560; Boyd, *Jefferson Papers*, 6:573–74; Francis Newton Thorpe, *The Federal and State Constitutions, Colonial Charters, and Other Organic Laws*

necessary, and Jefferson introduced one immediately after Congress accepted the Virginia deed of cession.

In February 1784, Congress had appointed Jefferson chairman of a committee to draft a plan for the temporary government of the West.[5] The committee was to prepare a bill to fulfill the terms of the state land cessions—particularly Virginia's, which Jefferson undoubtedly had greatly influenced. Congress agreed to recognize state land reserves in the Northwest and to divide the West into republican states which would be admitted to the Union as equal and perpetual members. Moreover, both the Congressional Resolution of 1780 and the Virginia Act of Cession required future states to be between 10,000 and 22,500 square miles in area—roughly between the present areas of Maryland (10,577) and West Virginia (24,181).[6]

The report presented by Jefferson on March 1, 1784, became the Ordinance of 1784.[7] Though he had solicited suggestions, the plan Jefferson offered was his own brain-child. It followed the general principles for a colonial policy laid down by Congress, but in drafting it, Jefferson had decided to exceed his instructions, and he wrote a compact suitable for imperial expansion. His rapid ideological transformation is evident in the various drafts of his report. Starting with George Washington's idea of establishing a single district in the eastern part of the Northwest Territory, he soon chose to carve six states, which he called A, B, C, D, E, and F, out of the territory now occupied by Ohio, Indiana, Illinois, and Kentucky. Kentucky was not within the ceded territory. Not long after drawing geographically unachievable boundaries for these states, he abandoned that plan in favor of one that di-

---

of the States, Territories, and Colonies Now or Heretofore Forming the United States of America (7 vols., Washington, D.C., 1909), 955–56, hereafter cited as Thorpe, *Constitutions*; Merrill Jensen, *The Articles of Confederation. An Interpretation of the Social-Constitutional History of the American Revolution, 1774–1781* (Madison, Wisc., 1962), 235–38.

5. Compare *JCC*, XXV:693n, with Boyd, *Jefferson Papers*, 6:584–85. Boyd contends that the editor of the *JCC* erred, that Congress in fact set up the committee for western government on February 3, 1784, not on December 18, 1783. Jefferson headed a committee created on the latter date, but it was not charged with devising a government for the West.

6. *JCC*, XVIII:915–16; Boyd, *Jefferson Papers*, 6:573–74.

7. Boyd, *Jefferson Papers*, 6:603–07; *JCC*, XXVI:118–20.

vided all the land between the Appalachians and the Mississippi north of Florida into squares, along lines of longitude and latitude, to form small states of 14,000 to 17,000 square miles. In this manner, Jefferson moved from the consideration of a governmental policy for the land possessed by Congress to the formulation of a broad colonial policy that embraced all the western lands he hoped Congress would someday control. If he was not yet thinking of expanding the national domain, he was clearly anticipating additional land cessions by the southern states to enlarge the public domain. In particular, he considered Virginia still too large, and felt that it ought to cede the area that roughly coincides with the state of West Virginia.[8]

Although the terms of the state land cessions would seem to have dictated the need to make some provision for the admission of states, Jefferson's instructions from Congress were simply to furnish a plan for "temporary government." Instead, he devised a four-stage process through which each of the proposed colonies would progress individually to statehood.[9] He made no provision for government during the early years or decades of settlement, which suggests he believed that either rudimentary local government would be unnecessary at that point, or that ad hoc arrangements would suffice. At an indeterminate point, the settlers were to establish a "temporary" government using the constitution and laws of one of the original states. During this second stage they could begin dividing the territory into counties and townships. The second stage would continue until the population within the prospective state reached 20,000. Then, upon receiving proof of the size of the population and of the desire of the people, Congress was to appoint the times and places for the election and

8. Ideas and proposals that preceded the establishment of Jefferson's committee may be found in *JCC,* XXV:690–93; Boyd, *Jefferson Papers,* 6:582–84; George Washington to James Duane, September 7, 1783, in John C. Fitzpatrick, ed., *The Writings of George Washington from the Original Manuscript Sources, 1745–1799* (39 vols., Washington, D.C., 1931–1944), 27:133–40, hereafter cited as Fitzpatrick, *Writings of Washington.* Boyd, *Jefferson Papers,* 6:585–600, has an excellent discussion of the evolution of Jefferson's thought, followed (600–16) by various forms of the draft ordinance. See also Edmund C. Burnett, *The Continental Congress* (New York, 1941, 1964), 597–99 (1964 ed.), hereafter cited as Burnett, *Congress.*

9. Boyd, *Jefferson Papers,* 6:587–88.

meeting of a convention to draw up a permanent state constitution. The third stage began with the inauguration of the permanent state government, but the quasi-state could not apply for admission to the Union (the fourth stage) until its population reached that of the least populous of the thirteen original states. In the meantime, during the second and third stages, the colony could keep a representative in Congress who would have the right to debate, but not to vote.[10]

Jefferson's plan was paradoxical. It gave the appearance of Congressional noninterference, yet it set up a loose empire. The settlers were to take the initiative and do all the work, and Congress was to assume no financial, administrative, or protective responsibility for the territories. On the other hand, the plan limited western self-determination by prescribing routes of development and restricting western action. Settlers were expected to obtain Congressional consent before organizing governments, and to enter the successive stages only at the times and in the ways authorized. Congress alone could set the time and place—and presumably the mode—of electing delegates to a constitutional convention. In all stages, the colonial governments were to govern the whole area of land within their future state boundaries and to respect the limits imposed by the Ordinance on their freedom of action. One of the most important restrictions was that Congress reserved to itself all matters relating to the disposal of public lands.

During the debates on Jefferson's report, it became clear that the delegates favored more Congressional control over the West than he had provided. They added three sections to the compact, making membership in the confederacy perpetual, requiring western governments to be republican, and prohibiting higher taxation on the lands of nonresidents than on those of territorial residents. This shift in thinking

10. The report of March 1 is in *JCC*, XXVI:118–20; and in Boyd, *Jefferson Papers*, 6:603–07. See also *ibid.*, 6:585; and an important interpretive letter, David Howell to Jonathan Arnold, February 21, 1784, in William R. Staples, *Rhode Island in the Continental Congress, with the Journal of the Convention that Adopted the Constitution, 1765–1790* (Providence, R.I., 1870), 479–81, hereafter cited as Staples, *Rhode Island in the Continental Congress.* Part of the Howell-Arnold letter is in Edmund C. Burnett, ed., *Letters of Members of the Continental Congress* (8 vols., Washington, D.C., 1921–1935), 7:452, hereafter cited as Burnett, *Letters.* Burnett, however, omits some important parts of the letter.

toward comprehensive Congressional participation in the development of the colonies, however, was most evident in the adoption of a general article which compromised the idea of western self-determination. On April 21, Jacob Read of South Carolina proposed an amendment to permit Congress to appoint magistrates and other officers for the territories until the settlers formed their own temporary governments. Jefferson voted for the amendment, but it lost. Two days later, Elbridge Gerry of Massachusetts offered another amendment, which Jefferson apparently wrote, to give Congress even greater powers. It provided[11]

> that measures not inconsistent with the principles of the Confedn. & necessary for the preservation of peace & good order among the settlers in any of the said new states until they shall assume a temporary Government as aforesaid, may from time to time be taken by the United States in Congress assembled.

Read immediately moved that Gerry's amendment be laid aside and that Congress reconsider his recently defeated amendment. The delegates denied Read's motion and, after altering it slightly, adopted the Jefferson-Gerry amendment. On the same day, April 23, by the unanimous vote of ten states, Congress enacted the Ordinance of 1784.[12]

Jefferson may have wanted the Gerry amendment in the Ordinance to provide leeway for future legislative needs and to enable Congress to intervene in territorial affairs if absolutely necessary. The wording of the amendment, however, suggests a broad construction, and in this sense, the Ordinance as he helped amend it both illustrates Jefferson's reconciliation of republicanism with imperialism and demonstrates the transition of his thought to advocation of a fully centralized empire. Construed broadly, the amended Ordinance did not simply transform the Confederation into an empire; it gave Congress unlimited control over its colonies. Subsequent events demonstrated that an increasing majority in Congress expected a broad interpretation to be necessary, if not desirable.

Though the Ordinance provided for the organization of an empire,

11. *JCC*, XXVI:274–75, 278; Boyd, *Jefferson Papers*, 6:613.
12. Boyd, *Jefferson Papers*, 6:612–13; *JCC*, XXVI:247, 274–79.

it was fraught with defects that precluded effective implementation. As in 1776, when he included the article on the disposal of the West in his constitution for Virginia, so in 1784 Jefferson intended the articles of the Ordinance to "stand as fundamental constitutions between the original thirteen states and each of the several states now newly described," not subject to basic change at the whim of Congress. This stipulation raised some serious constitutional problems. In the first place, Congress could not make a law part of the Constitution, but the Ordinance may have had to be incorporated in the Articles of Confederation before it could be operative, since the Articles did not specifically empower Congress either to create or to admit new states. A more practical problem was that a change in the number of states in the Union would require a change in the Constitutional majorities needed for the enactment of laws in Congress, and this could be accomplished only by amending the Articles.

The Ordinance could escape the charge of being *ultra vires* only through its lack of clarity in places. Jefferson wrote the Ordinance to include "the territory ceded or to be ceded by individual states," and to authorize the organization of states in lands not yet ceded, thereby depriving existing states of territory for the benefit of the United States—despite Congressional declarations to the contrary—unless they voluntarily ceded additional lands. Before passing the Ordinance, Congress had deleted two of Jefferson's provisions that lacked Constitutional bases: the abolition of slavery and the granting of hereditary titles in the West. Apparently none of the above Constitutional problems arose when Congress debated the Ordinance, but in 1787 and 1788 James Madison employed some of them as reasons for adopting the new federal Constitution. Unlike the Articles, he argued, the new Constitution would give Congress the authority to create and admit new states and to take any other actions it considered to be in the national interest. Gouverneur Morris put it more bluntly: the new Constitution would provide a sound foundation for the erection of any kind of empire Congress might choose to create.[13]

13. *JCC*, XXVI:278–79; Boyd, *Jefferson Papers*, 6:612–13; Francis S. Philbrick, *The Laws of Illinois Territory, 1809–1818* (Springfield, Ill., 1950), cxxv, hereafter cited as Philbrick, *Laws of Illinois*. Subsequently, Arabic numbers will be substituted for the Roman page numbers in citations to the introductions

If Jefferson believed he was writing higher law and sidestepping Constitutional issues, others were more pragmatic. Some members of Congress who supported the Ordinance did so possibly because they wanted to see if it would work. Probably others considered it to be inadequate, but backed it principally because it met the requirements of state land cessions and thereby completed the land transfers. Some of the Congressmen may have opposed a stronger law. With the seemingly inoffensive Ordinance, Congress could avert criticism while giving the states time to adjust to the idea of a stronger general government that would be manifested in Congressional administration of the public domain. In time, too, the states might yield to Congress the additional land Jefferson and others desired. Such considerations help to explain both the apparently innocuous nature of the Ordinance and Congress' failure to implement it.[14]

Whatever the thinking was in Congress, there were reasons for more positive Congressional action than the Ordinance envisioned, and others soon emerged. Some easterners, viewing the Illinois and Kentucky settlements, doubted the feasibility of allowing the alien and "half-savage" westerners to have unbridled representative government. On the other hand, if the frontiersmen of the isolated Kaskaskia and Wabash settlements in the Illinois Country had any idea of the provisions of the Ordinance, they might have discovered that their settlements fell in three or four proposed states instead of being united in one. Of more immediate concern, the settlements of the Northwest were too scattered, too poor, and too small to support representative governments, even if Congress had authorized them. Western settlers, though unable or unwilling or too preoccupied to form temporary governments, cried for government protection and for confirmation of their land claims. The Land Ordinance of 1785, which provided for the

---

of works by Philbrick and Pease. Citations to the introductions will be prefixed by R, to indicate Roman, and citations to the texts of laws will be prefixed by A, to indicate Arabic pagination. Thus the page number cited above becomes R125.

Boyd, *Jefferson Papers,* 6:587–88, discusses the Constitutional problems. James Madison argued against the constitutionality of the Ordinance in Federalist Number 38. On Morris, see Snow, *Dependencies,* 458–65.

14. See Boyd, *Jefferson Papers,* 6:598–99; and Staples, *Rhode Island in the Continental Congress,* 479–81.

survey and sale of land in eastern Ohio, anticipated new settlements in the territory that would add to existing needs for control. Such a migration could only aggravate Indian problems already in need of federal action; additional settlements in state land reserves in the Northwest would simply compound the anarchy and discord, and Congressional declarations alone would neither create order among the frontiersmen nor keep whites and Indians apart.

Congress was unwilling to act under the broad, discretionary powers of the Jefferson-Gerry amendment in the Ordinance of 1784 for several reasons. The law envisioned the creation of at least seven states in the Northwest, and consequently necessitated the organization of at least seven colonial governments. The boundaries of the proposed states, however, were not based on geographic features, and contemporary maps were so inaccurate that they could not be used to indicate even approximate locations. The boundaries, therefore, had to be established by survey. To Congress, soon to find its hands full surveying just the Seven Ranges provided for in the Land Ordinance of 1785, the idea of undertaking this larger task could not have been appealing. But since Congress reserved disposal of the public lands to itself, it would have to provide machinery for the survey and sale of land in each of the proposed states. Moreover, Indian relations and associated military affairs were international in character, making it necessary for Congress to control and coordinate their conduct in each state. All of these problems suggest that even if the Jefferson-Gerry amendment were not in the Ordinance, Congress would have found it absolutely necessary to assume some kind of direct administration over its western colonies, at least during the initial stages of settlement.

No rational person, however, would advocate that the impoverished Congress actually establish and maintain the apparatus necessary to give unity to Jefferson's system. The very idea of continental mercantilism, on which the empire rested, precluded lavish Congressional expenditures for the support of an unwieldy administrative system in a proliferation of territories. Like Parliament, Congress expected its colonies to be self-supporting, and not a burden on the national treasury. Congress' primary objectives were to settle the West at the least possible cost to itself and, through the sale of public lands, to raise money to avert financial embarrassment or bankruptcy. Thus, because of the prohibitive costs implicit in the Ordinance of 1784, Congress would not have acted under it, even if it were able to locate the proposed states and the settlers assumed the responsibilities of organizing and supporting their own governments.

Since Congress intended to administer some western policies directly, the supposedly autonomous western governments could avoid clashes and Congressional interference only if they cooperated closely with the central government. In any case, as creatures of Congress, the colonies were its inferiors regardless of the provisions of the Ordinance, and if they did not accept that status voluntarily, Congress could be expected to abridge their autonomy whenever it saw fit in order to assure the smooth execution of national policies. It is not surprising, therefore, that Congressional thinking moved steadily away from the idea of theoretically complete western autonomy toward the position that Congress should assume direct control over all sectors of colonial affairs, including local government.

By the end of 1785, a number of American leaders must have felt a curious sense of identification with Britain's colonial problems. The United States had just won its independence, after fighting a war born of the nature of the British colonial system and of Parliament's attempts to enforce centralized administration. Now Congress was on the verge of imposing the same kind of administrative system on its own inland empire. However, in moving from the denunciation of one empire to the implementation of their own, Congress seemed to have solved the British dilemma of what to do with mature colonies. Congress' solution of the problem was only apparent, however, since it could repeal the Ordinance at will, and did replace it in 1787 without changing the guarantee of statehood. The guarantees of eventual partnership in the empire that were written into the Ordinance could of course only be measured over the long run, but they undoubtedly made the temporarily inferior status of the territories more palatable to former "radicals."

In 1785 James Monroe returned from a tour of the West convinced that Jefferson's Ordinance should be changed. As it was, the size of the proposed states was too small and the population requirement for statehood too large. They would impede the growth of the West and might frustrate all efforts to organize state governments. Monroe especially noted the poverty of the Great Lakes area and its meager prospects for attracting settlers. He concluded that, under the Ordinance of 1784, none of the colonies there might ever acquire enough people to gain admission to the Union. If such areas were to be brought into the Union, they would have to be annexed to other areas having more economic promise. Immediately on his return, then, Monroe advised Congress to consider reducing the number of states to be created in the Northwest. To him a larger division of the territory, into from three to five states, was more judicious, for it would equalize resources by giving each of the more promising of Jefferson's states a larger hinterland and a responsibility for developing the poorer areas.

Congress took Monroe's proposal under consideration early in 1786. At the same time it set up a new committee to review the whole problem of government for the Northwest. The decision to organize the new committee probably grew out of Monroe's first-hand reports, which confirmed doubts about the general suitability of Jefferson's Ordinance. Monroe was certain that settlement everywhere in the West was going to be slow at best, and he thought federal direction would be essential in the early years—at least until frontiersmen could form their own governments—and probably would be desirable until statehood.

As heir apparent to Jefferson, who was abroad at the time, Monroe became chairman of the new committee. His recent tour of the West had gained him a reputation as an authority on western problems, and he was generally regarded as eminently well-qualified to draft a practical plan of temporary government that would be acceptable to both northerners and southerners.[15]

15. Thomas Jefferson to James Monroe, July 9, 1786, in Boyd, *Jefferson Papers,* 10:112–13; James Monroe to Thomas Jefferson, January 19, 1786, in Stanislaus Murray Hamilton, *The Writings of James Monroe* (7 vols., New York, 1898–1903), I:117–18, hereafter cited as Hamilton, *Writings of Monroe;* Monroe to Jefferson, May 11, 1786 (*ibid.*, I:127); Monroe to Jefferson, July 16, 1786 (*ibid.*, I:140–41); John M. Merriam, *The Legislative History of the Ordinance of 1787* (Worcester, Mass., 1888), 17, hereafter cited as Merriam, *Ordinance of 1787*; and, Jay Amos Barrett, *Evolution of the Ordinance of 1787, with an Account of the Earlier Plans for the Government of the Northwest Territory* (New York, 1891), 34–36, 38, hereafter cited as Barrett, *Ordinance of 1787*. Whether from Monroe's arguments or from two years' observation, Jefferson himself was convinced that his 1784 plan was not wholly adequate and that the ideal size of western states should be 30,000 square miles, rather than the earlier 15,000. In other words, by 1786 Jefferson had doubled his idea of a state of "moderate size," and had brought his thinking in line with Monroe's. The

On May 9, 1786, Monroe presented his committee's first report.[16] In its refined form the report constituted the governmental articles and part of the compact that became the Ordinance of 1787. Monroe unequivocally patterned the system of colonial government after the British model.[17] At the same time he gave form to Read's proposed amendment to the Ordinance of 1784 and developed the broad imperial construction implicit in the Jefferson-Gerry amendment. Unlike Jefferson, Monroe had kept the object of his work in sight, and his report furnished a relatively precise plan by which the West would pass through two stages of political evolution before admission to statehood. The plan explicitly applied only to the ceded western lands—the Northwest Territory—but Monroe, like Jefferson, clearly intended his proposed ordinance to serve as a constitution until the territories achieved statehood. In the first stage, for which Jefferson had provided no government, Monroe, by implication, made the entire Northwest into a single administrative district, thereby centralizing all elements of colonial government. Congress was to appoint a single territorial governor who would hold office for an unspecified number of years. He would be assisted by a five-man council and a secretary, each appointed by Congress for an unspecified term. In addition, Congress was to appoint five judges to a territorial supreme court. They would hold office during good behavior.

---

actual areas of the five states created in the Northwest are: Ohio, 40,972 square miles; Indiana, 36,185; Illinois, 55,930; Michigan, 57,019; Wisconsin, 54,705. Note that these are larger states, on the average, than those carved out of the Southwest Territory, that *all* of the states created from the public lands east of the Mississippi River were smaller than Virginia (about 63,920 square miles before the Civil War), and that a number of them were smaller than Massachusetts (about 38,850 square miles before 1820) and Pennsylvania (45,007 square miles).

16. The report of May 9 is in *JCC*, XXX:251–55. The committee was set up on March 27, according to Burnett, *Letters*, 8:vxx. Until the report of May 1787, the whole territory was not explicitly designated to be a single administrative district during the first stage, but this seems to have been Monroe's intent. The reasons for making the May 1786 report in what might be taken to be a multiterritorial form were that Monroe was following the letter of the cession laws while working to get Congress to alter its stand and the states to alter their cession acts. See the preface to the May 9, 1786, report in *JCC*, XXX:251; and Barrett, *Ordinance of 1787*, 36–38. For background see Burnett, *Congress*, 651–53.

17. James Monroe to Thomas Jefferson, May 11, 1786, in Hamilton, *Writings of Monroe*, I:127; Boyd, *Jefferson Papers*, IX:510–11; or Burnett, *Letters*, VIII: 359–60.

During the first or district stage, the governor was to administer the laws of one of the original states, divide the territory into counties and townships, and appoint all necessary civil officials and militia officers below the rank of major.[18] It would seem that Monroe intended to give the district-stage governor both absolute executive powers and, through the right to issue proclamations, complete legislative powers. In other words, Monroe's first stage was one of pure autocracy.

When the free adult male population reached an unstated number, the territory could enter the second or representative stage of colonial government. The transition to the second stage would begin with the first meeting of the General Assembly, following the election of a House of Representatives. Monroe provided for Congress to assign the time and places of the elections, but the governor would presumably make the initial apportionment of the territory, according to an undetermined, fixed ratio of representatives to free adult males.[19] Prospective representatives would have to meet a property and residence qualification for office, and only those adult males who had a fifty-acre freehold and were citizens or, if aliens, had been residents for one year, were to be eligible to vote.[20] Significantly, neither Monroe nor anyone else seems to have questioned the prudence of transferring these con-

18. The governor was empowered to commission all civil officials, but in this report the militia officers were to receive their commissions from Congress. In the report of September 19, 1786, and in all subsequent versions of the plan, the governor was to commission all militia officers he appointed (*JCC*, XXXI:671). In the May report the governor was charged with laying out counties and townships on petition from the settlers (*JCC*, XXX:253). The July 13, 1786, report, however, authorized him to make the necessary divisions of the territory as soon as possible, and nothing was said about petitions from settlers (*JCC*, XXX:404). The May report did not explicitly empower the governor to appoint local governmental officials, but the conclusion that that was the intent is inescapable in light of the governor's general powers to organize governments. The July 13 report made the intent fully explicit. It provided that "Previous to the organization of the general Assembly, the governor shall appoint such Magistrates and other civil officials in each county or township as he shall find necessary" and that all local officials were to continue to be appointed by the governor until statehood was achieved.

19. These conflicting and overlapping powers of the governor and Congress stated in the early reports were more apparent than real, and they were worked out in later drafts so that all executive functions were conducted by or through the governor.

20. In the final form of the Ordinance of 1787 the residence requirement for foreigners was raised to two years. (*JCC*, XXXII:313–20).

servative eastern residence and property requirements to western colonies, and this suggests that Monroe and the rest of Congress wanted to guarantee the development of conservative western governments dominated by substantial landholders.

Monroe's second stage was almost identical in concept to the royal colonial governments of the old British Empire. With the appointed governor and council, the House of Representatives would form a General Assembly. It was to be competent to legislate on all internal affairs, insofar as its acts were not inconsistent with the provisions of the Articles of Confederation, acts of Congress, the state land cessions, and other covenants. In essence, these restrictions were similar to those of Jefferson's Ordinance. Monroe's plan gave Congress absolute control over representative government through the governor, who had an unqualified veto and the authority to convene, prorogue, and dissolve the Assembly at will. Apparently no one questioned the propriety of giving the executive such broad powers, in spite of the complaints they had aroused before the Revolution when in the hands of the royal governors. In July 1787 Edward Carrington, then chairman of the committee reconsidering Monroe's plan, perhaps reflected the general attitude in Congress in a letter to Jefferson. Referring to the territorial governor's veto, he observed that during the British colonial period, "The negative which the King of England had upon our Laws was never found to be materially inconvenient."[21] Unlike the British system, however, there was no formal hierarchy of appeals beyond the governor in either stage of Monroe's plan. Under it, the governor would lose little if any power in the second stage. He would lose initiative in legislation, for example, only insofar as the requirement that all bills must originate in the lower house proved to be significant.

Monroe's May report was vague in several important respects. He did not specify whether the laws of the original state used during the first stage were to continue in force in the second stage until altered or repealed by the General Assembly. Nor did he indicate how or when a state constitution was to be formed. His provision for statehood simply

21. Edward Carrington to Thomas Jefferson, June 9, 1787, in Boyd, *Jefferson Papers,* 11:410. See also James Monroe to Thomas Jefferson, July 27, 1787. (*Ibid.,* 11:631.) The May 1786 provisions for second-stage government are the same as those in the Ordinance of 1787, except for the requirement that all bills originate in the lower house.

stated that a territory could be admitted to the Union by the seating of its delegates in Congress when its population equaled that of the smallest original state. In the meantime, the territory could keep a non-voting delegate in Congress during the second stage, as under Jefferson's plan.

Writing to Jefferson on May 11, Monroe noted that, "The most important principles of the Act at Annapolis [Ordinance of 1784?] are you observe preserv'd in this report." He added, "It is generally approv'd of but has not yet been taken up." It was not taken up again until July 13, 1786, exactly one year before Congress enacted the Ordinance. In the revised report all the blanks were filled. Monroe gave the governor and secretary three- and two-year terms respectively, and increased the governor's appointive power to include all militia officers below general rank. The second stage could now begin when there were 500 free adult males in the territory. The House of Representatives was to be elected annually on the basis of one representative for every fifty free adult males until its membership reached twenty. Thereafter, the legislature was to adjust the apportionment to maintain that number. Monroe also reduced the lower house's control over legislation by requiring only money bills to originate in it.[22]

There were two deletions of some consequence in the July report. Either Monroe or Congress, in earlier debates, struck out the requirement that the governor enforce the laws of one of the original states during the first stage. This probably grew out of a belief that the laws of none of the eastern states were likely to meet frontier needs fully. And, though not so stated in the draft ordinance, it may have been understood that the governor would adapt or proclaim effective in the territory, laws and parts of laws from various existing state codes to fill the statutory void until the second stage. Apparently the selection of laws was to be left entirely to the governor. Under the provisions of the May report, the governor might have chosen laws with the help of the council, but in July Monroe deleted the first-stage council from the plan. In a cost-conscious Congress, this was to be expected, for during the first stage the council would be a superfluous organ. The governor might ask it for advice about important matters, but he was not

22. *JCC*, XXX:404–06. See also note 17 above. As enacted, the Ordinance omitted even the requirement that money bills originate in the lower house.

obliged to consult it. Consequently, in the July revision Monroe provided that the council and the House of Representatives should come into existence simultaneously. At the beginning of the second stage, Congress was to appoint five men to serve on the council "during pleasure." Monroe did not prescribe residence or property qualifications for councillors, but since he required a 200-acre freehold and three years residence in the territory as a minimum to qualify for election to the lower house, it may be assumed that the council would represent the territory's largest landowners and speculators.[23]

In the two months after Monroe submitted his revised report, Congress debated the plan several times and sent it back to the committee to be reconsidered. This activity led to further changes, but work stopped short of completion early in September. By that time Monroe and several other members of the committee had left Congress and nothing more could be done until September 18, when Congress reconstituted the committee. William S. Johnson of Connecticut became chairman of the reorganized committee and Nathan Dane of Massachusetts was among its new members. On September 19 the committee presented a new version of Monroe's plan containing some important changes. Dane's hand was evident in the legal verbiage regarding property rights, and possibly in the inclusion of the first positive guarantees of civil rights, habeas corpus, and jury trial. In this report, the federal judges were empowered to adopt criminal laws from the existing state codes for use during the first stage. In light of Monroe's original provision and its deletion in the July report, this new provision suggests that there was some uncertainty in Congress as to who should exercise the legislative authority during the district stage. At this point, apparently the governor was to choose the territory's civil laws and the court its criminal laws.

23. *JCC*, XXX:404. The officeholding qualifications for the House are confusing. Citizens of a state may not have had to meet the residence requirement in the territory, but foreigners had to be residents for an additional year in order to be eligible for office. On the other hand, however, state citizens had to own fifty acres above the 200-acre requirement for residents. As a whole, the section gives the impression that Congress saw territorial settlers as neither citizens nor foreigners. If this were true, the section has important implications. Congress' attitude toward colonists in 1786 may have been comparable to that of Congress around 1900 and to that of the British Parliament.

Other unsettled issues also appeared in September. The article on representative government regressed almost to its original form. The size of the House, the representation ratio, and the population requirement for initiation of the second stage were again omitted. Finally, there was a new population requirement for statehood reflecting the so-called northern bias of the committee. All reports since 1784 had provided for statehood when a territory's population reached that of the smallest of the original states. Now the committee raised the admission requirement to one-thirteenth of the population of the thirteen original states at the most recent census.[24]

In debate, Congress reduced the number of federal judges from five to three and again filled the blank spaces in the section on representative government. These provisions appeared unchanged in the Ordinance when it was finally enacted. Congress decided that the territory could not enter the second stage until it had 5,000 free adult male inhabitants. This was a tenfold increase from Monroe's July report. Similarly, it authorized the election of one representative for every 500 free adult males, whereas in July the ratio had been 1:50. If it was more conservative, the new formula was also more realistic than the earlier one, given the size of the territory and the current wide dispersal of the predominantly French male population, which certainly exceeded 500, especially if it were now agreed that the entire Northwest would be a single administrative district not only in the first stage but also during at least part of the second.[25]

24. *JCC*, XXXI:502n, 561n, 563, 667n, 670–72; Barrett, *Ordinance of 1787*, 42–43. For a discussion of the North-South split on the population requirement see Staughton Lynd, "The Compromise of 1787," in *Political Science Quarterly*, LXXXI (June 1966), 230–38, hereafter cited as Lynd, "Compromise of 1787."

25. *JCC*, XXXI:670–72, 700–02; XXXII:242, 274–75; Barrett, *Ordinance of 1787*, 42–43. Congress also provided for the legislature to determine both the number and apportionment of the House when its membership reached twenty-five. The adopted Ordinance, however, simply limited the House to twenty-five.

It is generally overlooked that Jefferson's provision that a territory must have 20,000 inhabitants before it could enter the second level of representative government is essentially the same as the 5,000 free white adult male requirement of the Ordinance of 1787, and ten times Monroe's provision in the July 1786 report. Adult males constituted about a quarter of frontier populations. See Jack E. Eblen, "An Analysis of Nineteenth-Century Frontier Populations," in *Demography*, 2 (1965), 399–413. More important, however, is that the population requirement of the Ordinance of 1784 applied to each of the predetermined states individually,

After the September debate, Congress took no further action on the plan for seven months. During this time Congress witnessed the suppression of Shays' Rebellion and the triumph of the movement for revision of the Articles of Confederation, but it is impossible to say that these events had any political influence on the drafting of the Ordinance of 1787, since its governmental articles were already nearly settled. In April 1787, less than a month before the Constitutional Convention opened, the committee on western government presented another revision of Monroe's plan.[26] Now the entire Northwest was explicitly made a single administrative district until Congress chose to divide it. The revised report also raised the terms of the secretary and assemblymen to four and two years respectively, but, more important, it solved the problem of the divided first-stage legislative authority by providing that the governor and the judges would exercise it jointly. Meeting together, a majority of them was to adopt those civil and criminal laws from the original states' codes that they thought were best suited to frontier conditions. These laws were to remain in force until changed by the General Assembly in the second stage.

On May 9, 1787, the plan passed its second reading. Its final reading was scheduled for the following day but, for a variety of reasons, Congress did not enact the Ordinance until July 13. Just before its enactment, Congress added property qualifications for all federal appointed offices, changed the tenure of councillors to five-year terms, and lowered the population requirement for statehood. But in all other respects, the governmental provisions of the Ordinance adopted in July were identical to those in the plan read for the second time on May 9, which were in turn hardly more than a refinement of Monroe's original report of May 9, 1786.[27]

---

whereas the requirement of the Ordinance of 1787 was to apply to the entire Northwest, if it were still a single district when its adult male population reached 5,000.

26. Barrett, *Ordinance of 1787*, 43–45. See also *JCC*, XXXII:274–75; and Burnett, *Letters*, 8:xli.

27. See Barrett, *Ordinance of 1787*, 43–45; and compare *JCC*, XXXII:281–83, with 313–20, and 333–43; and with Thorpe, *Constitutions*, 957 ff; and Clarence E. Carter, ed., *The Territorial Papers of the United States* (Washington, D. C., 1934–), II:39–50, hereafter referred to as Carter, *Territorial Papers*. The property qualification for governor was a 1,000-acre freehold in the territory. For the secretary, judges, and councillors, it was a 500-acre freehold each, also to be

On May 9, 1787, the Reverend Manasseh Cutler arrived in New York City, where Congress was meeting. The following morning he appeared before that body to begin promoting his land scheme. No evidence should be needed to show that he did not influence the drafting of the governmental articles of the Ordinance other than the fact that there was little left in the whole Ordinance for him to affect by the time he arrived. On May 10, Congress postponed the third and final reading of the Ordinance. This and Cutler's appearance seem to be purely coincidental. The postponement emanated directly from the long-standing desire of a number of Congressmen to debate adjournment for a vacation and removal of proceedings to Philadelphia, where the Constitutional Convention was about to meet. Some members of Congress may have wanted Congress to be in Philadelphia in order to supervise the Convention and to keep it in check, but others wanted to be there because they were also delegates to the Convention. In addition, a final southern drive to strike out the one-thirteenth population requirement for statehood may have succeeded on May 10, thereby raising the need for further examination and amendment of the Ordinance. In any case, Congress took no action on May 11, and between then and July 6 it lacked a quorum. Obviously, a number of Congressmen were bent on leaving and would not be deterred either by the western need for government or by Reverend Cutler's lust for land.[28]

When Congress again had a quorum it moved quickly to complete the long overdue business of supplying colonial government for the Northwest. On Monday, July 9, it reorganized the committee on western government to make final revisions in Monroe's plan. The reconstituted committee had three new members, one of whom, Edward Carrington of Virginia, became its chairman, but Nathan Dane remained its most effective member. The reasons for recommitting the Ordinance are reasonably clear. Southerners had not willingly accepted the one-thirteenth population requirement for statehood, written into the plan after Monroe left Congress, and during debates either of May 10 or of July 9, they secured its deletion. This left the Ordi-

in the territory. Congress was to appoint the five councillors from a list of ten men nominated by the territorial House of Representatives.

28. See *JCC,* XXXII:283–97; Barrett, *Ordinance of 1787,* 46–50; Burnett, *Letters,* 8:xli; Lynd, "Compromise of 1787," 225–38; and notes 32 and 34 below.

nance without any provision for statehood. Simultaneously, a number of Congressmen from both the North and the South were pressing for amplification of the statehood provision. Like Monroe, they strongly believed that the population required for admission should be explicitly tied to the number of states to be created in the Northwest. They were about to have their way. So were those northerners who, since 1785, had wanted to reintroduce Jefferson's proposed prohibition of slavery into the frame of government for the West. The coincidence of these achievements suggests logrolling.[29]

In revising the Ordinance, the committee incorporated Monroe's 1786 proposal for the eventual division of the territory into from three to five states. For at least a year and a half, this idea for the division of the Northwest had been drifting aimlessly about in Congress attracting only occasional attention. Monroe had proposed it separately, and had deliberately omitted it from his plans of government. Although it was very desirable, he did not feel that its inclusion was essential to the adoption of a system of temporary government. On the contrary, he feared its inclusion would only delay the enactment of a law providing colonial government, since the size of potential western states could not be so increased without the consent of the states which had ceded land to Congress. By 1787, these states were receptive to the idea of creating larger states.

29. Barrett, *Ordinance of 1787*, 46–50, 75–80; Merriam, *Ordinance of 1787*, 14–16; *JCC*, XXXII:281n, 283; Lynd, "Compromise of 1787," 225–38, 246–48. Writing to Rufus King on July 16, 1787, Dane (Burnett, *Letters*, 8:622) claimed that Congress "tried one day to patch up M ——'s plan, but got some new ideas going and recommitted the whole" project. He implied that when he got it back in committee, he discarded most of the plan and drafted a whole new one himself. What probably happened was that, on July 9, when the population requirement was struck out of Monroe's plan in debate, someone suggested that the number of states carved out of the Northwest should be included in the Ordinance and tied to the admission requirement as in the Ordinance of 1784. Undoubtedly, someone also mentioned that the restrictive clauses from the latter Ordinance had somehow fallen from the new plan in the process of revision since Monroe first reported it. It would be surprising if someone else had not moved that, since the government was being explicitly framed (according to Monroe's original plan) to protect settlers' rights, their civil liberties also should be enumerated in the compact. Not even this last could remotely be called a new idea. All of these ideas had been around for some time, and all but the last had always been explicitly associated with plans for western government. (See notes 32 and 34 below.)

Although Monroe wanted to divide the Northwest into fewer states than Jefferson's Ordinance of 1784 permitted, in order to improve their chances of attaining statehood, he received support from several quarters for very different reasons. Both Cavaliers and Yankees assumed that all western states would have a southern bias. For this reason many northerners were bent on admitting the smallest number of states possible, as were other easterners who saw a general threat to their power in the West. Together, they had labored to amend Jefferson's Ordinance so as to raise the population requirement for admission and to reduce the number of states to be created in the Northwest. It was partially to gain the initiative and forestall attempts to reduce the number of states to two that Monroe had introduced his proposal, in 1786, for a three- to five-way division of the territory.

After Monroe left Congress, opponents of western statehood obtained the higher admission requirement they desired, but, this having been struck out of the Ordinance, they return with renewed interest in mid-1787 to the idea of reducing the number of states. Being less interested in the potential number of new states than in increasing their power in Congress with all deliberate speed, southerners would cheerfully have agreed to a reduction in the number of states in return for northern acceptance of a smaller population requirement for statehood.[30]

The statehood article, as it was finally written, seems to have been designed to please almost everyone concerned. Southerners could anticipate as many as five states emerging from the Northwest, which would add considerable strength to their voice in Congress, while northerners (or more generally, easterners) could continue to hope that only three states would be carved out of the land. This prospect seems to have caused some jubilation. To some people, the enlarged size of prospective states and the setting of the admission requirement at 60,000 inhabitants appeared to insure that not more than one of the three general divisions might ever qualify for statehood, and it was possible that that one might adopt "Eastern politics."

The article, however, also contained the important provision that permitted Congress to admit states with a smaller population if such action seemed desirable. Moreover, those people who thought the population requirement was high and possibly prohibitive erred badly. In

30. *JCC*, XXXI:738–39. See also note 15 above and notes 32 and 34 below.

reality the southerners got a better deal in 1787 than they had in 1784, because the entrance requirement of 60,000 people worked out to fewer than a population equal to that of the smallest original state. This should have been reasonably clear in 1787, but everyone apparently underestimated Delaware's population. In 1790, Delaware, the smallest state in the Union, had 59,096 inhabitants; in 1800, it was still the smallest with 64,273, and the first state was yet to enter the Union from the Northwest. Finally, the Ordinance of 1787 made statehood easier to achieve than it would have been under the Ordinance of 1784 in that the new plan required only a simple legislative majority in Congress for admission whereas the old one required the consent of two-thirds of the states in the Union at the time a new state petitioned for admission.[31]

In its final meeting, the committee expanded and added to the compact articles of the Ordinance. One of the new articles restored all the restrictions Jefferson had imposed on western states in 1784. Most of these had been in Monroe's first draft but had been gradually lost in revision. The other articles augmented the list of civil liberties incorporated the preceding September. On July 11, 1787, after two days' work, the committee presented its newly revised and enlarged Ordinance. At this point it might be called the Jefferson-Monroe-Dane Plan. Congress made some minor emendations and on Friday, the 13th of July, after adding an amendment prohibiting slavery in the Northwest, it adopted the Ordinance unanimously.[32]

31. Lynd, "Compromise of 1787," 242; *Historical Statistics of the United States, Colonial Times to 1957* (Washington, D.C., 1960), 13, 756, hereafter cited as *Historical Statistics*.

32. The delegates from Maryland and Pennsylvania (including Arthur St. Clair, President of the Confederation Congress, and soon to be Governor of the Northwest Territory) were absent during these debates and missed the final vote. (See *JCC*, XXXII:313–20, 333–43.) The compact article in Jefferson's Ordinance was restrictive only. Monroe specifically stated that a primary objective of his plan of government was the protection of settlers' rights. His positive emphasis and concern for governmental provisions in this context may indicate that he expected a bill of rights to be added to his plan at some point after the governmental articles were refined. The absence of concern over the deletion of the restrictions placed on the territory in the first draft reinforces the idea that Congress was operating on the same assumption. Then, too, Monroe had said, in effect, that he hoped the number of states to be created in the Northwest would be incorporated in the Ordinance before it was passed, although he was

The Ordinance of 1787 provided for three levels of government in place of the four outlined in Jefferson's Ordinance of 1784. The new law simplified some elements of the earlier plan and elaborated others. By eliminating the third stage of the 1784 Ordinance, the new plan allowed a colony to become a state at the same time that it adopted a permanent state constitution. Part of Jefferson's second stage and all of the third were to be covered by an elongated second stage in the Ordinance of 1787. The new second stage also developed ideas implicit in the Ordinance of 1784 by detailing the structure and operation of the temporary representative government. In this way, the new plan furnished a precise definition of republicanism upon which regular state governments were to be built. The most important change in the new law lay in the complete revision and elaboration of Jefferson's first stage. It is on this point that the Ordinance of 1787 has been subjected to the most severe criticism, but it was also on this point that Jefferson's plan was most deficient, and a strong authority was deemed crucial to assure the maintenance of order and the execution of national polices in the territory. The Ordinance of 1787 provided for external direc-

---

willing to see a plan of government adopted without it (see notes 15 and 30 above). Dane, in this sense, not only rounded out Monroe's plan, but also carried out his design when, in the report of July 11, 1787, he added the sections enumerating the positive rights of settlers, reintroduced the restrictive clauses from Jefferson's Ordinance, and incorporated Monroe's scheme for dividing the Northwest. Certainly, regardless of whose idea it was, Dane's inclusion of the guarantee of civil liberties was significant, not only because it gave balance to the Ordinance of 1787.

The question of whether or not Article 6 of the compact, the slavery amendment, was part of a North-South compromise over the statehood article is unclear. Dane claimed to have proposed such an amendment on July 11, but he did not include it in the bill submitted on July 13. It may be that by July 13 enough northerners had realized the negative ramifications (from their viewpoint) of the statehood deal that had already been made and, with those stalwarts who had always wanted its inclusion, threatened to withhold their approval of the plan unless the prohibition of slavery were added. Together, they may have had the power to force its inclusion. See Burnett, *Letters,* 8:622; Lynd, "Compromise of 1787," 246–48. In the letter to Rufus King, July 16, 1787 (Burnett, *Letters,* 8:622), Dane, however, not only said that he thought the population requirement was too small, but that it was not very important. At the same time, he expressed some surprise that the slavery amendment had been adopted without opposition. He leaves the impression that any deal involving slavery and statehood was made on July 13, did not include him, and was not evident to him. However, Dane is not very reliable.

tion in the person of the governor, who was intended to act as a stabilizer throughout the colonial period, but principally during the first stage. Jefferson's plan did not explicitly provide for continuous Congressional direction during any stage of development.

The Ordinance of 1787 was more in tune with the British colonial experience than the law it replaced. One can argue that Monroe extracted from his knowledge of pre-Revolutionary colonial history those elements he considered to have been central to the evolution of British colonial government and that he both systematized and institutionalized them in his draft ordinance. The American colonies passed through three stages of political development before the Revolution that roughly, but distinctly, parallel the three stages of the Ordinance of 1787. During the seventeenth century the colonies passed through a stage of strong executive control that can be equated with the first stage of the Ordinance. The first two-thirds of the eighteenth century was a period of executive eclipse and of the real emergence of representative government, authorized in the Ordinance's second stage. After 1763 the colonies moved into a period of rebellion that led to independence. The Ordinance sought to avoid rebellion by providing for quasi-independence through statehood as the third stage. In this light, the Ordinance cannot be viewed as innovative or progressive in any basic sense, even in the provision for statehood; on the contrary, its system of colonial government was decidedly more authoritarian than that of the British. In the first stage it did not afford even the most meager elements of popular government to be found in colonies during the seventeenth century. In the second stage the Ordinance did not simply revert to the second British stage of representative government; it incorporated all the changes made in the British system after 1763 that strengthened the governor's office. The British found it to be disastrous to introduce such measures after representative government was firmly established. Realizing this, Monroe may have considered a strong governor to be necessary from the beginning of representative government, both to get the people in harness and to prevent rebellions before statehood was attained.[33]

33. See Jack P. Greene, *The Quest for Power. The Lower Houses of Assembly in the Southern Royal Colonies, 1689–1776* (Chapel Hill, 1963), 3–4, hereafter cited as Greene, *Quest for Power.*

Monroe designed a relatively precise, operative system of colonial government that implemented Jefferson's general principles by returning to the experience of the old Empire. In adding a positive bill of rights, Dane supplied a valuable but perhaps unnecessary counterweight to the apparently rigid governmental forms and potentially stifling Congressional controls.[34] He also gave the Ordinance greater clarity by rewriting and rearranging parts of Monroe's plan, but as he

34. See *Essex Institute Historical Collections* (Salem, Mass., 1888), XXV:196–200. A vainglorious egotist, Dane denied, yet tacitly admitted, that Jefferson had formulated the ideas upon which the Ordinance of 1787 was based, when he noted that the Ordinance of 1784 was "A mere incipient plan, in no manner matured for practice." (*Ibid.*, XXV:196.) Arthur Butler Hulbert, ed., *The Records of the Original Proceedings of the Ohio Company* (2 vols., Marietta, Ohio, 1917–1918), I:xciii–xciv, called the Northwest Ordinance "a cumulative document" but, at the same time, tried to credit the whole of the Ordinance to New Englanders, particularly to Dane and Cutler. On the other hand, he contended that the Ohio Company was not interested in the Ordinance of 1787, and noted the significant lack of mention of it in the Ohio Company contract. The Company was only interested in land, Hulbert maintained, and ignored the existence of the Ordinance—there is only one insignificant reference to it in all the Company records—presumably because it was wholly uninterested in government (I:xcv–xcvi). Hulbert said that the Company wanted a positive bill of rights in the plan of government, but he offered neither reasons nor evidence. He also asserted that there had been a consensus favoring the kind of law adopted in 1787 at least as early as 1784, and again he offers no evidence (I:xciii–xciv). Whether this was so or not, it is clear that by the time Cutler arrived in New York in 1787, there was nothing really new to be offered. At the very most, he can be given credit for having provided part of the bill of rights and for having helped to lower the population requirement for new states and to change councillors' terms to five years. All of these were positive, or liberalizing, changes, and Cutler did not claim to be responsible for any of them. Consequently, the all-too-common and persistent interpretation of the origins of the Ordinance of 1787 (see, for example, Merrill Jensen, *The New Nation. A History of the United States During the Confederation, 1781–1789* [New York, 1958], 354, 358; Theodore C. Pease, "The Ordinance of 1787," in *Mississippi Valley Historical Review*, XXV [September, 1938], 167–80; John Bach McMaster, *A History of the People of the United States* [8 vols., New York, 1914], I:511–12), that conspiratorial land speculators were behind the writing of the Ordinance of 1787 and that the Ohio Company representatives forced Congress to draft the governmental articles in the way that it did merely to serve as an adjunct to their land grab, should be discarded. Interpretations similar to the one offered here are not new. (See Burnett, *Congress*, 598–686 *passim*, 711; and Philbrick, *Laws of Illinois*, R240.) Philbrick bluntly states that there is absolutely no evidence to support the claim that the Ohio Company influenced the writing of any part of the Ordinance of 1787. (See note 37 below.)

completed his work he unleashed his political conservatism, prescribing property qualifications for all office holders cited in the Ordinance. This was remarkable only in its enthusiasm, for the idea of requiring property qualifications had been in Monroe's first report. Since Monroe had required voters and representatives to own land in the territory, logic must have led Dane to complete the job.[35]

In March 1830, following the Webster-Hayne debates, Nathan Dane wrote Daniel Webster to explain the origins of the Ordinance of 1787. The law, he contended, was clearly the work of a Massachusetts lawyer, meaning himself. He said *he* had written the important parts of the plan, and that it owed nothing to the ideas of Jefferson or anyone else. Significantly, he dismissed the governmental articles of the Ordinance as irrelevant.[36] He argued, as other Congressmen may have in the 1780s, that in the history of a nation, brief periods of colonialism were inconsequential. Only things that were permanent mattered and, in Dane's eyes, these were the conveyance article that he wrote for the Ordinance and those parts of the compact articles that he claimed to have written. He thought almost any form of government would suffice temporarily, if at the same time appropriate machinery were provided to guarantee basic property rights and civil liberties. For this reason, in the 1780s as in the 1830s, Dane and others may not have considered it necessary to develop a more refined or democratic system of colonial government for the West, even though it was foolish to suppose that colonial institutions of government would not shape those of the states.

Monroe seems to have been well aware of the fundamental relationship between colonial and state institutions and Jefferson must at least have sensed it. Whatever the case, if native Americans from the East were going to settle the Northwest, as Jefferson sometimes anticipated, the Ordinance of 1784 should have been adequate. After the intellectual and physical upheavals and the Constitution-writing of the preceding decade, Anglo-Americans did not need the more elaborate Ordinance of 1787 to instruct them in their basic rights or in how to set up a republican government. Westerners might demand written

35. The property requirements for federal officials (see note 27 above) were universally ignored.

36. *Essex Institute Historical Collections*, XXV:196–200. (See note 34 above.)

guarantees, and Congress might respond almost automatically by writing them into law, but written or not, few Anglo-Americans going to the frontier were likely to believe that their rights and institutions did not accompany them. If, on the other hand, Congress expected the continued settlement of the Northwest by French-Canadians and other aliens unfamiliar with American political and legal institutions, Jefferson's Ordinance would clearly have seemed inadequate, if not a license to anarchy. A more rigid and centralized system of colonial government, as in the Ordinance of 1787, would have been deemed desirable. Through it, Congress would have sure control over the West during the period of "apprenticeship," in which frontiersmen would assimilate republican institutions, until they reached the level of conformity requisite for full partnership in the Empire.

These considerations apparently loomed large in the decision to rewrite Jefferson's Ordinance and pervaded every stage of the drafting of the Ordinance of 1787. Petitions from the French settlers of the Illinois Country in the 1780s gave force to arguments that Jefferson's Ordinance needed to be redone in greater detail. But, more important, Monroe said in effect that he wrote his governmental articles specifically for the government of such "foreigners," to initiate them into the mysteries of republicanism. In the latter sense, the Ordinance of 1787 was intended to teach non-English westerners what constitutes a republican government, how it should be organized and how it should operate. For Monroe, Dane, and others who seemed to take it for granted that non-English settlers would predominate in the West, the Northwest Ordinance satisfied the need, unmet in the Ordinance of 1784, for concrete Congressional supervision and a carefully worked out, clearly defined system of colonial administration.

Similarly, through the article on the descent and conveyance of property—which, as a law, did not belong in a fundamental document such as the Ordinance pretended to be—Dane explained in detail how real and personal properties were transferred and inherited in the United States legal system. Though Dane modestly boasted that this article was the first truly republican inheritance law in history, its inclusion in the Ordinance could be justified only on the assumption that western settlers would import ideas or institutions incompatible with Anglo-American practices and unacceptable to easterners, which should be prevented from taking root. Indeed, Dane was pessimistic when it came to the future of the West. The Northwest, he asserted, would be divided into three districts, and only the eastern one was likely to qualify for statehood within the foreseeable future. He was not confident that American institutions would successfully penetrate the two western districts. He thought, however, that there was some hope that enough easterners would settle in the easternmost district to form a majority, or at least a controlling minority. Then, by the time the district entered the Union, there would be an "equal" chance of its adopting a system of government similar to that of the original states, and "Eastern politics."[37]

37. See, for example, Nathan Dane to Rufus King, July 16, 1787, in Burnett, *Letters,* 8:622. Scattered evidence in other sources supports the stronger interpretation offered here than would seem warranted by the letter cited. Forty-three years later, in 1830 (see note 36 above), Dane contended that, since 1784, he and other northeasterners had been preparing the way for the New England settlement that they had anticipated in the Northwest Territory—a specious bit of hindsight. Significant northeastern or New England settlement in the Northwest probably was not anticipated much before the organization of the Ohio Company and Reverend Cutler's arrival in Congress. In fact, the formulation of the Ohio Company scheme may have been very important, precisely because it may have inclined northeastern Congressmen more favorably toward Monroe's plan of government by offering the pleasing prospect that new western states so settled might be sympathetically disposed to New England designs in Congress.

Monroe's views on the future of western settlement are not altogether explicit, but see his interchanges with Jefferson cited in note 15 above. See also James Madison to Thomas Jefferson, April 23, 1787, in Burnett, *Letters,* 8:588–89; R. H. Lee to Wm [?] Lee, July 30, 1787 (*ibid.,* 8:629–30); R. H. Lee to George Washington, July 15, 1787 (*ibid.,* 8:620); Edward Carrington to Thomas Jefferson, October 23, 1787 (*ibid.,* 8:660); John Jay to Thomas Jefferson, April 24, 1787, in Boyd, *Jefferson Papers,* 11:314; Thomas Jefferson to James Madison, June 20, 1787 (*ibid.,* 11:481); John Jay to Thomas Jefferson, July 24, 1787 (*ibid.,* 11:618–19); and Carter, *Territorial Papers,* II:39–40n.

Philbrick (*Laws of Illinois,* R458) concludes that the Ordinance was "a product of forthright political reactionaries, determined to control an assumedly untrustworthy (and potentially revolutionary and traitorous) population. . . . Its framers were logical—and, in view of their attitudes toward frontier society, not hypocritical."

The idea that general provisions in Organic Acts were insufficient for new citizens was explicitly expressed in reference to continental areas at least until 1822. In that year, Representative John Rhea of Tennessee successfully argued against an amendment to the Florida bill, which would have substituted for a detailed list of U. S. statutes applicable to the territory, a simple statement that

Dane and Monroe, two of the principal architects of the Ordinance of 1787, were supposedly well versed in western problems. They represented different northern and southern perspectives, but they firmly agreed that it would be difficult to transplant republican institutions in the hinterland of the Empire and that the success of any attempt was uncertain at best. Add to this their expectation, and Jefferson's, that settlement was going to be slow, and that statehood for even the easternmost part of the Northwest would be long in coming, and it is small wonder all three decided the Ordinance of 1784 should be redrawn. In fairness, then, politically controversial or deceitful motives cannot be attributed to these men. Their contributions to the Ordinance of 1787 did not emanate foremost from a desire either to further or frustrate whatever democratic tendencies there were on the frontier, but from their perception of what would constitute the most viable system of colonial government for the Empire in the West. In more general terms, the governmental articles may be called conservative or reactionary only if one is willing to use the same label to describe all American leaders during the mid-1780s. The Ordinance can hardly be considered the work of a band of conspirators, since everyone seems to have agreed on its basic content. This is not to suggest that there were no compromises between rather fluid factions in Congress, nor that all of them were unimportant, but to emphasize the essentially apolitical nature of the governmental provisions. The continuity and consensus of thought are obvious, yet they have been missed in the past because the history of the Ordinance has been overdramatized and its political significance has been obscured by irrelevancies. In light of the aura of intrigue that has surrounded the Ordinance, it is thus surprising to see how its history is apparently nothing more or less than that of a rather ordinary piece of noncontroversial legislation.

Early in October 1787, Congress implemented the Ordinance by appointing the necessary officials and by enacting a law to provide for their salaries. This law completed the concentration of power in the

---

Florida laws must conform to the Constitution. He contended that the new citizens of the former Spanish colony would not understand the compact language, and that restrictions and rights had to be spelled out in some detail. (See Carter, *Territorial Papers,* XXII:398.)

hands of the governor for, in addition to the $1,000 annual salary for his services as administrator of the territory, commander of the militia, and overseer of the disposal of public lands, it made the governor superintendent of Indian affairs in the territory, and allocated an additional $1,000 per year as payment for this service. Arthur St. Clair, Governor of the Northwest Territory, considered it a handsome salary, but then he was inclined to view this job as an immensely prestigious sinecure, as he had viewed his presidency of Congress. William Blount, Governor of the Southwest, who did not look on the governorship as a sinecure, also thought that the salary was generous at first.[38] But more important, the law set a precedent for all subsequent federal officials to receive their salaries from the imperial government rather than from the inhabitants of the territories. Though it was obviously necessary at the time of the organization of the Northwest, the practice continued in the second stage, spread to all the territories, and persisted to the present. In itself, this should give cause for neither acclaim nor alarm, as many frontiersmen realized; however, the law did help to give undue prominence to the more despotic potentialities of the Ordinance.

Until Congress chose to divide the Northwest—a territory covering well over a quarter million square miles—it was to be a single administrative district, and until its free adult male population reached

38. Arthur St. Clair, Winthrop Sargent (the secretary), and the three original judges of the Northwest were the only territorial officials appointed by the Confederation Congress. Beginning in 1789 the President appointed all officials with the consent of the Senate. The Ordinance of 1787 was reenacted in 1789 by the first federal Congress, which also enacted the Southwest Ordinance, without debate and without any alterations except those necessary to bring it into line with the new Constitution. This may be taken as an indication of the extent of Congressional satisfaction with the Ordinance of 1787. The Southwest Ordinance is identical to the Northwest Ordinance except that it does not contain the article prohibiting slavery. The absence of debate over the Ordinances is evident in the *Annals of the Congress of the United States* [1789–1824] (24 vols., Washington, D.C., 1855–1856), hereafter cited as *Annals of Congress*. The act of adapting the Northwest Ordinance to the federal Constitution is in Thorpe, *Constitutions*, 963–64; as well as in the United States *Statutes at Large*.

The secretary's salary was to be $750 a year. Those of the judges were to be $800. Congress later began appropriating a small "contingency fund" annually, usually of $350, out of which the governor was to meet the official expenses of office. (See *JCC*, XXXIII: 599–602; and William H. Masterson, *William Blount* [Baton Rouge, La., 1954], 178, hereafter cited as Masterson, *Blount*.)

5,000, it was to have a first-stage government. This consisted of a governor, a secretary, and three judges, who were responsible for the execution of all imperial policies and for the management of all governmental, judicial, military, and Indian affairs in the territory. All this would cost Congress just under $5,500 annually, when appropriated, if there were no extraordinary expenditures for the conduct of Indian and military affairs. At the end of the district stage, the normal annual cost to Congress would be between twenty-five and thirty cents per capita. Before Congress divided the Northwest, and when all five administrators were in the territory, there would be an average jurisdictional area of over 50,000 square miles for each federal official, but the theoretical judicial districts would range upwards of 85,000 square miles, roughly the size of Utah. Obviously, then, though the Ordinance provided for highly centralized administration, the sheer size of the Northwest and the many responsibilities of the officials left the people with considerable room for both self-help and self-determination.

Whatever the reality was to be, the governor was cast in the role of an autocrat. During both the first and the second stages of temporary government, he was legally responsible only to Congress—and, after 1789, to the President—from whom he received all his authority. Like the British royal governor, he wielded virtually absolute power within his realm, but unlike his counterpart in the old British colonial system, the American territorial governor received his salary from the imperial government and supposedly was protected from unsavory manipulation at the hands of the territorial legislature. The American governor had an absolute veto over legislation, as the British governor had, and Congress, like the Crown, reserved the right to negate laws the governor approved. But since the Ordinance did not provide a formal system of appeals, a veto in the American system could be overruled only by an act of Congress. Finally, all the early territorial governors were not only superintendents of Indian affairs, but commanded the regular army in their territories, and could requisition regular troops and militia from neighboring states.

The governor's civil powers alone were staggering. During the first stage, the Ordinance empowered him to create townships and counties, meaning that the governor could not only establish the boundaries and locate the seats of government, but that he had the power to create and fill by appointment all offices within the units of local government. This appointive power included the selection and commissioning of all militia officers below general rank. The Ordinance did not explicitly make the governor the executive, but it held him responsible for the enforcement of federal and territorial laws. Although he shared the district-stage lawmaking power with the three judges, the governor was the dominant legislator since he presumably had a veto. Early governors also assumed the right to issue licenses of all kinds.

It is difficult to tell whether or not the Ordinance curtailed the governor's powers significantly in the second stage. He continued to appoint all local officials and militia officers as in the first stage, and he had several means by which to control the General Assembly. On the one hand, he could veto its acts and convene, prorogue, or dissolve the legislature at will. He could also affect the selection of the legislative council in two ways. Using his favored position, he might influence Congress' appointments, and if he had a strong enough party following, he might determine who was nominated by the territorial House of Representatives. The representatives held the only directly elected offices in the territory, and the governor controlled their election. He issued the writs of election, which specified the times and places of elections. In addition, early governors normally apportioned their territories and occasionally decreed election procedures. After elections, the governor was final arbiter of their results, though the power was not enumerated in the Ordinance. This, with the power to issue commissions, could be combined into a powerful weapon, since only persons appointed by Congress could hold office in the territory without a commission from the governor. Following an election that did not turn out as he wished, a determined governor might, and sometimes did, use his authority as judge to pass over the candidate with the highest number of votes and commission someone else. Aside from manipulation of this kind, the governor's formal endorsement of candidates could be important. Once elected, the legislature had the power to alter county and township boundaries, and presumably to regulate the number of local officials and their duties. The power to create new counties and townships, however, did not clearly pass to the General Assembly, and Arthur St. Clair continued to exercise it alone for a time during the second stage—though not without raising a storm of criticism.

At the critical junctures of change from one stage of government to another, the governor exercised nearly absolute powers, akin to those respecting second-stage elections. The governor was to conduct a census to determine the size of the population and the number of free adult males when he thought the territory was ready for representative government, and, if he chose, he could poll the voters on the question of entering the second stage. If the territory had the necessary population, and a majority of the voters was not opposed, he was to apportion the territory, direct the election of representatives to the lower house, certify the results, and order the house to convene for the nomination of councillors. Although he was not specifically empowered to do so by the Ordinance, the governor might follow the same procedure to decide when his territory was ready for statehood, bring about the election of a constitutional convention, and if a constitution was adopted, oversee the election of a permanent state government.

In spite of the impressive breadth of the governor's powers, however, they were not so precisely defined in the Ordinance that they could not be construed disparately. Congress did not subsequently clarify the various realms of authority sufficiently, and only rarely did the federal government intervene in any way to enforce or preserve the governor's statutory powers. Consequently, the course of development actually followed by the American Empire depended heavily on Congress' choice of administrators, how the federal officials interpreted their powers, and how strongly they could make their interpretations hold. The early territorial governors used the British royal governors for their model, logically enough, and the federal government looked on without comment. The result was a quick repetition of the slow devolution of the pre-Revolutionary royal governors' powers, even though the territorial governor's office was stronger in law. The succeeding chapters explain this failure of the territorial governors to impose their interpretation of territorial government on the inland empire and analyze the pattern of colonial government that developed.

II

The Beginnings of Territorial Government

SHORTLY after it was put into operation in the Northwest, the district stage proved to be an ineffective and undesirable instrument for colonial government, unpopular both in the West and in Congress. The reasons for its inadequacies are not hard to find. No system held in contempt by the federal administration, the territorial officials, and the people could be expected to work as the authors of the Ordinance apparently had intended. The basic failing of the district-stage provision in the Ordinance was that it was inadequate to fulfill the governmental needs of the Northwest, since the conditions that had developed in the territory did not correspond to those for which the Ordinance was intended. Tightly centralized administration was impossible for territorial officials, whose multiple responsibilities in large territories could not all be fully met.

Congress, nevertheless, seemed reluctant to change or abandon the district-stage provisions of the Ordinance. Instead, the continual use of these provisions during the first twenty years of the federal period suggests either satisfaction with the first stage of the Ordinance or unwillingness to consider alternatives seriously. In 1789, the first federal Congress reenacted the Ordinance of 1787 without debate, amending it only as necessary to adapt it to the new Constitution. The principal change was to give the President power to appoint all general territorial officials, with the consent of the Senate. The following year, Congress extended the Ordinance to the Southwest, deleting the prohibition of slavery, and in 1804 the Ordinance became the organic law of the Louisiana Purchase north of the present state of Louisiana. Thus, the entire public domain came under the provisions of the Ordinance, in each case with a striking lack of debate in Congress over the suitability of using this system of government. Only seven district-stage governments, however, were eventually created in this huge land area: the Northwest (Ohio), Indiana, Illinois, Michigan, the Southwest (Tennessee), Mississippi, and Louisiana (Missouri).[1]

Although Congress continued to use the first-stage provisions as late as the early nineteenth century, it was always willing to allow territories to move to the second stage without regard for the population requirement. For a variety of reasons examined below, Congress did not fully abandon the district stage until the 1820s, but within a generation, just before the end of the First Empire, there were attempts to revive its use, and it was revived during the Second Empire for the administration of Alaska. Its application then was based on the same assumptions as had pertained in the late eighteenth and early nineteenth centuries. In the meantime, from about 1820 to the late 1830s, Congress experimented with other methods of organizing new territories, and during the last decade of the First Empire it completed the standardization of the system along the lines which prevailed throughout the Second Empire.

The characteristic pattern of first-stage government naturally influenced the government of the second stage, and it is therefore necessary to study the evolution of this pattern before turning to an examination of the abandonment of the district stage and standardization of the second stage. A general introductory discussion of the district stage, and some broad comparisons between it and second-stage government, will help to put the analyses of major elements of the first-stage governments in perspective. These elements include a correlation between the length of existence and growth factors. Because of its importance in terms of establishing precedents, the sequence of events leading to gubernatorial impotency during Arthur St. Clair's administration must be laid out in some detail. This will illustrate the

1. The omissions of Arkansas and Florida are discussed in Chapter V below. (See the *Annals of Congress,* at the respective times, for the lack of debate over the organic bills.)

surprising speed with which governors lost control over their principal statutory powers. It will also provide the setting for an analysis of the reasons for the loss of powers and why executive powers, once lost, were difficult or impossible to regain. Since the governor's position was that of an autocrat and the devolution of his powers was directly tied to his actions, the suitability of the laws he and the judges adopted, as well as the laws themselves, must be examined. The general inadequacy of legislation and the vacillation of federal attitudes had an immediate and cumulative effect. The weaknesses of district-stage governments that resulted from these factors and abetted the rise of local autonomy can then be studied.

In the broadest sense, the district stage was intended to provide a caretaker government for essentially transfrontier regions—the bare minimum of government for the small, relatively stable populations beyond the mainstream of expansion. Where this was the case, the government seems to have served its apparent purpose well enough. In other words, given the assumptions and expectations of Congress in the mid-1780s, the district stage was not an unreasonable solution to the problem of providing government, even if it was an autocratic one—especially when judged by the length of time it had taken to advance agricultural settlement as far as the Appalachian Mountains, which were in themselves a formidable barrier to expansion. More importantly, perhaps, the migration beyond the mountains during the 1780s was not only unspectacular, but was focused on lands *south* of the Ohio River, not within the Northwest Territory.

The principal inhabitants of the Northwest were the French, living in small groups scattered deep in the interior of the territory. The French may have lived in harmony with the Indians, but the Indians were anything but receptive to a large-scale Anglo-American invasion of their lands. They were no more enthusiastic about the increasing settlement south of the Ohio, and there were continual outbreaks of violence there between the Indians and the settlers. The federal government found it necessary to concentrate its limited resources on the Southwest in an attempt to pacify and remove the Indians. In the meantime it pursued a peace policy in the Northwest and made no effort to encourage migration to that territory. Consequently, given the expectation that Indian removal, which was a prerequisite to extensive Anglo-American settlement, would be difficult and lengthy, there was every reason to believe that the growth of the Northwest would be very slow. During the years of light settlement rudimentary government institutions would suffice. It was, of course, necessary to defend the frontier areas, but the settlers were expected to do most of this themselves through militia units organized by the governor.

In 1787, Congress thought that both the French and most Anglo-American settlers were untrustworthy and potentially dangerous. For at least a generation more, Anglo-Americans believed that the French, in particular, were not only unfamiliar with American institutions but were constitutionally unable to adapt to them, because they preferred their traditional forms of autocratic government. Thus Congress was being touchingly magnanimous in providing the district stage to fulfill the wishes of its French subjects in the West.

Few people in 1787 could have foreseen the rapid transformation of the Northwest from an Indian territory into five states which, in 1850, contained four and a half million inhabitants—a quarter of the white population of the United States. The unexpected rush of settlers quickly outgrew the capacities of the district-stage governments. The complexity of administration and the demands on territorial officials increased with the size of the population, but first-stage governmental services seem not to have become critically inadequate until the emergence of commercial economies, when people began concentrating around towns. In short, population growth, economic development, political awakening, and recognition of the inadequacy of first-stage government seemed to be directly related. In the territories that did not pass through the district stage, the situation was apparently analogous, and the discussion of district-stage evolution can be taken to reflect elements of growth in non-district-stage governments as well. In the early years of territorial development, the small population was apparently characterized by relative extremes in wealth and poverty, and it is probably correct to say that there was either no middle class or a very small one. Local government, insofar as it existed, was the preserve of the well-to-do.

Rapid settlement, however, ordinarily followed closely upon the organization of a new territory, and its origins were predominantly middle-class. The costs of farm or business relocation or of new starts in the West were such as to exclude the poor, and perhaps also a good share of the lower middle classes of society, as society was structured at the time of any given migration. Moreover, the wealthy tended not to migrate but to invest or buy in the West through agents. The middle-class migrants, then, not only made up the bulk of the settlers shortly after extensive settlement began, but seem to have been the people who created the real conflicts in district-stage government, or in the first decade or so of government in the territories that began with the second stage. The newer immigrants resented the monopolization of government by the earliest settlers and pressed for changes in the system by which they could obtain a share of power. In territories under the district stage, they generally directed their agitation toward the achievement of representative government. Agitation both in the territories that did pass through the district stage and in those that did not, however, was not structured along party lines.

During the early years in every territory, party factions of various sorts existed, but they seemed to be fluid, local in orientation, and organized primarily around specific issues. Not until a territory's economic development began in earnest did political parties emerge, and this development was closely allied to the migration of a substantial middle class to the territory. Political parties invariably assumed national party labels and often made use of national issues, but other than the patronage links, their relationship to a national party was usually tenuous, since their *raison d'être* was power in local and territorial government. It is difficult to determine which source of power was more important.

The quest for representative government can be interpreted in two ways that are not mutually exclusive. For the bourgeoisie, the second stage provided a means of bypassing the local oligarchies and sharing in the exercise of power, thereby broadening membership in the oligarchy. For the existing oligarchies, the legislature might be a mechanism for consolidating and extending their control over local affairs. It is clear that there were numerous, significant divisions between territorial and local oligarchies, and that local oligarchies, whatever their composition, could and often did resist territorial authority successfully. Consequently it is not clear whether the second stage simply raised the oligarchic power structure to a higher level or altered it.

Conflicts during the district stage were by no means limited to those between local magnates and the incipient or real bourgeoisie who wanted a share of power. When it existed, popular criticism of the first stage centered not only on the local oligarchies, but on the nature of the system itself, particularly on the governor's autocratic powers. A good deal of this criticism arose from the slowness of the imperial government and its administrative personnel to appreciate the magnitude of the changes occurring in the territories, and from their failure to adjust quickly enough to these changes. The bulk of criticism seems to have been directed toward governors' use of their appointive and proclamation powers to increase governmental services or to cope with pressing problems, since the use of these powers kept the noxious, absolutist nature of the district stage before the public eye. Of more practical and real importance, every time a governor used the appointive power, he showed himself to be the captive or ally of the original settlers, and this only increased the bitterness of the dispossessed. If he was not subservient to the original settlers, the governor still had a vested interest in their retaining power, and, with few exceptions, governors felt obliged to appoint from the ranks of the original settlers, because their leaders in fact controlled the governor's appointive power.

Undoubtedly one of the most important factors in explaining the course of government during the district stage and thereafter is the governor's attitude toward his position. During the initial years of settlement in every territory, the most fundamental problems were those of Indian removal or pacification, and land settlement, and these were naturally the governor's major preoccupations. But when settlers began arriving in large numbers, other problems became more pressing, and they quickly overtaxed the limited resources of the district governments. Large scale immigration necessitated the speeding up of Indian removal and land survey so that land could be distributed, but since the Indians would not graciously cede their ancestral lands and be pushed back into the territory of other tribes, who were often unfriendly anyway, a military problem emerged. When the Indians resisted, punitive action was taken both by the federal government and by the settlers themselves, and the governor found himself in the unenviable position of having concurrently to enforce a peace policy with the Indians and to obtain Indian removal so that Anglo-American settlers could occupy their lands. Thus, in the governor's eyes, the initial problem boiled down to a military one. He had to discipline the citizenry, organize it into militia units and, as both commander of the regular army and superintendent of Indian affairs, bring the Indians to their knees, protect them, and get their land.

If one were to gauge priorities by the volume of correspondence devoted to these subjects, he could only conclude that all early governors considered matters of civil administration to be secondary, at least as long as settlement depended on Indian removal. The federal government certainly gave most emphasis to the problems related to Indian removal and, in effect, early executives saw their role as primarily a military one. The early governors of the territories in both the Northwest and the Southwest, in fact, stated explicitly that they considered their primary function to be Indian removal. It comes as no surprise, therefore, that they paid relatively little attention to civil administration. Nor should it give cause to wonder that Governors St. Clair and Blount immediately limited themselves to the most general sort of supervision over the lesser governmental officials. By so doing they established a system of governmental relationships that subsequent governors found difficult to change. The early governors in succeeding territories accepted the system, if for no other reason than that, faced with the same problems, they also decided to concentrate on Indian and military affairs. But it was at precisely the time that immigration reached floodtide—the latter half of the 1790s in the Northwest Territory—that the problems of local government and land settlement grew beyond the control of the district governments.

The problems of governing a territory and of administering federal policies during the district stage were not simply the result of the personal strength or weakness of the governors. Rather, they resulted from a combination of the failure of the federal government to give the governors adequate support, the statutory and practical weaknesses of the governor's office and, perhaps most important, the necessity of performing many and varied duties, which often led governors to neglect their civil responsibilities. Furthermore, by limiting themselves to generalities or by ignoring civil administration, the first governors, as well as changing national patterns of deference to authority, contributed to the early rise of that autonomy which was to characterize local governments and make the governors mere figureheads in many respects. The rapid and permanent deterioration of the executive powers must have fostered absenteeism in all territories. If in this way the governors became the foremost symbols of federal impotence, who could blame them for absenting themselves from their territories when it was expedient for them to do so or when they were not needed?

Certainly as surprising as the events that occurred during the district stage was the speed with which they took place. While there are no simple relationships between the attitudes of the people, the sizes of populations, and the length of the district-stage governments, there are some generalizations that can be drawn from a comparison of these factors. In terms of population growth, the district stage was relatively brief in all seven territories, and transition to the second stage invariably followed hard on the heels of the citizens' demands for representative government.

The district stage of the Northwest officially lasted eleven years, but significant agitation for advance to the second stage developed only after 1795, when the population began to increase rapidly. During the three or four years between the initial demands and the realization of representative government, Governor St. Clair consistently resisted making the change. He based his opposition largely on the contention that the people were unprepared for representative government, but an equally important factor was his well-known and outspoken distrust of republican institutions. Nevertheless, the underlying cause for delay was the need for division of the territory before beginning the second stage. Leaders of all the political factions agreed on this matter, as did St. Clair, who as early as 1790 had called on Congress to split the territory into three districts, pointing out that it was impossible to administer the Northwest effectively as a single district. The problem was that the three principal factions—centered around Marietta, Chillicothe and Cincinnati—and the governor could not agree on how the territory should be divided. The three factions were at odds, partially because each wanted a division that would make its town the most suitable capital. St. Clair had formulated several plans aimed at postponing the second stage and statehood for as long as possible or, if it could not be delayed, to obtain a gerrymandered division of the territory which would assure Federalist domination in the more populous eastern portion. Until 1798, there was neither sufficient cooperation among factions nor enough general pressure generated to force St. Clair to call elections for an assembly, and then it was done before the territory was divided. In the meantime, petitions and lobbyists had been sent to Congress to promote the various plans. In 1798, Congress finally took up the question of division, and the following year, after the first Northwest General Assembly had met, temporarily settled the issue by dividing the Northwest into two parts along a line roughly corresponding to the provisions of the Ordinance.[2]

2. For a full discussion of the issues, see Randolph C. Downes, *Frontier Ohio, 1788–1803* (Columbus, 1935), 164–72, 178–80, hereafter cited as Downes, *Frontier Ohio;* Beverley W. Bond, Jr., *The Civilization of the Old Northwest. A Study of Political, Social, and Economic Development, 1788–1812* (New York, 1934), 101, 111–12, 435, hereafter cited as Bond, *Old Northwest;* Beverley W. Bond, Jr., *The Foundations of Ohio* (Columbus, 1941), 431–35, 449–55, hereafter cited as Bond, *Foundations;* Gordon L. Wilson, "Arthur St. Clair and the Administration of the Old Northwest Territory, 1788–1802" (unpublished Ph.D. dissertation, University of Southern California, June, 1957), 168–69, 175, 326, 334, 352, hereafter cited as G. L. Wilson, "St. Clair"; William Henry Smith, *The St. Clair Papers. The Life and Public Services of Arthur St. Clair . . . with his Correspondence and Other Papers* (2 vols., Cincinnati, 1882), II:480–84, hereafter cited as Smith, *St. Clair Papers;* Carter, *Territorial Papers,* III:62–66, 76–78, 86–88 and *passim.* The first Northwest legislature met in September 1799. When St. Clair was out of the territory after 1795, Sargent continued, in his correspondence, to hammer away at the need for division, emphasizing the rapid increase in population since the Greenville Treaty, and arguing that it was unrealistic to expect settlers from the whole territory to send representatives to a single seat of government. The acquisition of the population around the northwest posts, following the Jay Treaty, compounded the need for division. Though their numbers were small, the people were widely scattered. To give a semblance of United States sovereignty over the area and to assure territorial integrity, the population had to be brought under direct administration. By 1798 it became clear that the first-stage system could no longer handle the complexities of government on any level. By the end of 1797 Committees of Correspondence in eastern Ohio were promoting statehood and a private census. When they made preparations for a private census and seemed determined to pass directly to statehood, St. Clair capitulated, called a census himself, and prepared the way for second-stage territorial government. (Bond, *Foundations,* 88; Downes, *Frontier Ohio,* 166–168, 171–72, 178–80.) Bond (*Foundations,* 450) concludes that Congressional indifference in itself was an almost insuperable obstacle before 1798, and that thereafter the principal objection in Congress was to the added expense that would result from division. Downes (*Frontier Ohio,* 172) draws similar conclusions, and adds that the delay also resulted from the fact that there was no Congressional leader before 1798 who

In 1801, shortly after division of the Northwest Territory, settlers in the Illinois Country of the new Indiana Territory began pressing for second-stage government. Although they had apparently been content with the first stage, the Franco-Americans now saw in representative government a way to protect slavery. Initially, Governor William Henry Harrison opposed their demands because he did not want to be hampered by a legislature that might turn up with a Federalist majority. By 1803, however, the positions were reversed. When Ohio became a state, Congress annexed the relatively populous "gore" to Indiana, thereby significantly changing the political complexion of the territory. Following this change, the Franco-Americans became disenchanted with their idea for protecting slavery, since the eastern settlers had an anti-slavery bias and would probably control a representative assembly. In November 1802, they joined with Harrison on their common pro-slavery interest. Together they organized a convention and petitioned Congress for nullification of Article 6 of the Ordinance, which prohibited slavery in the Old Northwest, but this only prompted a group of easterners to fire off the first of a long line of anti-slavery petitions and to request Harrison's replacement by a governor whose principles were not "repugnant to Republicanism." At this point the Franco-Americans became completely opposed to transition to the second stage and petitioned Congress for a division of Indiana and annexation of the western half to the newly acquired Louisiana Purchase.

In the meantime, Harrison had been revising his views on the desirability of representative government. The conflicts between the western, pro-slavery Franco-Americans and the eastern, anti-slavery Anglo-Americans endangered his security, and Harrison decided that the safest political move was to elevate the territory to the second stage. In this way, he hoped to avoid division and at the same time to strengthen his position by standing aside and reaping the harvest while the sections of the territories played out their antagonisms against each other. Consequently, during August 1804, within a month after

---

would sponsor a bill for division. James Ross, Federalist senator from Pennsylvania and a heavy speculator in the seven ranges, sponsored St. Clair's ideas, while in 1799 Harrison, as the territorial delegate, successfully promoted the general consensus of territorial citizens. See also Bond, *Old Northwest*, 101.

receiving petitions for a change in government, Harrison ordered a poll of the voters. Of the 400 votes cast, a majority favored change and, despite charges that he had rigged the canvass, Harrison declared the question carried, apportioned the territory, and set the election of the lower house for December. The first full legislature met in July of 1805. Thus Indiana had representative government within three and a half years of the time the first demands were voiced. It came largely at the insistence of the governor who initiated it as soon as he was confident that a real demand existed, and before an organized movement developed. As a consequence, Harrison was to be accused "ten thousand times . . . [of having] thrust the people of the territory into the second grade against their will."[3]

The Franco-Americans continued agitating for a separate government in Indiana until 1809, when Congress obliged them by dividing the territory. The new Illinois Territory reverted to the first stage, but having achieved their primary goal, its inhabitants seemed reasonably content, and the district stage was not marked by conflicts of the sort found in Illinois' parent territories. Instead, there seems to have been a kind of ambivalence toward it, reflected by Governor Ninian Edwards. He was not really satisfied with the first stage, yet he resisted advance to the second stage, so he claimed, because he did not know of a single person in the territory who could meet the 200-acre freehold requirement to qualify as a representative under the Ordinance, much less the 500-acre requirement for the council. Moreover, he did not want to see a tenth of the population, the freeholders, choosing the representatives, as he felt would be the case under the Ordinance fran-

3. The quote is from Francis S. Philbrick, *The Laws of Indiana Territory, 1801–1809* (Springfield, Ill., 1930), R28–29, hereafter cited as Philbrick, *Laws of Indiana.* See note 13, Chapter I. The Illinois-Indiana conflicts are discussed thoroughly in *ibid.*, R19–30, R36–38, R44, R53–54, R117–18; Dwight G. McCarty, *Territorial Governors of the Old Northwest* (Iowa City, 1910), 76–77, 86–87, hereafter cited as McCarty, *Governors of the Northwest;* Carter, *Territorial Papers,* VII:240–47; Logan Esarey, *A History of Indiana* (2 vols., Indianapolis, 1915–18), I:159–61. The "gore" was the thin triangle bounded by the present Ohio western boundary, the Ohio River, and a line drawn from a point opposite the mouth of the Kentucky River to Fort Recovery (Carter, *Territorial Papers,* III:86). Michigan was annexed to Indiana when Ohio became a state.

Philbrick (*Laws of Indiana,* R20) feels that by his "democratic practice" Harrison "greatly checked . . . the [general popular] demand for transition to the second stage," but see Chapter V.

chise. Nevertheless, as war with England grew imminent, he felt that the territory urgently needed a full-time representative in Washington. Consequently, in 1811, while urging Congress to abolish property qualifications for the suffrage, or at least to provide for the direct election of a territorial delegate, he began taking the necessary steps to move the district into the second stage.[4]

In sharp contrast to the bare three years between Edwards' arrival in Illinois and the change to representative government, Michigan spent nineteen years in the first stage. Like the Franco-Americans in Missouri and in Illinois, except during 1801 and 1802, the Michigan settlers never demanded second-stage government and, as in the Southwest Territory, when Governor Lewis Cass conducted a referendum in 1818, the voters defeated his proposal to progress to the second stage. Cass then let the question lapse for a time and turned to Congress for modification of the government. By the early 1820s there was some popular interest in change and, following passage of the Florida Organic Act in 1822, some Michigan settlers petitioned Congress for the same form of government. In 1823, Congress provided Michigan, like Florida, with a semi-representative unicameral government. The Legislative Council met for the first time in June of 1824.[5]

The apparent apathy of the people does not alone account for the length of Michigan's district stage. Congress had created the Michigan Territory in 1805, partly because of the inconvenient location of Detroit, which had the major concentration of population, and which was far from the seat of Indiana government. But it was also primarily an area of fur trading and trapping, in which there was stiff international competition that called for close supervision. For a number of years,

4. McCarty, *Governors of the Northwest*, 86, 88, 92–94, 111–13, 116; Philbrick, *Laws of Indiana*, R40–52; R. Carlyle Buley, *The Old Northwest: Pioneer Period, 1815–1840* (2 vols., Indianapolis, 1950), I:79, hereafter cited as Buley, *Old Northwest*. The first legislature met in December 1812. Edwards obtained both a broader suffrage and direct election of the delegate. One obvious inference that can be drawn from Edwards' attitude toward transition is that he considered himself better qualified to look after the interests of the territory than the "upper tenth"—and this was probably true. He might also have worried that an assembly elected on a narrow suffrage would prevent or delay his desired broadening of the electorate.

5. Carter, *Territorial Papers*, X:769–71. (See Chapter V for a discussion of the unicameral system.)

Michigan was essentially a transfrontier territory with only a few thousand widely scattered people. As late as 1820, its white population was under 9,000, but by then it was becoming an area of active Anglo-American agricultural settlement, and less than four years later the district stage ended. Thus one finds roughly the same time lapse between the beginning of extensive immigration and the end of the first stage in Michigan as in the other territories of the Northwest.

Michigan's settlement was delayed for several reasons, only one of which was its location outside the mainstream of settlement in the Ohio River drainage area, whose rivers were the avenues for commerce. When William Hull, the first governor, reached Detroit in 1805, the town had just been destroyed by fire. Poverty and starvation stalked the land, and federal aid was necessary both to help feed the people and to rebuild the town. When the territory was about on its feet and the government was finally operating, the War of 1812 began, Hull surrendered Detroit, and the British occupied the territory. Consequently one can argue that the official length of the Michigan district stage is deceptive, that its real existence should be dated from the end of the War of 1812, for then the new governor, Lewis Cass, had to begin reorganizing the territory. Again federal subsidies were essential—and inadequate. In addition, after the war, Michigan continued to suffer from bad publicity, when federal surveyors advised against locating military bounty lands in the territory because they considered its soil poor for farming. Cass led a campaign to counter such reports and to encourage agricultural settlement in Michigan. He also helped launch internal improvement projects and, by 1820, his efforts to enhance the territory's image were succeeding.[6]

6. See McCarty, *Governors of the Northwest*, 122–27, 130–32; Elvin L. Valentine, "The American Territorial Governor" (unpublished Ph.D. dissertation, University of Wisconsin, 1928), 21–22, hereafter cited as Valentine, "Territorial Governor."

Unlike the Illinois Country, which was a transfrontier area under the Northwest government, the Michigan government was initially established in a non-settlement area. That is, it was a transfrontier area, but one not attached to and administered from a principal settlement area.

If the Illinois and Indiana district stages are considered to include the periods under other district governments, their first-stage existence extended over nineteen and sixteen years respectively. Similarly, Michigan's district period could be lengthened to thirty years.

Outside of the Old Northwest, the district period in Missouri, when it was called Louisiana Territory, paralleled that of Michigan. After a year under the jurisdiction of Indiana Territory, Congress gave it a separate government. Like Michigan, Missouri was a transfrontier area with a small Franco-American population that did not overtly object to the district form of government. Unlike Michigan, however, Missouri was sought out by immigrants from the east soon after the wave of immigration started, and by 1809 a campaign began to obtain second-stage government. In that same year Governor Lewis died, and his replacement, Benjamin Howard, did not arrive until September of the following year. Howard was out of the territory during much of his administration, and took no stand on the issue of second-stage government. However, the acting governor, Secretary Frederick Bates, previously a territorial judge of Michigan Territory, tacitly supported the popular movement.

It was the pace of Congressional action rather than gubernatorial obstructionism that accounted for the three-year delay between the beginning of a campaign and the attainment of representative government in Missouri. Whether intentionally or not, the 1805 Organic Act had omitted the usual provision for transition to the second stage. Although the explicit extension of the articles of the Ordinance to Lousiana-Missouri might have been interpreted to permit the organization of a second-stage government, apparently everyone assumed that a new Organic Act was necessary, so the requisite petitions were duly prepared and sent off. Congress took up the petitions for a new Organic Act in 1810, but did not enact one until July 1813.[7]

At the beginning of his administration in the Southwest Territory, Governor William Blount did not wish to see his authority divided by

7. See Chapter V and Carter, *Territorial Papers,* I:25–26; XIV:245–46, 249–50, 252–56, 328, 332, 337, 338, 357–62, 362–66, 366n, 390–93, 403, 403–04n, 428–31, 456–58, 468–69, 471–79, 483, 484–87, 490–93, 495, 496, 524–25, 548–50, 552–59, 552n, 547n, 657n, 693. The editor of the *Missouri Gazette* wrote on March 1, 1809, that the most important question to be considered, both by those opposed to and those in favor of second-stage government, was whether the first- or second-stage government at that time would "most facilitate our arrival at that wished for goal of political puberty, a state government." (*Ibid.,* XIV:252.) As a whole, the Missourians showed a very keen interest in the relationship of population size to government—especially as it related to cost factors.

the election of an assembly. Nevertheless, the territory had more than the required number of free adult males, so he polled the voters in 1791. The electorate obligingly defeated the proposal to inaugurate the second stage. Two years later, however, the people were demanding a new canvass, and Blount had changed his mind. In May 1793 he ordered a new poll and actively supported transition. His objective was to extricate himself from the uncomfortable position of having to cope with both the federal peace policy toward the Indians and the popular clamor for war by placing a large part of the burden of dealing with these problems on a General Assembly. This time the question carried, and on October 19 Blount apportioned the territory. He scheduled the election of representatives for December, but it was nearly nine months later, in August 1794, before the council was appointed and the first General Assembly convened. The district stage in the Southwest thus lasted four years, until the population had reached about 61,000, despite the apparent lack of barriers to the popular will.[8]

In Mississippi, the last of the seven territories, Governor Winthrop Sargent's autocratic behavior and the violent, sustained popular reaction he engendered precipitated change. In 1800, within two years of Sargent's arrival, Congress ended the first-stage government with an act that inaugurated representative government, even though the total population was under 9,000. President Adams reprimanded Sargent but did not dismiss him, nor did Congress formally sustain charges against him in 1799 or 1800, so he completed his term of office in spite of continued criticism. Jefferson removed him by simply not renewing his commission in 1801.[9]

8. Masterson, *Blount*, 209–10, 235, 242–43, 245, 256; Carter, *Territorial Papers*, IV:80, 264, 267, 309–10, 319, 326, 329. The assembly met in February 1794, but only to nominate men for the council. (*Ibid.*, IV:328.) The absence of a strong movement for second-stage government within such a large population is partly explained by the simultaneous settlement of several widely separated parts of the territory, their mutual suspicion, and fear of domination.

Blount hoped that a legislature, by giving vent to popular discontent, would generate enough pressure to force the federal government into adopting a war policy and forcibly removing the Indians—all of which would also help to further Blount's land schemes. Blount was, after all, a businessman (that is, a speculator) in government for the sake of business.

9. See Carter, *Territorial Papers*, V:67, 74, 79–82, 87–88, 95–99, 99–103, 141, 606; Thorpe, *Constitutions*, 2027–28. Max Farrand (*The Legislation of Congress*

The first stage was not significantly contested or criticized in any of the territories for more than three or four years before the second stage officially began, and in some territories it was not vigorously challenged at any time. The average contested period was less than three years. When considered in terms of the normal lethargy of any government to undertake fundamental changes, particularly in cases where an act of Congress is necessary, it must be concluded that the response to popular demands for representative government, when they existed, was rapid. This is especially true since a census, referendum, and apportionment preceded the call for elections, and the representatives had to meet and nominate councillors, whom the President had to appoint and commission, after obtaining Senate confirmation, before the first General Assembly could meet and officially begin the second stage. Consequently, if a year is deducted from the average time lapse to compensate for time lost in transition—time that cannot reasonably be attributed to resistance to the change, the average contested period drops to about eighteen months, a remarkably short time.

More remarkable are the demographic characteristics of the territories, and their relationships to provisions of the Ordinances of both 1784 and 1787. By interpolating between censuses and by making some allowances for differential growth rates, it is clear that only the Southwest, with 40,000 to 45,000 inhabitants, exclusive of Indians, exceeded the 20,000 population requirement of Jefferson's Ordinance when the governor or settlers started pressing for representative government. More relevant is that only the Southwest, with about 11,000 adult males, definitely had more than the 5,000 required by the Ordinance of 1787 when movements for transition to the second stage *began.* In Mississippi there were probably no more than 1,800 adult males at the beginning of 1799; in Indiana, Illinois, and Michigan, about 2,100,

---

for the Government of the Organized Territories of the United States [Newark, N. J., 1896], 19–20, hereafter cited as Farrand, *Legislation for Territories*) states that Congress dropped the 5,000 adult male requirement and advanced the territory to the second stage primarily to avoid the problems of first-stage lawmaking. This was an important reason but it was undoubtedly secondary to the personality conflict. The first assembly met in October 1800, but took no action because the council had not yet been selected (Carter, *Territorial Papers,* V:108).

2,650, and 2,400 to 3,600 at the respective dates when transition became an issue; in the Northwest between 2,700 and 4,000; and in Missouri from 4,500 to 4,800.[10]

Maximum estimates of the population of each territory at the *end* of the first stage show similar characteristics but include the Northwest and Missouri with the Southwest as having well over the prescribed 5,000 adult males (see Table 1). However, the straight line interpolation used for these estimates assumes a constant annual increment during the decade in which transition occurred, and in some cases the growth rate fluctuated significantly. In both Illinois and Missouri, the second stage began on the eve of the War of 1812, and a large majority of the immigrants must have arrived in the second half of the decade. Consequently, more accurate estimates for their populations at the end of the district stage would probably be about 15,000 and 22,000 respectively, making the numbers of adult males about 4,000 and 5,800 (the bracketed figures in the table).

If the same figures are reduced by one year's average increase, the approximate population and number of adult males in each territory at the beginning of the transition period can be determined. The figures for adult males also represent the maximum possible number of potential voters in each territory where a year's residence was necessary. In four territories, however, the Organic Acts required two years' residence. For them, the terminal estimates of the district stage are reduced by two years' growth in the table to indicate the maximum number of men who could have possibly qualified for the vote. The average for all seven territories is 5,800 men, and the average for the six, excluding the Southwest, is 4,760. Since all the figures are estimates and cannot be pinpointed to the months in which the changes began, there is no advantage or increased accuracy to be gained by reducing them by another year's growth to take full account of residence requirements. Thus the estimates are intentionally liberal, and they could be justifiably reduced further without risk of underestimation. This is especially true of the southern territories, in that all the estimates are based on whole populations, which include free Negroes and slaves.

10. The two figures for Michigan are estimates for 1818 and 1822. The latter is probably the more appropriate.

TABLE 1. TERRITORIAL POPULATIONS AT THE END OF THE DISTRICT STAGE

			Estimated Maximum Populations			
	Length of District Stage		*End of District Stage*		*End of District Stage Minus 1 or 2 Years' Growth*	
Territory	*Month/Year*	*No. Years*	*Total Pop.*	*Voting Age Males*[1]	*Total Pop.*	*Voting Age Males*[1]
Northwest	July 1788–Sept. 1799	11	43,000–46,000	11,400	36,000*	9,500*
Ohio (1801)[2]			39,000	10,300		
Indiana	July 1800–July 1805	5	14,500	3,850	10,400*	2,800*
Illinois	Apr. 1809–Dec. 1812	3	20,900	5,600 [4,000]	16,500	4,400 [3,100]
Michigan	June 1805–June 1824	19	17,000	4,500	14,600	3,900
Southwest (Tenn.)	Oct. 1790–Aug. 1794	4	61,000[3]	16,200	47,000*	12,500*
Mississippi	Aug. 1798–Oct. 1800	2	8,850	2,350	7,100*	1,900*
Louisiana (Mo.)	July 1805–July 1813	8	27,500–33,600[4]	7,300–8,700 [5,800]	22,800	6,050 [5,300]

* Indicates territories requiring two years' residence; these figures are for the end of the district stage minus two years.

[1] Voting age males are calculated on the basis of percentages estimated for the period 1830–1860, about 26.5%. See Jack E. Eblen, "An Analysis of Nineteenth-Century Frontier Populations," in *Demography*, II (1965), 405, Table 1. This percentage estimate may well be too high. A census of Hamilton County, Northwest Territory, July 1798, indicates only 23% of the population to have been voting age males. Cincinnati and Columbia, the largest towns of the county, had the extreme percentages, 29.8 and 18.3, respectively. Since the enumeration of Cincinnati may well have included the soldiers at nearby Fort Washington, the average of 23% may be high for the time. See census data in Carter, *Territorial Papers*, II:649. 23% of 36,000 is 8,300.

[2] These are estimates of the population in the Northwest after division of the territory. See *Historical Statistics*, 13 notes.

[3] The census of late 1795 showed the territory to contain 77,300 people. This includes 11,600 free Negroes and slaves. Carter, *Territorial Papers*, IV:404.

[4] Straight line interpolation for Missouri is very inaccurate; the larger figures are clearly too high. End of the district stage minus one year is calculated on the basis of the smaller figures, which are also probably too high. The population of the territory in 1810 was 20,800. See Carter, *Territorial Papers*, XIV:491.

Source: Population estimates determined by straight line interpolation of data in *Historical Statistics*, 13.

The residence requirement is a very inadequate measure of the qualified voters in a territory, since there were also property requirements which seem to have shrunk the electorate to at least half the number of men. In retrospect, therefore, when Congress abrogated the 5,000 free adult male requirement in the Indiana and second Mississippi Organic Acts, and substituted the provision for a majority of the freeholders—presumably qualified voters in all respects but residence—to decide when each territory was ready for the second stage, it accomplished nothing. The magic figure of 5,000 had clearly been meaningless in practice before 1800, and the new requirement assured neither earlier transition nor a more accurate expression of the popular will, since a small group of land owners (averaging less than six percent of the territorial populations) in each territory always controlled the decision. In the four territories where the adult male population was definitely under 5,000 when the change to the second stage began, the governors or Congress had been primarily responsible for initiating the transition.[11]

11. See the discussion of the suffrage in Chapter V below and in notes 4 and 9 above, and in McCarty, *Governors of the Northwest*, 76–77, 136–38; Carter, *Territorial Papers*, VII:7–10. See also Farrand, *Legislation for Territories*, 31–34; Valentine, "Territorial Governor," 30–31.

The assumptions that seem to have been implicit in the Ordinance suffrage requirements—that population growth would be slow enough, and of such a nature, that by the time the number of adult males reached 5,000 the electoral and economic bases would be adequate for self-sufficient representative government, while high property qualifications for officeholding would assure conservative control of government—did not entirely work out in practice, except in the latter case. The effects of abrogating the population requirement for the beginning of the second-stage government were mainly psychological.

In 1804, Indiana may have had an adult male population of about 3,300, but only 400 votes were cast in the referendum on second-stage government. As Philbrick (*Laws of Indiana*, R26) says, regardless of complaints that Harrison fixed the election, both sides had an equal opportunity to turn out their votes. Thus, if the number of votes cast is any indication of the number of qualified voters, then the decision rested in few hands indeed. (Four hundred is 14 percent of 2,800, the estimated maximum number of men who could meet the residence requirement, and 12 percent of 3,300, the probable number of adult males in the territory around the time of the elections, but in either case it is less than 4 percent of the total population of the territory. See the notes to Table 1.) John Welling Smurr, "Territorial Constitutions; A Legal History of the Frontier Governments Erected by Congress in the American West, 1787–1900" (unpublished Ph.D. dissertation, University of Indiana, 1960), 502, hereafter cited as Smurr, "Con-

Compared to the size of population, the rate of growth, and the speed of transition, the end of the district stage corresponded rather closely to the provisions of the Ordinance of 1787. In these terms, one may conclude that the district stage worked out pretty much as intended by the authors of the Ordinance, and that its length was neither prolonged nor severe. On the other hand, the overall length of a district-stage government is not a measure of the pace at which "aliens" were educated into the mysteries of American political institutions, but of the pace of Anglo-American settlement and of their reaching numerical superiority.[12] With the possible exception of St. Clair, the governors brought the first stage to an end quickly when substantial opposition or strong demands for representative government developed. This is not to say, however, that the system was necessarily adequate or that the nature of government as it evolved during the early years was unimportant. On the contrary, next to the relative brevity of the district stage, the most surprising characteristic of territorial government in the First Empire was the rapid deterioration of executive power and the pattern of political life that crystallized in the first stage.

The governors must bear a primary share of responsibility for the shortcomings of the district stage, since their general lack of interest in civil administration and their frequent absences are directly related to the political pattern that developed in practice. This relationship had profound consequences both in the Northwest and in every other territory.

---

stitutions," concludes that the franchise requirements of the Ordinance disqualified a majority of men. This may be behind the fact that, of the 676 adult males in the Illinois Country in 1808, only 322 cast votes in the election. (Carter, *Territorial Papers*, VII:609–10. Residence was certainly a negligible factor in Illinois around 1808.) Similarly, in the elections for the first Mississippi Territorial Assembly in 1800, only 239 votes were cast for eight of the nine representatives—that is, the representatives elected for the principal areas of settlement. Assuming that the two counties involved contained no more than 1,600 of the roughly 1,900 adult males who might have met the residence requirement, only 15 percent of the men (5.65 percent of the population) were eligible and voted. (See Carter, *ibid.*, V:96, 112.)

12. Philbrick (*Laws of Indiana*, R217–22) discusses the American attitude toward the Illinois settlers and the ways in which Anglo-Americans wrested control of government from the French as they moved into that territory.

Executive absences from the territories were common everywhere, and they presented administrative problems that were most distressing to President Washington; like a number of other Presidents during the First Empire, he was continually admonishing governors and other territorial officials to return to their posts. Sometimes Presidents ordered governors to return to their duties, threatening to remove them if they did not, and in the nineteenth century Congress joined the effort to keep governors in their territories. In one case, Congress adopted a law forbidding the governor of Florida to leave the territory without permission. Early in 1852, Congress passed a law under which a governor who was absent without a certificate from the President showing good cause would lose his salary for the whole year in which the absence occurred. From then on, through much of the Second Empire, Congress and the Departments of the Treasury and Interior periodically made similar declarations or renewed old ones, providing for losses of pay ranging from sixty days to one year. In 1873, the Interior Department even went so far as to issue a circular stating that any official absent without leave would be assumed to have tendered his resignation. None of these laws and declarations seem to have helped much. Instead, the greater ease of obtaining permission to leave the territory that came with improvements in communications in the post-Civil War period seems to have reduced the volume of absences without leave. But since total absences thereafter were as high as before, and permission for them seems to have been granted almost routinely when requested, the earlier concern would appear to have been largely a matter of federal punctiliousness rather than of wishing to maintain constant or tight supervision over the colonies. Thus the average absence of about a quarter to a third of every year, which seems to have characterized the First Empire during the first half of the nineteenth century, apparently continued throughout the Second Empire.[13]

13. The Florida law, passed May 3, 1823, was repealed May 26, 1824 (Carter, *Territorial Papers*, XXII:391n; 3 *Statutes*, 750–54; 4 *Statutes*, 47). Absences are discussed in Valentine, "Territorial Governor," 46–48, 83–84; Earl Pomeroy, *The Territories and the United States, 1861–1890* (Philadelphia, 1947), 9–10, 20, hereafter cited as Pomeroy, *Territories, 1861–1890;* Farrand, *Legislation for Territories*, 44–45; William M. Neil, "The Territorial Governor in the Rocky Mountain West, 1861–1889" (unpublished Ph.D. dissertation, University of Chicago, 1952), 43–45, hereafter cited as Neil, "Territorial Governors." See also Carter, *Territorial*

During the history of the territories, the term "absence" was never defined adequately. The federal government and most governors (St. Clair, for example), simply assumed that "absent" meant "outside the territory." But there was a significant difference between physical absence from the territory and practical absence from duties, or executive inaccessibility. Throughout the Northwest district stage, for example, there was neither a formal seat of government nor an archive; they were wherever St. Clair and Secretary Sargent happened to be. Distance alone made the governor virtually inaccessible to the more remote parts of the territory, except for periods of a few days at a time, when he or the secretary traveled to the outlying settlements. During these trips, which sometimes lasted several months or more, the governor's services were unavailable to almost everyone who was not in the executive entourage. In addition, there were times when both St. Clair and Sargent were outside the territory at the same time, and at least one occasion on which the governor, the secretary, and all three judges were simultaneously outside the territory. Finally, St. Clair's aloofness and arrogance alienated people, and he sometimes withheld his services deliberately.

Whenever the executive was inaccessible, or when the officer who was exercising executive authority lacked the seal, no territorial business could be conducted. Moreover, the absence of the governor and judges affected local administration both directly and indirectly, since both lawmaking and enforcement depended on their presence. The absence of public records or ignorance of their whereabouts also hindered local administration. Throughout the district stage, and often, if not generally, during the second stage in both the First and Second Empires, the publication and distribution of laws was either totally neglected or woefully inadequate. As a result, local officials were often, and territorial officials were at least occasionally, entirely ignorant of the laws of their territory. Even in supposedly mature territories, the situation was little better. For example, just before Montana achieved statehood, it lacked adequate storage for its public records

---

Papers, V:92; XIV:403–04, 448, 599–601; XIX:228; XX:406–07; XXI:438; XXII:539; XXV:617. Governors had a penchant for long absences in the East. They went not only for business and pleasure, but sometimes to lobby for their territories.

and was still having difficulty in raising enough money to publish its laws, despite federal printing subsidies. Aside from the problems created by these factors, the secretary, as acting executive in the governor's absence, lacked the funds, prestige, and clearly-defined authority to be wholly effective. Executive absences from the territory, then, resulted in a serious lack of administration for considerable periods of time, and, practically speaking, resulted at times in the nonexistence of territorial government.[14]

All of the above factors help to account for the rapid rise of local autonomy and diminution of the governor's power in the Northwest. St. Clair's absences from the Northwest and their effect on the administration of the territory are of primary interest, since they illustrate the precedent-setting devolution of the executive authority and the inability of a secretary to act effectively. The Northwest district stage officially lasted for a little more than eleven years, from July 15, 1788 to September 16, 1799. In the first nine years and ten months of that

14. See Philbrick, *Laws of Illinois*, R395–400; Downes, *Frontier Ohio*, 127–28, 134–47, 169; Bond, *Old Northwest*, 74–75, 77–78, 83–84; G. L. Wilson, "St. Clair," 408, 413; Bond, *Foundations*, 400–01, 423, 427–28; Neil, "Territorial Governors," 162; Pomeroy, *Territories, 1861–1890*, 32–33; Carter, *Territorial Papers*, XVI:373; XXIII:389, 535. On one occasion St. Clair entered and immediately left the territory, because he felt his presence in one part of the territory made Sargent's acts in another part illegal. (See Philbrick, *Laws of Illinois*, R397–99; Downes, *Frontier Ohio*, 169.) According to Bond (*Foundations*, 423, and *Old Northwest*, 74–75), Sargent made frequent trips east to lobby in Congress for extra compensation for the periods while he acted as governor. Sargent figured that the government owed him $6,939.03 for such services by the end of 1797. He seems to have collected $1,000 eventually. On at least three such occasions, the governor was also absent. Early in 1794 a House committee recommended that the secretary receive the governor's salary while acting as governor but the question was never settled. (See Carter, *Territorial Papers*, II:476, 648; McCarty, *Governors of the Northwest*, 38.) It should be added that the presence of the executive was not necessarily important. In the cases of trips to outlying settlements, for example, the governor or secretary did little more than proclaim counties, appoint officials, and make brief, ineffective stabs at settling land claims and conflicts.

The Ordinance of 1787 did not authorize the secretary to act for the governor in his absence, but in adapting the Ordinance to the Consitution, the first Congress authorized the secretary to do so. (Thorpe, *Constitutions*, 964.) In the meantime St. Clair had entered and left the territory, in order to watch Washington's inauguration, run for governor of Pennsylvania, and conduct private business, without anyone's being authorized to act as governor.

period, St. Clair was officially outside the territory for two-thirds of the time. During 1799 he was absent for an indeterminate period of time, carrying the territorial seal.[15] These do not include St. Clair's virtual absences within the territory and his unofficial absences from the territory. For example, it is estimated that he traveled about 10,000 miles within the territory. At an average rate of twenty miles a day, this amounts to five hundred days spent travelling. In addition, the accuracy of the official dates of absence is questionable. If anything, they were pared to reduce the periods of absence. The data, too, do not include all of the period when St. Clair was preoccupied with military preparations and the Indian campaign in 1791. These began in late spring 1791 and ended with St. Clair's defeat on November 4, 1791. If all absences of this sort are added, it seems St. Clair was unavailable for civil administration for nearly nine-tenths of his term. These considerations also omit periods when St. Clair was in the territory but was unable to act because Sargent had gone away with the official seal or records, or because of illnesses of which he constantly complained.

St. Clair's neglectful attitude toward his responsibilities typified a number of governors who seemed to consider the governorship a seasonal job, and who tended to leave civil administration to the secretaries while both inside and outside their territories. St. Clair apparently spent a good part of his absences on his estate at Ligonier, about forty miles east of Pittsburgh, which he felt was close enough to the territory so that he could return quickly, should his presence there be required. Not infrequently, St. Clair wintered at Ligonier, his return to the territory being delayed successively by frost, snow, spring thaw, and sieges of the gout. In the spring, "the Brimstone [having] proved once more too strong" for the gout, he reluctantly returned to the Ohio Country.[16]

15. Carter, *Territorial Papers,* II:312–13, 416, 418, 430–31, 437–42, 444, 450, 455, 463, 464, 476, 511, 558–59, 560, 564–66, but especially 471, 648, and 519. See also Downes, *Frontier Ohio,* 144. St. Clair was also absent frequently during the second stage. (See, for example, Smith, *St. Clair Papers,* I:241.)

16. Carter, *Territorial Papers,* II:312, 471; Neil, "Territorial Governors," 45. St. Clair apparently spent some time promoting himself for the Vice Presidency during absences in the early 1790s. (Downes, *Frontier Ohio,* 199.) During an eastern visit in 1791 he considered running for Congress from Pennsylvania but was persuaded not to do so. Two years earlier, on another absence from the territory, General Thomas Mifflin had defeated him in a race for the gover-

During St. Clair's extensive absences, Sargent acted as though he had all the powers of the governor—he held legislative sessions with the judges, created counties, appointed officials, and commanded the militia—and St. Clair accepted his actions as definitive. St. Clair thought that, in the absence of a clear definition of the extent of the secretary's authority as acting governor, he and the secretary could avoid conflicts over the use of the executive power during his absences through a simple understanding. Conflicts, nonetheless, arose between them and also, with more far-reaching effects, between the secretary and local officials.[17] Finally, in September 1797, St. Clair obtained an opinion from Secretary of State Timothy Pickering. The principal questions were whether the secretary could exercise all the governor's powers, and whether his actions were final or provisional. Pickering offered a partial interpretation, dealing only with Indian affairs and other matters that were essentially national or international in scope, and specifically exempted them from falling to the secretary during the governor's absence, except in cases of extreme need. In such cases, the actions or decisions of the secretary were provisional, subject to the governor's approval, alteration, or rejection. By inference, the secretary's authority in internal civil affairs was also provisional. Pickering concluded that the secretary had neither the same final authority exercised by the governor in person, nor that which he commanded when the office of governor was vacant, since he was not strictly speaking the acting governor but the governor's representative.[18]

Regardless of the inferences that could be drawn from Pickering's opinion, after 1797 St. Clair avoided conflicts over the use of executive

---

norship of Pennsylvania by a margin of eight to one. (Smith, *St. Clair Papers,* I:186–87; Frazer Ells Wilson, *Arthur St. Clair, Rugged Ruler of the Old Northwest; An Epic of the American Frontier* [Richmond, 1944], 50, an absurd volume hereafter cited sparingly as F. E. Wilson, *St. Clair.*)

17. For a discussion of conflicts between St. Clair and Sargent, see Bond, *Old Northwest,* 86–89.

18. Pickering to St. Clair, September 18, 1797, in Carter, *Territorial Papers,* II:629. Though Sargent acted as if all the governor's powers fell to him during St. Clair's absence he showed a marked lack of confidence in the legitimacy of some actions. (See, for example, *ibid.,* III:400, where he questions his authority to hold legislative sessions with the judges.) One indication of the practical extent of the secretary's authority is that secretaries did not remove undesirable officials while they were acting as governors. (See below note 28.)

powers by making it impossible for secretaries to act in his absence. Both St. Clair and Sargent were Federalists having similar attitudes, and their conduct as executives was compatible. This was not true after Sargent became governor of the Mississippi Territory in 1798. Republican William Henry Harrison replaced Sargent as secretary, and when the legislature elected Harrison as territorial delegate, another Republican, Charles Willing Byrd, assumed the secretarial post. At this time, national politics had a strong influence on the territory. The Republicans were rapidly gaining strength, and to prevent their taking advantage of his absences, St. Clair henceforth withheld all public records from the secretary and carried the seal with him wherever he went, inside or outside the territory. St. Clair thereby prevented a Republican secretary from appointing Republicans during his absences, but he also brought administration to a standstill. Apparently St. Clair felt that there would be less opposition to this course than to his leaving the seal behind and nullifying when he returned to the territory any Republican handiwork that he did not approve. In fact, such a naked display of autocratic power outraged even his friends and focused more diffuse animosities on the system of government that made such despotism possible.[19]

19. Philbrick, *Laws of Illinois*, R396–99; Bond, *Old Northwest*, 89–90. Philbrick, R399n; and Carter, *Territorial Papers*, V:402, cite other instances of governors' withholding seals and records from secretaries, and vice versa. Later in the history of the territories there were similar occurrences, and in one case the secretary's refusal to let the governor use the seal prompted the governor to have a duplicate made. There followed a fight over which seal was the official one, and which more closely conformed to legal specifications. (See Neil, "Territorial Governors," 149–53.)

President Adams may have blundered by appointing Republicans as territorial secretaries, but he may also have hoped to silence discontent with a bipartisan display that drew off leaders and made them impotent agents of the federal government. In practice, the appointments elevated the status of Republicans and provided a focus for popular opposition to the governor and the first-stage government. As national party politics invaded the territory, St. Clair also became a much more active Federalist. In 1798 he wrote two pamphlets to help his party fight the spread of democracy—an evil word in St. Clair's vocabulary. The pamphlets propounded the Federalist ideal and supported John Adams and the Alien and Sedition Acts. (See Smith, *St. Clair Papers*, II:442; Alfred B. Sears, "The Political Philosophy of Arthur St. Clair," *The Ohio State Archaeological and Historical Quarterly*, XLIX (Columbus, 1940), 49–50, hereafter cited as Sears, "Philosophy of St. Clair.")

After 1797, the secretary as acting governor was in fact impotent. Almost from the beginning, local officials in the Northwest Territory resisted, and then denied, the right of the secretary, during the governor's absences, to do more than create new counties and renew the commissions of officials in existing counties. By late 1790, a bare two years after the organization of the Northwest, the local officials made it clear that they did not consider the secretary authorized in the governor's absence to interfere in local affairs or to remove appointed officials for any reason. During the early 1790s they consolidated their claims and extended them, and by the middle of the decade they had effectively limited the prerogatives of the governor himself in local affairs. The weakening of the governor's office occurred early in the Northwest, and it is evident in many of the events that took place during St. Clair's administration.

As acting governor of the Northwest and as governor of Mississippi, the irritable, puritanical director of the Ohio Company, Winthrop Sargent, was the most autocratic executive to hold office during the first two United States empires, and for that very reason he failed to enforce his will upon either territory. Anxious to succeed and inclined to use martial law whenever civil law seemed to him to fail, Sargent seldom resisted the temptation to "stretch to the limit" his powers as acting governor of the Northwest during St. Clair's frequent absences.[20]

In the summer of 1790, Sargent moved from Marietta, Ohio, to Cincinnati.[21] When he arrived there, he found soldiers having a noisy cel-

20. Bond, *Foundations*, 400–01; Downes, *Frontier Ohio*, 127–28, 131–40. The following narrative draws heavily on Downes' detailed discussion of "The Reign of Winthrop Sargent" in *ibid.*, 127 *et seq.*

21. Sargent had married General Benjamin Tupper's daughter, Rowena, in February 1789, and left Marietta shortly after she died. Tupper was one of the organizers of the Ohio Company. There is some conflict in the sources between the dates of Mrs. Sargent's death and Sargent's subsequent move to Cincinnati. Compare B. H. Pershing, "Winthrop Sargent," *Ohio Archaeological and Historical Publications*, XXXV (Columbus, 1926), 593, hereafter cited as Pershing, "Sargent"; and Bond, *Foundations*, 427. The former places Sargent's wife's death in September, but it is clear from correspondence (Carter, *Territorial Papers*, III:329–30) that Sargent arrived in Cincinnati during the last week of August. There is also some question as to St. Clair's whereabouts during the second half of the year. Officially he was in the territory from mid-September to late December, but the lack of activity and Sargent's actions indicate that he was absent most of this time. (See *ibid.*, II:312; III:333.)

ebration and punctuating their nocturnal revelry with gunfire. Such disorder, especially the indiscriminate discharging of weapons in a time of Indian danger, appalled the secretary. General Josiah Harmar was presently off with an "army"—which the Indians would defeat handily in October—and in his absence Cincinnati's defenses had to be properly maintained. Sargent promptly issued a proclamation calling attention to two laws recently adopted at Vincennes that forbade the sale of liquor to soldiers and the discharging of firearms in towns except to warn of Indian attacks, and he ordered local officials to enforce them immediately.[22] His objectives were to make an example of the people of Hamilton County, in order to alert the whole territory of the need for keeping its defenses in constant readiness, and to warn that, if necessary, he would not hesitate to invoke martial law.

Sargent's proclamation was not greeted with enthusiasm. The frontiersmen did not take to its strong threat of rigid discipline, and surely would have reacted if it had been implemented, but George Turner, one of the territorial judges, intervened in time. After publicly denouncing Sargent, Turner humiliated the secretary by pointing out that the two laws in question were explicitly inoperative by their own provisions until January 1, 1791.[23] This left Sargent no choice but to retreat temporarily. In the meantime, local officials ceremoniously

22. See Carter, *Territorial Papers*, II:305; III:332–33; Theodore Calvin Pease, *The Laws of the Northwest Territory, 1788–1800* (Springfield, Ill., 1925), A28–34, A256 (see note 13, Chap. I), hereafter cited as Pease, *Laws of the Northwest*. The soldiers were drinking and Sargent concluded that they were drunk—as they may well have been.

Neither Sargent nor the judges signed the first law referred to, hence its legality was questionable. "Passed at Vincennes" on July 26, 1790, the "Act" forbade the sale or procurement of liquor for soldiers within ten miles of any military installation, provided fines of treble the value of articles involved, and added a month's imprisonment for each repetition of the offense. The law was repealed in 1795. The second law, passed August 4, 1790, forbade the firing of weapons in or about settlements and before sunrise or after sunset in certain other places, and contained a list of penalities. The Act included the statement that it was not intended to "restrain or impair [the right of citizens to] the peaceable exercise of any useful or rational amusement . . . whether the same be used to promote health, pleasure, or a laudable emulation to excel in feats of skill, strength, adroitness, or otherwise howsoever"—provided, of course, that gambling was not involved.

23. Pease, *Laws of the Northwest*, A29, A34; Philbrick, *Laws of Illinois*, R461–62; Downes, *Frontier Ohio*, 134–35.

dealt with the worst problems, and the governor returned before Sargent could renew his assault from a stronger position. St. Clair was of the same mind as Sargent, but he agreed with Turner that the secretary had acted improperly and without legal basis. St. Clair set about repairing the damage while attempting to improve defenses through personal suasion. In early November, the remnants of Harmar's army retreated from the north and the nature of the problem changed as winter set in.[24]

As spring drew near and the threat of Indian forays increased, Sargent prepared for a new attack on disorder and inadequate defenses.[25] Whatever the needs were for improving defenses, Sargent's methods were unjustified. By militia orders in March 1791, he attempted to turn the settlements of the territory into armed camps. He ordered daily inspections and used courts-martial to enforce his orders. His action amounted to direct rule by martial law, and local officials became openly hostile to his invasions into what they considered to be purely local affairs. Especially irritating were instances in which Sargent bypassed functioning local courts in favor of courts-martial, and threatened to mete out death penalties to persons who illegally fired weapons. Beyond gunshot of Cincinnati, however, people largely ignored him, and once St. Clair's army was organized and took to the field, controls were relaxed in Cincinnati.

After St. Clair's ignominious defeat in November there was again reason for constant vigilance. St. Clair left the territory under a cloud in December 1791, to defend himself before the President and Congress. He did not return until August 1793, leaving Sargent uninterrupted in the pursuit of discipline for over a year and three quarters. During this period, local authorities successfully defied Sargent and asserted their autonomy, decisively weakening the executive power.[26]

24. Carter, *Territorial Papers,* II:305, 312, 471, 648; III:333. St. Clair apparently returned on September 16.

25. St. Clair had left the territory well before Christmas 1790 and did not return until the following April. After a few days' stay he was gone again. During this visit to the territory he made Sargent a colonel of the militia. (Carter, *Territorial Papers,* II:312, 339, 471.) St Clair spent the remainder of the year on the military expedition, and when he was in the territory, he evidently took no part in civil administration.

26. See Downes, *Frontier Ohio,* 135–36; Carter, *Territorial Papers,* III:334–35.

In March 1792 Sargent faced open rebellion when a lieutenant colonel of the militia objected to fulfilling a fifteen-day quota of men for road construction, saying that such a deployment would weaken defenses. Sargent countered with an order to build a stockade to improve defenses if the men could not otherwise be spared, and when nineteen of the sixty men did not appear for the road construction detail, he had them court-martialed. Simultaneously, he began building up a loyal following by promoting his supporters in the militia. In June General James Wilkinson, the future territorial governor of Louisiana-Missouri, possibly at Sargent's request, imprisoned two civilians in Fort Washington at Cincinnati, and refused to honor a writ of habeas corpus. Sargent used the issue to mount a frontal assault on the civil courts. He denied the validity of the writ, contending that John Blanchard, the issuing clerk, had not been legally appointed. He then appointed a new clerk, but Blanchard refused to vacate his office and continued to act as clerk. Territorial judge John Symmes came to Blanchard's aid, proved that the clerk's tenure was legal, and forced Sargent to make another retreat.[27]

Twice in as many years, territorial judges had helped the populace to force Sargent to stop interfering in their local affairs. The next time, the people themselves thwarted him, even though Sargent made sure in advance that his legal ground was solid. The confrontation grew out of Sargent's obsession with the illegal firing of weapons after dark, during the Christmas celebration of 1792—which lasted until mid-January. During the Christmas season of 1791, Sargent had imprisoned four celebrants; in 1792 he had less success. On New Year's Eve he called out the militia and the constable, who promptly disappeared.

27. Downes, *Frontier Ohio*, 137–38; Carter, *Territorial Papers*, II:402–04; III: 367–68, 375–83. Sargent did not like Wilkinson any more than he liked Turner or Symmes at this time, but he certainly was willing to use him. Open animosities among federal officials had an increasingly adverse effect on administration during the 1790s, as the judges (Turner and Symmes; Putnam was of the same mind as Sargent) more openly championed and led factions against the executive. Besides those conflicts mentioned in the text, St. Clair, the federal official least involved in speculation, openly and frequently criticized the land activities of other territorial officers and their failure to attend to their duties. The most notable public rebuke occurred in 1792, when the governor issued a proclamation warning prospective settlers that Symmes was selling land at the mouth of the Miami that he did not own. (See Bond, *Old Northwest*, 81–90, particularly 85.)

When the militia took two prisoners, a crowd freed one of them. On January 6, Sargent worsened the situation when he ordered a constant patrol of the streets of Cincinnati to improve enforcement of his laws against drinking and the firing of weapons. On the following night, he apprehended one of the guards drinking outside the guard house, incarcerated him, and proceeded to court-martial him. Judge Symmes immediately issued a writ of habeas corpus to local authorities, and rumors went out that force would be used to release the man, if necessary. Sargent ignored the writ and got a conviction by court-martial, but only after encircling his house with guards and secretly removing the prisoner to prevent interference.

Unsatisfied with this action, Sargent next went after those leaders of the rebellious populace who were not in the militia. He presented a list of names and charges with supporting evidence and one witness to the Court of the Quarter Sessions, and demanded indictments. Over Sargent's objections, the court called a grand jury which, while he watched in impotent rage, refused to return indictments. He might have tried to fire the head of the court if St. Clair had not appointed the judge. Later, Sargent said that "if he had been my appointment I would have removed him." Having already suffered enough embarrassment for one time, he was probably unwilling to face the probability that the judge would defy his authority to remove him.[28]

Sargent occupied much of his time during the year in an unsuccessful attempt to undermine the power of the local hierarchy by gaining control of the Court of Common Pleas.[29] The three-man court needed expansion, and Sargent decided to appoint two new members at the beginning of February 1793. The three men on the court had commissions of unspecified tenure, but Sargent intended to appoint the

28. The quote is in Downes, *Frontier Ohio*, 140. See also *ibid.*, 138–40; Bond, *Foundations*, 427; Carter, *Territorial Papers*, III:390–97, 401–04. Like Christmas, Founders Day was always an occasion for jubliation.

29. The Court of the Quarter Sessions of the Peace was at this time the center of power, but since plural officeholding was common, Sargent could undermine it by asserting control over those members who were also on the Common Pleas Court. A frontal assault on the Quarter Sessions would have been foolhardy and the situation that arose with regard to the Common Pleas offered some hope of success. For a discussion of the entire court system see Philbrick, *Laws of Indiana*, R143–65. See also Chapter IV below.

new members with tenure during pleasure. To make all commissions uniform and make clear his interpretation of the meaning of the original commissions, he attempted to revoke the commissions of the old members and give them and the new justices a single commission specifying tenure during pleasure. The justices refused to accept the commission and the three already on the bench continued to sit under their original commissions. They protested that tradition and commissions having no stated tenure entitled them to hold office, like the territorial judges, during good behavior. Sargent asserted that *any* commission issued by the governor was during pleasure by implication if not explicitly stated. He then proclaimed that, in any case, the justices held office only because of the lack of intelligent, qualified personnel on the frontier, and that, for the good of the territory, they should always stand ready to step down whenever more qualified people appeared. In the standoff that followed, Sargent threatened to remove the recalcitrant justices forcibly, but in late July, before the situation reached a showdown, St. Clair returned to the territory.

While he was in full accord with the secretary, the governor was more tactful and was willing to compromise to get his way. He secured opinions from two lawyers saying that the justices were guilty of usurpation by remaining in office under commissions that had been superseded. With these, St. Clair talked the old justices into accepting a new commission "in the original form," thereby setting a precedent that might be used later to enforce his and the secretary's interpretation, but it was to be a hollow victory.[30]

30. Downes, *Frontier Ohio,* 142–44; Bond, *Foundations,* 427–28; Carter, *Territorial Papers,* II:432–33, 456; III:405, 408–11, 413. See also Chapter IV. On August 16, St. Clair issued a single commission, naming the same five men that Sargent had appointed. The meaning of the phrase "in the original form" is unclear. It seems to mean that the former justices continued in service without a defined tenure, and that the new ones served during pleasure. If this is the meaning, the precedent was simply that they accepted the new commissions.

One of the five justices did not hold office for very long; he was tried for refusing to subpoena a witness. (*Ibid.,* III:438.) Sargent's zeal knew no limits with regard to another judge: in April 1798 he attempted to revoke the justice's commission for "contemptuous" conduct, but for some reason he ordered his reinstatement a week later. (*Ibid.,* III:505–06.)

Before St. Clair returned to the territory, Sargent had gotten some satisfaction out of creating a special militia company of "Gentlemen"—that is, of his supporters, perhaps with a view to using them to enforce his will more completely,

Within a few months of St. Clair's next departure from the territory, Sargent precipitated another confrontation. In September 1794, following a "scuffle" between a party of Indians passing through the town and some inhabitants of Cincinnati, he ordered out the militia to preserve the peace and ordered the Quarter Sessions Court immediately to investigate the incident. The court again employed the popular grand jury and this time it indicted two men for assault and battery, but found evidence of no other disturbance. A jury subsequently acquitted one of the defendants when the principal witness against him mysteriously disappeared. In the meantime, Sargent took the matter to Judge Rufus Putnam, with the result that the territorial judge agreed that the civil authorities of Hamilton County—Cincinnati and environs—were incapable of protecting Indians or keeping the peace. He was unwilling to initiate any legal action for fear of being rebuffed. The territorial judges had earlier limited themselves primarily to appellate jurisdiction, in large part because they had no choice, and they carefully avoided interfering with local court practices. At the same time, local courts nibbled away at the powers of the General Court.[31]

Next, Sargent attempted to force the withdrawal of squatters west of the Great Miami, and he ordered out a unit of the militia for this purpose. In a public letter published in Maxwell's Cincinnati *Centinel*, Sargent ordered Israel Ludlow, the principal surveyor and speculator in the area, to prevent surveying until he was authorized to do so. Immediately below the letter, Maxwell printed a short notice saying that St. Clair had just returned to the territory. According to the understood meaning of absence, knowledge of the governor's return would make

while figuring out new ways to deal with local authorities (Downes, *Frontier Ohio,* 140–41). In late July 1793 St. Clair returned to the territory and stayed until the spring of 1794. The people heartily welcomed his return because it took control out of Sargent's hands, and his visit to the territory was characterized by carefully cultivated harmony. No doubt St. Clair was as anxious to have peace as were the people. His military defeat of 1791 had carried with it an enormous loss of prestige and, despite official exoneration by Congress (due largely to his friendship with George Washington), St. Clair could hardly have expected the warmth of his reception in the territory. After the ordeal with Congress, even the Northwest, which he detested, must have been a welcome sanctuary.

31. Carter, *Territorial Papers,* III:421–24; Downes, *Frontier Ohio,* 141–42; Philbrick, *Laws of Indiana,* R143–65 *passim.* The General Court is also referred to as the territorial Supreme Court.

Sargent's actions invalid. A newspaper battle ensued, in which the secretary charged that Maxwell's notice was deliberately premature, malicious, and designed to arouse contempt for him—all of which was probably true. The change in executive authority, Sargent contended, did not occur until he received official notice directly from the governor. Thus, since he had had no knowledge of St. Clair's presence in the territory when the letter to Ludlow was published, his action was valid. Obviously, the tenuous position of acting governor was always one of potential embarrassment, and Sargent helped it along by his inept handling of every situation. In this case, however, his opponents tried to make it much more than an embarrassment, and they plotted Sargent's final undoing. They brought suits against the secretary for usurpation of the governor's powers, but dropped them at St. Clair's insistence, apparently because everyone was relieved to see St. Clair supersede Sargent's authority and no one cared to face down the governor on the issue.[32]

Throughout the first half of the 1790s Sargent never learned to leave the courts alone. He continually tried to dictate to them and in other ways meddled directly in local affairs. Each rebuke carried with it a loss of executive power and prestige, and demonstrated the folly of territorial officials' attempting to impose autocratic controls or to interfere in local affairs. All of Sargent's mistakes helped to preserve some of St. Clair's prestige, despite his military disaster, but by 1795, after his sustained absences, the governor returned to find his executive authority drastically shrunk by local encroachment. Equally important, the powers of the secretary were fatally weakened. Henceforth, during governors' lengthy absences, secretaries were reduced to caretakers.[33]

After the middle of the 1790s, local leaders in the Northwest had achieved about as much as was possible by direct attacks on the executive powers, and they turned their efforts increasingly to obtaining a second-stage government. This change corresponded with a solution of the immediate Indian problem—Anthony Wayne's army defeated a force of Indians at Fallen Timbers on August 20, 1794, and he con-

32. Downes, *Frontier Ohio*, 144–46.

33. For an example of the extent to which this was true of another strong-willed secretary, see Carter, *Territorial Papers*, XIV:637–39, 646–47. See also Chapter IV below.

cluded the Treaty of Greenville on August 2, 1795—and the influx of large number of settlers.

Sargent's difficulties as acting governor are only a part of the story. The general ineffectiveness of district-stage governments was not simply an outgrowth of his conflicts with the judges, local authorities, and the people, or of his ineptitude. It was equally a consequence of the inadequacies of first-stage laws and of legislation by which the governors allowed their authority to be limited. These laws, in turn, help to explain why men like Sargent and the governors generally were unable to enforce their will in the face of any organized local opposition supported by the local hierarchy.

III

Territorial Government during the District Stage

ALTHOUGH the district-stage lawmaking provision included in the Ordinance of 1787 appeared to be clear enough, it was a perennial source of confusion, and had a debilitating effect on territorial government. The governors and judges questioned and argued both the extent of their legislative authority and the composition of a majority for enacting laws. The Ordinance's requirement that all laws be adopted from the codes of the original states also caused them concern, since they felt that none of the codes was fully suited to the needs of their territories. The federal government offered them no solace because its attitude vacillated and it failed to clarify the provision with any exactness. Moreover, the governors and judges ordinarily lacked sufficient copies of state codes from which to draw their laws. Consequently, left to their own resources, and in constant doubt as to the legitimacy of their actions, they limited themselves to the most general kinds of legislation, enacted as few laws as necessary, and employed several ruses in efforts to provide laws for their territories and avoid federal censure. The body of law, nevertheless, grew organically in each territory and was handed down from older territories to newer ones. As a result of the cautiousness, if not outright incompetence, of most district-stage legislators, however, the law developed haphazardly and was never adequate. Moreover, the laws were often unenforceable or irrelevant, either because of their nature or because of their unavailability to local authorities. A discussion of district-stage legislation that illustrates the character of territorial government is nonetheless requisite to an analysis of local government.

The Ordinance gave to the governor alone full legislative powers to create and divide counties and townships during the district stage, and to "appoint such magistrates and other civil officers in each county or township, as he shall find necessary. . . ." Presumably, the governor could also create all local offices, including courts, and define the duties of local officials, but he shared all other legislative powers with the judges. In other words, the Ordinance authorized the governor alone to create and regulate a system of local government, but required him to choose with the judges the laws to be enforced therein. These two realms of legislative authority were not fully separable, however, and the Ordinance did not explicitly empower the governor to do more than divide the territory into units of local government and appoint their officers. Moreover, it was obviously desirable to have the structure and functions of local governments and the duties of their officials fixed in law. Thus at the outset of his administration Governor St. Clair and the three territorial judges of the Northwest began enacting general laws which, in effect, restricted the executive power.

As published, the Ordinance provided that[1]

> the governor and judges, or a majority of them, shall adopt and publish in the district such laws of the original States, criminal and civil, as may be necessary and best suited to the circumstances of the district, and report them to Congress from time to time: which laws shall be in force in the district until the organization of the General Assembly therein, unless disapproved of by Congress.

Nothing in the Ordinance, or in subsequent Organic Acts, prescribed the length or frequency of first-stage lawmaking sessions, but during the early years in the Northwest, and in most other territories, the governor and judges met annually. Sessions usually lasted a few days to a week, but occasionally they continued intermittently over a period of several months. From the beginning, governors convened the judges by proclamation and they generally opened each session with a formal address recommending legislation. In the early years, St. Clair treated the judges as a wholly separate lawmaking body, retiring while

1. *JCC*, XXXII:334; Thorpe, *Constitutions*, 959; Carter, *Territorial Papers*, II:42–43.

the judges acted on his suggestions or drafted other bills for his approval. Later he sat with the judges and helped them to draft laws, the common practice in succeeding territories.[2]

The laws enacted depended heavily on the state codes available to the legislators, but since the governors usually assumed leadership in the adoption of laws, it is not surprising that the laws also reflected their backgrounds. Under St. Clair, most laws originated from those of his home state of Pennsylvania; Virginia laws were prominent in the legislation of Harrison's administration; and Ninian Edwards brought a number of Kentucky laws into the Illinois code. The real character of the law, then, as well as other aspects of territorial government, rested partly on the ability, background, and objectives of the governors. In the Northwest, these qualities in St. Clair were of primary importance, because there alone government had to be created *de novo*.[3] St. Clair's influence was great, despite his frequent absences, inasmuch as he presided over the adoption of the most important laws.[4]

The foremost problem at the beginning of every district government, and a constant source of uneasiness throughout the first stage, was the meaning of the Ordinance provision for adopting laws. In every territory except Louisiana-Missouri, the governor and judges debated whether the Ordinance allowed them to make laws anew or limited them to the literal adoption of laws of the original states. Basically, the question was whether or not district-stage legislators had full legislative competency. Logically, the question in the Northwest should not have been the meaning of "adopt," but the scope of original lawmaking intended by the Ordinance. Neither the federal government nor the territorial officials appreciated the background and purpose of the Or-

2. Valentine, "Territorial Governor," 12–13, 19; Philbrick, *Laws of Illinois*, R451–52.

3. See Valentine, "Territorial Governor," 12–13, 19; McCarty, *Governors of the Northwest*, 45; William L. Jenks, "Territorial Legislation by Governor and Judges," *Mississippi Valley Historical Review*, V (June, 1918), 36–50 *passim*, hereafter cited as Jenks, "Legislation"; Philbrick, *Laws of Indiana*, R104.

4. Note the subject matter and signatures of the laws in Pease, *Laws of the Northwest*, A1–315. Sargent helped frame three laws in 1790 (he presided over only half of the legislative session), twelve in 1792, and ten in 1798; most of the early laws did not continue in force for very long. Sargent avoided holding legislative sessions with the judges, it seems, because he doubted his authority to do so. See also Chapter II and Carter, *Territorial Papers*, III:400; XIV:637–39, 646–47.

dinance in this respect. Its framers were not so much interested in seeing identical institutions develop in the West as in transplanting basic American principles, and in insuring the growth of republican governments by requiring that territorial laws conform as closely as possible to those of the East. State codes were thus to be used as guides and their laws adapted as necessary to meet peculiar western needs. St. Clair might have known this had he not been absent from his post as President of Congress during the debates over the Ordinance.

Regardless of the intentions of the framers of the Ordinance, contemporary practices and the Ordinance itself made the semantic debate over literal adoption senseless, since lawyers and legislators used the terms enact, make, and adopt interchangeably. To legislate was to make law and, in common usage, a bill enacted became a law adopted. Every statute, then, was "made" law as distinguished from customary law. Besides, in order to adopt laws in the territories it was necessary to assume original lawmaking powers. Governors and judges had to add enacting clauses to every law adopted and adapt the wording of laws to their territory, for example by changing or deleting inapplicable specific references. Moreover, the Ordinance specified adoption in one place, and referred to laws "adopted or made" in another. In a like manner, Congress provided in 1792 for printing "enacted" territorial laws, and authorized the governor and judges to repeal laws they had "made."[5]

The debate over the meaning of adoption began with the first bill considered in the Northwest. St. Clair objected to a militia law drafted by the judges, pointing out that they had not taken it literally from a state code. He correctly argued that the judges were assuming original legislative powers. Giving a very limited meaning to the term "adopt," St. Clair contended that "The governor and judges . . . shall adopt laws of the original states" meant that they had to transfer statutes intact. *Any* alteration in wording would constitute law "making," which he took to be beyond their authority. The judges, on the other hand, assumed the position that the intent of the phrase was not to prevent lawmaking but simply to require that territorial laws be consistent with the laws and practices of the original states.

5. For a complete discussion of "adoption" see Philbrick, *Laws of Illinois*, R400–04. See also note 12 below.

Both the governor and the judges recognized that literal adoption was not feasible, even for laws of a general nature. On occasion, St. Clair expressed a desire to see the Ordinance changed to permit lawmaking, but he apparently never approached Congress for a remedy. Instead, throughout the first stage, he railed against the legality of a broad construction of the article, and demanded that "correct" forms be observed, while he grudgingly acquiesced to the judges' view insofar as it was absolutely necessary "for the sake of harmony." The extent of his uneasiness was shown when the first General Assembly met in 1799, and he insisted that it immediately reenact all first-stage laws to insure their validity.[6]

In view of the effect on legislation of St. Clair's concern with literal adoption, the most surprising aspect of the conflict is that apparently none of the governors or judges received, or even attempted to obtain, an official interpretation from the federal government. The federal government compounded the lawmaking problems by failing to give the governors and judges detailed instructions or any other systematic interpretation of the Ordinance. Before going to their territories, the governors invariably obtained copies of the Ordinance and sought advice, but their main objectives seem to have been to determine the extent of their powers and the procedures for setting up governments. Even on these points their advisors were vague, counseling the governors that their powers were great and should be used with the utmost discretion. Similarly, Congress never elaborated or clarified the first-stage legislative powers, although several bills were introduced for the purpose. As a whole, the statements, actions, and threatened actions that did emanate from the federal government were more restrictive than permissive, in spite of its increasingly lax attitude toward the territories in general. The federal government thereby tended to inhibit first-stage legislation and to prevent the passage of much needed laws or to cause the adoption of inadequate laws. Thus, though the judges of the Northwest seem to have had good legal training, they

6. Philbrick, *Laws of Illinois*, R408, R415; McCarty, *Governors of the Northwest*, 57; Valentine, "Territorial Governor," 14; Jenks, "Legislation," 39; G. L. Wilson, "St. Clair," 328. After 1795 the conflict over adoption was primarily political. St. Clair continued to acquiesce but then went on record in opposition to the "latitudinarian" interpretation, apparently in order to deprive the Republicans of a political issue. (See Philbrick, *Laws of Illinois*, R422.)

lacked confidence in their interpretation—a situation that resulted in no small part from St. Clair's claim that on one of his eastern trips he had gotten an unofficial opinion supporting his viewpoint. The sense of caution and uncertainty thus engendered in the Northwest was carried over into all of the other district-stage governments.[7]

In the absence of a firm interpretation of their powers, the governor and judges of each territory had several choices. Winthrop Sargent, as governor of Mississippi Territory, followed the Northwest example of the period before 1795 and openly made laws, but his offensive methods caused resentment and had repercussions in Congress. William Blount, in Tennessee, faced a somewhat different situation, since the Southwest Ordinance continued Carolina law in the area and extensive legislation was not necessary. He concurred with the judges' opinion that they were free under the Ordinance to legislate in any manner, but they went about their lawmaking quietly, and enacted only two laws during the first stage.[8]

Outside of Mississippi and Tennessee, the usual practice was to put up a front of compliance with St. Clair's literal interpretation, while engaging covertly in varying degrees of lawmaking. St. Clair began this himself in 1795, when he and the judges codified the laws that became known, under the name of their printer, as Maxwell's Code. The device was to give each law, as circumstances permitted, a more or less legitimate parentage in state codes, by attaching to each a statement that named the state or states of its origin. Not infrequently, not even a similar law could be found in the supposed parent code, and almost always the relationships that did exist were tenuous. Often, in laws of considerable length, no more than a few words or phrases bore any resemblance to a state law. Since the exact law of origin was not specified, the governor and judges undoubtedly intended to discourage Congressional interference by giving Congress the burden of determining the extent to which they had complied with the Ordinance. If this was the purpose, they succeeded completely.[9]

7. Masterson, *Blount*, 180–81, 183–84; Bond, *Old Northwest*, 56–57; Pease, *Laws of the Northwest*, R17–23. (See note 19 below.)

8. Philbrick, *Laws of Illinois*, R429–30; Jenks, "Legislation," 41–44; Valentine, "Territorial Governor," 14.

9. Pease, *Laws of the Northwest*, R28–31; Jenks, "Legislation," 36–50; Phil-

Success in avoiding Congressional nullification resulted in large measure from the inability of Congressmen to agree among themselves. In the early years, members of the House generally subscribed to St. Clair's interpretation of the meaning of adoption, according to which all first-stage laws were "nullities." Though a number of House resolutions were proposed or passed to nullify territorial laws of the Northwest and Mississippi, on grounds that they had been "made" rather than literally adopted, the Senate never concurred and the laws remained in force. After 1800 House interest declined sharply but the threat remained to inhibit first-stage legislators even after 1804. In that year, Congress attached the Louisiana Purchase, north of the 33rd parallel, to the Indiana Territory for administration, and explicitly gave the Indiana government the power to "make" laws for the Louisiana district. By extension, Harrison and the judges might have assumed the right to make laws for Indiana, but within the next year Indiana moved into the second stage, and Congress created a separate Louisiana Territory, again explicitly granting the right to make laws to the governor and judges of Louisiana-Missouri.

Congress did nullify two first-stage laws, but in both cases their content, rather than the method of adoption, was at issue. In 1792 Congress disallowed a 1788 Northwest law because the law provided a statute of limitations that it deemed unfair and contrary to established practice. Within six months of its passage, Congress nullified the Michigan law of 1806 chartering a Bank of Detroit, on the ground that it was a monopolistic grant.[10]

---

brick, *Laws of Indiana*, R106–09; Philbrick, *Laws of Illinois*, R418–20; Valentine, "Territorial Governor," 14–19; McCarty, *Governors of the Northwest*, 59, 67–68.

10. Valentine, "Territorial Governor," 16–17; Jenks, "Legislation," 39–41, 44; Charles Meyerholz, "Federal Supervision over the Territories of the United States," *Beitrage zur Kultur- und Universalgeschichte*, VI (Leipzig, 1908), 171–72, hereafter cited as Meyerholz, "Federal Supervision"; Philbrick, *Laws of Illinois*, R422; Carter, *Territorial Papers*, V:92–94, 94–95n, XIII:93. Contrary to Philbrick's assertions (*Laws of Illinois*, R422, R428), the question of adoption cannot be considered dead by 1804 or 1805. He argues that the question was ended by the explicit grant of lawmaking powers in the Orleans Organic Acts, but this assertion is unreasonable because of several important differences in the structure of the government. (See note 23 and Chapter V below.) Similarily, the explicit grant to Louisiana did not entitle governors and judges elsewhere to assume the extension to their territories—specifically Illinois and Michigan, the only district governments besides Louisiana-Missouri after 1805.

The courts offered no interpretation of the adoption article until all first-stage governments had ceased to exist. The reasons lay partially in the cautious attitude of the Supreme Court, but primarily in the nature of the territorial courts and the uncertain constitutional status of the territories. Territorial judges were not federal judges. Although the territorial courts were an arm of the Justice Department, they did not have the same jurisdictional realm as the federal courts because their functions were limited and unusual. By John Marshall's definition, territorial courts were legislative, rather than constitutional or United States courts, and were thereby limited in the kinds of cases they could handle. Initially, the territorial courts did not have clear jurisdiction over federal cases, and before 1805, no cases brought in them could be appealed to the United States Supreme Court. In 1805, appeals were permitted in a very limited number of areas directly involving the federal government. These areas were broadened somewhat in the mid-1820s, but the jurisdiction of territorial courts was never fully clarified because the constitutional status of the contiguous territories themselves was always ambiguous. The only certainty was that, because the territories were extensions of the national sovereignty and not sovereignties in themselves, suits could not be brought against them—that is, lacking full independence, a territory could not be a defendant. At the end of the nineteenth century Congress and the Supreme Court defined the status of colonies and the relationship of their courts to federal courts, but then the definitions did not apply fully to the three remaining contiguous colonies, but only to those of the Oceanic Empire. All of these factors were to affect procedures and cause confusion throughout the history of the continental colonies. They also made it difficult to know how or where to initiate test cases, especially in the first stage when confusion was greatest. On the other hand, even if someone had wanted to test a law during the district stage, there was little future in trying, because he would necessarily end up testing it before the men who had written it.[11]

11. See Philbrick, *Laws of Illinois,* R41–44, R169, R437; Philbrick, *Laws of Indiana,* R159–60; Meyerholz, "Federal Supervision," 122–23, 226; Farrand, *Legislation for Territories,* 32–35; John D. Hall, "The Administration of United States Territories and Island Possessions" (unpublished PhD. dissertation, Syracuse University, 1948), 162 and *passim,* hereafter cited as Hall, "Administration";

The only district-stage law tested in the federal courts was one from Michigan. In 1828, a federal court in New York upheld a Michigan law chartering a bank, even though the law was clearly "made." But when in 1853 the same question came before the Supreme Court in *Peck v. Pease*, the Court invalidated the law. As in the strongly political and sectional Dred Scott decision four years later, the Court's decision in *Peck v. Pease* respecting the powers of Congress over territories lacked both legal and constitutional justification. The Court ruled that, in the district stage, the governor and judges had had no legislative powers whatsoever and consequently were not entitled to alter or modify the laws adopted in any way. This necessarily meant that only adoption of whole laws was valid; to adopt only parts of laws was to modify them, since the parts alone had different meanings. Had the Court handed down such a decision while first-stage governments existed, the governors and judges would have been hamstrung as legislators.[12] Thus there were ample reasons for district-stage legislators to walk gingerly and to make use of any expedient that would enable them, with relative impunity, to provide the territories with needed laws.

One of the most significant and far-reaching legislative advances, however, occurred, at St. Clair's insistence, in 1795, in a rare instance of almost perfectly literal adoption. One of the governor's favorite topics was the perfection of common law. For years, he expounded its virtues while trying to find a way to implement English common law in the Northwest. The judges agreed on the desirability of doing so, but doubted their power to implement it, even though the Ordinance specifically gave common law jurisdiction to the Supreme Court (or

---

Smurr, "Constitutions," 37, 747–49, 763–64, 952; Snow, *Dependencies*, 400–73, 537–78; Pomeroy, *Territories, 1861–1890*, 51.

12. Philbrick, *Laws of Illinois*, R157, R444–45, R445n, *passim;* Valentine, "Territorial Governor," 18; Jenks, "Legislation," 50; *Laws of the Territory of Michigan*, (4 vols., Lansing, 1871-1884), I:xiii–xiv, hereafter cited as *Laws of Michigan*. The senselessness of the adoption question raised here is that, by inference, the decision invalidated the 1792 Act of Congress allowing the governor and judges to repeal laws. As Philbrick notes, the power to repeal whole laws logically carries the power to repeal parts. Thus presumably, the governors and judges might have adopted whole laws from a state and then repealed all but a few phrases, as a way of avoiding nullification. However, this practice was not consciously or deliberately followed anywhere.

General Court) of the territory and guaranteed common law proceedings to territorial inhabitants. St. Clair was persistent, however. He argued that the common law was always in force except where expressly superseded by statute, and by 1795 he overcame the judges' doubts and found a solution. In the legislative session of that year, he and the judges adopted nearly verbatim a 1776 Virginia statute that declared all English common law that was not inconsistent with American sovereignty, and which was enacted prior to the fourth year of the reign of James I, to be thereby in force in the state. The delay in adopting such a law may be illustrative of the debilitating effects of federal attitudes, and of St. Clair's literal mind. Given the lack of state codes in the Northwest, it may have taken the governor until 1795 just to find an appropriate statute to adopt. Of greater importance, the law had a strong influence on the course of territorial history. At one stroke, it made available a large body of law, but the beauty of the act was that no one knew precisely what constituted the common law. By defining it to suit themselves, the local courts could make their own laws to justify their actions and establish their autonomy.[13]

When the governors and judges doubted their authority to legislate on a given subject, or when they did not wish to make or adopt a law, they sometimes legislated by assumption or resolution, or the governor resorted to proclamation.[14] For example, the Ordinance specifically gave the General Court only common law jurisdiction, so the governor and judges of the Northwest injected chancery jurisdiction by following the Pennsylvania and Massachusetts practice of providing equitable relief through common law actions. They further assumed that the Ordinance's omission of chancery jurisdiction, which they took to be a restriction on the General Court, did not require them or

13. Regardless of their position, it is clear that the judges had condoned, if not engaged in, the local court practice of using familiar law long before 1795. In this respect, private and local lawmaking were well developed before the adoption of common law, and the real significance of the adoption of common law was that it broadened and strengthened the previously tenuous legal basis of decisions. (See Philbrick, *Laws of Indiana,* R100–02; Pease, *Laws of the Northwest,* A253; Bond, *Foundations,* 402.)

14. In practice, both proclamations and resolutions had the full force of laws, since all officials used the terms "law," "act," and "resolution" inexactly and usually interchangeably, and the distinction between laws and resolutions was lost once the deed was done. (Philbrick, *Laws of Illinois,* R109.)

the General Court to limit the inferior courts. Consequently, with their third act of 1788, St. Clair and the judges established equity courts. The General Court then allowed appeals from these courts, a practice unknown under common law jurisdiction.[15]

When Congress divided a territory, the officials of the new territory assumed that the laws of the parent territory continued in force. This was a logical and desirable assumption—and a necessary one to the continuity of law—since the Ordinance, in limiting adoption to the laws of original states, made it impossible to reenact the parent territory's code. Fortunately the federal government never questioned the legality of this practice. Thus Harrison and the Indiana judges assumed that the laws of the Northwest, through the first General Assembly, remained in force after division, and they repealed part of a 1799 law of the Northwest General Assembly as their second act of legislation. In Illinois, the first legislative action of the governor and judges was to adopt a resolution declaring all relevant Indiana laws to be still in force, and the second was to repeal some of them. Hull and the judges of the Michigan Territory made no pronouncement on the continuation of the Northwest and Indiana laws, and for a time it seemed that they did not intend to extend them. However, within the first several years, the courts made it clear that the laws of both parent territories, whatever they were, continued in force insofar as they were compatible with each other and with the laws enacted by the Michigan legislators.[16]

Governors occasionally used or threatened to use proclamations in lieu of legislation, when judges would not concur in the enactment of legislation. Proclamations were also used when governors were unable or unwilling to raise a quorum for a lawmaking session. In some territories, notably the Northwest and Michigan, governors abused the power, as in 1814 and 1815 when Lewis Cass used proclamations to

15. Pease, *Laws of the Northwest,* A9–10; Philbrick, *Laws of Indiana,* R163–68; Philbrick, *Laws of Illinois,* R39–41. Most of the drafts of the Ordinance had granted chancery jurisdiction, but in the final stages of revision Congress unaccountably struck out the provision. (See *JCC,* XXX:253, 404, XXXI:670, XXXII:242, 281; and note 1.) Not until the second Michigan Organic Act was passed in 1823 did Congress expressly grant the territorial courts chancery jurisdiction. (See Farrand, *Legislation for Territories,* 32.)

16. Philbrick, *Laws of Indiana,* R104–06, A2; Philbrick, *Laws of Illinois,* R434–36, A5; Valentine, "Territorial Governor," 15, 17; McCarty, *Governors of the Northwest,* 79, 110, 120–21.

"repeal and abrogate" all Michigan laws inconsistent with his decrees.[17] Both St. Clair and Sargent employed proclamations liberally on their trips to Illinois and other outlying parts of the Northwest. On these trips, proclamations were useful expedients, since it was impossible to convene the judges for lawmaking sessions; but they took on a different cast when the governor failed to replace them with laws during the next session. In 1789, St. Clair threatened to ignore the judges entirely and rule by proclamation if he did not get his way. Hull did rule by proclamation in 1809, forcing local officials to obey and enforce laws that he and one judge approved, but which the other two judges held to be invalid.[18]

Hull's resort to the proclamation in 1809 grew out of a second problem of interpreting the law-adoption article of the Ordinance: the recurring question of what constituted a majority for lawmaking during the district stage. St. Clair precipitated this debate, as well as the one over the meaning of adoption, when he refused to approve the first law proposed by the judges in the Northwest—the militia law already mentioned. The judges contended that in his legislative capacity the governor was just another legislator, without special privileges, and that the phrase "majority of them" referred to the governor and judges collectively. St. Clair argued correctly (in the technical sense), that the phrase meant a majority of the judges. In other words, the governor claimed a veto over the first-stage legislation, and the judges denied its existence. When the judges threatened to carry on under their own interpretation if the governor refused to accede, St. Clair threatened to rule by proclamation. At this juncture, a letter arrived from Charles Thomson, Secretary of the Confederation Congress, supporting the governor's interpretation. Because of the urgent need for legislation, the judges then relented, breaking the deadlock.[19] There-

17. See, for example, Carter, *Territorial Papers,* X:714; *Laws of Michigan,* I:323.

18. Philbrick, *Laws of Illinois,* R418–20, R448–49, R459–63; Bond, *Old Northwest,* 510 ff; Valentine, "Territorial Governor," 17. Philbrick (*Laws of Illinois,* R462) considers the 1809 episode in Michigan, which occurred nearly twenty years after similar use in the Northwest and Southwest territories, to have been "by far the most dangerous example of an improper resort to executive proclamation" in territorial history.

19. Charles Thomson to Winthrop Sargent, March 11, 1789, in Carter, *Terri-*

after the judges grudgingly recognized the governor's veto power, and St. Clair avoided using it. Within a few years, when St. Clair began sitting with the judges during lawmaking sessions, they avoided making a public display of their differences by arguing in private, and by not acting on proposals that they could not carry. Thus after the first few years in the Northwest it is impossible to gauge the governor's full

---

torial Papers, II:189–90. See also *ibid.*, II:39–49 and notes; Philbrick, *Laws of Illinois,* R446. Thomson (also spelled Thompson [See Carter, *Territorial Papers,* II:191]) examined the original Journal version of the Ordinance (*JCC,* XXXII: 336), in which the punctuation differed from the universally printed versions, and concluded that the original form supported St. Clair's interpretation.

Carter (*Territorial Papers,* II:42n) points out that Thomson was well known for his carelessness, and that an error in the Journal form of the Ordinance is by no means impossible. The punctuation of the original Ordinance is inaccurate and inconsistent. Carter (*ibid.*, II:40n, 42n) found over 140 differences in punctuation between the printed version and the original Ordinance. Over 130 of these variations occurred in the half of the Ordinance that Thomson transcribed, including the article here in question. Thus it seems that Congress felt it was necessary to clean up the Ordinance, to make it presentable and literate in printed form, or that the printer voluntarily undertook the task alone—possibly out of embarrassment for the Congress. In any case, the first published form has universally been the official printed form, and the *only* printed version of the Ordinance available until publication of the Journals in the twentieth century. In this sense, both Philbrick's discussion of the significance of the differences in forms (Philbrick, *Laws of Illinois,* R450–53: he concludes that the Journal form definitely gave the governor a first-stage veto) and Thomson's letter, based on reexamination of his own handicraft, are rather irrelevant. Certainly Thomson's opinion was of no official value—he was secretary to the rump Confederation Congress that had already been superseded by the Constitution, and he wrote the letter while waiting for the first Federal Congress to convene. The opening of the new Congress had been delayed, in his words, "the badness of the roads having prevented the attendance of the Southern Members." (Carter, *Territorial Papers,* II:190.) The principal differences in the phrase debated are as follows. Original Journal version: "The governor, and judges or a majority of them shall adopt . . . laws"; the printed form: "The governor and judges, or a majority of them, shall adopt . . . laws." Examination of earlier drafts of the Ordinance indicates that these differences in punctuation were unintentional and that the official printed form is the correct one. For example, the draft of July 11, 1787, follows the form of the printed version (*JCC,* XXXII:315), and there is no evidence of changes having been introduced prior to the passage of the Ordinance two days later. Reports of May 9, May 10, and July 9, 1787, also follow the punctuation of July 11 (and of the printed Ordinance) in the placement of the first comma, but they omit the second comma. (*JCC,* XXXII:281.) As a qualifying phrase, "or a majority of them" requires either the two commas or none at all, depending upon the interpre-

impact on legislation, though the threat of the veto could clearly exert a powerful influence.[20]

Outside the Northwest, the district-stage veto was not always contested, and St. Clair's interpretation apparently prevailed in all but one territory when conflict erupted. If the judges of the Southwest Territory questioned the existence of the veto or if Blount claimed it, no one cared to make an issue of it. Similarly, Harrison in Indiana and Edwards in Illinois were content to leave the question undisturbed and apparently neither used the veto. By contrast Sargent, as governor of Mississippi, reverted to St. Clair's early practice of issuing veto messages and used the veto often enough to cause bitter denunciations. In Louisiana-Missouri, in 1806, Governor James Wilkinson's similar attitude and the rephrasing of the lawmaking article brought on a new debate over the first-stage veto that paralysed legislation for a time, but the outcome was similar to that in the Northwest. As a whole, the use of the veto during the district stage, or extensive conflict over its use, represented a breakdown in relations between the governor and the other legislators—a generalization that can be applied equally well to second-stage government.[21]

William Hull's administration in Michigan, between 1805 and 1812, is the sole example of a district-stage government in which the governor definitely did not have a veto. At the outset, Hull and the judges interpreted the adoption article of the Ordinance in a way that raised questions that were not encountered in other territories. According to St. Clair's reading of the article, the assent of the governor and two judges was necessary to enact a law; that is, not only did the governor

---

tation intended (if the commas can be considered to make a difference) or the stylistic preference of the author. In either form the intention is confusing, and in 1805 Congress changed the wording of the Ordinance article (in the Louisiana Organic Act) without clarifying its meaning: "The legislative power shall be vested in the governor, and in three judges or a majority of them." In 1806 a bill was introduced in Congress to clarify the meaning of both forms but nothing came of it, and no other attempts were made during the period of first-stage governments. (See note 23 below and Philbrick, *Laws of Illinois,* R453, R453n; Carter, *Territorial Papers,* XIII:93, 270, 271, 420.)

20. Philbrick, *Laws of Illinois,* R451–52; Carter, *Territorial Papers,* II:207.

21. Philbrick, *Laws of Illinois,* R447, R450–53; Jenks, "Legislation," 36–50 *passim;* McCarty, *Governors of the Northwest,* 55; Valentine, "Territorial Governor," 19.

have a veto, but there could be no quorum or majority without his presence.[22] Hull and the Michigan judges, on the other hand, decided that the governor was simply another legislator and that he should have no veto. A quorum, then, consisted of any three members of the legislative board, and a majority of those present could enact laws. Consequently, in Michigan only two votes were necessary to pass laws when three members were present. In 1809 a conflict arose over some laws that Hull and one judge had approved. The other two judges declared the laws invalid because neither of them had been present when the laws were adopted, and there was therefore no legal quorum. Hull, however, contended that the laws were valid on the ground that only two votes were necessary for passage, and proceeded to use a proclamation to insure their enforcement.[23]

22. Philbrick, *Laws of Illinois*, R447, R450–51.

23. *Ibid.*, R447–50, R460; Jenks, "Legislation," 45; McCarty, *Governors of the Northwest*, 121; Carter, *Territorial Papers*, X:320–24. At least during the first few years, all members of the Michigan legislative board signed laws, whether they had approved them or not. This practice gave all laws—excepting, of course, those adopted in sessions made up of the governor and one judge or only two judges, wherein it seems laws that only one judge approved were adopted and had full force—at least a three-vote approval at law, since the approval of all signers was assumed unless the laws were contested on that ground. In January 1806, Thomas Worthington of Ohio introduced a bill in the Senate to alter the Ordinance and to clarify the entire district-stage lawmaking process in Louisiana-Missouri and Michigan. The bill expressly authorized lawmaking and would have formally abolished the first-stage veto. If the governor and all three judges were present, any three could pass a law; if only the governor and two judges were present, or only the three judges, decisions had to be unanimous. The Senate took no action on the bill. (Carter, *Territorial Papers*, XIII:420–21.) In November 1808 Hull and one or two judges adopted a law to validate existing practices. It specified that a quorum consisted of any three members and that laws could be adopted by two members if only three were present. The law supposedly came from Vermont, which was not an original state and which clearly had no relevant law. (*Laws of Michigan*, IV:21.) This law and some forty others were signed only by the governor (or acting governor) in his official capacity and as president of the legislature, without any indication of the nature of the majorities for passage. (See *ibid.*, II:13–81, IV:21–92; Philbrick, *Laws of Illinois*, R448.) Jefferson and his advisors seem never to have questioned the propriety of the Michigan practices, and, as in the cases of Indiana and Illinois, Congress never intervened. (*Ibid.*, R420–21.) I have not been able to find any laws signed by only one judge, or, for that matter, any that do not bear the signature of the governor or acting governor during the administrations of both Hull and Cass. Apparently, under Cass, all laws were adopted by three votes.

To increase the body of law available for adoption, and to minimize the necessity of outright lawmaking, Hull and the Michigan judges also redefined "the original States" to mean all of the states in the Union in 1805, the year Michigan became a separate territory. This required a rather liberal construction, since the Organic Act simply provided for a district government in accordance with the Ordinance of 1787, without repeating the pertinent words so that they could be construed as updated. But under such a definition, the Michigan government could adopt at will laws from the Ohio, Kentucky, and Tennessee codes, all of which contained well-developed and highly relevant laws, unmatched in the codes of the original thirteen states.[24] The Michigan government's presumption that the authors of the Ordinance intended to limit adoption only to more advanced areas was not unwarranted, either in theory or practice. The district governments of both the Northwest and Indiana had drawn from the Kentucky code, and Ninian Edwards, who had been chief justice of the Kentucky Supreme Court before becoming governor of the Illinois Territory, extended the practice after 1809. There were no repercussions from Washington in any of the cases.[25]

While the governors and judges were broadening their field of selection, the attitude of the federal government also changed. After 1800 Congress interfered less in territorial lawmaking and took no action on the laws of Indiana, Illinois, Michigan, or Louisiana-Missouri. Part of the explanation is that Congress had no procedure for the systematic review of territorial laws as they were received. Illinois officials, for example, may have avoided Congressional interference with their legislation just by deliberately failing to send any copies of district-stage laws to the federal government. But more important was the lapse of federal concern with the territories. Washington had shown a keen interest in the territories, and records were well kept during his administrations. Interest declined sharply under Adams, and the Jeffersonians seemed content to allow territorial officials to follow whatever reasonable policies they thought best suited local conditions. Thus it appears that Jefferson and his advisors did not question the propriety

24. McCarty, *Governors of the Northwest*, 121–23; Valentine, "Territorial Governor," 15; Philbrick, *Laws of Indiana*, R109–10.

25. Philbrick, *Laws of Indiana*, R106–07; Philbrick, *Laws of Illinois*, R418–20.

of the various interpretations of the Ordinance, or any other arrangements of the territorial governors and judges. The change in federal attitudes corresponds with the rapid increase of Anglo-American settlement in the West. Accordingly, the mood of the Jeffersonians in the early nineteenth century may be less a reflection of libertarianism than of the simple realization that native-born Anglo-Americans would predominate in the territories and that close supervision would not be necessary to assure the development of eastern forms of republicanism.[26]

The Southwest code was not affected by that of the Northwest, nor does the Southwest seem to have affected the early development of law in later territories. Instead, as a whole, territorial laws grew, in a haphazard manner and at an irregular pace, out of the legislation of St. Clair's administration. The core of territorial law was the Northwest code; district-stage legislation after St. Clair, or more specifically after 1795, was basically supplementary. This necessarily meant that it was both elaborative and corrective. Outside the Old Northwest itself, the Northwest code became the basic body of law in Mississippi, Alabama, and the Louisiana Purchase. Sargent carried Maxwell's Code with him to Mississippi Territory, which included Alabama, and there he added thirty-nine laws to it during the district stage. The trans-Mississippi area north of the 33rd parallel, principally the Missouri-Arkansas region, acquired the code in 1804 when Congress attached that region to the Indiana Territory for a year. In the meantime, and subsequently, the Indiana, Illinois, and Michigan governments elaborated the Northwest code. The product of their work was to have a more or less constant influence in the entire upper Mississippi Valley and trans-Missouri West, both by the explicit extension of the laws themselves and through the transfer of personnel, as it had had earlier in the Missouri region. But the fact that the Northwest code was to be the basic law in most territories does not mean that it or the supplementary legislation of district-stage governments was adequate or effective.[27]

26. Philbrick, *Laws of Illinois*, R420–21.

27. Philbrick, *Laws of Indiana*, R104–06. For a comprehensive analysis of the growth of laws see W. W. Blume and E. G. Brown, *Digests and Lists Pertaining to the Development of Law* (6 vols., Ann Arbor, University Microfilms, 1965). See also Philbrick, *Laws of Illinois*, R171, R337, R436–39; Valentine, "Territorial Governor," 98.

On paper, the first territorial officials of the Northwest were well qualified, in terms both of eighteenth-century standards and of the average of later territorial officials. St. Clair had attended the Univer-

The growth of law from the drafting of the Northwest Ordinance through Illinois' district stage may be illustrated as follows: shortly after St. Clair arrived in the Northwest he met with the judges. Between July 25 and December 28, 1788, in what was probably the longest single first-stage lawmaking session, they adopted only ten laws. (Pease, *Laws of the Northwest,* R22, A1–26.) The governor and judges did not meet again until July 1790. Between July 19 and August 4 (St. Clair being absent), Sargent and the judges adopted three laws. (*Ibid.,* A26–34.) When the governor returned, he met with the judges between November 4 and November 6, and they adopted three laws. (*Ibid.,* A34–41.) In June and July 1791 they adopted seven more laws. (*Ibid.,* A41–54.) Sargent met with the judges in St. Clair's absence during August 1792; they spent much time arguing, but adopted thirteen laws. (*Ibid.,* A57–119.) Despite the basic inadequacies of many of the laws and the continuing need for legislation, there were only two more sessions during the first stage—one in 1795 and the other in 1798. Maxwell's Code, drawn up in 1795, contained thirty-seven enactments, one repeal law, and eight resolutions. (*Ibid.,* A121–290.) The session of 1798 added eleven laws, Sargent again presiding in the governor's absence. (*Ibid.,* A291–315.) See also *ibid.,* R22–24, R25, R26–29, R31; Bond, *Foundations,* 408, 421–22; Bond, *Old Northwest,* 82; Carter, *Territorial Papers,* III:400. St. Clair's absences and Sargent's uncertainty that he was authorized to hold lawmaking sessions primarily account for the infrequent sessions. In addition, at the times when the governor was in the territory, between December 1788 and November 1790, he could not raise a quorum. This resulted from the absence of judges, the death of two judges, and the absence of their replacements. (Pease, *Laws of the Northwest,* R22.) Until 1795—that is, in the sessions of 1788, 1790, 1791, and 1792—St. Clair and Sargent played nearly equal parts, presiding over the adoption of twenty and sixteen laws, respectively. Together, during the entire district period, they approved eighty-four laws, acts, and resolutions.

The number of laws, of course, gives no indication of the progress or significance of legislation, and includes a number of repeal acts and resolutions. St. Clair and the Northwest judges began repealing laws in 1790 (thus assuming the right, two years before Congress specifically granted it) and the power was thereafter used in every district-stage legislative session in the Northwest, Indiana, and Illinois, excepting only Indiana's 1802 session. (See McCarty, *Governors of the Northwest,* 66; G. L. Wilson, "St. Clair," 141; Philbrick, *Laws of Indiana,* R109–10; Pease, *Laws of the Northwest,* A35, A37.) In addition, the governors and judges frequently adopted new laws that altered existing statutes or superseded them without explicitly repealing them, or that implicitly superseded existing laws with which they were incompatible. Often the repeal acts themselves affected more than one law. As a whole, Maxwell's Code superseded all previous enactments, but it also contained a repeal act nullifying all or parts of twenty-six separate statutes—that is, over two-thirds of the existing laws. (Pease, *Laws of the Northwest,* A255–57. At least one law

sity of Edinburgh before entering the British army, and had held a number of colonial and state offices in Pennsylvania, serving as a justice and in other court offices, before entering the Confederation Con-

---

had been repealed in 1792, and several earlier, in whole or part, leaving no more than thirty-four laws in force at the time Maxwell's Code was adopted.) At the end of the district stage in the Northwest there were no more than eight resolutions and sixty-four laws in force. At least nine of the latter were partially repealed. Moreover, most of the resolutions and a few of the laws dealt with matters specific enough as to be inapplicable in subsequent territories.

When Harrison and the judges launched the government of the Indiana Territory in January 1801, they assumed that in addition to the laws of the district stage, the enactments of the first Northwest General Assembly had full force in Indiana. These laws of 1799 consisted of thirty-nine titles. The first proclaimed all Northwest district laws in force, while the last repealed six district laws in their entirety, three in part, and all resolutions. The last were repealed as unconstitutional. (Pease, *Laws of the Northwest*, A337–40, A515–16.) A number of the laws and the four resolutions of the first General Assembly were redundant, purely local in character, or implicitly amended existing laws. Thus it can be estimated that the body of law assumed to be in force in Indiana at its beginning contained, at most, eighty-six operative statutes, eleven of which had been explicitly repealed in part. To these, the governor and judges of Indiana added twenty-five laws and resolutions, but adopted two repeal acts and four resolutions of repeal. The former annulled seven laws and one resolution, all but one section of another law, and repealed a repeal act. (Philbrick, *Laws of Indiana*, A15, A64–66.) The repeal resolutions nullified all of one law and parts of three others. (*Ibid.*, A30–31, A85–86.) Thus the net statutory growth during the Indiana district stage was eighteen laws, bringing the net total, in 1805, to 104 laws (of which fifteen were partially annulled). The first two sessions of the Indiana Territorial General Assembly continued the process of piecemeal addition to and alteration of the Northwest Code. In 1807 the legislature repealed all statutes in force within the territory and enacted the first thorough revision of territorial laws. Besides codifying and revising the legislation of the previous nineteen years, the Code of 1807 legalized, or recognized in law, arrangements and practices in local government that had previously existed only in custom. (*Ibid.*, A217, A222–642, A608–609 [repeal law].) The Code contained ninety-five statutes or chapters, besides the repeal act, and resolutions for indexing, printing, and distribution.

This Code, with the twenty-three acts and resolutions of the fourth session of the Indiana General Assembly, which were mainly local in character, became the inheritance of Illinois Territory when Congress created it in 1809. The principal job of the Illinois governor and judges was to adapt the Indiana code more completely to local needs. For this purpose, during the three and one-half year Illinois district stage, they added twenty-four laws and one resolution. They also adopted nine repeal acts that voided at least four laws (one of which was a repeal law) and parts of eleven others. (Philbrick, *Laws of Illinois*, A5–6, A8, A12–14, A22, A25, A25–26, A35–36, A39, A47; McCarty, *Governors*

gress.[28] Though he was not a trained lawyer, Sargent had graduated from Harvard.[29] Samuel H. Parsons, of Connecticut, also a Harvard graduate, followed a legal career before becoming a judge in the Northwest. James M. Varnum, of Rhode Island, the second judge, was a Brown graduate and a practicing lawyer. He had served in Congress intermittently from 1780 to 1787.[30] John C. Symmes of New Jersey was the least qualified of all, having obtained only a partial education. Nevertheless he served two terms in the Confederation Congress, and had been a New Jersey Supreme Court judge for almost a decade before his appointment to the Northwest bench.[31]

All of the territorial officers also came to the territory with some

---

of the Northwest, 95–96, 97. Edwards had perhaps the best legal training of any territorial governor east of the Mississippi River, and as might be expected, his district legislation refined Indiana laws especially in the courts.)

In Michigan the continuity of law was not as evident. The courts assumed that the Northwest and Indiana codes were operative, but the governors and judges enacted hundreds of additional laws on specific subjects and made no effort to implement either most of their own laws or those of the parent territories. Thus between 1805 and 1812 Hull and the judges enacted some 124 laws, creating a cumbersome body of law that made the systems in the Northwest and Indiana simple by comparison, without establishing a corresponding court system. Until after the War of 1812 only a few district courts existed to administer the complex legal system. Michigan was divided into several districts, each having a single court, until 1815, when Cass began dividing the territory into counties and creating a regular county court system. Until this time the laws of the parent territories, as well as those enacted under Hull, were essentially in suspension. (See Jenks, "Legislation," 45–48; *Laws of Michigan*, I:17–19, 184–86, 186–92, 211, 323–36, 716; II:7–9, 68–73, 109, 125, 130, 131, 132; IV:96.)

28. Pease, *Laws of the Northwest*, R17; Randolph C. Downes, "Arthur St. Clair," *Dictionary of American Biography* (New York, 1935), XVI:293–95, hereafter cited as Downes, "St. Clair."

29. Benjamin H. Pershing, "Winthrop Sargent," *DAB*, XVI:368–69, hereafter cited as Pershing, "Winthrop Sargent." Sargent was from Massachusetts.

30. Pease, *Laws of the Northwest*, R17–18; Frederick W. Coburn, "James M. Varnum," *DAB*, XIX:227–28; *National Cyclopaedia of American Biography* (New York, 1869), VI:158–59.

31. Pease, *Laws of the Northwest*, R18; Beverley W. Bond, Jr., "John Cleves Symmes," *DAB*, XVIII:258–59. Bond feels that influence rather than ability accounts for Symmes' success. The New Jersey judgeships were apparently elective. Symmes was an associate justice of the New Jersey court, not, as Pease states, the chief justice. (Philbrick, *Laws of Indiana*, R15n.) Symmes' appointment was dated February 19, 1788, four months later than the others, because the commission initially had been offered to John Armstrong of Pennsylvania, who declined. (Carter, *Territorial Papers*, I:25–26.)

military experience, and the military background was so prominent in the early laws as to make the officials' legal knowledge seem deficient. Symmes had served briefly as a lieutenant colonel of militia and Sargent was a brevet major, but the other three were generals. The ten laws adopted during the first lawmaking session in 1788 were drafted more in the form of general orders than laws. They lacked enacting clauses and were not divided into sections. Poorly phrased, they contained incredible definitions and were pious, verbose preachments often devoid of penalties or means of administration.[32] The form im-

32. Pease, *Laws of the Northwest*, R18–19, A1–26. See also Bond, *Old Northwest*, 56–57; Philbrick, *Laws of Illinois*, R459. Varnum's health was poor when he went to the territory; he died on January 10, 1789, at the age of 41. Parsons drowned when he was 52, on November 17, 1789, when his canoe capsized. They were replaced by George Turner and Rufus Putnam whose commissions were dated September 12, 1789 and March 31, 1790 respectively. Both men had some military background: Turner had been an officer in the Revolutionary Army and Putnam, in 1792, became a major-general of the regular army. (Carter, *Territorial Papers*, I:25–26; II:217, 217n; Beverley W. Bond, Jr., "Rufus Putnam," *DAB*, XV:284–85; Pease, *Laws of the Northwest*, A23.) Putnam had been in and out of the territory since 1785 as a surveyor for Congress and as a representative of the Ohio Company. (In 1796 he resigned the judgeship to become Surveyor-General of the United States. Jefferson peremptorily replaced him in 1803.) He was a self-taught man, having no legal background. Nothing is known of Turner's antecedents other than that he was a major and came to the territory from South Carolina, and there is no evidence of his having had any legal training. Despite the weak legal training of the seven legislators who held office until 1796, Philbrick (*Laws of Indiana*, R14–15) concluded that they were all superior to the governor, secretary, and judges of Indiana Territory in legal and adminstrative training and in experience.

The ages of the territorial officials of the Northwest in 1790 were: St. Clair, 54; Sargent, 37; Symmes, 48; Putnam, 52; Turner, unknown, but judging from his wartime rank, he was near Sargent's age.

Besides the fact that the Northwest officials all held or had held military commissions—which is not of great consequence in itself, since the Americans had just fought a Revolution—all of the seven men, except Symmes, were original members of the Society of Cincinnati. St. Clair was president of the Pennsylvania branch and Varnum was president of the Rhode Island branch. Moreover, and again excluding Symmes, all of the officials were connected with the Ohio Company. Turner, least involved, was apparently a member but not a shareholder of the company. Besides being secretary for the Ohio Company, Sargent was the company land agent who sold the most Ohio land. He retained six shares for himself and sold another to St. Clair, which represented the governor's only apparent involvement in the company. Varnum,

proved after the first lawmaking session but such irregularities persisted throughout the district stages of the Northwest and Indiana and were to be found in territorial legislation throughout the nineteenth century.[33]

More important, however, was the way in which the governors and judges continually made and remade laws, adding piecemeal to the number of titles, without direction and often without improving the law. Thus, despite the number of statutes, district-stage legislators dealt with very few subjects and often had incompatible laws in force simultaneously. This situation led to great confusion, at least until 1807, when the Indiana legislature revised and supplemented existing laws.[34] That few district-stage laws were either relevant or adequate is indicated by the fact that at the beginning of the second stage every legislature, with the exception of Illinois which benefited fully from the

---

Parsons, and Putnam were land agents and directors of the Ohio Company. They held four, five, and two shares, respectively. (See L. A. Alderman, *The Identification of the Society of the Cincinnati with the First Authorized Settlement of the Northwest Territory at Marietta, Ohio, April Seventh, 1787* [Marietta, Ohio, 1888], 20–22; and Albion Morris Dyer, "First Ownership of Ohio Lands," *The New England Historical and Genealogical Register* [Boston, 1911], 65:60n.) Given these connections and Symmes' private land operations in the territory, one might conclude that Congress had made a deal whereby land company officials could control or find representation in the territorial government. However, while it is clear that land speculations interrupted and interfered with government in the Northwest, there is no evidence that the governor, secretary, or judges tried overtly or extensively to use their powers for such purposes. Rather, in light of their associations, what is remarkable is the extent to which they were fair and objective in their official functions—especially during the years when both Symmes and the Ohio Company ran amok and were most apt to abuse their authority in order to save their investments. St. Clair undoubtedly was a healthy influence in this respect. He was always willing to use his office to expose and broadcast the illegal activities of speculators. (See, for example, Bond, *Old Northwest,* 83; Carter, *Territorial Papers,* II:342–43, 347–48.) That he did not often feel obliged to do so indicates that the Ohio Company officials, at least, were careful about their activities or that they benefited from the governor's absences, which placed one of their number in command. Nowhere in the Northwest is there an example comparable to the unrestrained avarice, abuse of power, and complete subservience of official activities to the land speculative mania displayed by William Blount while he was governor of the Southwest. (See Masterson, *Blount, passim.*)

33. See Chapter VI.

34. Philbrick, *Laws of Indiana,* R111.

work done in Indiana, codified and added to all district laws. This in turn suggests that, once there were enough people in a territory to organize a representative government, the assembly could make better laws than the governor and judges, which is not to say that they could govern a territory better.

Of all the district laws of the Northwest and Indiana, probably the most important and enduring legislation was embodied in two acts: the 1795 law adopting English common law, and the 1790 act empowering the justices of the Courts of the Quarter Sessions of the Peace to divide counties into townships, to establish boundaries, and to appoint local officials.[35] The latter is discussed in detail below. As for the rest, the governors and judges expended a great deal of energy adopting laws that created and regulated an extremely elaborate county court system. By 1805 the system was so unwieldy that the Indiana General Assembly, as one of its first acts, simplified it by consolidating the various courts.[36] Similarly, the governors and judges constantly tampered with militia and tax laws, and again improvement did not come until the second stage. Tax laws were an especial problem, since no one seemed to take them seriously except the lawmakers, but this was often, if not generally, true in the second stage as well. Nevertheless, it is difficult to say whether the tax laws were any less effective than the criminal and civil laws during the district stage, because most of them were simply not suitable, and there is little evidence that local officials even attempted to enforce them. By the beginning of the Indiana period, for example, the legislation of the Northwest district stage had

35. The first Northwest General Assembly readopted the common-law statute in 1799, and the Indiana Territorial Legislature incorporated it in the Code of 1807. In the meantime, of course, it had been in force. (Pease, *Laws of the Northwest*, A253, A340; Philbrick, *Laws of Indiana*, A323.) Similarly the first Northwest General Assembly readopted the second statute. In 1805 the first Indiana Territorial General Assembly reorganized the courts, but readopted the statute with a change in wording that vested the same powers in the new Court of Common Pleas rather than in the Quarter Sessions, which it absorbed. (Pease, *Laws of the Northwest*, A37–41, A338; Philbrick, *Laws of Indiana*, A255–56. The last citation is to the 1807 Code wherein the 1805 law was readopted.)

36. Philbrick (*ibid.*, R146–47, R161) contends that nevertheless, "the real improvement" in the administration of justice came through Harrison's appointing "fewer and better men to the reconstituted courts."

created a system of law and local government on paper that was too complicated to operate efficiently, except where it had been long familiar, and which bore only a superficial resemblance to local government in practice.[37]

Aside from the factors already discussed, the inadequacy and ineffectiveness of first-stage legislation can be attributed to the failure of territorial officials to provide themselves with copies of federal laws and state codes, or to see that local officials had copies of territorial laws. The first problem was not overcome during the district stage in any territory, and the territorial officials were not solely at fault. For one thing, in the early years no adequate collections of state codes existed. More important, federal money was not often forthcoming, and never in sufficient quantities, for the purchase of state codes. Nor did the federal government equip territorial officials with all (or, more frequently, any) United States statutes. In addition, territorial officials were underpaid and either could not or would not buy codes for themselves, and when Congress did give them money to buy laws they apparently used it for other purposes. In the case of the Northwest, Congress gave the judges extra money in advance of their departure for the territory so that they might procure copies of state laws, but none of them did so. When they met with the governor for the first lawmaking session, the only available code was one from Pennsylvania that St. Clair had remembered to bring along. However attractive the prospect of being able to pick the best laws from any of the states may

37. The very volume of work in Michigan, in the absence of even the inadequate court system of Indiana and the Northwest, suggests that these conclusions are especially true of that territory. (See the laws in Pease, *Laws of the Northwest*, A1–552; in Philbrick, *Laws of Indiana*, A1–87; and in *Laws of Michigan*, I: in entirety; II:ix–xiii, 1–180; IV:iii–v, 3–107. See also Philbrick, *Laws of Indiana*, R126–41, R222–23.) The statutes not enumerated in the text attempted to regulate fencing of animals and fields, fees, licensing, the Indian trade, and sale of liquor; they pretended to tax bachelors, provide imprisonment of vagrants, debtors, and bigamists, to protect orphans and the poor, to control divorce, usury, Negroes, slaves, and servants, and to prevent vice, crime, profanity, and drunkenness—all without notable effect. The governors and judges of Michigan added to these a multitude of elaborate procedural laws of questionable utility; the definitions alone must have made most court actions nearly impossible. See also Carter, *Territorial Papers*, IX:379–80, for a discussion of legislative problems in Orleans.

have been, the laws were not available, and therefore useless. Sargent used this situation to justify his outright lawmaking in Mississippi.[38]

Within the territories, the principal problem was the chronic shortage of printed laws that caused local officials to be ignorant of their content. Initially, the only way a governor could make laws known was to have them read in open General Court. In the Northwest, St. Clair and the judges did not enact a law providing for the publication of laws until 1791, and then they were unable to raise the funds to implement it. They repealed the law the following year, after Congress passed an act appropriating money for the purpose. Until 1795, when William Maxwell set up the first print shop in the territory, the Northwest laws had to be printed outside the territory, which delayed their distribution. But even with federal subsidies and a printer in the territory, distribution continued to be a problem until the territory was divided, because copies of the laws were never available in sufficient quantities. Sargent, of course, exaggerated the problem by his habit of carrying territorial laws with him, instead of establishing a public depository, and by his reluctance to make handwritten copies of them on request. During his trip to Illinois, for example, Sargent appointed county judges and justices, but refused to give them copies of the territorial laws, thereby leaving behind him a new county government

38. Bond, *Foundations*, 402; Philbrick, *Laws of Illinois*, R406–97; Jenks, "Legislation," 41–42; Valentine, "Territorial Governor," 14; Carter, *Territorial Papers*, XVI:373; Pomeroy, *Territories, 1861–1890*, 11. Surprisingly, the lack of state codes persisted in the territories until the Wisconsin period when, beginning with the Wisconsin Organic Act in 1836, Congress provided funds at the outset of each territory's existence for the purchase of a permanent library of state codes for legislative use. Michigan lacked state codes during the district stage and no amount of pleading could convince the federal administration to furnish them. (See, for example, the correspondence of 1818 in Carter, *Territorial Papers*, X:831–32, 713, 737.) Cass and the other officials apparently did not get any state laws from the federal government; John Quincy Adams stated that his office had no money for the purpose and that there was no federal law to permit him to provide the territory with state laws. Cass and Woodbridge also wanted copies of United States statutes, which they apparently did not have. They eventually received three volumes of the statutes but these were of no help in lawmaking, since they only made federal law known to territorial officials. Federal laws were always impossible to obtain in sufficient numbers, and the question of whether federal laws applied uniformly to the territories invariably arose and added to the confusion.

whose officials had no knowledge of what the law was, much less of their duties or of the procedures to be followed.

The problem of printing and distributing laws varied only slightly in other territories. Although there was no printer in Indiana until the end of the district stage, conditions were probably worst in Michigan. It is possible that no one there ever saw a Northwest or Indiana law before Michigan became a separate territory in 1805, but then few people seem to have seen Michigan laws during the district stage, either. Perhaps most of the Michigan laws were not published in their entirety until late in the nineteenth century. A number of Michigan laws were apparently lost during the district stage, and Lewis Cass had considerable difficulty in determining what was the law when he assumed the office of governor. When the Michigan district government did publish its laws, it published them in "codes"—that is, periodically in groups rather than continuously or as enacted—and as late as 1816, Cass included only the titles of many laws in his code, in order to save money. Yet even these austerity measures seem to have helped little, and laws remained in short supply.[39]

A final hindrance to effective legislation was St. Clair's insistence that all laws enacted under his adminstration must apply explicitly to the entire Northwest Territory. In this way, he deliberately limited the scope of lawmaking to the most general kinds of statutes, and even these were often inappropriate for parts of the territory. St. Clair thus prevented the adoption of specific laws to solve local problems, though such measures were obviously desirable in such a vast territory, having widely differing conditions and needs. In the meantime, local authorities took matters into their own hands, but the problems were not wholly solved until Congress divided the Northwest and the amount of diversity decreased within the territories.[40]

The statutes themselves, of course, do not represent the whole of territorial law. The Ordinance gave the governor broad powers by way of proclamations. Throughout the district stage, governors used

39. Apparently these were no less important problems in Mississippi, Missouri, and Illinois. (See Bond, *Old Northwest*, 79–80; Bond, *Foundations*, 419; Philbrick, *Laws of Indiana*, R113–14; Philbrick, *Laws of Illinois*, R394; *Laws of Michigan*, I:xiii, 226; II:v–vi, vii. Laws that were presumed to have been lost were later found and published in 1884 in *ibid.*, IV:vii, 3–107.)

40. Bond, *Foundations*, 402, 422; Valentine, "Territorial Governor," 20–21.

proclamations extensively to create counties and, at the beginning of government in the Northwest, St. Clair used both proclamations and less formal, unrecorded orders to deal with other matters, such as the powers, duties, and jurisdiction of the courts and local officials. In spite of the clarity with which gubernatorial powers were granted in the Ordinance, however, President Washington disapproved of St. Clair's broad use of his powers, and as early as 1790 he began warning him against overusing them. Consequently, the governors were soon inhibited by the federal government, and the use of proclamations declined quickly. In the meantime, a system of relationships and controls developed in local governments which were only partially recognized in law, both in the first and in the second stages.[41]

Altogether, then, the general ineffectiveness, and in some cases the virtual absence of district governments, resulted only in part from the preoccupation of territorial governors with military and Indian affairs. It grew equally out of the inadequacies of the laws, the lack of publication of laws, and the indifference of territorial officials toward their civil responsibilities. The upshot, if not another cause, of the weaknesses of territorial government was the rapid emergence of a high degree of local autonomy, which transformed the early failure of territorial officials to control local governments into the inability to do so.

41. G. L. Wilson, "St. Clair," 407; Valentine, "Territorial Governor," 17.

IV

Local Government during the District Stage

BECAUSE territorial officials failed to regulate local governments effectively, local officials defined their powers to suit themselves, and acted as they pleased. The rapid rise of local autonomy did not reflect emerging democracy, however; even when local governments became more democratic in form, they remained oligarchic in operation. A small group of men controlled government in each county and the high degree of plural officeholding, at least in the early years, made local governments far less complex and diverse in practice than the laws of the various territories would suggest.

Aside from the pattern of appointments to local offices, the continuity of oligarchic control was evident in local court practices, in the assessment and collection of taxes, and in the results of the elections held. The courts were the heart of local government, and they were highly political. Moreover, the courts were in the hands of the upper class, principally the landed gentry, so that when justice was egalitarian, it was a function of expediency rather than of democracy. Similarly, there were few elective offices, and when governors held preferential elections prior to making appointments, their motives were not necessarily to further democracy. As governors well knew, the existing oligarchies controlled all elections and could be counted on to run their own candidates. Consequently, through the use of preferential elections, governors often sought both to avoid conflicts over their appointments and perhaps to undermine the entrenched oligarchies by providing newcomers to the territories with the means to gain a share in power. Concurrently, this device both permitted and encouraged the rise of political organizations, which were potentially useful to the governors. Whatever their objectives were, during the district stage, and perhaps equally in the second stage, personalities, policies, and political styles seem to have changed a good deal more than the underlying realities of the possession and exercise of power in local governments.

While the governor's control over local governments during the district stage was potentially absolute, the Ordinance left all matters pertaining to their organization, operation, and real powers *vis-à-vis* the territorial executive, entirely within the governor's discretion:

Previous to the organization of the general assembly, the governor shall appoint such magistrates and other civil officers in each county or township, as he shall find necessary for the preservation of the peace and good order in the same: After the general assembly shall be organized, the powers and duties of the magistrates and other civil officers shall be regulated and defined by the said assembly; but all magistrates and other civil officers not herein otherwise directed, shall, during the continuance of this temporary government, be appointed by the governor.

For the prevention of crimes and injuries, the laws to be adopted or made shall have force in all parts of the district, and for the execution of process, criminal and civil, the governor shall make proper divisions thereof; and he shall proceed from time to time as circumstances may require, to lay out the parts of the district in which the Indian titles shall have been extinguished, into counties and townships, subject however to such alterations as may thereafter be made by the legislature.[1]

St. Clair chose not to make the most of his powers over local government at the outset of his administration, when tight control would seem to have been most easily established. Instead, he delegated most of his powers to local officials, thereby setting the pattern for local government that prevailed throughout the district stage in all of the territories.

The customary practice at the beginning of the first stage in each territory was for the governor to create several large counties having nominal jurisdiction over all or most of the territory. He placed the seats of government at the centers of population, charged the county

1. Thorpe, *Constitutions*, 959; Carter, *Territorial Papers*, II:43–44 and notes.

officials with responsibility for organizing township governments, and expected them to use their authority to expand local government to keep pace with the rate of settlement. When new concentrations of settlement arose at inconvenient distances from the county seats, the governors usually created new counties. In making the county, rather than the township, the basic unit of government, the governors not only avoided any involvement in township administration, but also limited themselves to supervision over counties. This course was probably the wisest, since it left the governors free for other activities and minimized the friction that was virtually inevitable, no matter what course they followed. However, St. Clair rapidly lost to county oligarchies whatever control over local government he might have exercised.[2]

2. The location of the county seat nearly always caused discontent, regardless of whether it was fixed by a governor or by a legislature. In 1886 Congress attempted to end conflicts by requiring territorial legislatures to locate county seats by general acts; that is, Congress forbade special acts for the purpose. Meyerholz, "Federal Supervision," 242. Philbrick (*Laws of Illinois*, R475) argues that it required a liberal interpretation of the Organic Acts to include the fixing of the county seat as one of the powers of creating counties. But, as illustrated by the county seat wars in Iowa and by the fights that occurred in territorial legislatures, the governor's fixing of county seats probably gave the least cause for unnecessary squabbling. In any case, the locations of the county seats during the district stage were often temporary, subject to the redivision of the county as the population increased. See also Bond, *Foundations*, 428. Agitation for new counties became prominent in the Northwest after 1795 when settlement, especially from New England, increased rapidly, and may be associated with the impotence or virtual nonexistence of the familiar township system of government. (See G. L. Wilson, "St. Clair," 108–10, 123–36, 168; McCarty, *Governors of the Northwest*, 50–54; Philbrick, *Laws of Indiana*, R213–22; Bond, *Foundations*, 406–08; Bond, *Old Northwest*, 80–81; Downes, *Frontier Ohio*, 151–52.) Winfred B. Langhorst ("The Puritanic Influence in the Northwest Territory, 1788–1803," *Ohio Archaeological and Historical Publications*, XLII [Columbus, 1933], 415 ff) contends that Puritans dominated territorial life in the Northwest through control of government, but this seems exaggerated, since he concentrated on territorial officers. Pease (*Laws of the Northwest*, R33) calls New Englanders generally the backbone of settlement.

The glaring exception to the generalization about the process of county creation is the Western Reserve. Connecticut retained jurisdiction over the area until October 1797, despite St. Clair's contention that the Ordinance passed control to him. In the years before 1797 the area was a no man's land, without civil officers, laws, or courts since Connecticut refused to pay for government in the Reserve. (See G. L. Wilson, "St. Clair," 95–96; Carter, *Territorial Papers*, III:84–86.)

All power in local government was concentrated initially in the county courts. Until 1805, governors appointed for each county the following court officials: three or more judges to a Court of Common Pleas, who had jurisdiction in civil cases; three justices of the peace to a Court of General Quarter Sessions of the Peace; and one Probate Court judge. A law of 1795 added an Orphans Court in each county, to which the governor might appoint several judges. Most often, the same men sat on each court, and the courts held sessions concurrently. Consequently, the distinction between courts was not always apparent, and in 1805 the first Indiana Territorial General Assembly officially combined them, vesting all powers in the new Court of Common Pleas. The Illinois government continued this simplified court system, and control over local government remained in the hands of three to five county court justices or judges—the terms are used interchangeably in the laws—from the beginning of territorial government in the Northwest through the Illinois territorial period.[3]

The Michigan local court system differed in law from that of the other Northwest territories until after the War of 1812, but in fact it was always similar. Before 1815, the territory was divided into several

3. Philbrick, *Laws of Indiana,* R144–52. Above the Quarter Sessions courts were the circuit courts, held by one territorial judge, and the General (or Supreme) Court of the territory. The territorial judges consistently argued that they should exercise only appellate jurisdiction, that the volume of business made it an essential limitation. While this may have been true, even early in the territorial period, the judges' absences from the territory did not help the flow of business. Nor did their reluctance to ride circuit. Before 1800 circuit courts were not held regularly; the Supreme Court not only did not meet regularly, it never held a full court west of Cincinnati. Under these circumstances, the county courts were bound to gain prestige at the expense of the General Court. After 1800 circuit courts seem to have met annually, but they remained inadequate. The only solution was to divide the territory or add more judges, and the burden was eased only when Illinois and Michigan were set off as separate territories. See also McCarty, *Governors of the Northwest,* 54; Smith, *St. Clair Papers,* I:195; Philbrick, *Laws of Indiana,* R157–59; Philbrick, *Laws of Illinois,* R28. For a full discussion of the court system see Philbrick, *Laws of Indiana,* R143–65.

The county was not officially declared the basis of government until 1807 in Indiana; in 1812 the Illinois legislature reenacted this Indiana law. (See McCarty, *Governors of the Northwest,* 111.)

There seems to be no evidence to support G. L. Wilson's claim ("St. Clair," 103) that St. Clair "used the establishment of counties as a means of bringing the land companies under governmental control."

court districts rather than into counties. Each district had a "Supreme Court" consisting of a chief justice and two associates. When Governor Cass began laying out counties in 1815, the district courts became county courts with only a change of name. Two years later, Cass and the judges transformed the county courts into Courts of General Quarter Sessions of the Peace, and in 1818 they replaced them with county Boards of Commissioners. Throughout the Michigan district stage, each of the courts and boards consisted of three men and each exercised the same powers. These powers were roughly the same as those of the Indiana courts after the reorganization of 1805, except that the Michigan county officials could not create townships or appoint other local officials.[4] In practice, this exception was of little consequence.

In 1778 Virginia had enacted a law to provide government for the Ohio Country, under which most offices were elective. Ten years later, when St. Clair arrived in the Northwest, he adopted instead the Pennsylvania system, which also had numerous elected offices, as his model for local government. But there was only a superficial resemblance between county government in the Northwest and that in either of the states or, for that matter, even in colonial Pennsylvania. In the early eighteenth century, the county assessors or commissioners, sheriffs, coroners, and presumably any township officials of colonial Pennsylvania, were selected by ballot. By comparison, the United States colonial system was retrograde in the extreme. Almost all local offices were filled by appointment under every district-stage government, and both the method of appointment and the breadth of jurisdiction made these county governments far more centralized and powerful than those of either Pennsylvania or Virginia.[5]

4. *Laws of Michigan*, I:17–19, 184–86, 186–92, 716; II:7–9, 68–73, 109–14, 125, 130, 131, 132, 485–87. The district court scheme claimed its origins in the laws of Maryland, Massachusetts, Connecticut, North Carolina, Virginia, and Vermont. The laws establishing the Quarter Sessions courts and vesting the same powers in the County Boards of Commissioners came from Ohio. After attaining statehood Ohio had abolished the Quarter Sessions courts and given their powers to elected Boards of County Commissioners. This reorganization amounted to the single county court system adopted by Indiana in 1805, under a different nomenclature. Cass had studied law in Ohio and practiced there until he became governor of the Michigan Territory. (See Downes, *Frontier Ohio*, 154.)

5. Compare *Statutes at Large of Pennsylvania, 1682–1801* (Philadelphia, 1898),

As one of his first acts when he arrived in the Northwest in 1788, St. Clair created Washington County, which embraced most of the present state of Ohio, and delegated broad powers to the county courts. Two years later he and the judges began enumerating these powers in law. Under the 1790 act the justices of the Quarter Sessions courts were to appoint all township officials and any county officers not appointed by the governor. The act empowered the justices to divide their counties into townships, to locate the seats of government, to define boundaries, and to redivide or subdivide their counties at will. For each township, the justices were to appoint one or more constables and overseers of the poor annually, a superintendent of highways, and one clerk during good behavior. Maxwell's Code gave them the power to appoint three county tax commissioners, one of whom the justices were to replace annually after the first year, and two overseers of the poor for each township.

The Northwest had no revenue law until 1792. In that year, the judges of the Courts of Common Pleas were authorized to appoint from one to three commissioners or assessors for each township. Three years later, Maxwell's Code reduced the number to one, and made the office elective by ballot. This was the first elective office provided by law in the Northwest. When the freeholders of each township elected the assessor, they were also to select three of their number to review the previous year's accounts of the overseer of the poor. If the office was ever filled, the significance of elected township assessors was minimal, because Maxwell's Code left de facto control over taxation in the hands of the county courts, through the provision for the Quarter Sessions courts to appoint three tax commissioners for each county.[6]

---

especially II:34–39, 212–14 [basic electorial law of 1705–06], 272–75; IV [1729–30]:10–26, 183; V[1744–59]:16–22, 134–38, 153–58; Thorpe, *Constitutions*, 3076 ff; and W. W. Hening, comp., *Statutes at Large . . . of Virginia . . . 1619–1792* (Richmond, 1822), IX:552, with the following discussion.

6. Pease, *Laws of the Northwest*, A37–41, A71, A201–03, A216, A338, A402, A480–81, A483; Bond, *Foundations*, 405–06. In 1799 the Northwest General Assembly raised to two the number of township assessors and called them appraisers. Occasionally, they were also referred to as commissioners. The same terms were sometimes used in reference to county commissioners. Philbrick (*Laws of Indiana*, R150–51) says that the office of county commissioner is surrounded by obscurity in the early period. It was a new office and "its

Nevertheless, by 1799, a rather elaborate system of township government had come into existence in law. The first Northwest General Assembly reenacted the pertinent laws, and Indiana Territory carried the system unchanged through the first stage and into the second. But the pattern of strong county governments continued. In 1807 the Indiana Assembly made a single change in the Northwest system when it replaced the three-man county board of commissioners with a single county assessor appointed by the principal county court for a four-year term.[7] Two years later, immediately after its separation from Indiana, the new Illinois district government abolished the office of township assessor and handed its duties over to the county sheriff. This system prevailed until Illinois attained statehood, but in 1818, the year Illinois became a state, the General Assembly found it necessary to order the Common Pleas courts in each county to appoint township assessors, in order to facilitate the collection of the 1817 taxes, after the existing arrangement failed to bear fruit. In the meantime, the legislature had created the new office of town assessor. Beginning in 1814, acts incorporating towns empowered the town trustees to appoint one person to the office annually.

Altogether, by 1818 local government in these territories would seem to have regressed to the point that the township no longer existed as a unit of government, and that the county courts directly controlled all phases of government outside incorporated towns. There continued

---

differentiation from the quarter sessions was new and insecure" until the early nineteenth century. The Quarter Sessions justices may have appointed county commissioners before 1795, while sitting as the judges of the Common Pleas court, but they normally exercised the powers of tax commissioners themselves. (See Pease, *Laws of the Northwest*, A70–71, for the Act of 1792 that authorized the Common Pleas judges to appoint commissioners.) This practice continued after 1795, since the justices of the Quarter Sessions, which court was now vested with the power, tended to appoint themselves as county commissioners.

7. Pease, *Laws of the Northwest*, A467–94; Philbrick, *Laws of Indiana*, R149–52, A255–56, A308, A592–93. Philbrick (*ibid.*, R151–52n) says that Indiana did not carry over the township arrangement, despite abundant laws to the contrary and the obvious continuation into the early Illinois territorial period. (See, for example, the act in Philbrick, *Laws of Illinois*, A13, that repeals part of the Indiana system. Both Indiana and Illinois, however, eventually abandoned the township as a unit of government altogether.)

to be no provision in law for the election of any local officials. Thus, if democracy is to be measured by provisions for the popular selection of governmental officials, the statutes of the period from 1797 to 1818 illustrate anything but growth from its very meager beginnings under St. Clair.[8]

By 1818, laws covering local government in Michigan were roughly equivalent to those of Illinois at the same time. The principal difference was that, as the Michigan laws evolved, the county courts theoretically lost power rather than gaining it. Under a law of 1809, each district court was to appoint three assessors and a district treasurer. In 1817, Cass and the judges withdrew these powers, and the governor began appointing a single assessor and one treasurer for each county. During the same year, the district-stage legislators made the first provisions for subdividing counties in an act that empowered the governor, rather than the county courts as in other territories, to divide counties into townships. He was also to appoint constables and a township supervisor for each township, whose tenure was to be during pleasure. However, Cass did not lay out townships during the remainder of the district stage, and not even rudimentary township government developed.

The only elective local offices provided during the entire first stage in Michigan were district commissioners. Under a law of 1810, five commissioners were to be selected annually in each district, but Governor Hull seems not to have implemented the act before the War of 1812. After the territory went through a period of British occupation and American martial law, the new governor, Lewis Cass, repealed the law as one of his first civil acts.

Even if Cass was "the Last Jeffersonian," the statutes of his district-stage administration in Michigan were more retrograde than those of the other territories. The township government law of 1817 is a good example. It provided for the appointment of local officials during the governor's pleasure, a tenure that had gone out of style sometime earlier in the other territories of the Northwest. Moreover, the law

8. See Philbrick, *Laws of Illinois,* A13, A67, A133, A267, A322. Illinois retained constables and may have continued overseers of the poor in townships, but there is no mention of the latter in the Illinois laws. Most evidence indicates that if the provisions remained on the books they were meaningless. (See below.)

did not make provision for complete township governments; it mentioned only the appointment of supervisors and constables. This oversight did not, of course, preclude the appointment of other officials with the same tenure, and that others were intended is indicated by the absence of a statute to cover even the appointment of county sheriffs. Under the 1817 law, however, the governor was to appoint township officials on the recommendation of the county courts, and in practice this requirement probably would have placed the essential appointive power in the hands of the county judges, as did the laws of the other territories.[9]

Though the Northwest, Indiana, and Illinois had elaborate township governments in law, the county courts seem to have been the only significant units of local government during the first stage. This is not to say that the county courts did not fully exercise their powers to create townships and appoint officials, but that the townships were wholly the creatures of the county courts. Township governments seem scarcely to have existed or functioned as distinct political units, and it is doubtful that the few elective offices were ever filled. The same nonelective system of county government apparently continued in Indiana and Illinois until they achieved statehood. On the other hand, in January 1802 the Northwest General Assembly enacted extensive reforms in local government, making most offices elective, and in 1825 Congress revamped the Michigan system. Since Governor Cass had done nothing about local government, Congress finally gave Michigan completely elective township governments, made some county offices elective, and required the legislative council's consent for the governor's appointments to the remaining offices.[10]

In light of the fact that no local official or militia officer could hold office without a commission of appointment from the governor, one would suppose that the governors had a great deal of control over in-

9. See Chapter V, note 35; and *Laws of Michigan,* I:211; II:93, 109–14, 279–83, 317, 477–81; IV:40, 42, 96; Carter, *Territorial Papers,* X:428; 767–68, 773, 774; XI:39–40, 310–11; Frank B. Woodford, *Lewis Cass. The Last Jeffersonian* (New Brunswick, N. J., 1950), 74–171 *passim,* hereafter cited as Woodford, *Lewis Cass.*

10. *Laws of Michigan,* I:318–20; Downes, *Frontier Ohio,* 154–55; Philbrick, *Laws of Indiana,* R149–50; Salmon P. Chase, *Statutes of Ohio and of the Northwestern Territory from 1788 to 1833 Inclusive* . . . (3 vols., Cincinnati, 1833–35), I:344–46. hereafter cited as Chase, *Statutes of Ohio.*

ternal affairs. This would seem to be especially true when governors made their appointments during pleasure or for short terms, the latter being more common after the first years, and since they always claimed the right to remove appointees at will. Indeed, the volume of appointments was impressive. St. Clair eventually appointed about 700 officers in the Northwest; in the Southwest, William Blount appointed 208 civil officials and 269 militia officers during the first six months of his administration. If Ninian Edwards' record of 128 appointments in an eight-month period can be considered typical, governors normally issued about 200 commissions of appointment each year.

Executive appointments, however, were not distributed evenly over time. They came in bunches when the governors created new counties, enlarged the staff of existing county governments, renewed expiring commissions or appointed replacements, and when they organized or expanded the militia. Perhaps more than half of all appointments were to the militia, and not directly associated with civil administration, although instances such as Sargent's use of militia appointments to reward friends, punish enemies, and build up loyal units must have affected civil government. The remarkable aspect of governors' appointments, however, was not their number and distribution, but how infrequently they were contested and how seldom governors removed appointed officials. The reasons for this lack of protest also serve to illustrate how little control the governors really exercised over their appointments.[11]

Conflicts over appointments during the early years of first- and second-stage governments, when political factions were immature or absent, usually involved "imported" appointees. An imported candidate was one drawn from outside the territory or the county, or from the ranks of recent arrivals, the distinction being largely academic in the eyes of the "original" settlers who always felt that they had a prior claim to any office. No matter how new settlement was when a governor organized a new county, there was sure to be an outcry if he appointed anyone who, as a matter of fact or expediency, fit the definition of an imported candidate. Sargent's experience indicates the danger of such conflicts. His unfortunate personality and his habit, like St.

11. Philbrick, *Laws of Illinois,* R465, R467; Valentine, "Territorial Governor," 25–26, 72–76.

Clair's, of calling the people settlers—by which, as everyone knew, he meant semi-savages—were grating, but the insult of importing candidates who were qualified to his satisfaction was intolerable. This practice was a primary source of complaint against his administration in Mississippi, and it eventually led to his removal. W. C. C. Claiborne, as governor of Orleans, imported candidates with greater success, but he apparently had the full support of the national administration. He unnecessarily dragged national politics into county government by appointing only Republicans to local offices, regardless of their qualifications, even if it meant going outside the territory for politically correct candidates, to avoid appointing well-qualified Federalists.

St. Clair and the other district-stage governors, probably all for the same reason, apparently did not import appointees. As Harrison put it, he would not import candidates or endorse the idea of importing them because the people "Complain So bitterly." This was especially true when the inhabitants felt that someone in the area qualified for the job, and it was seldom that they would admit that they lacked a qualified resident.

District-stage executives, like many second-stage governors, occasionally appointed friends and relatives to territorial or local offices. St. Clair seems generally to have been careful about avoiding this, perhaps for lack of friends and relatives, but in 1795 he faced severe criticism when he appointed his son Attorney General of the Northwest with tenure during good behavior. St. Clair had deliberately appointed his son during good behavior because he had not received a new commission and did not expect to be reappointed governor. In this way, St. Clair hoped to protect his son from removal by his successor, and he undoubtedly anticipated the denunciations for nepotism and for granting tenure inconsistent with that common to the territory, although he probably did not expect President Washington and his cabinet to condemn his action. This strong federal reaction seems to have had a lasting effect, since no other governor followed St. Clair's example of granting unusual tenure to relatives or friends. A greater number and variety of office-seekers apparently followed new governors and other federal officials to the territories west of the Mississippi River during the Second Empire, and they often received appointments, but the appointment of such individuals figured prominently in memorials requesting the removal of governors throughout territorial history.[12]

There were several other important reasons why governors did not import local officials, even if the alternative was to appoint wholly unqualified residents. One was that when a new county was created, even at the beginning of each territorial period, there were already some recognized leaders among the settlers, if not a formal oligarchy more or less in control. This was as true in 1788 in the Northwest as when a new territory was created by dividing another one. If governors did not appoint or reappoint the existing leaders, they ran the risk of having their authority challenged or denied. As it was sometimes difficult enough to convince the settlers to accept the authority of a territorial government anyway, this was no small matter. At the same time, governors of new territories, and generally their successors, seldom were able to acquaint themselves with all candidates for office. Consequently, they always sought advice before making appointments, particularly from the existing leadership, and appointed men from its ranks—perhaps on the assumption that they had popular support because they had power. As a matter of expediency, then, St. Clair was not being inconsistent, even though he was an implacable aristocrat who considered it a crime against his class "to lean toward" or be "tinctured with democracy," when he felt what he thought was the popular pulse before making his appointments to offices in the Northwest.

At the beginning of his administration, St. Clair reappointed those men who had been acting as magistrates before his arrival, and there-

12. Valentine, "Territorial Governor," 24–25, 133–35; Philbrick, *Laws of Illinois*, R467, R471; Carter, *Territorial Papers*, VII:708–09, 710, VIII:43, 57–58; Smith, *St. Clair Papers*, I:195–96.

Territorial judges disputed the governor's right to appoint clerks of the General Court on grounds that it was their prerogative in common law to chose their own clerks. They eventually had their way. (See Philbrick, *Laws of Illinois*, R465, R469–70.)

Occasionally governors made appointments to offices before the passage of acts creating the offices. St. Clair contended that the office of Attorney General was essential and could be assumed to exist under common law. Thus he argued that he could appoint someone to the office in the absence of a statute. He agreed, however, that he lacked the power to give the appointee a salary. (See Philbrick, *Laws of Indiana*, R106; Philbrick, *Laws of Illinois*, R472. For illustrations of similar occurrences in later territories see Valentine, "Territorial Governor," 74–75.)

after he solicited nominations for local offices from residents of counties or proposed counties. This became the custom in all territories and settlers in the Northwest labored to extend the practice. They were usually free with advice and often offered nominations before vacancies occurred or without being asked. As settlement increased, they sent petitions to the governor requesting or demanding "reforms" such as the creation of new counties or an increase in the number of offices in an old county. As often as not, the objective of these petitions was to create a new center of power or to add new members to the current power structure, and governors usually resisted reform of this type. St. Clair constantly resisted pressure for the creation of new counties except when such action was clearly warranted. In 1799 he stated that he preferred large counties because they minimized the cost of government to the people. Nevertheless, he seemed willing enough to increase the number of offices in existing counties whenever population increases made it desirable.[13]

The only significant conflicts over the governor's appointive powers in the Northwest, other than those noted earlier, occurred near the end of the district stage. Having failed in all his attempts to reenter national politics in the East, St. Clair sought unsuccessfully to develop a strong Federalist following in the territory in the hope of securing himself a job after the territory attained statehood. But even here the conflicts had more to do with national party differences and the governor's attempts to prevent or delay statehood than with abuse of the appointive power per se.[14]

13. Downes, *Frontier Ohio,* 149–52, 155; Philbrick, *Laws of Illinois,* R467–68; Bond, *Foundations,* 428; G. L. Wilson, "St. Clair," 331; Carter, *Territorial Papers,* II:67. Quotes are from Sears, "Philosophy of St. Clair," 48–50. Valentine ("Territorial Governor," 77–78) discusses some of the problems of gaining recognition of territorial government in some territories. In Montana, for example, the vigilantes refused to yield to the territorial officials and Governor Ashley had to leave them to their summary methods. Utah was perhaps the most difficult case. In 1870, after Utah had been a territory for twenty years, Governor J. W. Shaffer still complained about the Mormons' open ridicule and defiance of federal authority.

14. Sears, "Philosophy of St. Clair," 44–50; Smith, *St. Clair Papers,* I:186–87, 192; II:442; Downes, "St. Clair," *DAB,* XVI:295; B. A. Hinsdale, *The Old Northwest: with a View of the Thirteen Colonies as Constituted by the Royal Charters* (New York, 1888), 305; F. E. Wilson, *St. Clair,* 50. St. Clair was incapable of becoming a democratic leader, and he was unable to secure a division of the ter-

William Blount was a more adroit tactician than St. Clair. When he reached the Southwest, the population was larger and the political factions were well defined. In a sense, this made the job of developing a personal following more difficult than in the Northwest, where St. Clair had a nearly virgin field to till. But Blount immediately made an informal alliance with John Sevier, leader of the larger faction, and he avoided opposition from the other principal faction by reconstituting local governments as they had existed under North Carolina. By reappointing the current officeholders under the new territorial authority, Blount left members of both groups in office and gained support from each. Whenever possible, as government grew and vacancies occurred, the governor carefully appointed close, loyal friends who were leaders of public opinion and associated with one of the factions. In this way Blount was able to build a personal following essentially independent of the main political groups and to use them without becoming involved in most factional squabbles. On occasion he also used or fabricated crises to dilute popular or factional discontent that endangered his position. The reward for his adept maneuvering was a seat in the United States Senate when Tennessee joined the Union.[15]

The pattern in Indiana and Illinois was similar in some respects to the early years of both the Northwest and the Southwest. Territorial division did not bring a break in administration or change of personnel in either Indiana or Illinois. The secretaries, acting before the new governors arrived, proclaimed counties and appointed officials, but in each case they merely renewed the status quo in the new jurisdiction. Secretary John Gibson of Indiana apparently exercised full powers of appointment, however, whereas Secretary Nathaniel Pope of Illinois pointedly issued only temporary commissions, pending the governor's arrival.[16]

Under Governors Harrison, Edwards, and—after the War of 1812—

---

ritory that would assure Federalist control in the eastern state wherein he hoped to become governor. Frustrated and embittered, he made the treasonous outbursts during the Ohio Constitutional Convention that led Jefferson to fire him.

15. See Masterson, *Blount*, 188–90, 192–93, particularly 219. Blount's Senate career nevertheless was short. His improprieties and speculations got the best of him, the Senate censured him, and, like St. Clair, he died a pauper.

16. Philbrick, *Laws of Indiana*, R104, R106; McCarty, *Governors of the Northwest*, 97–98.

Cass, a degree of popular participation in the selection of local officials became institutionalized. The immediate significance of this occurrence is impossible to determine, however, because the sources note that the people made recommendations or held elections without specifying whether or not participation was limited to the freeholders. The suffrage requirements of the Ordinance and other laws during the first stage would suggest that only freeholders took part, and if this were the case, the preferential elections and nominations would have involved few if any people outside the oligarchies in the early years. Nevertheless, in the long run, these elections and nominations were to be important.

Harrison encouraged recommendations for appointments and the holding of informal elections. Though he always reserved final decisions to himself, he appointed the majority choice in preferential elections, when it was consistent with his objectives. Like Blount, Harrison made appointments to enhance his own prestige and influence, but he got carried away by the slavery issue in Indiana. He used his appointive power to build support for his pro-slavery position, openly took part in the debate, and was roundly criticized. Several factors that saved subsequent governors helped Harrison to survive the intense opposition engendered by the issue. He was certainly less arrogant than his predecessors in the Northwest Territory, he had a respectable military record, and he was something of a demagogue. He had also made important concessions to the people and had championed their causes as the Northwest Territory delegate to Congress. Altogether, the people seem to have accepted Harrison as one of them, a "genuine" territorial citizen.

By contrast, both Edwards and Cass were outsiders, albeit from states adjacent to their territories. They won the respect of many people by discreetly avoiding overt involvement in local politics and by using their office and money to advertise and develop their territories. Edwards went beyond Harrison's practice in letting the people elect their local civil officials, and the militia its officers, and by appointing the winners uniformly, without making any apparent effort to develop a personal following. His decision to permit the election of militia officers was a wise one. Militia commissions carried a great deal of social prestige, and in Illinois perhaps no other appointments were as likely to lead to open animosities. Cass gradually adopted Edwards' expedients in Michigan and, when the people were reluctant to elect their own officials, he sent out blank commissions with orders that elections should be held and the blanks filled.[17]

By using preferential elections for appointive offices governors yielded to popular demands and more easily avoided conflicts, but they also helped to undermine the power of local oligarchies. Extremes of wealth and poverty characterized society in the Northwest, and the aristocratic St. Clair naturally made political magnates of the county gentry by appointing them to the courts even though they had no special educational, moral, or other qualifications.

St. Clair was not alone in appointing the economic magnates of counties to key government offices, for the lack of qualified candidates was acute during much of his administration in the Northwest, and at least during the early years in every other territory. Semi-literacy alone virtually qualified individuals for licenses to practice law, and since a degree of literacy and a claim to acquaintance with law were desirable qualifications for judges, most of the few practicing "lawyers" were also judges, often serving simultaneously on several benches in the Northwest and Indiana before 1805.

Regardless of the absence of alternative candidates for office, the power of county oligarchies left governors little choice but to appoint or reappoint persons whose improprieties and malfeasance in office were well known. Though the governors appointed the court judges in law,

17. Philbrick, *Laws of Indiana,* R19, R106; Philbrick, *Laws of Illinois,* R56–60, R466; Valentine, "Territorial Governor," 24–25, 133; Clarence W. Alvord, *The Illinois Country, 1673–1818* (Springfield, Illinois, 1920), 431; McCarty, *Governors of the Northwest,* 98–100, 139; Carter, *Territorial Papers,* X:769–71. Harrison seems to have felt that the Ordinance provisions granting broad appointive powers to the governor precluded any elective arrangements, but the intent was merely that no one was to exercise office without a commission of appointment from the governor. St. Clair clearly understood this, but was not inclined to encourage democracy.

Of all the governors, Cass alone made all new appointments when he became governor. This action was undoubtedly necessary, since Hull's appointments were allegedly poor choices and were all made before the War of 1812. The situation changed drastically during the War; many people were dispersed, and officials resigned or left the territory. Those individuals who had remained in office during the British occupation were suspect as traitors or fellow travelers. (See, for example, McCarty, *Governors of the Northwest,* 130.)

in practice they were seldom able to control their appointments to the courts, much less those to the other offices. Consequently, any enumeration of executive appointments at face value tells only how many commissions a governor issued. The judges continually nominated each other for appointment and their recommendations, which went far beyond the judgeships themselves, could not easily be ignored. Characteristically, county judges recommended as fit to hold offices or run public houses men who were under indictment for illegally selling liquor to Indians or some other offense, and governors seem to have honored their recommendations. Governor Harrison appointed at least one nominee of this kind to a judgeship on a Court of Common Pleas, two months after his second indictment. For such reasons, plural officeholding and oligarchic control continued in the countries long after any possible justification had passed. In the second stage of government for example, the same men frequently sat both on the courts and in the legislatures, despite laws forbidding plural officeholding.[18]

Whether or not one of the governors' objectives in allowing preferential elections was to undercut the power of local oligarchies, there was a gradual movement in that direction. The slow pace resulted partially from the governors' policy of limiting popular nominations to the nonjudicial offices in a system where county court judges controlled all phases of local government. In addition the gentry vigorously resisted attempts to reduce their power over local government. Usually large landowners, land speculators, and tavern keepers, they had vested interests in retaining control over the extensive powers of tax assessment and collection and over licensing, which were lodged exclusively in the county courts and their agents.[19] Among the latter were the sheriffs. They received their commissions from the governor but were

18. See Philbrick, *Laws of Indiana,* R35, R180–81, R192–95, R203–05, R206–09, R225.

19. During the first stage, governors assumed the power to issue licenses and charters for taverns and ferries, but the application of power is unclear. It seems that much of the power fell to local courts, either in the form of recommending licenses to the governor or of actually issuing licenses. Beginning with St. Clair, governors allowed their powers to be defined and limited somewhat by law in this respect. In any case, it is clear that governors received fees for these services and that such fees were an important part of the income of local officials. (See Philbrick, *Laws of Indiana,* R160; Valentine, "Territorial Governor," 25–26, 53–54.)

nonetheless controlled by the county courts that nominated them. The sheriffs, of course, conducted elections. Thus, soon after Harrison began allowing preferential elections in Indiana, he received complaints that local officials controlled them to their advantage. Through the control of elections and their own mutual nominations, the county gentry retained control of local government in Indiana until well into the second stage of government, and no doubt they perpetrated it in some form long after statehood was achieved.

Inequitable taxation was one consequence of local autonomy and oligarchic control. The difficulty of getting county governments to make assessments and collect taxes was always a problem, and collections were often delayed, incomplete, or not made at all. Examples of this problem can be found throughout territorial history, in both district- and second-stage governments. For example, just a few years before Montana, Wyoming, and Idaho became states, their governors and legislatures were still attempting to force tax collections and to end private lawmaking. Nevertheless the problem of collecting taxes was extremely critical for the impoverished first-stage governments, and it was more serious for second-stage governments that were responsible for their own support than for such later ones as the federal government subsidized heavily.

Legislation was usually ineffective, and legislators were constantly remaking tax laws. Harrison's experience in Indiana illustrates the nature of oligarchic control during both the first and the second stages. He and the judges before 1805, and the legislature after 1805, rewrote tax laws almost annually without significant results. In 1806 the assessors of St. Clair County in the Illinois Country refused to assess or collect taxes, and the tax law of 1805 had not been observed punctually in any county. Tax delinquency, as one might expect, was primarily a privilege of the well-to-do. The published list of delinquents for Randolph County in 1805 included all the magistrates. Five years later, when the territory was divided, the assessments remained unpaid and were turned over to Illinois for collection. At that time the list included four court justices, the wealthiest merchant and landlord, and, an addition since 1805, the sheriff. Indiana legislation did, however, force counties to reduce their levies in some degree. In 1808 Harrison delivered a strong address to the General Assembly, complaining that taxes were too heavy for most citizens to pay and were unfairly assessed. The tax law of that year defined procedures more precisely and abolished some taxes, but Harrison was never able to get the legislature to enact equitable taxation. Taxes on horses, for example, remained relatively much higher than those on land, a situation that certainly reflected the mutual interests of the legislators and local officials.[20]

In time, the nature of county oligarchies changed, even if the amount of autonomy did not. As the population increased and the economy developed, land and legal problems became relatively less important than other service functions of the government. Concurrently, government got more complex and officials who were not entirely subservient to the courts became increasingly important. With these changes, the preferential elections began to take on real significance, and they helped to reduce the political power of the courts and antipathy toward the government. In short, as the nature of government changed, the courts became less political, their services improved as the governors were able to appoint better qualified candidates, and local government as a whole became more acceptable. Until these changes occurred, however, the control of the local gentry was so complete that, despite their unlimited powers in theory, governors apparently never removed corrupt or undesirable officials, especially judges. Even after 1805, when the Indiana General Assembly enacted the first law on the subject, no county judges were successfully impeached. Altogether, then, general improvements in local government, as measured by increased popular participation in government or the broadening of the bases of power, were as much the result of population growth as of the governor's actions.[21]

A major contributing factor to the extensive local autonomy was the vague definition of powers. When St. Clair proclaimed Washington County in 1788 he merely outlined in hazy terms the jurisdictions and duties of county officials. Within the next few years he and the judges

20. See Philbrick, *Laws of Indiana,* R114–16, R119–20; Neil, "Territorial Governors," 17–19. Masterson (*Blount,* 241–43) discusses some aspects of attempts to levy taxes in the Southwest Territory in 1793; and Downes (*Frontier Ohio,* 142) discusses corruption in local government during the Northwest district stage.

21. See Philbrick, *Laws of Indiana,* R34–35, R151–52, R160, R180–81, R209, R218, R265, A123–24, A520; Valentine, "Territorial Governor," 24, 90.

began defining them for all local officials in law, and this became almost an occupational pastime for lawmakers during both the district and the second stage everywhere in the Northwest territories. Nevertheless, the laws remained incomplete, inadequate, and contradictory, at least until they were overhauled after the territories attained statehood. Equally important, the relationships of the county courts to the territorial courts were always unclear and the practices of the high courts encouraged local court autonomy. The Northwest territorial judges held circuit and general court sessions infrequently, as did the judges in the other territories, and they limited themselves to an ambiguous appellate jurisdiction that they continually tried to narrow. Before 1795 the governor and judges did not even designate territorial seats of justice, and at all times the judicial circuits were too large and the dockets too overloaded to permit effective supervision of lower courts.

Besides the inattentiveness of territorial officials and their failure to define adequately the duties and powers of local officials, the languid pace of legislation and its content generally encouraged county courts to take matters into their own hands. As district- and sometimes second-stage legislatures added new laws to the books, inconsistencies arose that were not wholly rectified by early codes. Such inconsistencies persisted throughout the Indiana territorial period, for example. The district-stage laws did not harmonize with the Northwest code, and they precipitated some confusion in Indiana courts. Much of the continuing problem arose not only from the erratic publication of statutes but also from the manner in which the legislatures codified and repealed laws. The extensive Indiana revision of 1807 added to the confusion insofar as the acts and resolutions repealing laws or declaring them in force usually cited the laws in question incompletely or neglected to specify either the date of the laws or the authority under which they had been enacted. Furthermore, legislators often left laws on the books without formally declaring them repealed or in force. Problems growing out of these circumstances were acute enough to prod Congress into enacting a remedial law in 1815, but a final solution came only after statehood. Thus, well into the Indiana period county governments looked after themselves and made many of their own laws.

From the outset of government in the Northwest, county officials seemed to make a conscious effort to wrest control over local affairs from the governor's hands. Initially they justified their independent administration and lawmaking as necessary. They assured St. Clair that they had no intention of undercutting his authority. Pointing out that the territorial laws were grossly inadequate, they claimed that their actions were temporary, meant only to serve pressing needs until the governor and judges filled the void. After a few years they dropped this pretext and argued that the powers and autonomy they claimed were traditional.[22]

The nature of local problems and the strength of the oligarchies were such that local lawmaking occurred in the courts rather than in the streets. The courts also controlled law enforcement, and there were few instances of lynchings or vigilante actions. Nevertheless justice, such as it was, was not entirely iron-handed. On the contrary, county courts dispensed different kinds of justice to different classes by tailoring it to the means if not the needs of litigants.

The county gentry brought by far the largest number of cases before the courts, yet the amounts involved almost never exceeded $1,000, and were often trivial. In these cases, as in all others, the county courts followed indifferent forms. Argumentation lacked technicality and demonstrated the general lack of legal knowledge. Written opinions were rare and were not even required of the Indiana Territory Supreme Court until 1808. Occasionally the presiding justice did not have a commission. There were at least two justices who held courts without commissions in the Indiana district period. One man sat on courts for about a year after Congress created the territory, and the other sat on one court until 1803 and on another until 1805. Moreover, justices often were litigants before themselves and argued their own cases. In these instances the decisions were predictable, and it is not surprising that the courts earned a reputation among outsiders for injustice and tyranny.[23]

22. See McCarty, *Governors of the Northwest*, 50–51, 80–81; Downes, *Frontier Ohio*, 128–30, 151–52, 157–63; Philbrick, *Laws of Indiana*, R157–79; Philbrick, *Laws of Illinois*, R22. Downes (*Frontier Ohio*, 146–47) discusses the Ohio court reform movement before admission to statehood. His conclusion that St. Clair delayed or prevented major court and administrative reforms, however, is not entirely justified.

23. See Chester J. Attig, "Some Governmental Problems of the Northwest

Of necessity, the courts apparently dealt out more equitable justice to people of lesser means, both in criminal and in civil cases. Criminal actions were limited by the poverty of governments, confusion over boundaries, and problems of extradition, all of which made apprehension and prosecution impossible at times. When persons were tried for criminal offenses, the courts dispensed summary justice, applying common sense as they understood it, rather than strict statutory or common law. This was so largely because all laws prescribing heavy fines or confinement were impossible to enforce. There were no jails in the Northwest Territory until 1798, at least (and often during the early years in other territories), and after that date the inadequacy of jails made escape easy. Sending prisoners to a territorial prison was out of the question since no territory ever built one. Thus, regardless of the punishments theoretically possible under the laws, there was little to suggest brutality in their application. Whippings, small fines and losses of licenses or other privileges were the common penalties meted out by the courts. Nevertheless, judges sometimes went to unusual lengths to find a law they could adapt to a case at hand. During the Northwest district period, justices tried a man for murdering a hog when they could not find a law to cover the killing of animals, and in 1799 a court entertained an indictment that charged a man with being a common nuisance for living with another man's wife.[24]

Territory, 1787–1803," in *Transactions of the Illinois Historical Society for the Year 1921* (Springfield, 1922), 83, hereafter cited as Attig, "Governmental Problems"; Philbrick, *Laws of Indiana*, R181, R186–91, R196–212. Apparently the two men who did not hold commissions had acted as justices during part or all of the Northwest territorial period. Philbrick (*ibid.*, R201–02 and notes) speculates that confusion over jurisdiction might explain why one of the men who had no commission held court: he was also a justice of the peace. An alternative explanation, though remote, is that both men had received appointments to judical offices in the Virginia period with tenure of good behavior, and that these appointments might have been regarded as entitling them to sit on courts of the Northwest and Indiana territories. In any case there seem to have been no attempts to unseat the men.

24. Pease, *Laws of the Northwest*, R35–36; Attig, "Governmental Problems," 84; Bond, *Foundations*, 430. For an excellent and thorough analysis of the lax court practices, the range of crimes tried before courts, and punishments see Philbrick, *Laws of Indiana*, especially R126–27, R173–85, R210–12. Escapes from jails were frequent enough to result in laws making jailors liable for fugitives' penalities (*ibid.*, R182). Philbrick (*ibid.*, R183–84) says "the records do not

The county courts adhered to strictly correct legal procedures least frequently in civil cases involving only the poorer people and their small claims. Common sense led the courts to refer them to extra-legal boards of arbitration for settlement out of court. The results were generally satisfactory and arbitration became so popular for settling disputes cheaply that in 1799 the first Northwest General Assembly provided for it in law.[25]

But of all court practices one of the most important was the treatment of debtors, in view of the fact that the courts represented the creditors if they represented anybody. The frontier propensity for litigating debts was abundantly evident: "The same persons occur over and over, litigating debts until one wonders who ever paid voluntarily, and torts until one wonders more over the relation of neighbor to neighbor." These actions, of course, primarily reflect the activities of the relatively well-to-do, yet, despite their zeal for litigation, "the practical nonexistence of jails substantially abolished debtor imprisonment" and there were apparently few attempts to prosecute the poor debtors or to confine them. In 1795, St. Clair and the territorial judges recognized the importance of debtor relief in an area of marked poverty by including a law in Maxwell's Code which limited imprisonment or confinement to about a year. A "truly remarkable statute for its time," it was also one of the few examples of progressive territorial legislation. Moreover, debtor imprisonment remained a legal possibility in the territories until 1837, when Wisconsin's General Assembly became the first to abolish it in law.[26]

---

support a contention that criminals were either numerous or active" and concludes (*ibid.*, R181) that "the courts made the statute-book ridiculous by the fines they imposed." G. L. Wilson ("St. Clair," 115–16) says that criminal laws showed a strong New England influence, but Philbrick (*Laws of Indiana*, R127–28) says only that it is surprising that legislators should have done no better: "The statutes are typical of the time."

See also Pomeroy, *Territories, 1861–1890*, 43–44. The federal government built penitentiaries in some territories of the post-Civil War period and allowed territories to keep their prisoners there at cost. The general inadequacy of prisons throughout territorial history, however, is suggested by the Congressional act of 1880, which permitted territories to lodge their prisoners in other territories.

25. Pease, *Laws of the Northwest*, A354–56; G. L. Wilson, "St. Clair," 170–71; Attig, "Governmental Problems," 85; Philbrick, *Laws of Indiana*, R126–27, R187.

26. Pease, *Laws of the Northwest*, A286–87; Philbrick, *Laws of Indiana*,

By and large, however, the county courts served only a small minority of the population. For a number of years a great majority of the people could not afford to take cases to court. Both the poverty of the people and the county governments' lack of interest, if not of capacity, in serving the needs of the masses of people were pathetically evident in Maxwell's *Centinel of the North-Western Territory*.[27] A major share of the advertisements offered rewards or simply pleaded for the return of "lost" items. As might be expected, people offered rewards for missing slaves and livestock, but there were also relatively large numbers of advertisements declaring the loss of provisions, such as a barrel of flour or dry goods, or asking finders to return a greatcoat, shirts, "small clothes," and handkerchiefs. The scarcity of goods and money in the territory were such that most people seemed happy to get things back and pay a small reward without asking questions.

The chronic poverty of territories during the initial years of settlement and the inadequate tax bases perhaps delayed transition to second-stage governments for as long as those governments had to be self-supporting. The inability or unwillingness of both local and territorial officials to use available resources efficiently could also be employed as arguments for retaining the district stage. However, the very nature of the district stage provided stronger arguments for its abandonment. The Ordinance simply did not provide enough people to make territorial administration effective, with the result that local oligarchy rather than executive autocracy characterized first-stage governments. Nevertheless the governors symbolized a disagreeable form of government that worked only to the benefit of the wealthy, and strong opposition to the district stage developed early in both Congress and the territories. Consequently, early in the nineteenth century Congress began experimenting with alternative means of organizing new territories and eventually abandoned the district stage.

R131–33, R187, R202–03; McCarty, *Governors of the Northwest,* 149. The quotes are from Philbrick.

27. Established in 1793 in Cincinnati. The author used the microfilm copy for November 1793 to June 1796 in the Wisconsin State Historical Society Library. See also Attig, "Governmental Problems," 84–85.

V

Transformation and Standardization of the First Empire

FUNDAMENTALLY, the transformation of the colonial system occurred as the federal government revised its concept of empire and imperial objectives. As the rate of western settlement sharply increased early in the nineteenth century and its dominant Anglo-American character became apparent, the previously assumed need for strong centralized colonial governments dissipated. Concurrently, if it did not become more liberal, Congress at least came to see the greater long-range value in encouraging the settlement of the West, which would eventually raise federal revenue by accelerating the growth of a national economy, than in realizing higher immediate returns by selling public lands at high prices, which tended to retard settlement and development. As these changes were taking place, the district stage of territorial government became increasingly objectionable, and when its gross inadequacies could no longer be ignored, Congress started modifying the colonial system in ways intended to make it more viable and acceptable, if not more attractive, to settlers. Ultimately, Congress abandoned the district stage and adopted in its place a standard second-stage government, differing in some important respects from that of the Ordinance, for the initial organization of new territories. It did not, however, go directly from one to the other.

Elimination of the first stage depended on Congress' making certain changes in the second, since a number of the provisions of the Ordinance made the latter unsuitable for the government of a territory during the early years of settlement. Until Congress modified the Ordinance, transition to the second stage was primarily a function of growth, and no matter how inadequate it may have been, the district or some other interim form of government was necessary. When Congress began altering the colonial system, however, it acted hesitantly and moved in several directions simultaneously, since the most obvious solution to the problem of government was not necessarily the most acceptable one. Nevertheless, Congressional thought passed through stages that are evident in Congress' successive decisions to support more and smaller territories, experiment with several methods of organizing territories to bypass the first stage, expand the suffrage and number of elected offices, assume the burden of financing representative governments, and in its finally making a modified second-stage government standard throughout the Empire.

The pace and nature of the transformation of the colonial system were such that the First Empire can be divided into four periods. Of the thirteen territories in the Empire, seven passed through the Ordinance first stage, three began their existence with unicameral governments, and the rest started at the second stage. The four territories created during the first phase (1787–1804) started with the district stage as provided in the Ordinance, and two of them became states before Congress made more than minor changes in the plan.

The transformation of the Empire really began during the second period (1804–1823), when the last district-stage government passed out of existence. The period began with the Orleans Act and ended with the Florida Organic Act and the second Michigan Organic Act, all of which provided for unicameral governments. Congress created two territories having first-stage governments in 1805, another in 1809, and, toward the end of the second decade of the century, organized two other territories whose governments began at the second stage. During the twenty-year period, Congress made piecemeal changes in the system, primarily broadening the second-stage suffrage and increasing the number of elected offices, but they were not applied uniformly to the territories. At the end of the period, Congress began assuming the costs of government in the unicameral systems.

Congress organized only one new territory in the third period, which extended from 1823 to 1838. Wisconsin began its government at

TERRITORIES OF THE FIRST AND SECOND EMPIRES

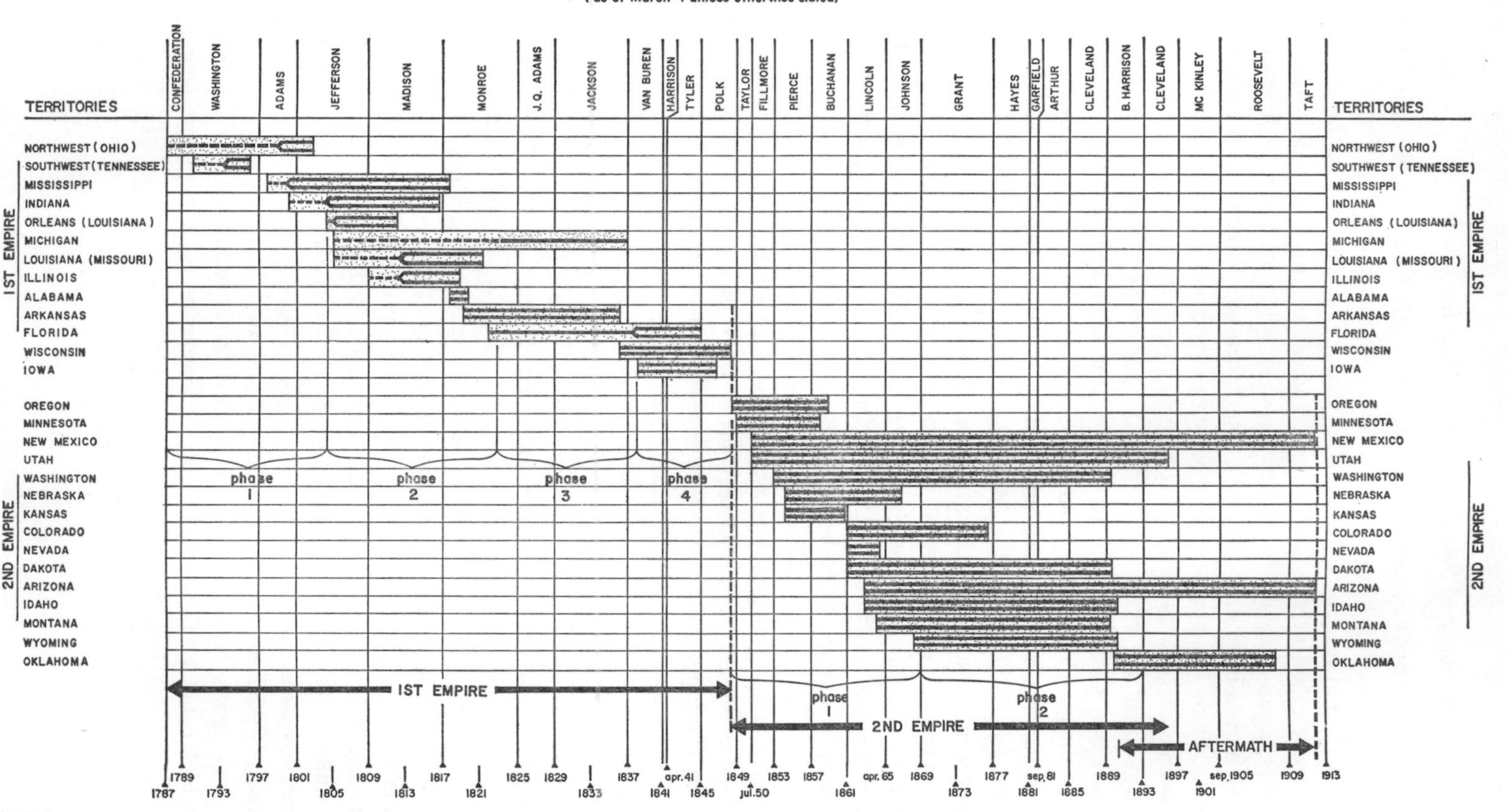

LEGEND:

- - - - - - DISTRICT STAGE GOVERNMENTS

——— UNICAMERAL GOVERNMENTS

the second stage and Congress paid its legislature's expenses from the start, as it did in all territories established subsequently. Both unicameral and bicameral governments existed during this phase; however, Congressional modifications were increasingly applied uniformly to all the territories and by the end of the period the last remaining unicameral government was made over into a standard bicameral one. The trend toward standardization was also evident in the unsuccessful efforts begun in this period to extend the bicameral system to the Indians. Bills for this purpose were continually introduced in Congress from 1834 until the federal government decided to convert the Indian Territory into a white settlement area and created the Territory of Oklahoma.

Between 1838 and the end of the First Empire, Congress created only one territory, Iowa, with a second-stage government like those of the other two territories already in existence. By 1838 the system had been standardized, and during the last decade of the Empire it underwent only minor modifications and refinements. By the end of the Empire the system to be used throughout the Second Empire was fully formed. Nevertheless, in the fourth period of the First Empire there were attempts to revive the extinct district stage for the government of two essentially transfrontier areas, Oregon and Nebraska. In the 1880s it was used again in a modified form for Alaska, and subsequently in other parts of the Oceanic Empire.

The pace of the transformation of the colonial system in the First Empire was irregular until Congress abandoned the first stage. All changes ultimately involved the attitudes of various groups toward the district and second stages, and they were not the same everywhere. Moreover, there were a number of reasons both for eliminating and for retaining the first stage. Thus the impetus for abandoning or keeping the district stage as well as for modifying the second sometimes came from the West, sometimes from the East and occasionally from both simultaneously, depending on the particular balance of opinion in any given place or time.

At times conflicting groups of territorial inhabitants shared the fear that a second-stage government would be more effective than the governor alone, and therefore opposed transition from the first stage. A second-stage legislature was sure to increase taxes and, possibly for the first time, effectively enforce their collection, both of which were necessary for the efficient operation of representative governments in territories that had to finance themselves. In Illinois, Tennessee, and perhaps to a lesser extent in Michigan, these were important reasons for opposition to transition. In addition, settlers in outlying regions often dreaded domination by the more populous area of the territory, which could be expected to control the legislature. Similarly, local oligarchies sometimes opposed the second stage, anticipating that a General Assembly would control local administration more effectively than the governor, thereby reducing their own power and autonomy.

A few district-stage governors argued that the inhabitants of their territories were unfit or unready for representative government, or that they could not bear the costs, but generally when governors raised objections to transition to the second stage, they echoed the feeling of various groups of settlers. Some governors, like most of the local oligarchies that opposed transition, did not want to see their powers divided or reduced as they assumed they would be in the second stage. Their soundest and commonest objections, however, related to the property and residence qualifications for second-stage government. Basically, given the provisions of the Ordinance, it was hard to find any advantage in the second stage during the early years of settlement. When the population was small, and for some time while settlement was rapid in a territory, a large majority of the people lacked clear land titles. As a result, they were ineligible to vote, even if they could meet the residence requirement, because they could not meet the property qualification. Moreover, resident landholdings were rather small, and few voters owned enough land to qualify for the few elective offices. In practice, then, the Ordinance limited voting and officeholding to a handful of territorial inhabitants and thereby simply increased the power or status of the existing local oligarchies and a few other wealthy people. Consequently, when territories were poor, as they always were in the early years, the costs of representative government were an extra burden that could be expected to fall heaviest upon those least able to afford it or to benefit from it. In short, for the average man, the returns would in no way be commensurate with the cost of the second stage as provided in the Ordinance.

Altogether, the Ordinance second stage was not feasible and offered no advantage over the first until relatively large numbers of people had lived in a territory long enough to vote and hold office, and until the economy developed sufficiently to support representative government. The second stage could be made viable earlier only if Congress modified the Ordinance by reducing the voting and officeholding requirements so that there would be a real choice and more truly representative governments, and by assuming the responsibility of paying for them, at least until the territories could become self-supporting. Once Congress made these changes, there would be no reason for retaining the district stage as an essential part of the colonial system. But Congress was no trailblazer. Instead, significant reductions in the suffrage and officeholding requirements tended to follow reforms made in eastern state governments.[1] It was not until the 1820s that Congress revised its philosophy regarding the territories to the degree that it was willing to use federal funds to support representative governments in the colonies—and then it attempted to hold down expenses by adopting a modified first-stage, unicameral system of government.

In the meantime, even if the district stage was as good as any other form of government for the early administration of transfrontier regions or new settlement areas, no form of government was adequate for very large and heterogeneous territories, particularly those like the Northwest, Louisiana, or Oregon. Within a year of his arrival in the territory St. Clair pointed out the basic problem: that the Northwest was too large to be administered effectively under the district stage as provided in the Ordinance. That effective administration was impossible became a recurring complaint of governors, secretaries, and judges, who usually recommend the creation of more governments (hence smaller territories), or the appointment of additional officials.[2]

In 1793 Governor Blount of the Southwest most expansively expressed the general gubernatorial disenchantment with the district stage. During one of his frequent indulgences in overstatement, he exclaimed "No body will say the Ordinance [,] the temporary constitu-

1. See Chilton Williamson, *American Suffrage: From Property to Democracy, 1760–1860* (Princeton, 1960), especially 208–22, hereafter cited as Williamson, *Suffrage*, in conjunction with the following discussion.

2. See Bond, *Foundations*, 449–50; Downes, *Frontier Ohio*, 166–72; and Chapter II, present volume. On the size of territories see Randall D. Sale and Edwin D. Karn, *American Expansion. A Book of Maps* (Homewood, Ill., 1962).

tion of this country [,] is a good one. . . ."[3] Such outspoken criticism of the system by the governor himself could not but engender more general dislike of the district stage and reduce its effectiveness. It was also unlikely that executives who shared this view of the district stage would do their best to make it work as well as it might have. Rather, their negative attitudes, frequent absences, and inattention to civil administration suggest that they tended to give up early. Thus, perhaps in part to overcome the weaknesses of their position or with a view to undermining the power of local oligarchies, governors besides St. Clair increasingly sympathized with popular demands for change to the second stage as general opposition to the district stage grew.

Popular criticism of the first stage in each territory developed as the population became large enough to have complex needs, by which time the governor had lost most of his control over internal affairs and could not cope with them effectively. Nevertheless, though people singled out the oligarchic local governments for condemnation, they usually dwelled on the despotic nature of the first-stage system and focused on the governor. They denounced the governor's powers and blamed him for allowing a few older settlers to monopolize local government by continually appointing them to local offices. In addition, critics of territorial government constantly attacked the governor's personal conduct. For example, the citizens in the Northwest called St. Clair a "British Nabob." More commonly they tried to discredit governors by comparing them to George III or accusing them of all kinds of moral depravity, but since second-stage governors were often similarly libeled, these personal vilifications cannot be taken very seriously.

Washington had frowned on autocratic colonial rule during his administration and Adams had shown little concern for the territories, but strong objections to the first stage of the Ordinance as such did not arise in the federal government until Jefferson's ascent to the Presidency. Consequently, governors never received much support from the federal government for strong district-stage administration and by the early nineteenth century, the federal government helped to under-

3. In the same vein, he wrote that his only concern was "to please the people [,] always [keeping] in view their happiness [because] The pleasure of pleasing to me is a great one. . . ." Blount to Sevier, May 31, 1793, in Carter, *Territorial Papers,* IV:266.

mine its slight remaining effectiveness. After becoming President, Jefferson pointedly referred to the first stage as a "despotic oligarchy without one rational objective."[4] Characteristically, however, he was ambivalent. Writing to Albert Gallatin on November 9, 1803, about providing government for the Louisiana Purchase, the President said that after "examining" the Ordinance, "I find that it will not do at all" for the southern region (which became Orleans Territory), because it would turn all the laws there "topsy-turvy." Nevertheless, in the same letter he concluded it was "best to appoint a governor & three judges, with legislative powers; only providing the judges shall form the laws, & the Governor have a negative only, subject further to the negative of the National legislature"—that is, a district-stage government functioning exactly as that of the Northwest during the early years of St. Clair's administration![5]

In spite of Jefferson's vacillation, as the district stage came under increasing attack and the general attitude of federal officials changed, Congress showed a willingness to do away with this form of government. The move toward abandonment of the first stage might be dated from the act of Congress in 1800 that began the second stage in Mississippi, except that the change seems to have resulted primarily from personality clashes. Moreover, by 1803 a majority in Congress may have come to view the change as premature. Immediately after transition, a significant body of settlers in Mississippi petitioned Congress for nullification of the second Organic Act and return to the district stage, arguing that the change was against the will of a majority of the settlers, that the small population lacked the means to support representative government, and that they could derive no benefits from a legislature controlled by a handful of landowners.[6] The Orleans Act of

4. Quoted in G. L. Wilson, "St. Clair," 352. This contrasts sharply with his tacit support of the system at the time Monroe wrote the basic governmental provisions.

5. Carter, *Territorial Papers*, IX:100.

6. *Ibid.*, V:110–17, particularly 112–13. The heavy debts are strongly emphasized and the fear of taxes is clear. In 1803 there was another petition complaining about the burden of taxes. (*Ibid.*, V:293.) As late 1809 Congress received a petition including complaints about the "enormous taxes for the support of" representative government. (*Ibid.*, V:733.) It should be added, however, that other petitioners of 1800 gave the impression that the territory was doing well enough financially. (*Ibid.*, V:101.) Despite claims of financial hardship, the

1804, on the other hand, was a decisive break with the past. It was the first Congressional experiment with an alternative form of government for the organization of a new territory. Unlike previous territories, the southern part of the Louisiana Purchase had a large non-Anglo-American population that made the district stage seem inappropriate. This might make Orleans seem to be a special case, were it not for the events of the following year that confirmed the shift away from the use of the first stage.

When Congress created the Orleans Territory in 1804 it provided for a unicameral government, which might be called a modified first-stage government rather than a modified second stage, in that it closely resembled the district stage in Monroe's first draft of the Ordinance of 1787, and its legislature was not a representative body. Perhaps the reaction of a number of settlers to second-stage government in Mississippi helped prompt Congress into devising the unicameral system, but it is clear that Congress both wanted to overcome the incomplete legislative powers of the regular first stage when drawing up the Orleans Act, and felt that the inhabitants were not ready for full representative government. As a compromise, Congress provided only a legislative council of thirteen men, to be appointed annually by the President and paid out of the federal treasury. With the governor, it would have full legislative powers. The Organic Act did not give the governor a veto, nor did it make the council a legislature in the usual sense. The governor was to frame laws and submit them to the council for advice and consent. W. C. C. Claiborne, however, reversed the procedure. He acted as the governor of a typical second-stage government and treated the council as a real legislature. He made recommendations and the council formed laws that he acted upon, an absolute veto being assumed and accepted.[7]

Congress debated the legislative articles of the Orleans bill extensively before enacting it on March 26, 1804. In the Senate there were a

---

legislature seems to have met annually in accordance with the Organic Act. (*Ibid.*, V:254).

7. See Valentine, "Territorial Governor," 30; Carter, *Territorial Papers*, IX:204, 247. The council was only one man smaller than the contemporary total of both the houses of the Mississippi legislature.

series of unsuccessful attempts to amend the bill to permit the election of councillors after one year, to allow a representative assembly as soon as the population reached a certain size, and to authorize the territory to have a delegate in Congress.[8] The following year, however, with little debate Congress passed a new Organic Act giving the Orleans Territory a regular second-stage government. Congress hoped this would silence the inhabitants' objections to the appointive council and the clamor for immediate statehood which, as Governor Claiborne repeatedly advised, was beyond the capacity of a people so recently lifted out of despotism.[9]

Probably as a result of its decision to pay the expenses of the Orleans council, and in order to save money, Congress in 1804 annexed the rest of the Louisiana Purchase, the 800,000 or more square miles north of the 33rd parallel, to Indiana Territory. Whatever Congress' motives, the idea of having one district-stage government for a land area of over 1,000,000 square miles was ludicrous. So the next year Congress detached the region west of the Mississippi River and organized it separately, with a first-stage government, as the Louisiana Territory, thus making the situation somewhat less absurd.

The Louisiana Territory, which was renamed Missouri when the Orleans Territory entered the Union as Louisiana, came close to getting a second-stage government in 1805. The Senate bill of February 7 provided for omission of the district stage and the immediate election of a ten-man assembly, but it was amended during floor debates on February 28 or March 1, when the bill passed. The amendment replaced everything but the enacting clause. It simply gave the territory a first-stage government and omitted the Ordinance provision for transition to the second stage. More important than the amended bill that passed, however, is that the original Senate bill passed through committee and had the support of enough senators to get to the floor. In a similarly casual fashion the previous month, Congress had divided Indiana to create Michigan Territory. In 1809 it again divided Indiana to create Illinois, and in both cases Congress adopted Organic Acts starting the new territories at the Ordinance first stage without any

8. See Carter, *Territorial Papers*, IX:204–05n.
9. *Ibid.*, IX:312, 314, 405–07.

apparent debate. Illinois, however, was the last territory to begin at the district stage.[10]

However uncertain Congress' mood may have been in the first decade of the century, its acts illustrate a significant shift away from the very conservative economic approach of the late eighteenth century. Proponents of a more positive economic policy gained ground, arguing that additional, smaller territories would be more efficient and in the long run would be well worth the extra expense to Congress. With a liberal land policy they would attract settlers more rapidly, accelerate economic development, raise land values, and ultimately increase federal revenues, thereby strengthening the entire national economy. That Congress was coming to accept this view was clear by the end of 1805, when it had five territories in operation rather than two or three. Indiana, Mississippi, and Orleans had second-stage governments, but their cost to the federal treasury was the same as the first-stage governments since the federal government still paid only the salaries of the five territorial officials in each territory, who were appointed by the President. For the five territories, these salaries totalled about $36,000 a year. Thus, regardless of Congress' general indifference to the territories, after the turn of the century it was usually willing to accede to demands or recommendations for changes in territorial governments. Nevertheless, while the progress toward the abandonment of the district stage after 1805 and the standardization of second-stage governments after 1823 may appear in retrospect to have been logically directed, in reality the changes occurred casually.

For eight years after it created Illinois, Congress organized no new territories. Then, between 1817 and 1823, it created three territories—Alabama, Arkansas, and Florida—and ended the last remaining district-stage government, that in Michigan. Each of the three new territories was initially organized in a different manner, but not even Arkansas passed through a district stage as previous territories had.

At the beginning of March 1817, after some debate over whether or not to divide the Mississippi Territory before admitting it to state-

10. Farrand, *Legislation for Territories,* 21, 24; Carter, *Territorial Papers,* X:5–7; XIII:87–90, 92–95. On the lawmaking power, see Philbrick, *Laws of Illinois,* R428; Carter, *Territorial Papers,* XVI:6–8. On the Illinois Organic Act see *Annals of Congress,* 10 Cong., 2 sess., 1093–94.

hood, Congress decided to divide it and create the Territory of Alabama. The Alabama Organic Act was the first under which a new territory explicitly began its existence at the second stage and, except in the manner of constituting the first General Assembly, the act established the precedent for the creation of Wisconsin and most territories west of the Mississippi River. In Wisconsin and the others, Congress armed the governors with extensive temporary powers to apportion the territory and direct the election of the first legislature. For Alabama, Congress ordered the representatives and councillors from the eastern half of the Mississippi Territory to meet and nominate six men for the council, three of whom the President would appoint, to round out the first Alabama territorial legislature. But most important, and probably a direct result of the very rapid population growth in Alabama, there was evidently no debate over the idea of bypassing the district stage.[11]

Two years later, when the Missouri statehood bill came up for consideration, Congress set off the Arkansas Territory. As in the case of Alabama, there is no evidence that it debated the form of government, but in contrast to the Alabama Organic Act, Congress simply extended the provisions of the Ordinance of 1787 to Arkansas as it had to Indiana and Illinois. Arkansas was to have a district-stage government until a majority of the freeholders voted for transition to the second stage. The tone of the Arkansas Organic Act, however, suggests that the intent of Congress was for the governor and judges to use their powers as district administrators to carry out the transfer of authority from Missouri and to organize a separate second-stage government. This, at least, is what happened. Governor James Miller was slow in accepting his appointment and in getting to the territory. When he arrived on December 26, 1819, almost ten months after the enactment of the Organic Act and five months after it became operative, he faced a *fait accompli.*

Secretary Robert Crittenden, acting as governor, had inaugurated the district government on July 28. With the judges he passed the single act of the district stage, an act creating the Arkansas court system, which amounted to reconstituting the old Missouri courts in

11. See Thorpe, *Constitutions,* 91; Carter, *Territorial Papers,* XVIII:36–39 and notes; *Historical Statistics,* 13.

Arkansas under the new jurisdiction. Crittenden similarly recommissioned all officials. Within a short time he and the judges decided, on petition of the "legal number of freeholders," presumably a majority, that it was time to enter the second stage. On October 20, Crittenden issued the necessary proclamation and writs of election for November 20. Thus in less than four months, before the governor had even accepted his appointment, the district stage in effect ended. Three days after his arrival, on December 29, Governor Miller issued a proclamation declaring it "expedient" to begin the second stage as soon as possible and ordering the legislature to convene in February 1820.[12]

This was the last time even so tenuous a district-stage government was used in the contiguous United States, but not the last time it was considered in Congress. A House bill of 1822 would have created a first-stage government in Oregon, contrary to the joint occupancy treaty with Great Britain. The 1822 bill contained no provision for a second-stage government. The same articles were reintroduced in another House bill for Oregon in 1824. A series of bills were introduced in both the House and Senate between 1842 and 1848 which would have made the Ordinance of 1787, in its original form, the organic law for the territories of Oregon, Nebraska, New Mexico, and California. The bill introduced in July 1848 for the organization of Oregon, California, and New Mexico, authorized first-stage governments for California and New Mexico and included no provision for their change to the second stage. Except for the 1848 bill, which was introduced by William Clayton of Delaware representing a select committee of the Senate, the bills of the 1840s were introduced by senators or representatives from public lands states. The Senate bills were all introduced by senators from states that, as territories, had passed through the first stage of the Ordinance (Stephen A. Douglas of Illinois, and David

12. See Carter, *Territorial Papers,* XIX:44–50 and notes, 133, 133n, 204; Thorpe, *Constitutions,* 261–64. The only Congressional debates that Carter mentions (*Territorial Papers,* XIX:44n) regarding the Organic Act involved slavery. Until the white adult male population reached 5,000, the Organic Act limited the assembly to nine members. Governor Miller dickered with the federal government for some time over his appointment, in part because he did not wish to be required to go to the territory immediately. In June he asked to be exempted from going until September. He apparently did not formally accept the appointment until November. (*Ibid.,* XIX:78, 102–03, 104, 119.)

Atchison and James M. Hughes of Missouri), a fact that has devastating implications for the idea of the West as a seedbed of democracy. Similarly, Senator Benjamin Harrison of Indiana was the principal Senate supporter of the Alaska Organic Act passed in 1884, which provided a cruelly modified first-stage government and made no provision for eventual representative government.[13]

13. I have used the original bills and amendments in the National Archives whenever extant, rather than the printed bills in the Library of Congress, because they are more useful. Numerous notations, alterations, and amendments, which help to trace the evolution of thinking, are included with the draft bills in the National Archives and do not appear with the bills in their printed form in the Library of Congress. For convenience, and to help distinguish between bills from the two sources, the following system will be used. Bills in the Library of Congress are bound and will be cited as *House Bills* or *Senate Bills*, followed by the Congress, the bill number and the date of the bill. Bills in the National Archives will not be cited by their Legislative Branch record group number (Senate bills are Record Group 46; House Bills are Record Group 233), but simply as *NA*, followed by the bill number, preceded by an S to indicate Sentate bill and H to indicate House bill, and succeeded by the Congress and date of the bill. The bills relevant to the discussion above are *House Bills*, 17 Cong., H-47, Jan. 18, 1822; *ibid.*, 18 Cong., H-67, Jan. 19, 1824; *NA*, S-27, 28 Cong., Dec. 28, 1843; *NA*, H-21, 28 Cong., Jan. 4, 1844; *NA*, H-444, 28 Cong., Dec. 17, 1844; *NA*, S-45, 28 Cong., Dec. 19, 1844; *NA*, S-170, 30 Cong., Mar. 15, 1848; *NA*, S-324, 30 Cong., July 18, 1848. Several of these bills were introduced more than once under different numbers. See also the *Congressional Debates*, 18 Cong., 2 sess., I:26–27, 35–36; and notes 14 and 25 below.

Fifteen years elapsed after the acquisition of Alaska before Congress seriously debated the question of organizing any government in the territory. In the meantime, some twenty-five bills were introduced and died in committee, while visiting naval officers in Alaskan ports administered a casual kind of law and provided intermittent services. The course of the Senate bill of 1882–1883, which launched semi-serious discussion and led to the law of 1884—indeed the whole of the Alaskan territorial period at least until the 1930s—illustrates that lack of leadership in Congress could be disastrous, not because of malice but because of indifference. The original bill proposed to vest both the executive and judicial powers in one man, as in Monroe's May 1786 report of the draft Ordinance of 1787. Apparently a legislative branch was not to be included. The Senate committee, however, reported out a substitute bill which is interesting as a hybrid of the original Ordinance district stage and the 1804 Orleans system. There was to be a governor, a secretary and a host of other appointed federal officials. The legislative authority was to be vested in the governor, the one-man Supreme Court (called the chief justice!), the territorial marshal, surveyor-general, and collector of customs—all of whom the president appointed. The only elective territorial office was that of delegate to Congress, an idea not related to either the Orleans or Ordinance systems, but probably a result of committee readings of the Florida

In practice, the district stage in Arkansas was similar to the military governments used briefly in other territories, where military commanders were temporarily vested with the same powers as territorial governors for the purposes of receiving populated land cessions and overseeing the organization of civil governments. In Orleans and Florida military rule lasted only a few months, but in California and New Mexico it lasted several years, from the period of occupation toward the end of the Mexican War until 1850, when Congress made more permanent provisions for the government of the Mexican Cession.

The military regimes were under the President's exclusive control as commander-in-chief of the armed forces until Congress created territories with normal civil governments. Under the Constitution, the

---

or Michigan legislative histories. Unfortunately, inadequate as the bill may have been, Congress adjourned without action and the next year enacted an Organic Act that prohibited both a legislative branch and a delegate to Congress. For another twenty-nine years there was no legislature. In the meantime, under the act of May 17, 1884, Alaska was "a civil and judicial district" with a governor, one district federal judge, four lesser judges and other officials, all of whom were given multiple jobs in an area one-fifth the size of the United States. The marshal, for example, was to act as surveyor-general despite the lack of legal provisions for a land system. The officials were to administer laws of Oregon and those written for the territory by Congress. But administration of some territorial affairs was to be carried out directly from Washington. The Secretary of the Interior, for example, was to direct education in the territory.

When Congress finally gave Alaska a legislature in 1912, it had over 64,000 people. Even then they lacked sufficient influence and support in Congress to overcome fully the opposition to representative government. As a result, the legislature was more severely limited in its field of action than the legislature of any other territory had ever been, whether under a district-stage or second-stage government. (See Ernest Gruening, *The State of Alaska* [New York, 1954], 33–293, particularly 47–52, 141, 151–52, 157, hereafter cited as Gruening, *Alaska;* 23 *Statutes,* 24.)

Benjamin Harrison, chairman of the Senate Committee on Territories in 1884, was apologetic about the Organic Act. His statement, with appropriate changes, might almost have been made by some proponents of the Ordinance of 1787: "Indeed, I am willing to confess upon the challenge of almost any Senator that all of the provisions of the bill are inadequate. It is a mere shift; it is a mere expedient; it is a mere beginning in what we believe to be the right direction toward giving a civil government and education to Alaska. I hope more will follow, but the committee in considering this matter adjudged what they believed to be the probable limit of the generosity of the Senate." *Congressional Record,* 48 Cong., 1 sess., January 23, 1884, 597, quoted in Gruening, *Alaska,* 52.

prior consent of Congress was not necessary for the establishment of military governments in ceded or conquered territories, but Congress could direct the President to establish them. It did so for the initial occupation of Florida in 1821—at the same time that a twenty-five year campaign began in Congress for the enactment of a similar law to order the President to occupy Oregon.

In the four territories temporarily ruled by the military, the predominance of non-Anglo-American inhabitants and the fear that they might resist the change in sovereignty suggested the need for a stronger authority than that of the district government. Yet, one wonders if, in 1786, James Monroe did not in fact intend the first stage of the Ordinance to be no more than a military government. The Ordinance did not specifically make the governor the civil executive, although his powers clearly implied that he would be, just as military governors were. Thus, as President, when Monroe ordered the occupation of Florida, he organized the military government exactly like the Ordinance first stage, and this is probably why the military period in Florida is sometimes referred to as one of district-stage government. While Governor Andrew Jackson was in the territory, the government had martial overtones, but he stayed there barely two months, just long enough to proclaim the treaty of cession and to set up a rudimentary government. After he left, the government under the secretaries, one each for East and West Florida, was indistinguishable in operation from a first-stage civil government. Nevertheless, by 1821 Monroe certainly no longer believed in the efficacy of the first stage as more than an expedient. On December 3, 1821, in his annual message he said that he had organized the territory as he had, making the fewest possible appointments "to avoid expense," because "radical change" would have to be made, and he urged Congress to provide a more appropriate form of civil government quickly.[14]

14. Meyerholz, "Federal Supervision," 195–201, 225–26; Valentine, "Territorial Governor," 9–10, 17–18, 28–29; Herbert J. Doherty, Jr., "The Governorship of Andrew Jackson," in *The Florida Historical Quarterly*, XXXIII (1954), 3–31, hereafter cited as Doherty, "Andrew Jackson"; Thorpe, *Constitutions*, 656–57; James D. Richardson, ed., *A Compilation of the Messages and Papers of the Presidents, 1789–1897* (20 vols., Washington, 1917–1920), II:103–05, hereafter cited as Richardson, *Messages*. Organic Acts drafted after the enactment of the Ordi-

nance explicitly made the governor the civil executive in all respects. (See the Organic Acts in Thorpe; and Valentine, 68.)

The Oregon bills are extremely interesting both in their provisions and in that they all provided for a United States takeover of the region in violation of the joint occupancy treaty. Nearly all of them, beginning in 1821, would have offered generous homesteads as incentives to settlers, in some cases for women as well as men. The bill of 1821 was almost identical to the Florida occupation law. It did not define the limits of the Oregon Country, but the bills of 1822 and 1823, which provided for a first-stage government, and that of 1824, which provided for a unicameral government like Michigan's, declared it to include all the land west of the Continental Divide north of the 42nd parallel. The bill of 1828 established the northern boundary as 54° 40′. During debates over the bill, James K. Polk underwent an interesting transition. First he called for a postponement of consideration of the bill, which began with the northern boundary at 44° 40′, because it contravened the treaty with Great Britain, then proposed an amendment to it that would have extended the civil or criminal jurisdiction of the Michigan government to the entire Oregon Country as far north as 54° 40′. The idea of the unicameral government of Michigan, at Detroit, governing the immense slab of land west of the Mississippi River to the Pacific Ocean from southern Oregon to Alaska surely shows Polk to have been in an unusual state of imperial ecstasy, even for him. The size of the proposed territory did not diminish from that area west of the Continental Divide between 42° and 54° 40′ in subsequent bills until 1843, but by the late 1830s Congressional exponents of occupation had returned to the idea of organizing it separately under a quasi-military government. The bill of 1842 was an odd combination. The military government was to be supplemented by attaching the territory to the Iowa Supreme Court for the administration of justice. In 1843 the northern boundary dropped to 44° 40′, climbed to the 49th parallel in a bill that was introduced early the following year, and in late 1844 returned to 54° 40′. During the last three years of joint occupancy the bills reverted to the governmental system of the Ordinance of 1787. The bills are: *House Bills,* 16 Cong., H–222, Jan. 25, 1821; *ibid.*, 17 Cong., H–47, Jan. 18, 1822; *ibid.*, 18 Cong., H–67, Jan. 19, 1824; *Senate Bills,* 26 Cong., S–7, Mar. 31, 1840; *NA,* H–12, 20 Cong., Dec. 18, 1828; *NA,* S–206, 25 Cong., Feb. 7, 1838; *NA,* S–52, 25 Cong., Dec. 11, 1838; *NA,* H–976, 25 Cong., Jan. 4, 1839; *NA,* S–331, 26 Cong., Apr. 28, 1840; *NA,* S–191, 26 Cong., Jan. 8, 1841; *NA,* S–58, 27 Cong., Dec. 16, 1841 and Feb. 3, 1842; *NA,* S–22, 27 Cong., Jan. 3, 1842 and Dec. 19, 1842; *NA,* S–23, 28 Cong., Dec. 21, 1843; *NA,* S–27, 28 Cong., Dec. 28, 1843; *NA,* H–21, 28 Cong., Jan. 4, 1844; *NA,* H–4, 28 Cong., Jan. 4, 1844; *NA,* S–45, 28 Cong., Dec. 19, 1844; *NA,* H–439, 28 Cong., Dec. 16, 1844 and Feb. 3, 1845; *NA,* H–7, 29 Cong., Dec. 9, 1845; *NA,* S–99, 29 Cong., Mar. 2, 1846; *NA,* H–533, 29 Cong., Aug. 6, 1846; *NA,* H–571, 29 Cong., Dec. 23, 1846; *NA,* S–41, 29 Cong., Dec. 23, 1846; *NA,* S–59, 30 Cong., Jan. 10, 1848; *NA,* S–324, 30 Cong., July 18, 1848; *NA,* H–201, 30 Cong., Aug. 2, 1848. Many of these are in fact the same bill, reintroduced in the same or another Congress, with or without amendments, under a new number. And, of course, the House and Senate bills are often the same. See also the *Annals of Congress* and *Congressional Debates* at the respective dates at which the bills came up. On Polk, see especially *Congressional Debates*, 20 Cong., 2 sess., V:129, 143.

Congress was unwilling to give Florida a regular second-stage government, but as in 1804 when Orleans was organized, it expected that the governor would need help to frame appropriate laws for the non-Anglo-American inhabitants, and a first-stage government did not seem suitable. Thus, almost as a matter of course, in 1822, Congress provided Florida with the same unicameral government, consisting of an appointed legislative council, that it had provided for Orleans eighteen years earlier. This made Florida the third territory to be created in five years which did not pass through the usual period of district-stage administration and, as in the cases of Alabama and Arkansas, Congress evidently did not debate its form of government at any length.[15]

Except for the single year of unicameral government in the Orleans Territory, Congress did not pay the expenses of any territorial legislatures before 1822. In the Florida Act, however, it agreed to pay the councillors $3.00 a day during legislative sessions and $3.00 for every twenty miles traveled to and from them. Congress probably did this because of the poverty of the territory and the difficulties of traveling to the seat of government, but whatever its reasons, the idea of the federal treasury paying these expenses was immediately popular in Michigan. Apparently at the people's request, in 1823 Congress passed a new Organic Act for Michigan, giving it a unicameral government like Florida's, and assumed the same expenses. Once it was begun in earnest, the process could not be stopped. In 1828, Congress started paying a per diem and travel allowance to both the representatives and the councillors of Arkansas, and continued to do so for all subsequent

---

Something like a casual military regime existed intermittently in Alaska before 1884, and such governments have been commonly used in the United States insular possessions. In Hawaii the military government seems to have been primarily supervisory to a provisional government set up by the inhabitants, much like that of California. (See Gruening, *Alaska*, 33–43; William C. Dill, *Statehood for Hawaii* [Philadelphia, 1949], 3–25, hereafter cited as Dill, *Hawaii*.)

While military governments in wartime are theoretically limited only to the observance of international law and may subordinate civil liberties to the main objectives of the war, they are not necessarily premised on the application of martial law. A military government may administer either civil or martial law. In the contiguous territories of the United States, military governments were purely transitory and accomplished their principal purpose of replacing a suspended civilian sovereignty without significant recourse to martial law.

15. See Thorpe, *Constitutions*, 657–62; Carter, *Territorial Papers*, XXII:389–

territorial legislatures. This gave territorial governments a greater economic significance, insofar as Congress appropriated the money and it was spent by the recipients in the territories or for the development of them, but it could not have made politics into a livelihood because the pay was small. Even for a large territorial legislature, the annual cost to the federal government never exceeded a few thousand dollars and was normally far less than the total salaries of the five principal territorial officials.[16]

---

99 and notes; Farrand, *Legislation for Territories*, 21–22, 31; Valentine, "Territorial Governor," 30–31.

16. Travel pay varied somewhat and the per diem allowance ranged from $2.00 to $4.00, depending on the territory, until after the Civil War, when it was somewhat higher. (See Carter, *Territorial Papers*, XXII:397; XI:404; XXI: 68, 290–92, 575; Farrand, *Legislation for Territories*, 22, 32, 35, 45–47; Valentine, "Territorial Governor," 31; Lamar, *Dakota Territory*, 98; 3 *Statutes*, 769–70; 4 *Statutes*, 80–81; 5 *Statutes*, 263–64.) Farrand (*Legislation for Territories*, 35) suggests that the Congressional limitations on the length and frequency of sessions grew out of the assumption of paying salaries and was followed by limitations on the kinds of legislation, but whatever the associations among the three, they are not significant in the broader perspective of the nature of the system and Congress' objectives. Where sessions were not limited, thirty-day (legislative, not calendar) sessions were normal and apparently worked no hardships. In 1868 Congress limited all legislatures to forty-day biennial sessions, but allowed sixty-day sessions, which should have been adequate, beginning in 1880. (*Ibid.*, 45–47; Pomeroy, *Territories, 1861–1890*, 39–40. In 1823 Congress had also limited the Michigan legislative council to sixty-day annual sessions. 3 *Statutes*, 769–70.)

In his elaborate letter of November 23, 1811, to the editor of the *Louisiana Gazette*, the anonymous Alknomack argued that Missouri Territory could easily afford a representative assembly. He noted that a forty-five-day session was "fully as long as an ordinary session of a state legislature." Alknomack also contended that people should not oppose the second stage while clamoring for statehood, because the former was cheaper. He estimated that, on the basis of the 1810 population of about 22,000, the per capita expense of the second stage was about ten cents as compared to thirty-three and one-third cents per person for a state government at a population level of 60,000. His figures did not all jibe but his estimates were realistic. In 1829 the federal government paid $2,127 to the seventeen Arkansas councilmen; $2,787 to twenty-three representatives; and $720 for clerks and other expenses of the thirty-day session. The total cost for the thirty-day session of 1832 for the some territory was $6,273, and the legislature now had twenty-three councillors and twenty-eight representatives. Since the Arkansas sessions were biennial, the annual cost of the legislature to the federal government was, even for a relatively large territorial legislature, much less than the salaries of the appointed federal officials. In Michigan and Florida the unicameral

Congressional abandonment of the Ordinance first stage in favor of organizing new territories with unicameral or bicameral legislatures, and the assumption of basic legislative expenses, did not necessarily affect the governors' legislative control. As long as councillors were appointed and the voting and officeholding requirements for the lower houses were restrictive, the governors retained roughly the same powers over legislation as they had had during the first stage. They rapidly lost power, however, as Congress broadened the franchise, reduced officeholding requirements, and made the councils elective. Congress began making these changes in the territories of the Old Northwest and west of the Mississippi River earlier, but it was not until the period between 1822 and 1836 that it standardized such changes in the provisions of the Ordinance and applied them uniformly to the three territories then in existence.

Under the Ordinance of 1787, as adapted to the Constitution, the President appointed five men to the legislative council from a list of ten nominees submitted by the territorial House of Representatives. This method of selecting councillors prevailed throughout the territorial periods of the Northwest, Southwest, Mississippi, Alabama, and Orleans, and until 1816 in Missouri, without significant opposition. Altogether, councils of second-stage governments remained appointive until 1819, when Alabama entered the Union. In the early territories, governors exerted extensive control over the selection of councillors. During the year that Orleans had a thirteen-man appointed council in place of a second-stage government, President Jefferson sent four blank commissions to Governor Claiborne. Thus the governor chose four of the councillors himself, and his recommendations were necessarily very important to Jefferson's appointment of the others.[17] The following year, 1805, Jefferson waived his right to appoint the five councillors for five-year terms in the new second-stage Indiana legislature and let the

---

legislatures met annually but were much smaller. (On costs above see Carter, *Territorial Papers*, XIV:390–93; XXI:290–92, 574–75; Philbrick, *Laws of Indiana*, R52–53, R53n.)

17. Valentine, "Territorial Governor," 30. The original Orleans bill provided for the governor to appoint councillors but was changed shortly before passage to appointment by the President. (See Carter, *Territorial Papers*, IX:204n.) Congress occasionally enlarged second-stage councils beyond five men. It did so in Mississippi in 1814 (3 *Statutes*, 143), and in other territories. (See note 23.)

governor appoint them. He delegated this power secretly, however, to prevent ill-feelings toward Governor Harrison.[18]

In time, the normal practice that evolved in the southern territories was for the President to appoint the nominees receiving the largest numbers of votes in the lower house, which could have the effect of removing most of the governor's influence over their selection. If a President did not appoint the top-ranking nominees, there was strong criticism. In early 1816, for example, when President Madison passed over John G. Heath in favor of Benjamin Cooper to fill a vacancy on the Missouri council, Heath wrote the President a biting letter of protest. Characterizing Cooper as an individual "who can neither *read nor write, a very ignorant old man, in his dotage* (being about 70)," Heath declared that "the house of Rep[s] expected you would commission as usual, 'the first in nomination' " and hinted darkly that the governor—"men in high places at Saint Louis"—was responsible for this insulting act which brought "disgrace" on the office of President.[19]

While Presidents continued to appoint the councillors to the southern territorial legislatures, a concerted effort in Indiana quickly brought about their direct election. President Adams appointed only one council to the Northwest General Assembly; Ohio became a state before its term expired.[20] Similarly, Governor Harrison appointed the first Indiana council and before it came up for renewal, Congress made the post of councillor elective. In October 1808, the council itself directed the territorial delegate to press for the enactment of a law to permit the direct election of both the delegate and the councillors and to limit the terms of councillors to four years. A few months later, petitioners requested Congress to allow the voters either to choose the ten nominees for the council or, preferably, to elect the five councillors. With surprising speed, Congress passed a law granting everything the territorial delegate had requested, and in mid-1809 the delegate,

18. McCarty, *Governors of the Northwest*, 87.

19. Carter, *Territorial Papers*, XV:133–34. See also *ibid.*, IX:277–78, 281, 284, 291, 307–08, 346, 363, 424, 426, 511, 523–24, 525–26, 580, 622–23, 659, 763, 830, 869, 872; XIV:554, 802; Farrand, *Legislation for Territories*, 21–24; Thorpe, *Constitutions*, 91, 2027–28. The largest number of council appointments occurred in Orleans (Carter, *Territorial Papers*, IX) but there were no movements for popular election.

20. Carter, *Territorial Papers*, III:15–16.

councillors, and representatives were elected simultaneously on the same franchise.[21]

When Congress divided Indiana in 1809, it did not explicitly extend the direct election of the delegate and councillors or the broader Indiana suffrage to the new Illinois Territory. This was one of Governor Edwards' primary excuses for resisting advance to the second stage in Illinois until 1812 when, armed with petitions, he obtained the same concessions from Congress for Illinois that had been granted to Indiana.[22] The same year, however, in passing a new Organic Act for the Louisiana Territory, which was renamed Missouri, Congress provided for an appointed legislative council. In the new Missouri government, the House of Representatives was to nominate eighteen men, nine of whom the President would appoint. These two acts clearly indicate the extent to which Congress could be influenced in this period, by popular agitation led or supported by the governor, to enact a basically different law for one territory from the law in another. On April 29, 1816, however, Congress did provide for the election of the Missouri council with two-year terms, to begin in 1817. With the exception of Alabama, which was created in 1817, the councils of all bicameral legislatures organized thereafter were elected directly by the voters.[23]

Congress did not initially provide for the election of the councils of unicameral governments created after 1820. In the Florida Act of 1822, Congress authorized the President to appoint a thirteen-man council annually, as it had in the first Orleans Act. The next year, under the Michigan Act, however, the President was to appoint nine out of eighteen men nominated by the eligible voters. Agitation immediately began in Michigan for full direct election of the council and its en-

21. Valentine, "Territorial Governor," 33; Carter, *Territorial Papers,* VII: 608, 633–34, 653.

Previously, in 1804, W. C. C. Claiborne had recommended that the councillors in the brief, unicameral Orleans government be made elective, but the reason differed significantly: he was concerned with making the government more acceptable in order to quiet agitation for statehood. (See his letters to the President and Secretary of State in Carter, *Territorial Papers,* IX:314, 312, respectively.)

22. Buley, *Old Northwest,* I:79; McCarty, *Governors of the Northwest,* 111–13; Thorpe, *Constitutions,* 966–67.

23. Carter, *Territorial Papers,* XIV:554; XIX:118; 3 *Statutes,* 328. Compare the Organic Acts, but see especially Thorpe, *Constitutions,* 262–63, 2140, 2144–45.

largement to the size of Florida's, but by the time Congress acted, the councillors had begun their second two-year term. In 1825 Congress enlarged the Michigan council by directing the President to appoint four additional councillors from a list of eight nominated by the voters. During the following year, Congress made the Florida council elective and in January 1827 it also provided for the direct election of the Michigan council.[24]

By 1827, then, all territorial legislators of both unicameral and bicameral systems were elected directly by the eligible voters. In the next decade, the unicameral governments passed out of existence and all the territories having bicameral governments were given uniform suffrage and officeholding requirements. Michigan remained under a unicameral government until it became a state in January 1837, even though the 1823 Organic Act authorized the council to poll the voters and establish a second-stage government whenever a majority of the electors wanted one. The council apparently never polled the voters, but it did petition Congress in 1828 for permission to create a bicameral legislature, without results. On the other hand, in July 1838 Congress reorganized Florida under a typical second-stage government. Congress acceded to a twelve-year-old call from the territorial delegate to increase the size of the Legislative Council to twenty-seven by enlarging and dividing it into a sixteen-man House and an eleven-man Senate, but the name of the legislature was not changed.[25]

24. Valentine, "Territorial Governor," 31; Farrand, *Legislation for Territories*, 31–33; Carter, *Territorial Papers*, XI:404, 610–11; XXIII:619n; Thorpe, *Constitutions*, 1926n; McCarty, *Governors of the Northwest*, 138; *Laws of Michigan*, I:315–20; 3 *Statutes*, 769–70; 4 *Statutes*, 80–81, 166, 200–01.

25. 3 *Statutes*, 769–70; 5 *Statutes*, 263–64; Carter, *Territorial Papers*, XI:1191; XXIII:619n; XXV:532 and note. The only attempt to revive the appointed unicameral council in the contiguous territories seems to have occurred on March 16, 1860, when Representative Lawrence O'Brien Branch of North Carolina, nephew of John Branch, the territorial governor of Florida, unsuccessfully tried to amend a House bill designed to make polygamy a crime in Utah. Branch's idea undoubtedly was to abolish the elected legislature and replace it with a more obedient council appointed by the President. The offered amendment is in the National Archives with H–433, 34 Cong., June 26, 1856, which was reintroduced as H–7, 36 Cong., Feb. 15, 1860.

In 1846, Morgan L. Martin, territorial delegate from the Wisconsin Territory, introduced a bill which, according to notations on it, passed the House July 17, 1847, with Douglas' support. It provided an elective, nine-man, unicameral

First-stage governors were the chief spokesmen and lobbyists for their territories, but during the second stage they lost much of their influence and control to the territorial delegates. Federal patronage and credit for any federal acts beneficial to the territories rapidly fell to the delegates, and in some territories this gave them more real power than the governors had. Consequently (though it may have occurred earlier), in Wisconsin and subsequent territories, governors occasionally sought election to Congress as territorial delegate, and a few men seem to have accepted the governorship for no other reason. But before the delegates were elected directly by the voters, they were not fully competitive with the governors. Thus the dilution of the governors' power can be measured crudely by changes in the election laws for territorial delegates, as well as by the general expansion of the suffrage in the early nineteenth century, even if, as was especially true in the early years, the requirements were often ignored.[26]

All second-stage governments and the unicameral governments of Florida and Michigan had delegates in Congress. Orleans had the only unicameral government without a delegate and Congress probably would have added one to it eventually, had it not decided to give Orleans a second-stage government in 1805.[27] Michigan was the only territory to obtain an elected delegate during the district stage. After the voters rejected Cass' proposal of 1818 to advance to the second stage, the governor, convinced that it was vital for the territory to have a full-time representative in Washington, urged Congress to provide a delegate. Entirely at the governor's behest, it seems, Congress passed a law for that purpose on January 16, 1819.[28]

In the territories covered by the original provisions of the Ordi-

---

legislature for Minnesota but did not provide for the eventual establishment of a regular second-stage government. *NA*, H–568, 29 Cong., Dec. 23, 1846.

26. For examples of the delegates' and governors' patronage in the early period see Downes, *Frontier Ohio*, 216–25. Pomeroy (*Territories, 1861–1890*, 23, 41–44, 67–68, 79–89) and Neil ("Territorial Governors," 93–97) discuss patronage in the period after 1860 and the governors who sought election as delegate. A good general discussion of these points is in Valentine, "Territorial Governor," 84–86, 125–34. See also Chapter IX below; Masterson, *Blount*, 265; and Williamson, *Suffrage*, 208–14.

27. Carter, *Territorial Papers*, IX:312.

28. *Ibid.*, XI:919–20; Thorpe, *Constitutions*, 1926n; Farrand, *Legislation for Territories*, 32.

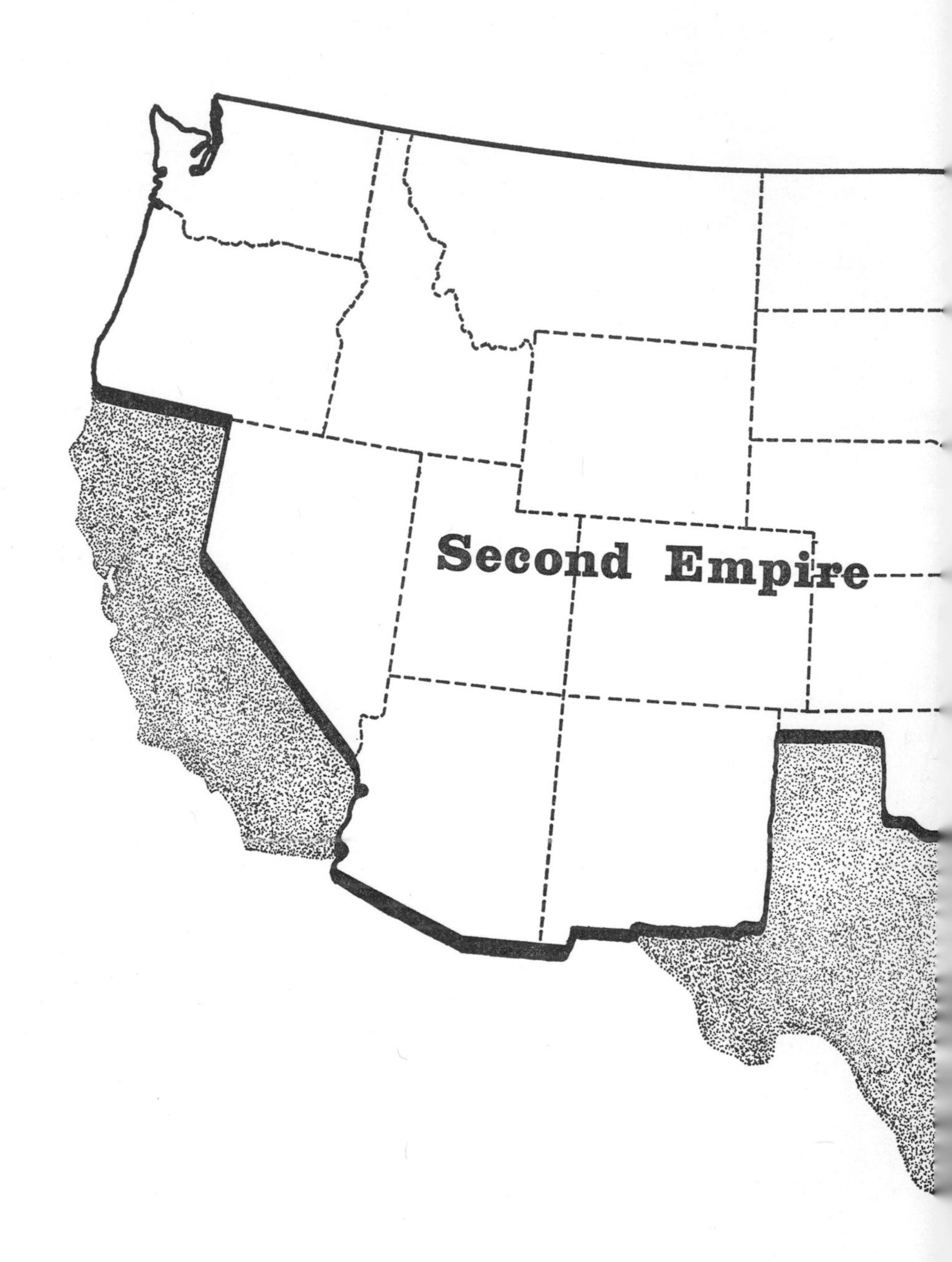
Second Empire

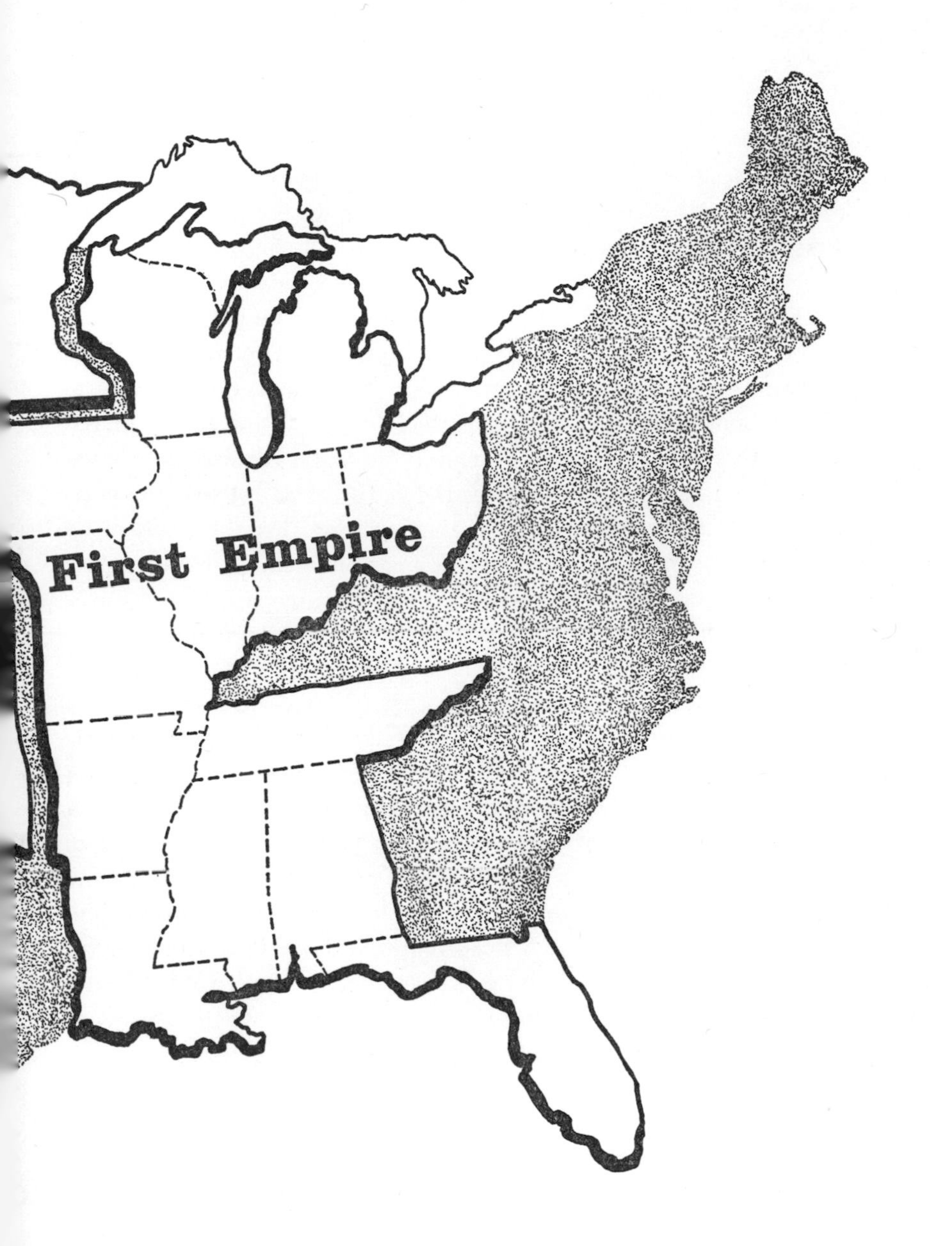
First Empire

nance of 1787, only the lower house of the General Assembly was elected directly by the voters, who consisted of those adult white males with a fifty-acre freehold who had resided in the territory for two years. Western settlers considered these suffrage requirements too restrictive and soon began agitating for their reduction. The property qualification was especially difficult to meet because the government took so long to survey and open land for sale. Consequently, in 1800 the first Northwest General Assembly instructed the territorial delegate to work for the passage of a law requiring only one year's residence and the payment of either the territorial or the county tax, but Congress took no action before Ohio entered the Union. Similar demands were soon to be voiced in Mississippi, Indiana, and elsewhere. Proof of having paid a tax was the usual substitute for the property qualification, but a variety of alternative residence requirements were suggested by petitioners and territorial legislatures. Mississippi petitioners for example, proposed in December 1803 that the suffrage be extended to all residents or citizens. A year later the legislature indicated that it would be satisfied with the two-year residence requirement of the Ordinance if the property requirement were dropped.

When Congress finally acted, it provided a *mélange* of laws with differing provisions for the territories that had second-stage governments between 1805 and 1820. In 1808 it reduced to one year the residence requirement for voting and authorized the direct election of the delegate in Mississippi. The next year it extended the same provisions to Indiana and added the right to elect the council in that territory. In acts of 1811 and 1812, Congress abolished the property qualifications for voting in Indiana and in Illinois and Missouri, the two territories just entering the second stage, and instead required the payment of either a territorial or a county tax. Two years later Congress extended this suffrage to Mississippi, and it also applied to Alabama when it was organized in 1817. None of these reforms affected the Orleans Territory. Moreover, while both the delegates and the councillors of Indiana, Illinois, and Missouri became elective, in Mississippi and Alabama only the delegates were directly elected and neither the delegate nor the councillors of Orleans were elected by the voters.[29]

29. Farrand, *Legislation for Territories,* 25–26; Valentine, "Territorial Governor," 33; 2 *Statutes,* 455, 525–26, 659–70, 741–42; 3 *Statutes,* 143, 328, 348, 371;

At least as important as the changes discussed above were those made in the officeholding requirements and the concomitant legal extension of territorial autonomy. In the Missouri Act of 1812, Congress eliminated some distinctions between voting and officeholding by making all qualified voters eligible for office. Voters with one year's residence were qualified to be representatives, but a minimum age of twenty-five and a 200-acre freehold were required for the council. These qualifications were not changed in the act permitting the election of the council in 1816.[30] Six years later, in the Florida Act, Congress left the suffrage requirements for the territorial delegate to the governor and the appointed council. The next year, 1823, it prescribed a year's residence and the payment of a territorial or county tax as qualifying persons both to vote and to run for the Michigan council—the delegate was already elective. When Congress made the Florida council elective in 1826, it required only a year's residence for office and left the suffrage up to the territorial legislature.[31] By 1832, Congress had further extended the franchise and eligibility for office. It abolished the taxpaying requirement for voting in the territories and reduced the residence requirement to six months. Beginning with the Wisconsin Organic Act of 1836, Congress went all the way, giving the vote to all free adult white males residing in the territory at the time of the first elections and making them all eligible to hold all offices. Under the Wisconsin and subsequent Organic Acts the legislatures were to prescribe suffrage requirements, Congress only requiring that the vote be limited to citizens of the United States.

On its face, this restriction was innocent enough, but in practice it

---

Carter, *Territorial Papers*, V:279, 361–62; VII:335, 608, 651–52, 667–68; XIV: 558; Thorpe, *Constitutions*, 2029; Bond, *Foundations*, 458–59; Bond, *Old Northwest*, 104–05. Compare the above discussion with Williamson, *Suffrage*, 213–14. Carter (*Territorial Papers*, IX:824–25, 982–83) lists no writs of election for the Orleans territorial delegate either in 1809 or 1811, but (*passim*) lists council nominations through 1810.

30. Carter, *Territorial Papers*, VIII:111–12; XIV:554–56, 558; 3 *Statutes*, 328; Buley, *Old Northwest*, I:79; McCarty, *Governors of the Northwest*, 111–13; Thorpe, *Constitutions*, 262–63. The old Ordinance officeholding requirements apparently remained in force in Mississippi and Alabama until statehood.

31. Thorpe, *Constitutions*, 662; 3 *Statutes*, 659, 769; 4 *Statutes*, 166; Farrand, *Legislation for Territories*, 31.

was another matter. It had the effect of disenfranchising persons who could have qualified to vote and hold office under the Ordinance and intervening suffrage laws. Moreover, the new laws could be used to give free rein to Anglo-American xenophobia, as in Florida, where things went well until 1826 when the legislature disenfranchised all Spanish-Americans on the ground that they were not citizens under the federal Constitution. Other devices were used after the Civil War to prohibit Negroes from voting in the territories despite federal laws and a Constitutional amendment guaranteeing them the vote. A few territories, on the other hand, used their freedom to determine voting qualifications to enfranchise women, and two bills introduced in Congress in 1869, both reported adversely, would have given the vote to women. One bill was to apply to all territories. The purpose of the other was "To discourage polygamy in Utah by granting the right of suffrage to Women in that Territory." As a whole, however, the territorial legislatures seem to have ignored the stipulation that only citizens be entitled to vote, except when it suited their purposes, since a number of bills were subsequently introduced in Congress to require citizenship "hereafter" or "henceforth" and to nullify all territorial laws to the contrary.[32]

As governors lost control over legislation to enlarged electorates and much of their patronage to territorial delegates, Congress took away most of their statutory powers to make appointments. Early in the district stage governors had found their appointive powers sharply curtailed in practice, though they remained broad in law. Consequently, the statutory loss of power was more apparent than real until the second quarter of the nineteenth century, when Congress went beyond the limits imposed on the governors' powers by local governments and territorial legislatures. In 1825 Congress began reducing the governors' powers and expanding those of legislatures. In a law of that year, Congress provided for the election of all township and nonjudicial county officials in Michigan. Moreover, it required that hence-

32. Farrand, *Legislation for Territories,* 34, 40–41; Smurr, "Constitutions," 506; Thorpe, *Constitutions,* 4067–68. Compare the section of the Wisconsin Act with that of any subsequent Organic Acts. On Florida, see Carter, *Territorial Papers,* XXIII:528n, 763–64. The suffrage bills mentioned are *NA,* H–119, 35 Cong., Jan. 18, 1858; *NA,* H–64, 41 Cong., Mar. 15, 1869; *NA,* H–68, 41 Cong., Mar. 15, 1869.

forth all the governor's appointments of county judicial officers and sheriffs have the consent of the legislative council, thereby leaving no local office in Michigan appointive solely by the governor. Recommendations that Congress take this action had been voiced intermittently in the territories since 1800, when it was first suggested in Mississippi.[33]

Within a year of the Congressional act of 1825, Michigan's voters began holding elections for county judicial officers and sheriffs despite the provision that they be appointed with the council's consent. Acting Governor William Woodbridge did not appreciate such forwardness, but he and Governor Cass undoubtedly felt obliged to appoint the winners of the elections, since they had earlier encouraged similar preferential elections for lesser offices, and the legislative council, soon to become elective itself, was unlikely to overlook their results when approving the governor's appointments to these offices.[34]

In 1829 Congress further broadened the system of elective local government and extended it to Florida and Arkansas, the other two territories in existence between 1821 and 1836. Under the act, all civil and militia officers were to be elected by the voters. County judicial officers, and the territorial treasurer and auditor were to be elected by the legislature in each territory. Any remaining territorial officials, in addition to those provided in the Organic Acts, were to be ap-

33. Farrand, *Legislation for Territories*, 34; Valentine, "Territorial Governor," 32–33; McCarty, *Governors of the Northwest*, 137; *Laws of Michigan*, I:318–19. The Congressional act (4 *Statutes*, 80–81) also authorized the governor and legislative council to divide the territory into townships, which had not previously been done, despite a district-stage law of 1817 (*Laws of Michigan*, II:93) authorizing the governor to do so. The legislative council began laying out townships in 1827. (*Ibid.*, II:477–81.) A Michigan law of 1825 made county commissioners, treasurers, and coroners elective annually and gave the commissioners the responsibility of determining the number of township constables to be elected every year. (*Ibid.*, II:279.) In the electoral law of 1827 the legislative council decreed that each township should have, in addition to the constables, a supervisor, a clerk, three to five assessors, one collector of taxes, an overseer of the poor, three highway commissioners, a number of fence-viewers, and other officers, all of whom were to be elected yearly. (*Ibid.*, II:317.) Obviously this was to be a township system well endowed with elected officials. Their powers and some election returns of local officials are cited in Carter, *Territorial Papers*, XI:182–84, 858, 859, 900, 1033.

34. See, for example, *ibid.*, XI:1026–28, 1186.

pointed by the President. Thus, in 1829 Congress removed the last of the governor's appointive powers, making him little more than a bureaucrat issuing commissions of appointment.[35]

With the Wisconsin Organic Act of 1836, however, Congress partially returned to the principles of the 1825 law by providing for the election of all township and county officials except county judicial officers, sheriffs, militia officers, "and all civil officers not herein provided for." These, according to the section on local government, the governor was to appoint with the consent of the legislative council.[36] But the executive article of the act did not give the governor appointive powers. It only empowered him to "commission all officers who shall be appointed to office under the laws of the said Territory."[37] Although "the laws of the said Territory" necessarily included the Organic Act, its provisions were somewhat confusing and might be construed to permit the legislature to determine the mode of selecting all officials not appointed by the President. Congress made this construction definitive in the Oregon Act of 1848: "all township, district, and county officers not herein otherwise provided for shall be appointed or elected in such a manner as shall be provided by the legislative assembly." The new wording may have resulted from uncertainties over the meaning of the Wisconsin Organic Act provisions, which were evident in 1840 when Governor Henry Dodge urged the legislature to petition Congress for clarification and modification of the Organic Act expressly to permit the election of all local officials without exception.[38]

35. *Ibid.*, XIX:46n; XXIII:1050–51n; Valentine, "Territorial Governor," 34; Farrand, *Legislation for Territories*, 34; Lonnie J. White, *Politics on the Southwestern Frontier: Arkansas, 1819–1836* (Memphis, 1964), 102, hereafter cited as White, *Arkansas*.

36. Thorpe, *Constitutions*, 4068. The phrase "and all civil officers not herein provided for" presumably applied to territorial offices which might be created by the legislature and paid for out of territorial revenues. If it were to apply to any township and county officials not explicitly named it would be in direct conflict with the elective provision. The term "judicial officers," of course, includes justices of the peace.

37. *Ibid.*, 4066. There was similar confusion in the Florida Act of 1822, whereby the governor was to appoint and commission all officers in accordance with territorial law. (*Ibid.*, 657.)

38. *Ibid.*, 2990; Valentine, "Territorial Governor," 73. The Iowa Organic Act provisions were identical to those in the Wisconsin Act. (See Thorpe, *Constitutions*, 1114.)

In the Minnesota Organic Act of 1849 Congress changed the wording of the section on local government. This time, it simply gave the legislature the power to enact laws for the election or appointment of all county and township officers without exception, but its basic meaning was identical to that of the same section of the Oregon Act of the previous year. All offices named in the Minnesota Organic Act and those not otherwise covered by a territorial law were to be appointed by the governor with the consent of the legislative council. This section of the Minnesota Act appears virtually unchanged in the Organic Acts for the thirteen territories subsequently created in the continental United States.[39]

Each time Congress reduced the governor's appointive power it increased that of the legislature and increased territorial home rule. By the early nineteenth century the governor's power to make appointments had been drastically reduced by territorial laws and local practices, often beyond the provisions of the Organic Acts. During the 1830s and the 1840s legislatures quickly took advantage of federal laws affording the further reductions of the governor's appointive power and went to the limits of the Organic Acts—or beyond. As they took away the governor's appointive powers they also reduced his ability to remove officials. Custom and law limited the governor to the removal of officials he had appointed during pleasure, a tenure that rapidly fell into disuse. Moreover, in practice, early in the history of the Old Northwest, governors lost the power to remove persons with that tenure, or more generally, anyone appointed by a predecessor. Later, governors were sometimes prohibited from removing any officeholder serving for a term or during good behavior unless specifically authorized to do so by the law covering the office. Thus, with expansion of the suffrage and of the number of elected offices, the governor's

39. Thorpe, *Constitutions*, 1938–84. The thirteen do not include Alaska. Compare Section 7 of the Organic Acts. The Oklahoma Act of 1890 (*ibid.*, 2943), for example, has wording identical to that of the Minnesota Act. The only difference between the two is that the former has additional elaborations at the end of the section that were unnecessary and are irrelevent to the discussion here. Bills in the National Archives, which were introduced in Congress for the creation of new territories after 1836, commonly consist of the Organic Acts for previous territories with the names changed and a sheet of paper pasted over the first section of the old law, defining the boundaries of the new territory.

prerogatives and patronage were rigidly circumscribed. By the middle of the nineteenth century and thereafter it was rare that any township or county offices were not elective.[40] By the end of the First Empire, home rule was a reality—but not solely for the reasons discussed above.

40. Neil, "Territorial Governors," 130; Meyerholz, "Federal Supervision," 193; Valentine, "Territorial Governor," 71–72, 75–76, 106–08.

VI

Federal Supervision during the Second Stage

UNTIL the second quarter of the nineteenth century, governors had absolute control over territorial legislatures in law, but since they did not exercise it fully, or were unwilling to run the risks of doing so, the pattern of local government during the district stage appears to have continued unchanged. After Congress withdrew most of the executive controls, it and the federal courts began playing a greater regulatory role with regard to the territories. Nevertheless, their part was not so large or significant as to bring increased centralization because federal interest was sluggish and irregular. On the contrary, though governors lost most of their powers and the federal government began to participate more in territorial affairs by the end of the First Empire, home rule characterized the Second Empire to perhaps an even greater extent than it did in the First. As the governors' appointive and patronage powers declined in the early nineteenth century so did their direct control over territorial governments of the second stage.

The governor who organized a second-stage government, either in a territory evolving out of the first stage or in one beginning at the second, briefly exercised great powers. Often in the First Empire and consistently in the Second, he apportioned the territory and appointed all necessary election officials. Except in Mississippi, Alabama, and Florida, the governor apportioned the territory, but Congress normally specified the number of representatives and, when elective, the number of councillors to be elected. Sometimes in the First Empire, as in Mississippi in 1800 and in Missouri in 1812, Congress also set the dates for the election and convention of the first General Assembly, but in the Wisconsin Act of 1836 and thereafter it consistently left these matters to the governor.[1]

In over half of the territories, primarily those in the Second Empire, Congress authorized the governor to pick the meeting place of the first General Assembly. Only governors of the first and last territories of the First Empire were entitled to designate temporary seats of government. The Northwest and Southwest Ordinances and the first Mississippi Organic Act did not expressly give the governor the right to locate a capital but the governors assumed the power. St. Clair, who did not establish a capital during the district stage, convened the first Northwest General Assembly at Cincinnati, whereas early in his term, Blount planted that of the Southwest at Knoxville, where he was heavily invested in land speculation.[2] In 1800, however, Congress had a change of heart. Except in the first Louisiana (Missouri) Territory Act of 1805, from the turn of the century until 1836, it chose the temporary capitals. In the second Mississippi Organic Act and the Northwest Division Act of 1800, is designated the capital in each territory and empowered the legislatures to change it at will.[3] The same year, in creating the Indiana Territory, Congress began locating the district-

1. Valentine, "Territorial Governor," 27–28, 90–94; Thorpe, *Constitutions*, 2027–28 (Mississippi, 1800), 2141 (Missouri, 1812). Congress apportioned Mississippi. The representatives and councillors from the part of Mississippi that formed Alabama apportioned its new legislature. (*Ibid.*, 90–91.) The Florida council was originally appointed, and when it became elective it similarly apportioned itself. (*Ibid.*, 658.) To see the consistency of provisions beginning in 1836, compare section 4 of the Organic Acts—excepting Kansas, section 22 of the double act, and New Mexico, where it is section 5—in *ibid.*, 465, 907, 1113, 1163, 1170, 1371, 1983, 2141, 2283, 2393, 2618, 2847, 2941–42, 2988, 3688, 3965, 4067, 4107.

2. G. L. Wilson, "St. Clair," 168–69; Masterson, *Blount*, 190–91, 198–99, 207–08.

3. Thorpe, *Constitutions*, 965, 2027–28, respectively. The first Northwest legislature met in 1799. The Division Act of 1800 moved the capital to Chillicothe, and the legislature began trying to move the capital back to Cincinnati. (See Smith, *St. Clair Papers*, I:217; Bond, *Old Northwest*, 111–12.) The second Mississippi Act inaugurated representative government and named Natchez the temporary capital.

stage seats of government, which could be moved only by an act of Congress (or of the General Assembly after the second stage began).[4] This became the usual provision, but Congress did not always explicitly authorize the legislature to move the capital, and in Michigan it inferentially withheld the power.[5]

Beginning with the Wisconsin Act of 1836, Congress, with three exceptions in the Second Empire, empowered the governor of every new territory to select the meeting place of the first General Assembly. In Minnesota, Kansas, and Oklahoma, Congress specified the location, but in sixteen of the seventeen territories concerned, it explicitly gave the territorial legislature the right to relocate the capital. Only in the Kansas half of the Kansas-Nebraska Act did Congress omit this provision.[6]

Once second-stage government began, the powers to apportion a territory, regulate elections, and with a few exceptions, to establish a capital passed to the General Assembly. The extent of the governor's long-range influence, then, depended in large part on the level of political development at the time the second-stage government was organized, his capacity for political organizing and leadership, and his support and ability to control the legislature. In general, the territories were politically undeveloped and the actions of the first second-stage

4. The Northwest Division Act (in Carter, *Territorial Papers,* III:86–88, and Thorpe, *Constitutions,* 964–65) designated Vincennes as the capital "until it shall otherwise be ordered by the legislature." With the same wording the Indiana Division Act of 1809 made Kaskaskia the seat of government in Illinois (Thorpe, *Constitutions,* 967). The Mississippi Division Act of 1817 similarly made St. Stephens the temporary seat of the new Alabama Territory. (*Ibid.,* 90–91.)

5. *Ibid.,* 1925. The 1805 Michigan Act made Detroit capital until Congress directed otherwise and the second Organic Act was silent on the matter. Congress designated New Orleans the capital of Orleans in 1805, St. Louis the capital of Missouri in 1812, and Pensacola the capital of Florida in 1822. None of the acts of those dates expressly gave the legislature the power to move the seat of government. (See *ibid.,* 1372, 2141, 658, respectively, and 1373–74 for the 1805 Louisiana [Missouri] Act.)

6. See the provisions of the Organic Acts, usually section 12 or 13: Thorpe, *Constitutions,* 468, 911, 1116, 1167, 2287, 2396, 2621, 2850, 2993, 3692, 3969, 4070, 4110; and Valentine, "Territorial Governor," 94. Congress named St. Paul, Leavenworth, and Guthrie as the seats of government for the first legislatures of Minnesota, Kansas, and Oklahoma, respectively. (*Ibid.,* 1986, 1175, 2948.)

executives were not long-lasting. The governor might hope to encourage the growth of a town and to bolster or build support in an area by locating the capital in a sympathetic stronghold. But the initial seat of government was not necessarily permanent. Legislatures in some territories had a penchant for moving the capital, and strong support in the General Assembly was always essential to prevent its being relocated. Moreover, movements to change the seat of government invariably engendered strong feelings, and few governors wanted to run the risks associated with partisan involvement of this sort.

Though the power of apportionment ordinarily belonged to the General Assembly, Congress or the legislature sometimes directed a governor to redistrict a territory, in both the First and the Second Empires. Neither the Northwest nor the Southwest Ordinance specified procedures for reapportionment, but this had no effect on the Southwest Territory since its house was not reapportioned during the second stage. In the Northwest, on the other hand, the first General Assembly enacted a law requiring the governor to conduct a census of adult males and reapportion the lower house accordingly every two years.[7] The Indiana and Illinois legislatures continued to use the Northwest law in their territories until 1814. Then, following complaints against Governor Thomas Posey's reapportionment of Indiana and a federal House of Representatives committee report expressing the opinion that the reapportionment had been illegal, Congress forbade executive reapportionments in both Indiana and Illinois.[8] Beginning with the Mississippi Act in 1800, Congress had included a provision in the organic laws for other territories directing the legislatures to apportion themselves.[9] Thus, after 1814 second-stage governors could not legally reapportion legislatures anywhere without instructions from Congress. These usually came after a legislature failed to reapportion

7. Pease, *Laws of the Northwest*, A404–14, particularly A408; Bond, *Old Northwest*, 93–94.

8. Philbrick, *Laws of Indiana*, A175, A397; Philbrick, *Laws of Illinois*, A51, A186, A197, A216, A219, A249, A255, A291, A313, A326–27, for legislative apportionment acts of Illinois beginning with the 1815–1816 session. The federal law is in 3 *Statutes*, 103.

9. Thorpe, *Constitutions*, 2027–28; Carter, *Territorial Papers*, V:96. Compare the Organic Acts but see especially the Orleans Act of 1805 (*ibid.*, IX:406) and the Missouri Act of 1812 (*ibid.*, XIV:555).

itself as prescribed by law. Nevertheless, there were a few instances after 1814 in which legislatures ordered governors to make new apportionments and Congress did not react. The Wisconsin General Assembly, for example, twice ordered the governor to redistrict it.[10]

In the early years of the First Empire, second-stage governors had four basic powers, expressly intended to give the federal government absolute control over the activities of territorial legislatures. These were the governor's right to convene, prorogue, and dissolve the General Assembly at will, and the veto. By the end of the second decade of the nineteenth century, however, Congress had withdrawn the first three, and before the First Empire ended it qualified the veto.[11]

Only in the six territories covered by the original provisions of the Ordinance of 1787—the Northwest, Southwest, Mississippi, Indiana, Illinois, and presumably Alabama—was the governor entitled to convene, prorogue, and dissolve the legislature. The governors of Illinois and Alabama never used any of the three powers and whether they actually had them is not clear. The governors of the other four territories used them sparingly and usually at the request of the General Assembly.

The most arbitrary of the three powers, the power to dissolve the General Assembly, was used only three times, twice in Mississippi and once in Indiana. Governor Harrison's use of the power was the only correct one, however, and then he dissolved the Indiana legislature at its own request. When Congress divided Indiana in 1809, Harrison reapportioned the truncated territory and called elections for the lower house instead of simply convening the representatives and councillors from the districts left in the smaller Indiana. When the new legislature met in October 1809, a minority of its members questioned the legality of Harrison's actions and complained that the apportionment had been inequitable. As a result, the legislature drew up a petition asking Congress either to certify Harrison's apportionment or to authorize him to make a new one immediately. On the same day the legislature asked the

10. Valentine, "Territorial Governor," 95–96; Meyerholz, "Federal Supervision," 173.

11. Valentine ("Territorial Governor," 103) notes a House report of March 18, 1800, stating that the governor had the powers to permit strong federal control over the territories.

governor to dissolve it, thereby making new elections necessary since, through dissolution, all commissions and terms of office in the General Assembly were revoked. Shortly thereafter Congress directed Harrison to constitute a new Assembly.[12]

Governor Robert Williams dissolved the Mississippi General Assembly once in 1808 and again in 1809. In 1808 he dissolved the legislature after deciding it had had enough time to conduct its business and was up to no good. This act met with the approval of Secretary of State James Madison. The next year Williams resigned, and he was unwilling to leave the legislature in session. Nonetheless, in dissolving it as his last act in office, he declared again that it was not doing the "proper and ordinary business of the territory." In each case, Williams could more appropriately have adjourned the legislature by proroguing it, as he had in 1807, at its request. In both 1808 and 1809, he acted as if he doubted his authority to prorogue, even though the Organic Act clearly provided the power. The federal House bill for a second Mississippi Organic Act in 1800 had explicitly withdrawn the powers to convene, prorogue, and dissolve the legislature, but the Senate struck out the clause and the act that was passed simply required that the government of Mississippi conform to the provisions of the Ordinance of 1787 in every respect.

Instead of falling back on the Ordinance for the power to prorogue, Williams made a lengthy verbal excursion into the colonial past under Great Britain. He claimed the right to dissolve the legislature from English common law and argued that he exercised the King's power in Mississippi as the Bishop of Durham. He might have used the same logic to derive the power to prorogue, of course, and that he did not indicates that he just did not want to do so. Williams created unnecessary problems by using dissolution in place of prorogation. According to the legislature, when the governor dissolved it he appropriated the right to remove Presidential appointees. Thus, each time he dissolved the legislature, the governor had to call new elections for the lower house and it had to nominate ten men for the council, five of

12. *Ibid.*, 104; Philbrick, *Laws of Illinois*, R455; Carter, *Territorial Papers*, V:633; VII:694n, 694–703. Whether Harrison dissolved the Indiana legislature or not the President presumably would have had to appoint a new council for the smaller territory.

whom the President had to appoint after getting confirmation from the Senate.[13]

Occasionally, sharp conflicts were associated with the use of the power to prorogue the legislature, but they do not seem to have been direct outgrowths of its use. The outcry following St. Clair's prorogation of the lame duck session of the Northwest General Assembly on December 9, 1800, for example, was allied with, if not a function of, the continuing campaign of a coalition of his opponents to prevent the governor's reappointment. St. Clair prorogued the legislature when his new commission did not arrive, on the day his old one expired, to ward off disagreeable legislation which the Republican Secretary Byrd might approve as acting governor. Other governors used the power frequently without precipitating conflicts. Normally they prorogued the General Assembly only at its request after it had completed its work.[14]

Though opposition to the right to prorogue the legislature was manifest at the beginning of the nineteenth century, it was over a decade before the right was clearly excluded from the governor's prerogatives. The Mississippi Act of 1800 authorized the legislature to adjourn itself, and the governors tended to assume that this meant they could not prorogue it. Yet neither the Mississippi Act nor the 1804 and 1805 Orleans Acts specifically withdrew the power, and in each case it could be inferred from the application of the Northwest Ordinance to the territory (in the case of the 1805 Orleans Act through the requirement that the Orleans government conform to Mississippi's). In the Missouri Act of 1812, Congress expressly withheld the power from the governor by providing that the General Assembly "shall sit on its own adjournment from day to day." The wording necessarily eliminated the power to dissolve the legislature as well. From 1812 onward, Congress included the same provision in the organic law of every new territory created, except Alabama. In Alabama, a two-year extension of the territorial period of Mississippi, the Organic Act

13. Carter, *Territorial Papers,* V:579–80, 590–91, 614, 633, 634–36, 640, 713–14; Valentine, "Territorial Governor," 104; Thorpe, *Constitutions,* 2027–28.

14. Bond, *Old Northwest,* 105–06; Bond, *Foundations,* 460–61; G. L. Wilson, "St. Clair," 340–41; Masterson, *Blount,* 258; Philbrick, *Laws of Illinois,* R455; Carter, *Territorial Papers,* V:590–91.

continued the governmental system of the parent territory without change, and if the governor believed that he held the powers, he never used them.[15]

The right to convene General Assemblies was the most short-lived of the governor's powers outside the Old Northwest. It was used only in the Northwest, Southwest, Indiana, and Illinois territories, and in these areas its use was a matter of form never contested. The Northwest and Southwest Ordinances did not specify when the legislature should meet, and the General Assemblies passed no laws requiring regular sessions. Legislatures of the four territories nevertheless met annually, at about the same time each year, and the governors continued to convene those of Indiana and Illinois at least until 1815. In the meantime, in 1800 Congress gave the Governor of Mississippi authority to convene the General Assembly only for extraordinary sessions.[16] It similarly restricted the governors of about half the subsequent territories in the First and Second Empires. Governors of the other half could not convene even special sessions of the legislature without special authorization in advance from the President or Congress. In some cases, extraordinary sessions could not be held until Congress appropriated money for them. Beginning in 1800 with Mississippi, however, Congress also required legislatures to meet annually or biennially, either at a time specified in the Organic Acts or at a time picked by the legislatures.[17]

During the district stage, the governors and judges established and regulated inferior courts and a few functions of the circuit and general courts and, though these powers were not enumerated among the powers of the General Assembly, the governors of the Northwest, Southwest, and Mississippi surrendered them to the second-stage legis-

15. Carter, *Territorial Papers,* V:97 and note; IX:406; XIV:556; Farrand, *Legislation for Territories,* 27; Valentine, "Territorial Governor," 33, 104–05.

16. See Philbrick, *Laws of Indiana,* R20–29; Logan Esarey, ed. [Indiana Territory] *Governors Messages and Papers* (2 vols., Indianapolis, 1922), I:378–83, hereafter cited as Esarey, *Messages;* Thorpe, *Constitutions,* 2027; Carter, *Territorial Papers,* V:97. The 1805 Orleans Act (*ibid.,* IX:406), however, does not include the power to convene extraordinary sessions except insofar as the government was to conform to that of Mississippi.

17. See Valentine, "Territorial Governor," 105; Pomeroy, *Territories, 1861–1890,* 26; and compare the relevant sections of the Organic Acts in Thorpe, *Constitutions.*

latures without contest. Congress did not explicitly give the powers to the legislature before the Orleans Act of 1804, and did not extend them to all territories until 1815. Nor did Congress clearly define the realm of the territorial legislatures' authority to establish and regulate courts before 1815. The extension of full powers to the legislatures followed a controversy in 1814 surrounding an attempt by the Illinois General Asembly to alter the judiciary system. The General Court, asked for an opinion by some assemblymen, stated that the legislature could not enact the law proposed because it did not have the power, especially insofar as the act would modify provisions of the Northwest Ordinance. Governor Edwards told the legislature that he thought it could pass the law, but it decided to petition Congress for a change in the Organic Act. Instead, in 1815 Congress adopted a general law and thereafter, during the remainder of the First Empire and throughout the Second, every territorial legislature could establish and regulate its courts in any way it wished without Congressional interference, as long as it did not abuse its powers.[18]

Whenever the lines of jurisdiction between the executive and the legislature were not clearly drawn, there was room, or at least an excuse, for conflict. Since the lines were never too clear there was always room, but even when the executive power was beyond question, as in the use of the veto, it could become embroiled in controversy, and in any conflict between the governor and the legislature or a political faction, each party could be counted on to seize every means at hand to discredit the other. Because they possessed only limited patronage, there was not much governors could do when legislatures refused to enact laws or programs they recommended, but the governors could always hinder or prevent the enactment of bills they opposed by resorting to the veto, and criticism tended to focus on the use of this power during the second stage.

Nevertheless, disputes between governors and legislatures more often centered on policies—how the powers were used—and personali-

18. Farrand, *Legislation for Territories*, 21–24, 27; Philbrick, *Laws of Illinois*, R44–45, R54, R468–69; McCarty, *Governors of the Northwest*, 114; Meyerholz, "Federal Supervision," 227–28; 3 *Statutes*, 237, 327. In 1828 Congress nullified an attempt of the Arkansas legislature to add a judge to the territorial Supreme Court (Meyerholz, "Federal Supervision," 172). For other examples of legislatures' abusing the powers see Pomeroy, *Territories, 1861–1890*, 51–61.

ties than on their respective powers per se, regardless of the rhetorical devices used. Intraterritorial sectionalism and rivalries of all sorts, including slavery in Indiana and Kansas, served as vehicles for conflict. The most general sectional problems, however, occurred in the territories of the Second Empire during the period of the Civil War and Reconstruction. The most prominent series of clashes arose from the appointment of Radical Republican governors during Reconstruction and the single issue of the test oath for legislators. In Montana and Idaho, the governors had to threaten legislators with force and face down insurrections in order to administer the new oath to moderate Republicans and Confederate sympathizers.

Sharp conflicts were virtually inevitable whenever a federal administration sent out a governor, who was necessarily a strong-willed and determined individual, to carry out specific, often unpopular, policies. President Cleveland, for example, precipitated a vigorous political contest in Wyoming. He appointed a governor, Thomas Moonlight, who attempted to inaugurate agricultural and conservation reforms in the territory where the Stock Growers' Association had long controlled the legislative and executive branches of government. Governors pursuing unpopular policies not infrequently encountered strong opposition from within their own party. Intraparty conflicts, in fact, were at times much more important than interparty rivalries, and Presidents sometimes appointed governors primarily to overcome them and rebuild party strength. Finally, national party cleavages were often evident, especially in well-developed territories, and friction sometimes followed the appointment of a Republican governor to a territory dominated by the Democrats or vice versa. Consequently, in any analysis of the veto it is not always possible to determine the real reasons behind its use.[19]

Ostensibly, governors vetoed bills as illegal invasions of their prerogatives, as inappropriate legislation, and for being in conflict with higher authority, meaning acts of Congress or the Constitution. In veto messages or other explanatory statements, they most often argued against the constitutionality of legislative acts, but all three reasons, and especially the first, sometimes reflected political differences be-

19. Valentine, "Territorial Governor," 99, 129; Neil, "Territorial Governors," 101–02, 116–36; Philbrick, *Laws of Indiana*, R20–55 *passim.*

tween the governor and a majority of the legislature. While it is clear that some governors used the veto almost exclusively as a political weapon and others used it in a strictly legal manner, the legal and political motives were frequently intertwined and the more fundamental of the two cannot be determined. In 1808, for example, when the Indiana General Assembly enacted a law requiring the governor to remove any court clerk on petition from the court, Harrison vetoed it on the plausible ground that it was contrary to the Organic Act, yet with equal plausibility one of his critics contended that the governor's real objective was to preserve his prerogatives. A few governors, like the tendentious Mason Brayman of Idaho, vetoed legislation designed to curb their appointive powers by making offices elective, even though the legislatures were within their rights. More often, governors vetoed as unconstitutional acts to make offices elective that were appointive by provisions of the Organic Act, but these vetoes could just as well have been intended to safeguard the executive authority.[20]

The most significant early use of the veto to protect prerogatives occurred in the Northwest. Just as the first session of the Northwest General Assembly was about to adjourn in 1799, St. Clair returned eleven bills with veto messages, destroying the harmony that had existed throughout the session. Six of the vetoed acts created new counties, and though St. Clair argued that they violated provisions of the Ordinance, his primary concern was to retain the power he had exercised during the district stage. The legislature contended that the power to create counties fell to it once the second stage began, but St. Clair continued to set off new counties on his own authority until 1801. In the meantime, strong opposition to the governor developed and in 1800 the General Assembly proposed that the question of who had the power be submitted to the territorial courts for settlement. St. Clair did not like the idea but the next year he asked the President for an opinion. He in turn queried the Attorney General who, surprisingly, could find neither grounds nor principles, in or out of

20. Valentine, "Territorial Governor," 106–09; Carter, *Territorial Papers*, VII:502, 548, XVII:285–87; Neil, "Territorial Governors," 130. There is no thorough study of the use of vetoes in territories or in the states. The most adequate analysis of territorial vetoes is in Meyerholz, "Federal Supervision," 179–94, and it is obviously in error in places. (See notes below.)

the Ordinance, for a confident decision. Nevertheless, he sided with St. Clair. Since the power to create and divide counties had been the governor's during the district stage and since the Ordinance contained no explicit provision for change, the Attorney General concluded that it continued to reside with the governor during the second stage. President Jefferson was not of the same opinion and said as much through Secretary of State Madison. Nor would the legislature accede to the governor's or the Attorney General's interpretation. Except for the first county, apparently, the legislature thwarted the governor by not providing in law for counties he proclaimed, and in 1802 St. Clair acquiesced.[21]

The vetoes of two of the other bills, which St. Clair vetoed at the end of the first session as impractical or unnecessary, had strong political overtones. One was an act to move a county seat from its original location, established in 1798, when the governor had proclaimed the county, to the home town of a leader of the Republican opposition. More arbitrary and generally resented was St. Clair's veto of a bill to take a census of the eastern portion of the territory in hopes that it could qualify for statehood. St. Clair opposed statehood but could argue convincingly that the census of the previous year, preparatory to the election of the House of Representatives, clearly indicated that there were not enough people in the area to warrant statehood. Moreover,

21. In 1800 St. Clair had said that he would approve county division acts if they met with his understanding of needs, and he more or less agreed from the outset that the legislature had the right to alter or adjust county boundaries after he had created them. His actions, however, were incompatible with these statements. The county creation conflict is discussed in Philbrick, *Laws of Illinois*, R474–75; Bond, *Old Northwest*, 92–99, 104–07; Bond, *Foundations*, 447–48; Burnet, *Notes*, 375–79; McCarty, *Governors of the Northwest*, 71; G. L. Wilson, "St. Clair," 158, 174–75, 330–31. See also Attorney General Levi Lincoln to President Jefferson, February 2, 1802 (Carter, *Territorial Papers*, III:208–11), and Secretary of State James Madison to Governor Arthur St. Clair, June 23, 1802. (*Ibid.*, III:231.) Probably correctly, for Federalist control was one of the governor's obsessions at the turn of the century, G. L. Wilson ("St. Clair," 333) implies that St. Clair feared that the creation of more counties would undermine the dominance of the two Federalist counties of Washington and Hamilton. Therefore, he wanted to retain the power to create counties so that it could be used to minimize the power of the Jeffersonians. By 1802, however, the cause was lost; the Jeffersonians were then too numerous and St. Clair's arbitrary conduct had cost him heavily in support.

it was unnecessary because the federal government would conduct its decennial census in 1800.[22]

In the other territories that passed through the district stage as well as in all the territories that began at the second stage, the legislatures assumed the power to create counties without question, even though Congress did not explicitly give the power to second-stage legislatures before the Missouri Act of 1812. Recognizing the lesson of St. Clair's experience, governors assiduously avoided, insofar as possible, conflicts with legislatures over the powers to create counties and to locate county seats. Governor Harrison even found it to be politically expedient, following a strong hint from the first Indiana General Assembly, to go so far as to tell it that he construed the Ordinance in such a way as to give the power to the legislature during the second stage.[23]

Governors nevertheless vetoed a number of laws creating counties and locating county seats as unnecessary or unwise, thereby getting themselves embroiled in local political issues. But legislatures often gave vent to the most petty forms of local politics with the enactment of a seemingly endless stream of such laws. As a result, during the early years in many territories, and sometimes extending well beyond statehood, county boundaries undulated while county seats lolloped from one site to another according to the changing fortunes of the various factions involved. During the first session of the Wisconsin General Assembly, Governor Henry Dodge began vetoing bills to change county seats, and he reprimanded the legislature at length for spending so much time on legislation he considered unnecessary and unjustified.[24] Dodge proposed that the voters in the counties be allowed to choose the county seats, but when this was tried in other territories

22. G. L. Wilson, "St. Clair," 333; Bond, *Old Northwest*, 98–99. The 1800 census showed the territory, after division, to have 45,400 people, well under the 60,000 requirement. Bond, *Old Northwest*, 107–08.

23. See Carter, *Territorial Papers*, XIV:554; Philbrick, *Laws of Illinois*, R476; Philbrick, *Laws of Indiana*, R29. Compare the Organic Acts in Thorpe, *Constitutions*.

24. McCarty, *Governors of the Northwest*, 149–50. In this case Dodge's position seemed calculated to thwart the ambitions of townsite boomers and speculators as well, but some governors (for example Dodge's successor, James Duane Doty) were among these individuals.

the court houses often proved to be no less mobile and veritable county seat wars were endemic. Legislatures wasted so much time drawing county lines and especially in locating county seats that eventually, in 1886, Congress required legislatures to locate county seats only by general laws. Four years later Congress went further by defining seven counties and providing for their seats of government in the Oklahoma Organic Act.[25]

Governors vetoed a wide variety of other acts as unfit or undesirable. These included inequitable apportionment acts, laws that would be incompatible with existing statutes, and poorly framed laws which, being defective or unclear, would lead to confusion. Governors sometimes vetoed acts granting special privileges for being in conflict with existing laws, but they usually vetoed them as undesirable or beyond the realm of legislative authority. Few governors thought they should have the prerogative to veto the divorce bills, which were quite common, and in some territories they passed unchallenged, but most governors felt compelled to veto them because they considered such private acts unfit legislation. These governors argued that grant-

25. Thorpe, *Constitutions*, 2940–41; Meyerholz, "Federal Supervision," 242. In some territories west of the Mississippi River the legislatures adopted something akin to a master plan for county government early in the territorial period, thereby avoiding the worst problems of county creation. Well before Indians had ceded more than the eastern third of the Iowa Territory, and while settlement and the surveys were still in the eastern quarter of the present state, the Iowa legislature divided the whole territory south of the present northern boundary into counties of nearly equal sizes. According to the plan, county governments were to be organized when enough people entered any predetermined county, whose boundaries would be defined along township lines when surveys were completed. Presumably, township governments could begin whenever a township had a sufficient population. Iowa counties were to average from twelve to sixteen townships each. With relatively few changes, other than adjustments to the surveys, the counties grew and remained as outlined at the beginning. (In the Wisconsin State Historical Society Library Manuscript Room there is a series of early maps of Iowa showing the evolution of the plan and changes in county boundaries.) In a sense, the adoption of this general plan by the Iowa legislature represents the true application of second-stage ideas to local government. The large counties of the Northwest were essentially the district-stage concept operating on a county level. By defining counties in advance and establishing the governments as needed, the former period of intracounty tutelage and intercounty animosity was somewhat avoided. Nevertheless, Iowa had its share of county seat wars.

ing divorces was strictly a court function. Congress eventually agreed and in 1886 outlawed divorce by special act of territorial legislatures.[26]

In the last phase of the First Empire, Congress began forbidding certain kinds of territorial legislation. Shortly after it passed the Wisconsin Act in 1836 Congress enacted a general law forbidding territories to incorporate banks or other institutions having banking powers except with its express approval.[27] At the beginning of the Second Empire, and again in the Washington Act of 1853, Congress prohibited without exception the granting of banking powers. In 1867 it broadened the prohibition to include a wide variety of private acts awarding charters and special privileges, but gave territorial legislatures the right to enact general incorporation laws for industrial purposes. During the early 1870's the law was construed to permit the enactment of general incorporation laws for railroads, wagon roads, and for educational, scientific, and charitable organizations, and in 1885 Congress empowered legislatures to adopt general laws for the incorporation of banks and canals.[28]

26. Valentine, "Territorial Governor," 109; Meyerholz, "Federal Supervision," 192; Neil, "Territorial Governors," 98–99, 124–28. Neil (*ibid.*, 98–99) notes that in some territories legislatures routinely overrode divorce bill vetoes, perhaps implying that the veto was largely a formality by which governors salved their consciences. On the other hand, Neil cites governors whose concern was such that they gave great attention to these bills. Meyerholz ("Federal Supervision," 242) states that "As a rule the Governors of the Territories were stringently opposed to the granting of divorce by the legislatures and in most cases vetoed. . . ." He also cites one instance, in 1885, when the Idaho Territorial Supreme Court nullified a divorce law passed either with the governor's consent or over his veto. Such court decisions are rare. Valentine ("Territorial Governor," 116) however, notes that at least two governors (A. P. K. Safford of Arizona and Fayette McMullin of Washington) obtained divorces by special act while in office.

27. Farrand, *Legislation for Territories*, 41. It is not clear that this excluded general incorporation acts, but it precedes their widespread enactment by state legislatures. Late in the nineteenth century the courts concluded that laws requiring Congressional approval for enforcement also required its approval before being repealed. This decision could not have been very important to the remaining contiguous territories but it was a real burden for territories of the Oceanic Empire. Under the Alaska Organic Act of 1912, for example, a broad range of legislative acts, including all acts for county government, required Congressional approval in order to be valid. (See Meyerholz, "Federal Supervision," 173–74; Gruening, *Alaska*, 151–52.)

28. Valentine, "Territorial Governor," 115; Farrand, *Legislation for Territories*,

In spite of federal legislation to the contrary, a majority of all legislative acts in many, if not all, territories continued to be private in nature. A number of governors apparently deplored this practice and continued to veto the laws, changing their reasons from the undesirability of the laws to their being in conflict with higher authority, after the federal government prohibited them, but by the end of the First Empire they were often powerless to stop private laws. If they vetoed the laws the legislatures overrode their vetoes, and few governors cared to arouse antagonism by making the gesture when it was futile. Thus, in the Second Empire, Congress and the federal courts were forced to play a larger part inasmuch as they wanted to bring about the repeal of unsound or undesirable legislation which, increasingly, also ran counter to the Constitution, Organic Acts, and other laws of Congress.[29]

As in the case of private laws, governors more or less regularly vetoed general acts that were in conflict with a higher authority, such as attempts of territorial legislatures to make offices elective that were appointive by provisions of the Organic Acts or to create new territorial offices and have their salaries paid out of the federal treasury. Governors vetoed laws of all kinds that were enacted during illegal legislative sessions and others they considered to be in violation of the Constitution, ranging from acts infringing individual rights in court to those appropriating public monies for the support of parochial schools.[30] In addition, they vetoed laws contrary to acts of Congress. For example, the governor of Idaho vetoed an attempt of the legislature to supersede the federal Reconstruction test oath with one of its own. A fracas ensued and the governor called out the army to restore order, but after the legislators vented their anger in a wild melee, in which they broke up the furniture in the legislative chamber and threw it

42–43, 47–48. Farrand (*ibid.*, 48) says that by 1878 municipal incorporations were permitted by interpretation of the 1867 law. If this is true, it means that a right assumed and exercised in the earlier territories had been withdrawn, lost, or simply not used after mid-century. (See Chapter IV.)

29. Neil ("Territorial Governors," 45–48) cites examples of the continuing enactment of private laws in the far Northwestern territories and quotes Governor Ashley of Montana to the effect that a majority of all laws were private or granted special or monopolistic privileges.

30. *Ibid.*, 49; Valentine, "Territorial Governor," 105–08.

out the windows, they finally realized they would not get paid otherwise and took the Congressional oath.[31]

In the meantime, during the latter part of the First Empire, Congress began qualifying the governors' veto power and correspondingly reducing the governors' control over legislation. Until 1822 the governors of all territories had had an absolute veto. In that year, perhaps inadvertently, Congress failed to provide them with any veto power in the Organic Act. The following year it remedied this oversight and provided a limited veto. Under the law of 1823, the legislative council of Florida could overturn a veto by a two-thirds vote. Six years later Congress similarly qualified the governor's veto over the bicameral legislature in Arkansas. There, as in all subsequent second-stage governments where the veto was limited, the General Assembly could override a veto by a two-thirds vote in each house. In 1839, Congress also qualified the veto power in Wisconsin and Iowa, so that between then and the end of the First Empire the power was limited in all three territories in existence. Thus, the only territory in which Congress did not limit the governor's veto between 1820 and 1848 was Michigan.[32]

Congress did not provide governors of territories in the Second Empire with a uniform veto power. In some territories the governor had an absolute veto, in others a limited one, and initially, neither the Oregon nor the Washington governor had any veto power. Why these two should have been exceptions is unclear. All of the Oregon bills, including the one that became the Organic Act, provided for an absolute veto. For some reason, however, the Senate struck out the provision before enacting it, and a few months later it passed a similar bill, also excluding the veto power, for the organization of California. Nevertheless, the trend was toward giving all governors a qualified veto and after 1860 Congress limited the veto in almost all territories either in the Organic Acts or supplemental legislation.[33]

31. Neil, "Territorial Governors," 116–21.

32. Valentine, "Territorial Governor," 30–31, 34, 110; Farrand, *Legislation for Territories,* 31, 42; Carter, *Territorial Papers,* XVII:390; Philbrick, *Laws of Illinois,* R453n.

33. Neil, "Territorial Governors," 100–01; Valentine, "Territorial Governor," 108–09. Congress provided the Washington governor with a qualified veto in 1864. *Congressional Globe,* 38 Cong., 1 sess., vol. 34, pt. 4, pp. 2510–11, 3063. See

Limitation of the veto power corresponded with changing state practices and federal attitudes, but it seems to have been associated largely with a desire on the part of Congress to pacify territorial inhabitants. Popular outcries against the absolute veto and its use, and agitation for its limitation, which began in the first Northwest General Assembly, continued intermittently to the twentieth century. Some governors supported such demands and St. Clair, of all people, was among them. In 1800 he offered to join the legislature in petitioning Congress to reduce the veto power to that of the President, until it added a demand for virtual manhood suffrage. He then demurred, so the legislature on its own ordered the territorial delegate to press Congress for these changes in the Ordinance. In the same year, the first Mississippi General Assembly barely seated itself before drafting a similar proposal. In 1807 and 1808 Harrison's use of the veto prompted letters and petitions from Indiana calling for limitation of the veto and, in at least one instance, the complete withdrawal of the power. Eventually Congress probably received petitions for its abolition or limitation from every territory where the governor had an absolute veto and from most of those where it was qualified.[34]

---

the 1848 Oregon bills (*NA* S–324, 30 Cong., July 18, 1848; and *NA,* H–201, 30 Cong., Feb. 9, 1848) and California bill (*NA,* H–685, 30 Cong., Dec. 20, 1848). Neither the Nebraska bills of 1844 and 1848 (*NA,* H–444, 28 Cong., Dec. 17, 1844; *NA,* S–170, 30 Cong., Mar. 15, 1848 [the same bill reintroduced]), nor of 1853 (*NA,* H–353, 32 Cong., Feb. 2, 1853; which became S–22, 33 Cong., Dec. 14, 1853), explicitly gave the governor a veto. See sections 2 and 6 of the amended S–22, 33 Cong. Compare these bills, those cited in notes 13 and 14 of Chapter V, and other territorial organization bills cited in David W. Parker, *Calendar of Papers in Washington Archives Relating to the Territories of the United States (to 1873)* (Washington, 1911) with the Organic Acts and other statutes, to see the trend toward a qualified veto. (It should be noted that Parker's notations are dated. All extant bills, regardless of the location he indicated for 1911, are now in the National Archives.) The lack of a pattern in the veto power provided is suggested by a bill like *NA,* S–555, 35 Cong., Feb. 4, 1859, also dated Feb. 23, 1859, for the organization of Arizona and Dakota, wherein the governor of one territory was to have an absolute veto while the governor of the other was to have a limited one. In this case, the difference arose from the sponsor's literally pasting together two separate bills, one from the House and the other from the Senate, which had been introduced earlier in the same Congress.

34. See Valentine, "Territorial Governor," 32, 108–10; Smith, *St. Clair Papers,* I:239; Bond, *Foundations,* 458–59; Philbrick, *Laws of Indiana,* R30; Philbrick, *Laws of Illinois,* R453n; Carter, *Territorial Papers,* VII:502, 548; Bond, *Old North-*

Almost as if by mechanical response when a governor issued a veto, a body of people or the legislature fired off a petition to Congress condemning the governor and asking for his removal or for revision of the veto power. The ease with which petitions for a governor's removal sometimes bore fruit dampened executive enthusiasm for use of the power and undoubtedly limited the value of threats to veto as a means of influencing legislation. Regardless of protests against its use, in the territories where governors had only a qualified veto, it was usually little more than an irritating hurdle obstructing the path of legislation. In the face of a determined legislature the governor was helpless to prevent legislation contrary to higher authority, much less to stop bills granting divorces or other special privileges, and legislatures dominated by the opposition political party sometimes went to extremes to embarrass the governors. In the 1888–1889 session, for example, the Republican majority in the New Mexico General Assembly unseated enough of the Democratic members to assure a two-thirds vote to override a veto at any time. During the session of that year Governor E. G. Ross, a Democrat, vetoed "nearly all" of the 145 bills passed and the legislature overrode every one. Legislatures in territories where the governor had an absolute veto sometimes tried to legislate by resolution to outflank the executive. The first Iowa legislature did this, before Congress limited the veto, but Governor Robert Lucas vetoed the resolutions anyway, declaring them illegal.[35]

Territorial legislatures nevertheless had several effective weapons at hand for countering or forestalling executive vetoes. They could normally meet the threat of vetoes with equally potent threats to withdraw the governors' extra compensation or to reduce their income from fees for services. The governors' legal income from the federal government was woefully inadequate and legislatures, during periods of harmony, early adopted laws to supplement their salaries

west, 104–05. Generally, legislatures followed the course set in the Northwest by instructing the territorial delegate to press for veto revision (Bond, *Old Northwest*, 104–05).

35. See Valentine, "Territorial Governor," 110–11. Neil ("Territorial Governors") has scattered references to similar occurrences. Lamar (*Far Southwest*, 182) claims "Ross vetoed more bills . . . than any governor in territorial history." This is not improbable, but it is an impossible generalization without a complete tabulation. See below, notes 39, 41 and 42.

from territorial revenue. The practice began with the first Northwest General Assembly which appropriated at least $833.33 to St. Clair for "services extraordinary" and house rent.[36] Legislatures continued to grant gratuities to governors under a number of guises throughout the nineteenth century, despite Congressional acts in 1873 and later years banning them. In the meantime many governors became heavily dependent on legislative subsidies and could hardly afford their loss. Some governors nonetheless welcomed the federal prohibition because they found the system of extra compensation humiliating and felt that the practice left them open to indirect and unsavory manipulation by the legislature.[37]

When all else failed to win over recalcitrant governors, legislatures mobilized public opinion against them and occasionally threatened them with violence. In one instance an angry mob surged about the governor's house in Minnesota until he signed a bill he did not wish to approve. In another, after threats of violence, Governor Sidney Edgerton decided to leave Montana "to see his daughter in Ohio." He had vetoed a reapportionment bill which the legislature stubbornly refused to change, thereby making it impossible for the legislature to reconvene without a special act of Congress. The legislature was glad to be rid of him and he never returned from Ohio. Governor Caleb Lyon of Idaho found that the minority party could also mobilize opposition and that the veto was double-edged. He narrowly escaped the wrath of a mob as he was slipping out of the territory after he *refused* to veto a bill as demanded by a minority of the legislature.[38]

36. See Bond, *Old Northwest,* 93–94, and Pease, *Laws of the Northwest,* A447, A512–13. The legislature authorized the territorial auditor to issue certificates of indebtedness before passing the tax laws and made appropriations totalling around $50,000 before ending the session (Pease, *Laws of the Northwest,* A384, A386–87, A446–47, A496–97, A512–13). Beginning with the Oregon Act, Congress forbade the legislature to pledge the people for loans or to issue certificates of indebtedness, and in 1886 Congress limited the total territorial indebtedness to one percent of the assessed values of taxable property—without notable effects. (See Farrand, *Legislation for Territories,* 42–43, 48–49.)

37. Farrand, *Legislation for Territories,* 45–46; Valentine, "Territorial Governor," 53, 115–16; Pomeroy, *Territories, 1861–1890,* 40, 46–50; Neil, "Territorial Governors," 20–23.

38. Neil, "Territorial Governors," 100–40, especially 115, 124–25; Valentine, "Territorial Governor," 112.

Altogether it is difficult to judge how frequently governors used vetoes or what influence their use and the existence of the veto power exerted on legislation. The number and distribution of known vetoes suggests that the use of the power in the territories was neither as significant nor as widespread as the anguished outcries of the people indicated. The average territorial governor probably used the veto less than the average state governor in any given time period and territorial governors in the Second Empire used the power significantly less often than those in the First. As governors became more conservative in the exercise of the veto power, they tended to change their reasons for using it. In the early territories governors more characteristically vetoed laws as impractical, unwise, or unbeneficial whereas in the Second Empire they more commonly vetoed laws for being in conflict with higher authority. As the century progressed, governors increasingly vetoed laws on sounder legal grounds largely because Congress broadened the constitutional basis for vetoes. Simultaneously, governors forsook efforts to prevent improper legislation, a responsibility Congress tended to assume. However, because of the enlarged categories of Congressional restrictions, the changing reasons for the use of vetoes may have been more apparent than real. In any case the declining use of the veto must reflect the weakening of the governor's office in general and limitation of the veto power in particular.[39]

39. I have relied heavily on Meyerholz's discussion ("Federal Supervision," 179–94), which is obviously in error. In some cases he apparently dealt only with sustained vetoes, since his total for New Mexico to 1902 is 77, whereas Valentine ("Territorial Governor," 111) found more than that during the session of 1888–1889, all of which were overridden. Similarly, Meyerholz apparently did not include figures for Dakota, Idaho, Montana, Nevada, Oklahoma, Utah, Washington, Wyoming, and Wisconsin in his calculations. The following discussion attempts to gauge all vetoes, whether sustained or not, by extrapolation from Meyerholz's data, based on the use of a number of other sources, such as Valentine, "Territorial Governor," 108–11; Neil, "Territorial Governors," 100–37; Philbrick, *Laws of Indiana,* R29–30; Philbrick, *Laws of Illinois,* R452–54; Carter, *Territorial Papers,* V:529:30; XXI:438n, and *passim.* As in Meyerholz, the following discussion does not go beyond 1902—which coincides closely enough with the end of the Second Empire—both because his data cannot be reduced to a point in the 1890s and because there is no real value in trying to carry the analysis to 1912. By the beginning of the twentieth century the three remaining territories were states in suspension and the veto power took on a meaning no different from that in the states.

Average figures, of course, conceal the wide range of frequency with which different governors used the veto. There were lengthy periods in many territories when governors did not use the veto and the governors of the Southwest Territory and Missouri, at least, never used it. During periods when there was no governor or when the governor was absent—periods sometimes lasting as long as several years—the secretaries, as acting governors, seem never to have used the veto, probably because the inherent weakness of their position made its use inadvisable. In sharp contrast, some governors vetoed nearly every bill, but they seldom stayed in office long if they persisted in doing so. Typical governors, like Ninian Edwards of Illinois, vetoed acts infrequently and then with reluctance.[40]

In the thirteen territories of the First Empire, governors probably vetoed between 250 and 320 unicameral or bicameral legislative acts. The territories existed for a cumulative total of 127 years, under unicameral or bicameral governments, so governors vetoed an average of two and a quarter laws annually. However, between 1832 and 1845, Florida governors vetoed 121 bills, which account for 38 to 48 percent of the total number. By excluding these 121 vetoes and that period of thirteen years as exceptional, the annual number of vetoes drops to an average of fewer than one and a half. Considering that there were no vetoes in the Southwest and Missouri, it seems reasonable to assume that, exclusive of the district stage, the average governor who used the power vetoed no more than two laws annually during the First Empire.[41]

40. See Meyerholz, "Federal Supervision," 189; Philbrick, *Laws of Indiana*, R29–30; Philbrick, *Laws of Illinois*, R452–53; John Bakeless, *Lewis and Clark, Partners in Discovery* (New York, 1947), 440; and notes 41 and 42 below.

41. Meyerholz ("Federal Supervision," 192) indicates that the Michigan average for 1827–1836 was three vetoes a year. The number of vetoes is based partly on Meyerholz's figures, but it is not clear whether he included the 121 Florida vetoes in his calculations. Nor is it clear whether the 121 were only sustained vetoes or included vetoes that were overridden. It seems likely, however, that that figure includes both kinds. (See Farrand, *Legislation for Territories*, 41.) The distribution of reasons for the 121 vetoes, as stated in Meyerholz ("Federal Supervision," 190–91) is probably representative of other territories before 1848, even if the quantity is atypical. The governors vetoed sixty-one acts as impractical, ten for defects, eight for conflict with acts of Congress, five for violation of existing territorial laws left unrepealed by the bills, four for conflict with the Constitu-

From 1848 to 1902, that is, throughout the Second Empire and during the early aftermath, a total of about 344 years of second-stage government in fifteen territories, governors must have vetoed between 600 and 700 acts. This works out to an annual average of about two vetoes a year, as in the First Empire. However, it seems that the legislatures of the Second Empire overrode vetoes far more frequently than did those few of the First that had the power to do so. As many as half the vetoes of the Second Empire may have been overturned, which results in an average of about one sustained veto per governor each year. Thus, though the figures used are crude estimates, it seems justified to conclude that while the average annual number of vetoes was the same in each empire, the effect of the veto was twice as great in the First.[42]

---

tion, three for being contrary to provisions of the Organic Act and the remaining thirty primarily as unwise, unnecessary, or unfair legislation. If the last thirty vetoes are assumed to fall in the same general category as the sixty-one, about 75 percent of the total number of vetoes was for unfit legislation for nonlegal reasons; excluding the thirty, it was 50 percent. In a sample study of the veto in states between 1945 and 1947, F. W. Prescott ("The Executive Veto in American States," *Western Political Quarterly* [March, 1950], 109, hereafter cited as Prescott, "Executive Veto") placed 67 percent of the vetoes in similar nonlegal categories, and 69 percent if the miscellaneous vetoes are included. He also listed 17 percent of the vetoes for defective drafting, confused wording or incomplete drafting, 8 percent for conflict with or duplication of existing laws and 6 percent as unconstitutional acts. Comparable percentages, respectively, for the above Florida vetoes in these three categories are 8 percent, 4 percent, and 12 percent.

42. The estimates were arrived at by manipulating Meyerholz's figures ("Federal Supervision," 191–92). His total of 296 vetoes was increased to take account of overturned vetoes that he clearly omitted and doubled to account for territories he did not include in his calculations, nearly all of which had a limited veto that was frequently overturned. The extreme case of New Mexico's 1888–1889 vetoes already cited is apparently unparalleled, but it lends support, as do other occurrences of legislative retaliation to vetoes, to the suggestion that probably half or more of all vetoes were overridden in the period after 1848. Meyerholz's categorization (*ibid.*, 193–94) of vetoes in this period is very incomplete, but the data clearly suggest the increasing use of Constitutional grounds for vetoes. Fifty-seven percent of Iowa vetoes, 74 percent of the Kansas vetoes, 46 percent of the Nebraska vetoes, 40 percent of the Colorado vetoes, 36 percent of the Minnesota vetoes, 61 percent of the New Mexico vetoes, and 39 percent of the Arizona vetoes were based on the argument that the bills conflicted with higher authority. These are percentages of a total of 182 laws vetoed. Presumably, all of them were sustained, and this raises the question of the reliability of the

Yet the apparent halving of the average annual number of definitive vetoes in the Second Empire reflects only a small part of the real decline in the use of the power. The disproportion between the use of the power in the two empires would be much greater if the numbers could be expressed in terms of the number of bills passed annually by the legislatures, for it is clear that the yearly volume of business increased both as individual territories developed and as the nineteenth century progressed. The only new contiguous territory in the last quarter of the century was Oklahoma. Moreover, the substantial decline in annual vetoes in the Second Empire runs counter to the trend toward the more frequent use of the power by state governors in the second half of the nineteenth century. In the twentieth century, when it "came into its heyday," state governors evidently used vetoes with even greater regularity. In 1915, governors of 39 states vetoed 1,066 measures, an average of 27 each. In 1923, 44 governors averaged 25 vetoes apiece, and in 1937 and 1945, 47 vetoed an average of 31 and 28 respectively. During this period the volume of legislation increased to the extent that the percentage of acts vetoed declined from seven in 1915 to five in 1949. Although these data for the first half of the twentieth century are highly inadequate for comparison, it may be assumed that they represent a continuing trend from the nineteenth century. As such, they and the other data strongly suggest that relative to the total volume of bills the veto power could not have played a very significant part in territorial legislation, and certainly did not warrant the criticism its use occasioned.[43]

---

percentages. Legislatures were far more reluctant to override vetoes based on Constitutional arguments and it is probably safe to assume that relatively few vetoes of this sort were overturned. If the vetos overturned did not involve Constitutional issues, the percentages above must be halved to reflect accurately the changing use of vetoes in order to compare them with the Florida figures in the preceding note.

Meyerholz's figures for the Second Empire suggest that, as in the territories of the First Empire, there was an average annual range of from one to three vetoes when exceptional territories are omitted. The principal exception during the Second Empire was Kansas, which saw 62 laws vetoed in seven years—an average of nine vetoes a year, as compared to the Florida average of 10.7 between 1832 and 1845.

43. The data for state vetoes are in Prescott, "Executive Veto," 98–112. Prescott concluded that between half and three-quarters of all vetoes up to 1950

As the governors' veto power and its significance declined, Congress and the courts took more direct action, but this does not mean that they took up more than a part of the increasing slackness of federal controls, much less that they brought about a higher degree of efficiency or centralization in the administration of the territories during the nineteenth century. Before the organization of Florida in 1822, when it began limiting the veto, Congress apparently did not nullify any second-stage laws. During the next eighty years, on the other hand, it enacted 35 or more laws which nullified an indeterminate number of territorial statutes. Most Congressional nullification acts were adopted during the Second Empire, and Florida accounted for a majority of the few laws disallowed in the First. Quite possibly, the total number of territorial laws affected directly and indirectly by the Congressional acts approximated the number vetoed by governors during the Second Empire.[44] With few exceptions, however, the machinery of federal nullification worked slowly. Moreover, it was irresolute, and many territorial laws escaped nullification altogether or remained in force for considerable lengths of time before they were disallowed.[45]

Congress nullified few laws during the First Empire, and then it generally did so because it found them to be in conflict with federal laws or considered them to be impractical or undesirable. Most prom-

---

had occurred since the beginning of the twentieth century. This unsupported statement should be viewed with some suspicion. Presumably, he counted only state governors' vetoes [since Independence?]. With the number of states and the volume of state legislation increasing throughout the nineteenth century, it is not surprising that, in absolute numbers, more vetoes should be found in the more recent period, but Prescott's claims seem exaggerated.

44. See Meyerholz, "Federal Supervision," 170–74.

45. Pomeroy, *Territories, 1861–1890*, 99–100; Philbrick, *Laws of Illinois*, R455. There was no time limit within which Congress had to nullify laws, and all laws were assumed to be valid until they were disapproved. Apparently only James Duane Doty of Wisconsin contended that every law required validation from Congress before it could be enforced. This was not feasible, of course, but Doty used the argument as an excuse for ignoring laws of which he did not approve. Doty did not get on well with the legislature and was charged with usurping legislative powers after he denied the legislature's powers over appointments and its right to convene without his express permission. (See McCarty, *Governors of the Northwest*, 152–53; Alice E. Smith, *James Duane Doty, Frontier Promoter* [Madison, Wisc., 1954], 256–97.)

inent among the last were bank chartering acts. Congress forbade in all territories the enactment of laws chartering banks after disallowing a Florida banking act, but legislatures tended to ignore the prohibition. After discovering two Wisconsin acts chartering banks in 1837, for example, Congress invalidated them with a act of its own. Congress also invalidated the laws of three territories that were designed to borrow money on public credit, and in 1828 voided an Arkansas statute which sought to add a judge to the territorial Supreme Court in contravention of the Organic Act.[46]

During the Second Empire, Congress nullified relatively more laws for being in conflict with higher authority or having technical defects, but impractical and undesirable laws continued to account for a significant number. The most striking example of the imposition of moral sanctions by Congress was the campaign against the Mormons, which came to a head in 1887 when Congress nullified the Utah laws regarding polygamy and the Mormon Church corporation. More characteristic was the disallowance of at least nine laws for imposing unjust taxes and the eight Congressional acts nullifying territorial laws that repealed acts that Congress considered desirable. Congress also nullified at least four laws granting special privileges that were contrary to the Organic Acts and other laws of Congress, and two New Mexico laws dealing with slavery. Finally, it voided several statutes that attempted to add appointive territorial officers not provided for in the Organic Acts, whose salaries were to be paid out of the federal treasury, and several others making existing offices elective that were appointive by provisions of the Organic Acts.[47]

46. Meyerholz, "Federal Supervision," 171–72, 190; Farrand, *Legislation for Territories*, 41; Philbrick, *Laws of Illinois*, R445. Borrowing money on public credit presented a peculiar problem in the territories, since they were not sovereign and any pledge became a federal responsibility. Thus, when a territory pledged its credit, it assumed a power of Congress. Smurr ("Constitutions," 685) says that the courts never considered the problem, but Congress clearly took it to heart.

47. Farrand, *Legislation for Territories*, 49–50; Meyerholz, "Federal Supervision," 172. Meyerholz (*ibid.*, 170n) concludes that Congress gave up its right to review and annul the territorial legislation of Colorado, Dakota, Idaho, Montana, and Washington in the *Revised Statutes of the United States* of 1874. This could hardly have been the case, though neither Meyerholz nor Neil ("Territorial Governors") cites any Congressional nullifications in those territories after 1874.

Perhaps the most common impetus behind Congressional action in the Second Empire came from the desire, if not the need, to invalidate laws that governors had not been able to keep from being passed and those enacted during illegal legislative sessions. When Congress nullified acts passed over a governor's veto, in effect it sustained the governor's decision. Congress disallowed such acts often enough to suggest that this was its purpose, but the correlation is a loose one at best. By far the largest number of territorial laws nullified were those adopted in unauthorized legislative sessions. In 1842 Congress declared that territorial legislatures could not convene until Congress appropriated funds. The new policy presented no problem insofar as Congress routinely provided money for the regular sessions, but the law also prohibited extraordinary sessions unless special appropriations were made or money was left over from the regular appropriation for the year or biennium. This made it practically impossible to hold special legislative sessions.

In 1874 Congress helped overcome the difficulties of calling extraordinary sessions in emergencies, especially when Congress was in adjournment, by empowering the President to authorize them. This eliminated Congressional nullifications arising from one kind of illegal session, since the Presidents habitually approved extra sessions. In the meantime, legislatures of at least two territories—Montana and Colorado—met without appropriations. The Montana legislators did not get paid. The governor had doubted the legality of the session but it was the federal government that ordered the territorial secretary not to issue pay and expense vouchers to legislators. Consequently, the session was in vain. In Colorado, the legislature determined to hold an extra session despite warnings from the judiciary and the Treasury Department that it would be unlawful and its members could not be paid. Fortunately, the United States Attorney General decided that circumstances warranted the session and it was authorized. When the first Montana legislature failed to apportion itself before its term expired, as required by the Organic Act, the governor first declared that a special act of Congress would be needed to permit the election of a new General Assembly, but he soon reversed his stand. The legislature subsequently held three sessions, using the governor's apportionment, without enacting an apportionment law of its own. Finally, Congress acted. It nullified the laws of all three sessions, directed the governor to make a new apportionment and call new elections, and again ordered the legislature to reapportion itself when it convened.[48]

Congress did not always play a negative role when it acted on territorial laws. Defective legislation was common, especially in the territories of the First Empire, and during the early years in later territories. Congress or the governors annulled some of these laws but most of them passed by unnoticed, to be repealed or nullified by the courts, usually after the territory became a state. After the Civil War, however, Congress began validating acts which would otherwise be illegal and which could not be sustained in court. For example, after the courts declared null and void all laws of the third, fourth, and fifth Arizona legislatures because the legislatures had not been apportioned in accordance with provisions of the Organic Act, Congress passed a special act validating the laws in order to prevent chaos. Similarly, in 1884 Congress perfected ten Washington laws to make them enforceable. These acts lacked the governor's approval and dates of enactment, and other irregularities that had commonly been ignored in laws of the Old Northwest.[49]

Most of the time there was difficulty in bringing problems involving territorial legislation to the attention of Congress, and at times the executive branch of the federal government handled these problems. Presidents, either personally or through one of their department heads, occasionally let governors and legislatures know that they considered some kinds of laws undesirable and that, if such laws were enacted, they would ask Congress to abrogate them. In this way, they could sometimes stop legislatures from overriding governors' vetoes or even from passing bills in the first place.[50]

A sizable majority of all laws contrary to higher authority seem to have escaped detection and nullification by the governors or Congress. A number of them, however, eventually made their way through the

48. Neil, "Territorial Governors," 49, 107; Valentine, "Territorial Governor," 96, 105, 110–11; Pomeroy, *Territories, 1861–1890,* 26; Farrand, *Legislation for Territories,* 41–42, 47; Meyerholz, "Federal Supervision," 192–93.

49. Meyerholz, "Federal Supervision," 174–75; Valentine, "Territorial Governor," 96.

50. Meyerholz, "Federal Supervision," 182; Neil, "Territorial Governors," 119–20, 130.

judiciary during the Second Empire, and the courts specifically struck down at least 34 laws between 1850 and 1902. This is an extremely small fraction of territorial laws, and though the decisions assuredly affected a number of other laws, it is impossible to determine either how many were affected or how much attention the government of one territory paid to rulings on the laws of other territories that were also applicable to its own.

The United States Supreme Court, to which only cases involving questions of law could be appealed, invalidated only six territorial statutes. Territorial Supreme Courts nullified the remaining 28 laws. The courts held 17 of the 34 laws to be in conflict with provisions of Organic Acts and ten to violate acts of Congress. They invalidated four more as being contrary to the federal Constitution and the other three for miscellaneous reasons. Most of the court decisions came late in the life of a territory, or after its territorial period was well advanced, and some occurred after statehood. In 1850, for example, the courts declared null and void an 1839 Iowa law for violating the Seventh Amendment of the United States Constitution. The act had denied the right to jury trial in certain kinds of litigation. Similarly, courts invalidated at least four laws in as many territories that provided for less than unanimity in jury trial verdicts involving common law cases. Six laws—three of Utah's, two of Idaho's and one of Montana's—were struck down for creating territorial offices or making them elective contrary to provisions of the Organic Acts. In the Montana law, the legislature made elective the offices of territorial auditor and treasurer who, according to the Organic Act, were to be appointed by the governor with the consent of the council. In 1869 Governor James M. Ashley brought suit in the territorial court, lost, and appealed to the United States Supreme Court. The Supreme Court at first refused to hear the case and the elected officers served their terms. Later the Court changed its mind, took up the case, and ruled in favor of the governor. In 1885 the Idaho Territory Supreme Court nullified a divorce act as unfit legislation. In another instance the Supreme Court, using ingenious reasoning, declared a female suffrage law contrary to the Organic Act; it argued in essence that it was the responsibility of Congress to pass the appropriate law if women were to have the vote.[51]

51. Meyerholz ("Federal Supervision," 233–42) says that the range of cases

Since the governors effectively lost their most vital statutory prerogatives early in the nineteenth century, the federal government began to step in, but as a whole it was only partially successful in filling the void of federal control over territorial governments. In the absence of strong federal supervision, and in the presence of an increasing federal desire to have no friction in its colonies or trouble from them, the governors were compelled to reach an accommodation with the legislatures by which, in imitation of the states, territorial governments achieved home rule. The territories, nevertheless, were at best states in suspension, without full autonomy and voting representation in Congress. The other basic difference between territorial and state governments in the late First Empire and throughout the Second was that the territorial governors were appointed, often from outside the territories, and were subject to removal at any time. As such, they lacked strong support within their territories. That the governors fully appreciated the fundamental weakness of their situation is indicated by the infrequent and circumspect use of their statutory powers. In light of the number and kinds of laws vetoed, and the apparent reasons for vetoing them, for example, one is led to the conclusion that with few exceptions, the governors were cautious and legally correct. The use of the veto does not show governors to have been petty or vindictive. Nor does the evidence suggest that they used the veto for political purposes on other than rare occasions. Essentially the same generalizations can be made with respect to the actions of the federal government. There was neither a desire nor an effort on the part of the federal government to assert its power to make its colonies subservient, outside of Utah and a few isolated episodes elsewhere. On the contrary, the federal government in effect encouraged autonomy in the continental colonies.

---

illustrates that the courts normally followed a strict construction of the Organic Acts and the laws of Congress: "In but a few cases if any, [have] the territorial courts shown any tendency to uphold the territorial legislatures against the authority of Congress as represented in the Organic Acts or in other laws passed for the territories." Smurr ("Constitutions," 873) notes that despite vigorous debates over Wyoming's female suffrage law of 1869, it was never tested in the courts. See also Valentine, "Territorial Governor," 106–08.

VII

Second-Stage Accommodation and Statehood

THERE were many sources and manifestations of executive-legislative accommodation during the second stage of government in the territories, ranging from extremes of collusion to studied correctitude that bordered on complete mutual disregard. Many governors tried to develop a political following and some succeeded, but as officials with an uncertain tenure in areas in flux, they generally encountered difficulty in cultivating a stable base of power equivalent to that of state governors, who were usually leaders in their party. Always the potential victims of movements to obtain their removal whenever they aroused the antagonism of a significant body of inhabitants, territorial governors had to be more discreet, subtle, and adroit than state governors in order to stay in office. In short, governors discovered that the surest way to succeed was to work harmoniously with the legislatures, while trying to lead or nudge them along paths compatible with federal policies. It was never easy to do both; consequently, even though they were often adept politicians and strong executives, by the end of the First Empire territorial governors tended to serve as administrators, primarily carrying out territorial rather than federal policies, or equivalent to weak state governors, and this seems more and more to have been what the federal government desired.

As federal representatives, or intelligence officers for the federal government, territorial governors were not capable of executing federal policies on their own, as is illustrated by the conduct of Indian relations. Despite the inherent weakness of their position, however, they were often successful as territorial officials. Though they were anything but universally effective, the second-stage governors were, as a whole, sincerely interested in the future of their territories. They made considerable efforts, frequently promoting ideas and policies that ran counter to the whims of the legislatures, to convince them to enact and to help enforce legislation that would further territorial development.

The governors' caution in the exercise of their statutory powers during the second stage resulted from the extreme resentment that the use of even the least objectionable power was liable to arouse. Occasionally there were popular outcries following the governors' apportionment of the first General Assembly. When this occurred in Wisconsin, the legislature sided with Governor Dodge and ruled that his apportionment was as equitable as possible, but in other territories the governors were not always treated so charitably. In the post-Civil War period, governors were at times subjected to strong criticism for pardoning or reprieving persons convicted of crimes, and in Idaho and Montana, at least, vigilantes mobilized to wreak vengeance on such individuals. In some cases they hanged released prisoners and in others, fearing that the prisoners might escape, they forcibly removed them from jails to make sure there would be a hanging. Nevertheless, even in Montana, the governors pardoned a substantial number of persons on the petition of a judge and a few leading citizens, but undoubtedly because of the threat of violence, they normally required the prisoners to pledge to leave the territory immediately and never return.[1]

1. The Wisconsin apportionment controversy involved Crawford County, to which the governor did not give a seat on the thirteen-man council because it did not have one-thirteenth of the population. As compensation, however, Dodge gave the county two house seats even though its population did not warrant them. (McCarty, *Governors of the Northwest*, 146–47.) In Indiana and Kansas, the first General Assembly unseated members certified by the governor in favor of their opponents. (Valentine, "Territorial Governor," 95.)

The State Department Territorial Papers, Montana, 1864–1872 (Washington, National Archives Microcopy 356, 1961), Roll 1 (Official Correspondence), and Interior Department Territorial Papers, Montana, 1867–1889 (Washington, National Archives Microcopy 192, 1956), Roll 1 (Executive Proceedings), con-

Less innocuous causes of conflict between governors and the citizens or the legislatures were the manipulation of elections and patronage. These issues were also more dangerous politically since they were likely to embroil governors in heated inter- and intraparty contests that could be risky for their prestige or tenure. Partly for this reason, Presidents normally expected governors to be nonpartisan in most territorial affairs, and governors avoided involvement in territorial controversies which, as President Adams warned St. Clair in the 1790s, would occupy all of their time. Nevertheless, in the first territories and thereafter, governors at various times plied their talents to bring about the election of legislators or territorial delegates who would be sympathetic to their point of view; not infrequently friends, relatives, and other office-seekers followed new governors to a territory, hoping to benefit from their patronage. Patronage figured prominently among charges leveled against unpopular governors in the territories west of the Mississippi River, in spite of the fact that by the time they were organized, the governors had lost most of their appointive powers. Occasionally, governors tried to control both elections and appointments by withholding commissions to office. In the former cases they were, in effect, assuming appointive powers they

---

tain lists and copies of pardons. The vigilante activities are discussed in Neil, "Territorial Governors," 55–58. The Ordinance of 1787 did not specifically empower the governor to pardon, reprieve, or extradite persons, but the governors assumed the powers from the beginning, in imitation of state governors. The Northwest judges expressed the opinion that St. Clair had these powers, and St. Clair, Blount, and Sargent used them in the Northwest, the Southwest, and Mississippi before 1800. In the Orleans-Louisiana Act of 1804 Congress expressly provided the governor with the power to pardon offenses against territorial law and to use reprieves for federal offenses until the President's will was known. Thereafter, Congress included the two powers in all Organic Acts except that of Michigan, which simply renewed the Northwest Ordinance. Congress never enumerated extradition among the governors' powers. (Carter, *Territorial Papers*, IX:203. Compare the executive article of the Organic Acts, which is usually the first or second, but see especially the Oklahoma Act of 1890 in Thorpe, *Constitutions*, 2939–40.) The question of the right of governors in the Old Northwest to grant pardons and reprieves to criminals and to extradite suspects was not settled until 1809. In that year Governor Hull of Michigan hesitated to use them. He asked for an official interpretation, and the United States Attorney General agreed that they were among the governor's powers. (Valentine, "Territorial Governor," 68–70, 90; Farrand, *Legislation for Territories*, 21–22, 36; Philbrick, *Laws of Illinois*, R463–64.)

did not have. In a few instances, governors also attempted to appoint people to vacant elective offices. Most audacious and unwise was Governor Robert Mitchell's appointment of a territorial delegate in New Mexico shortly after the Civil War.[2]

Before the 1820s, the restrictive suffrage and officeholding requirements may have made for more conservative and tractable legislatures than after that date. Similarly, well-chosen appointments to local offices could be used in early territories, for example by Blount in the Southwest, in cementing alliances with political factions either to bring the legislature under executive control or to narrow the range of conflict between the executive and the legislature. Nonetheless, even before the 1820s the governors' powers and patronage were severely limited in practice once the second stage began, and were exceeded both by those of the General Assembly and by those of the delegate. The delegate became the territory's spokesman in Congress and the principal dispenser of federal patronage, while the legislature took over the power to create counties and local offices, all of which had been sources of potentially enormous patronage and power to governors during the district stage. Equally important, legislatures nearly always went to the limits of the Organic Acts by making offices elective whenever they could, and during the second half of the First Empire, as Congress expanded their authority to do so, they made virtually every local office elective. By the late 1820s all the Congressional changes had the effect of reversing the power relationships between governor and legislature that were evident in the Ordinance

2. Valentine, "Territorial Governor," 120–21; G. L. Wilson, "St. Clair," 119, 368. See also Chapter IX. When petitioning the President to remove Governor Robert Lucas, the Iowa General Assembly charged that the governor had appointed to office intimates from the states over local candidates. (Valentine, "Territorial Governor," 133–35.) Valentine (*ibid.*, 74–76) also cites attempts of governors to appoint executive secretaries and clerks, not provided for in law, to be paid out of the federal treasury. These attempts always miscarried, since the Treasury Department uniformly denied their validity and never honored the salary drafts. The ease with which well-placed bribes could sometimes affect the election of a territorial delegate is illustrated by a case in Indiana (Carter, *Territorial Papers*, VII:335), but the election of the first delegate from the Northwest Territory is a classic, if unsuccessful, example of executive manipulation. In that election St. Clair bent his every effort to obtain the job for his son. (See Bond, *Old Northwest*, 92.)

of 1787. Instead of the legislature coming under the absolute control of the governor, the governor was more likely to be controlled by the legislature. Aside from the expansion of legislative powers, given the combination of an uncertain tenure and weak federal support, it is not surprising that, with rare exceptions, the governors scrupulously observed and stayed within the statutory limits of their powers. The result was that harmony and cooperation rather than conflict far more commonly characterized executive-legislative relations.[3]

Though Congress and the legislatures removed the power to appoint local officials, the governors were not left entirely without patronage. The Organic Acts of the last part of the First Empire and throughout the Second normally required that all general territorial officials not appointed by the President be appointed by the governor with the consent of the legislative council. Any territorial officer, for example the Commissioner of Education, not enumerated in the Organic Act, was to be paid out of territorial taxes. Consequently the number of additional territorial offices created in a territory depended on the willingness of the governor and legislature to impose taxes, the strength of the tax base, and the ability of the territorial government to collect taxes—assuming, of course, that the officeholders were to be paid regularly, if at all. In the early territories there were few such territorial offices, but the number increased rapidly after the Civil War. Nevertheless, the 112 territorial officials appointed by the governor and legislative council in Dakota Territory by 1880 is probably well above the average number for other territories.[4]

3. Compare McCarty, *Governors of the Northwest*, 78, 82, 91, 150–54; Philbrick, *Laws of Indiana*, R30–31; Masterson, *Blount*, 264–66; Valentine, "Territorial Governor," 74–76, 96–98, 112–13; Neil, "Territorial Governors," 84, 129–32, 136. Neil (*ibid*., 84) says, nevertheless, that Secretary Thomas Meagher, as acting governor of Montana in 1865–1866, was called a dictator because he so effectively created his own legislature and ran it absolutely.

Only Arthur St. Clair tried to create counties at the beginning of second-stage government, but he dropped his claim following a reprimand from President Adams and no subsequent governor attempted to revive it. Thus, a second-stage governor could do no more than recommend the creation of new counties to legislatures and veto county-creation bills. (See Philbrick, *Laws of Illinois*, R475–76.)

4. Valentine, "Territorial Governor," 73–74. Lamar (*Dakota Territory*) has scattered references to executive patronage in different political contexts, but compare especially his conclusions on pages 40, 122, 146.

Generally, the amount of appointive patronage a governor controlled or influenced depended on the number of territorial offices the legislature created and the degree of harmony existing between the governor and legislature. In some cases, however, neither harmonious relations nor the fact that the governor and a majority of the legislature belonged to the same party produced much real executive patronage. Under Governor William Jenkins of Oklahoma, the party chose the governor's appointees and, given the nature of territorial politics, this practice must have been widespread. In more specific terms, then, the governors controlled appointments only insofar as they selected the nominees approved by the legislative councils. Sometimes they used bribes to obtain approval of their candidates. In New Mexico it was common for governors to offer councillors future appointments in return for confirmation of current nominees. In addition, governors occasionally took advantage of the power to make recess appointments to install candidates with the hope that, once the appointees were in office, the council would be less likely to deny confirmation.[5]

Not infrequently in the post-Civil War period, both governors and legislatures were either controlled by or heavily involved in business interests.This was apparently more common in undeveloped territories lacking diversified economies, but even in those areas the range of harmonious relations between governors and legislatures covered the entire spectrum. Thomas Bennett, who was governor of Idaho from 1871 to 1875, represented one extreme. A jovial Hoosier, "far more interested in horseplay and local politicking than anything else," it was claimed that "in three days he knew everyone in Boise and in three weeks was equally well acquainted with everyone in southern Idaho." He showed a monumental disinterest in legislation and established a blissful relationship with the legislature by letting it do whatever it pleased.[6]

At the opposite end of the spectrum was the high incidence of executive-legislative connivance in some territories during the 1860s

5. Valentine, "Territorial Governor," 74–76.

6. The quotations are from Neil, "Territorial Governors," 129–30. See also *ibid.*, 130–32, 136 and *passim;* Lamar, *Far Southwest*, 132–33, 162 and *passim;* Pomeroy, *Territories, 1861–1890*, 70; Valentine, "Territorial Governor," 96–98, 112.

and 1870s. These joint ventures in corruption, which took maximum advantage of the remoteness of the territories, the poor communications, and lax federal supervision, primarily involved chartering and speculating in improvement companies. In the mid-1860s, for example, Governor Newton Edmunds and the Dakota General Assembly chartered a railroad company. He and every member of the legislature were incorporators and Edmunds was its president. Congress forbade this sort of private chartering in a law of 1867 and supplementary legislation during succeeding years, without stopping speculation. In some cases federal laws simply brought about a change in tactics. In 1872, Governor John Burbank of Dakota helped obtain a Congressional charter for a railroad of which he was the president and an incorporator. Coincidentally, during the same year he was elected to the board of directors of another railroad, after having helped to secure federal approval for the extension of its terminus to Springfield, where he had large interests.[7]

Governors and legislators always agreed that their salaries were inadequate, and during periods of harmony, legislatures often appropriated territorial funds to provide extra compensation both for themselves and for the governors. By the time Congress outlawed the practice, it was one of the largest items in territorial budgets and a primary cause of the heavy indebtedness of some territories. The Montana debt of $104,000, incurred between 1865 and 1871, could be attributed entirely to the appropriation of extra compensations since they totalled $175,000 during the same period.[8]

Territorial indebtedness was not simply a product of the legislatures' increasing the number of territorial officeholders to unseemly limits and voting themselves and the governors additional salaries. It also resulted from poor tax legislation and enforcement. During the early years in most territories, debts increased rapidly because the tax bases were insufficient to support expenditures, but even as their economies developed, tax laws and especially collections tended to lag badly be-

7. Valentine, "Territorial Governor," 114–15; Lamar, *Dakota Territory*, 101–02, 132–34.

8. Pomeroy, *Territories, 1861–1890*, 40, 46–50; Valentine, "Territorial Governor," 53, 115–16; Farrand, *Legislation for Territories*, 45–46; Meyerholz, "Federal Supervision," 173; Neil, "Territorial Governors," 21.

hind the demands of appropriations. The reasons are not hard to find. Legislatures usually undervalued or otherwise improperly taxed livestock and land, the chief sources of revenue, while the citizens evaded or refused to pay their taxes, and there was little the governors could do about either problem. Although a few governors, like Blount of the Southwest, actively opposed equitable taxation, most showed a genuine concern and did what they could to remedy the problems. Many governors apparently did not vigorously press the matter, even if they constantly harped on the need for tax reform and enforcement, perhaps because they too often had their hands full trying to thwart regressive legislation in other areas. Nevertheless, under the prodding of numerous executives, such as Harrison of Indiana, legislatures continually rewrote tax laws. Frequently, if not generally, when they did not ignore governors' recommendations, legislatures responded slowly and half-heartedly. Thus the Union Pacific Railroad lands in Wyoming were not "properly" taxed before 1886. Moreover, when legislatures did enact more equitable tax laws they were not notably well enforced.[9]

By mid-century, most governors were intensely interested in education, but before the Civil War, legislatures usually made provisions for its advancement without much encouragement from the executive. This was especially true of the first territories, where the governors sometimes exhorted the legislatures to take the necessary action to secure and safeguard Congressional land grants but advocated little else. That St. Clair, Blount, Sargent, Harrison, and Edwards were reasonably satisfied or unconcerned with the rate of progress is suggested by the lack of references to education in their messages and correspondence.

St. Clair, for one, showed strikingly little concern for education in the face of the all-too-obvious inadequacy of schools in some areas of the territory, and their total absence in outlying portions of the Northwest. Though a number of petitions during his administration highlighted these shortcomings, St. Clair simply stated in his first address to

9. Compare, for example, Neil, "Territorial Governors," 9–17; Esarey, *Messages*, I:157–58, 229–31, 380–81; Benjamin Potts to Carl Schurz, November 16, 1878, in Interior Department Territorial Papers, Montana, 1867–1889 (Microcopy 192), Roll 2 (Miscellaneous correspondence); and Governor E. G. Ross of New Mexico, 1887, Report to the Secretary of the Interior, in *House Executive Documents*, 50 Cong., 1 sess. (S.N. 2541), 872.

the General Assembly, after more than a decade as governor, that the need to secure the Congressional school lands was self-evident. He then turned to John Symmes and his associates, who in 1794 had received a land grant from Congress for the establishment of a college, and dwelled at length on the need to force them to start organizing it. St. Clair's primary motive in developing this issue, it seems, was to embarrass or discredit his old enemy and, as he probably anticipated, the legislature took no action. Nevertheless, in succeeding messages, St. Clair continued to stress the necessity of making Symmes comply with the terms of the grant.[10]

At least one petition written while St. Clair was governor of the Northwest came from the vicinity of Detroit, an area devoid of educational facilities. Conditions there apparently did not improve significantly or attract much attention before December 1808, when Governor William Hull began using his office to promote the establishment of schools in Michigan. This may mark a turning point, for within the next decade, other governors began to evince an increasing interest in education. The executives of poorer and more slowly settled territories like Michigan and Florida were normally the most vocal campaigners for improvements. A number of governors, following Hull's example, developed educational programs and sought federal aid to supplement the regular land grants for schools.[11]

Toward the end of the First Empire and throughout the Second, executives emphasized the continuing need to improve and establish schools and to safeguard land grants for their support, but in the post-Civil War period governors in some territories also had to reckon with regressive legislators who wanted to economize by making cutbacks in education. This was done in Idaho at the end of the war in part by abolishing the office of Superintendent of Education. The legislature

10. Carter, *Territorial Papers,* III:26, 67, 105, 119, 197. St. Clair's messages and the replies of the legislature are in Smith, *St. Clair Papers,* II:446–62, 501–23, 534–42. Harrison's messages through 1809 are in Esarey, *Messages,* I:152–61, 199–200, 229–37, 304–10, 378–83. The messages of most governors are scattered and some are lost, but the Wisconsin State Historical Library has extensive holdings of the published messages.

11. Compare the governors' messages. There are scattered references to education throughout Carter, *Territorial Papers,* but see especially, X:249, 256; XIV: 176–81; XXIV:402–03, 957–58.

turned its duties over to the Comptroller, who received no salary as Superintendent, and for two decades or more, education in the territory languished from the combination of poor school legislation and inadequate enforcement. In the meantime, Idaho governors harped on the need to enact better laws and to reestablish a separate office of Superintendent of Education, while the governors in Montana and Wyoming, as late as 1881, were still resisting legislative efforts to abolish the office, as long as the territorial legislators were not disposed to enact favorable school laws and it was unlikely that governors could force them to do so. Faced with inadequate laws and legislative backsliding or inaction, frustrated executives of numerous territories not infrequently accused legislatures of deliberately denying children their birthright. They also claimed at times that the legislatures wanted to abolish education, but since schools barely existed in many areas, this was probably a slight exaggeration. School systems, which in practice almost always came under the exclusive control of local governments, differed greatly in quality. Nevertheless, in the early 1880s school terms were still short and the schools were not the superlative institutions suggested by the official reports of the decade. In many parts of Idaho and other territories, school terms lasted only a few weeks, facilities were primitive, and the salaries, and probably the quality and performance, of teachers were extremely low.[12]

Throughout territorial history governors generally took an active interest in other kinds of legislation and had some influence on the laws passed. They usually delivered a formal address to the legislature at the beginning of each session, and maintained a rather close working relationship throughout the session. At times they explained and defended

12. Neil, "Territorial Governors," 48–53; Lamar, *Far Southwest*, 167–69, 178, 187–89, 386, 459–60. In addition to the governors' messages, the annual reports to the Secretary of the Interior are sometimes revealing, even in the 1880s, by which time they had become primarily propaganda tracts describing every aspect of the territories in glowing terms. (See, for example, reports of governors to the Secretary of the Interior, from Montana, 1879, 1883, 1889, in *House Executive Documents*, 45 Cong., 2 sess. [S.N. 1850], 1108–09; *ibid.*, 48 Cong., 1 sess. [S.N. 2191], 547; *ibid.*, 51 Cong., 1 sess. [S.N. 2726], 443; from New Mexico, 1881, 1885, 1890, in *ibid.*, 47 Cong., 1 sess. [S.N. 2018], 1000; *ibid.*, 49 Cong., 1 sess. [S.N. 2379], 1012; *ibid.*, 51 Cong., 2 sess. [S.N. 2842], 619; from Utah, 1885, 1886, in *ibid.*, 49 Cong., 1 sess. [S.N. 2379], 1029; *ibid.*, 49 Cong., 2 sess. [S.N. 2468], 989–90.

their actions in the address or avoided making any commitments by dwelling on the "blessings of democracy," but as a rule they provided a detailed analysis of territorial conditions and outlined a program which frequently guided lawmaking during the session. In almost every address governors discussed Indians and the militia, taxation or debts, and election laws, and generally pointed to the need for court and local government reforms, in each case making recommendations for appropriate legislation.[13]

Governors normally considered Indian and militia problems jointly. Blount and Harrison, for example, tended to encourage punitive legislation designed to cow the Indians or force their removal. Harrison helped to whip up enthusiasm for his aggressive Indian policies by castigating the British at length for spoliating United States shipping and for stirring up Indian restlessness. But most governors followed St. Clair's example of urging conciliation and fairer treatment of Indians. A large majority of the governors continually called on legislatures to enact laws for the more effective restriction of the sale and distribution of liquor to Indians. They all sought to reduce friction, but their auxiliary objectives in controlling the flow of alcohol ran the gamut from St. Clair's emphasis on protecting Indians against unsavory manipulation and abuse by whites, on the one hand, to Harrison's primary interest in extending Anglo-American hegemony over the Indians on the other. Similarly, the motives for promoting militia reforms extended from St. Clair's concern with improving defenses to Harrison's and Blount's rather strong desire to take aggressive or punitive actions against Indians. Whatever the objectives, legislatures seem to have enacted new militia reform laws almost as often as governors recommended them, but throughout the nineteenth century the militia remained largely ineffective and generally unreliable.

While the constant revision of electoral and apportionment laws probably brought some improvements, progress in most other areas was more closely associated with social and economic development in the territories than with the frequent alteration of statute books. Immigration, leading to increased prosperity and a broader tax base, for instance, undoubtedly did at least as much to overcome chronic

13. Valentine, "Territorial Governor," 96–97.

debt problems as better tax legislation and its improved enforcement.[14]

If most second-stage laws proved to be inadequate or ineffective, it was not the result of the failure of governors and legislatures to cooperate in lawmaking. On the contrary, as a comparison of executive addresses and statutes indicates, legislatures followed governors' recommendations rather closely, and ordinarily allowed neither personal nor party differences to stand in the way of fundamental legislation. This is illustrated by the political history of the second stage in the Northwest, where St. Clair and the General Assembly, though in sharp disagreement on a number of other matters, could agree on broad legislative programs.[15]

The elections for the lower house of the first Northwest General Assembly were notably nonpartisan, and a similar relationship prevailed between the governor and legislature until St. Clair vetoed eleven acts at the end of the initial session. When the first General Assembly met in 1799, St. Clair delivered a conciliatory address containing a number of specific recommendations, most of which were written into law. The legislature passed laws to create the territorial offices of treasurer and auditor, to provide a salary for the territorial attorney general, to levy territorial taxes on land, and to open and regulate public roads. In addition, it adopted a law to prevent usury, which set maximum interest rates at six percent, and a debtor relief act. The latter limited imprisonment for debt to no more than one year and required complaining creditors to contribute twelve and a half cents a day toward the sustenance of destitute debtors who were jailed. Although this law was superficially remarkable, in that it seemed very progressive, its limiting of the length of imprisonment for debt

14. Compare the messages and laws. For the examples of St. Clair and Harrison used here, see Smith, *St. Clair Papers,* II:446–57, 501–10, 534–37; Esarey, *Messages,* I:152–59, 199–200, 229–36, 304–10, 378–83; Chase, *Statutes of Ohio,* I:211–350; Philbrick, *Laws of Indiana,* A91–674; and Louis B. Ewbank and Dorothy L. Riker, eds., *The Laws of Indiana Territory, 1809–1816* (Indianapolis, 1934), hereafter cited as Ewbank, *Laws.* See also Bond, *Foundations,* 465.

15. As one would guess, except for a few cases in Kansas, Utah, and elsewhere, a new governor's administration usually began peacefully, while he and the legislature felt each other out, and, depending on the degree of tension that developed and the nature of the personalities involved, when the two could not reach a working agreement, or the agreement broke down, the governor was forced out of office. (See Valentine, "Territorial Governor," 68–70; Smurr, "Constitutions," 713–14; Neil, "Territorial Governors," 131–32 and *passim.*)

in no way released the debtor from his obligations. In his opening message, St. Clair also indicated a readiness to see the executive prerogatives limited, particularly the appointive powers, and as it revised all the territory's district-stage laws according to his suggestion, the General Assembly restricted the governor's powers somewhat more than they had been previously.[16]

While the legislature was acting on the governor's recommendations, a major controversy was developing over the question of territorial division. Both St. Clair and the legislators were actively interested, and as soon as the General Assembly adjourned, battle lines began to form. Initially, St. Clair took a wholly negative position, opposing not only division but statehood as well. However, after he failed to draw Harrison into an alliance to prevent the first division by offering to join the territorial delegate in a campaign to ruin Cincinnati's future, the governor went out of his way to obtain a division contrary to the Ordinance—one that would create a small, Federalist-controlled territory in the eastern portion of the Northwest and delay statehood. St. Clair's intransigence at each step of the way, in the face of mounting opposition, cost him heavily in prestige during the bitter contests that followed, while Republicanism rapidly gained in popularity. Nevertheless, up to the end of the second stage, he and the General Assembly continued to agree on constructive legislation.[17]

The second session of the first General Assembly convened in November 1800. If ill feelings still ran high, the General Assembly apparently wanted to avoid a confrontation with the governor. The goal of territorial division, which diminished the membership of the legislature, had been realized and the representatives for the second General Assembly were already elected. St. Clair, however, refused to budge from his position on county creation, and shortly after the session began he balked at a house request that he return all vetoed bills

16. St. Clair also spoke at length on the need for adequate jails and county court houses, but, as matters of local responsibility, improvements were slow in coming. (See Smith, *St. Clair Papers,* II:446–62; Bond, *Old Northwest,* 89–92, 95; Bond, *Foundations,* 438–42; G. L. Wilson, "St. Clair," 169, 328; McCarty, *Governors of the Northwest,* 70; Pease, *Laws of the Northwest,* A337–517, but especially A352–54, A384–88, A448–51, A452–67, A467–78.) The same laws are in Chase, *Statutes of Ohio,* I:211–87. There were 39 acts and four resolutions adopted, including an act proclaiming the district laws in force and a repeal act.

17. Bond, *Foundations,* 449–54; Bond, *Old Northwest,* 99–105.

within five days, stating his reasons. Thereafter, relations between the governor and legislature deteriorated and by early December, when St. Clair prorogued the General Assembly, they were at the breaking point. The increasing tensions notwithstanding, the legislature followed the governor's advice by enacting laws supposedly designed to improve the militia and taxation, assure more equal justice for Indians, and replace *viva voce* voting with the paper ballot.[18]

The complexion of the second General Assembly, which met in November 1801, differed little from that of the legislature during the preceding session. The membership of the council was the same, and the new House of Representatives had been elected over a year earlier on the same narrow franchise. The Republicans, who now controlled the national government and apparently had the sympathy of at least half the people in the Northwest, lacked a majority in either house. Consequently, the main difference in 1801 was that animosities toward the governor were much sharper, but they were balanced by an equally strong desire on the part of the legislature to reach an accommodation. This was evident both in the replies of the two houses to St. Clair's opening address and in the way the legislature acted on his recommendations during the session. The nature of the legislature's accommodation with the governor, however, suggests that the constructive legislation may have been little more than the by-product of a campaign to thwart statehood.[19]

Between May 1800, when Congress divided the territory, and the end of 1801, statehood emerged as the dominant issue in the Northwest, and St. Clair cast about frantically for a new plan and new associates with which to check the burgeoning statehood movement. He found both during the legislative session of 1801. The governor fashioned an odd tripartite alliance with the leaders of the flocks in Cincinnati and Marietta. The glue that bound them together was St. Clair's

18. See Bond, *Old Northwest*, 103–07; Bond, *Foundations*, 455–65; Smith, *St. Clair Papers*, II:501–23. Chase (*Statutes of Ohio*, I:287–310) lists twenty laws passed during the session, most of which amended earlier acts.

19. Chase, *Statutes of Ohio*, I:310–50; Smith, *St. Clair Papers*, II:534–42; Bond, *Old Northwest*, 107–09; Bond, *Foundations*, 463–67; Downes, *Frontier Ohio*, 201–25; G. L. Wilson, "St. Clair," 342–43. Chase (*Statutes of Ohio*, I:311 ff) lists twenty-five laws enacted during the session that ended on January 23, 1802. See also Bond, *Foundations*, 456–61.

scheme for a new division of the Northwest which offered the irresistible prospect of making Cincinnati and Marietta each the capital of a new territory, at the expense of the current capital, Chillicothe. The plan also satisfied the governor's requirements in that the Federalists would probably control the small eastern territory and, if the new division did not delay its admission to the Union as anticipated, St. Clair could at least expect to become the state's governor.

Through the alliance, St. Clair obtained a working majority in the legislature, which set out to implement the governor's plan just before Christmas 1801, by passing a law to move the capital to Cincinnati. Next, on January 1, 1802, it adopted an act calling on Congress to amend the Ordinance and redivide the territory. At this point, the Chillicothe residents and dissident Republicans began bombarding Congress with petitions intended to prove that a majority of the people supported the existing division of the territory, statehood, and removal of St. Clair. To these, the Republicans added a list of specific charges against the governor. In the territory, St. Clair's opponents took direct action and became violent. During two nights of vigorous demonstrating outside the governor's residence in Chillicothe, while the local lawmen standing along the sidelines ignored St. Clair's orders to disperse the crowd, a group of people broke through the front door of his house, but the governor escaped bodily harm.[20]

St. Clair was undoubtedly relieved to see the legislature adjourn, but when it did, the battle shifted to Congress, where the statehood advocates had a decisive advantage. Thomas Worthington, the territorial delegate, was not just a shrewd politician. He was a Republican pleading a popular case for statehood before a Republican government. In contrast, St. Clair was a Federalist swimming against a strong Republican tide, who had also alienated many of his earlier followers by his scheming. In short, by 1802 St. Clair's support was rapidly melting away in Washington as well as in the Northwest and the effect was immediate. Within three weeks, both houses of Congress passed the

20. Bond, *Foundations,* 451–52, 467–69; Chase, *Statutes of Ohio,* I:336, 341–42; Downes, *Frontier Ohio,* 202–04; Bond, *Old Northwest,* 112–13. While St. Clair was strong enough to get the two bills through the legislature, he could not prevent the lower house's passing a census bill with the objective of hurrying statehood. His friends, however, stopped it from passing in the council.

Ohio Enabling Act, and Jefferson signed it. It was not clear whether the proposed state contained 60,000 people, but if anyone really cared, the statehood advocates gave assurance that, at the current rate of growth, Ohio's population would reach the figure specified in the Ordinance by the time it entered the Union.[21]

The statehood issue aside, throughout the nineteenth century movements or laws to change the location of territorial capitals invariably precipitated crises that were sometimes accompanied by violence. Unlike St. Clair, who was an active participant from the beginning, most governors tried to avoid involvement, but they were almost always drawn into the struggles. Governor Henry Dodge, for example, wanted to leave the location of the capital of the new Wisconsin Territory entirely up to the legislature, but the bitter competition for supremacy between speculators finally forced him to take part. When the Oregon governor found he could neither remain aloof from a capital removal conflict nor guide it to a solution, the federal government had to step in. That the Oregon governor had no veto seems to have been immaterial in this instance. On the contrary, Governor Caleb Lyon's experience early in the Idaho territorial period suggests that he was better off without the power. In Idaho, a minority threatened to do violence to the governor if he did not veto an act of the legislature to move the capital from Lewistown to Boise. When Lyon refused to veto the law and sought to comply with it, the minority tried to prevent his departure and the removal of the territorial records. The governor, however, somehow slipped out of town—albeit empty handed; a mob forcibly detained the territorial secretary along with the archives until compelled to release them by the federal government.

Often, for example following a disagreement with the governor, when the legislature defiantly voted to move its sessions to another town, battles over the seat of government were petty and senseless. The federal courts were occasionally called upon to determine the legitimacy of a move. In some instances they sided with the legislature; in others they supported the governor. The Northwest Removal Act, however, did not raise any legal questions. As it turned out, it was sim-

21. Bond, *Old Northwest*, 113–16; Downes, *Frontier Ohio*, 216–33.

ply a futile gesture, damaging to St. Clair's already weak position. The General Assembly did not reconvene, in Cincinnati or anywhere else, between the session of 1801–1802 and statehood, and then the state constitution moved the capital back to Chillicothe.[22] Nevertheless, unlike similar conflicts in most other territories, capital removal in the Northwest was intimately related to the larger issue of statehood. The adoption of the removal law and the act calling for a new division of the Northwest galvanized the statehood enthusiasts. It also gave St. Clair and his allies, who formed the General Assembly's anti-statehood majority, a false sense of power that led them to think they could prevent statehood, after Congress passed the Ohio Enabling Act, at the constitutional convention.

To this end, St. Clair diligently promoted the election to the Ohio constitutional convention of delegates who opposed statehood. The primary objective of these delegates would be to prevent statehood, but if this proved to be impossible they could at least see that the convention did its work "intelligently"—in other words, guarantee that it drafted a constitution that would keep any democratic proclivities in check and, incidentally, make St. Clair a likely prospect for the state governorship. St. Clair failed miserably. He did not seek election to the convention himself and the candidates he backed did not do well, either in getting elected or in controlling the convention's proceedings. In addition, St. Clair was not invited to participate in the convention or preside over it as a number of governors were in other territories. The delegates, in fact, were so hostile to St. Clair that only after extended debate did they grant his request to address the convention, and then it was pointedly as a private citizen—"Arthur St. Clair, sen., Esquire"—rather than as the governor.

In the debate over whether to permit St. Clair to address the convention, the governor's request found support among the Republicans. One Republican leader summed up the situation in that remarkably worn cliché, hopefully not so stale in 1802, "Give him enough rope and he will hang himself." Figuratively speaking, St. Clair did just

22. Valentine, "Territorial Governor," 101–02, 111; McCarty, *Governors of the Northwest*, 148–49; Neil, "Territorial Governors," 113–15; Thorpe, *Constitutions*, 2908. For contrast, see the discussion of the Florida compromise in Carter, *Territorial Papers*, XXII:453, 621.

that. The governor came before the convention and explicated a theory of federal–territorial relations, or more accurately territorial autonomy, harking back to arguments of the Radicals of the Revolutionary period—one often to be propounded, in a slightly modified form, by disgruntled citizens of later territories. St. Clair began with the indisputable fact that the Northwest Ordinance had been adopted and implemented before the federal Constitution was ratified; moved to the questionable, if universally agreed-upon argument that the Organic Act was a compact agreement; then got to the heart of the matter, and in so doing parted company with all but his like-minded fellow Federalists. He argued that, as a covenant antecedent to the Constitution, the Ordinance was both inviolate and beyond the purview of the Constitution, and since the Constitution was necessarily inoperative in the territories of the Northwest until they became states, Congress had no authority over them. Therefore, when Congress passed the Ohio Enabling Act it broke the compact and, according to Rufus Putnam, the territory became a free agent. St. Clair was not so explicit. He did, however, call on the convention to draft a constitution for the whole of the Old Northwest and hinted at secession and forcible resistance to the federal government if it should try to stop such a move.

The arguments of the Federalist opponents of statehood were incongruous. St. Clair's analogue to the states' rights doctrine was especially curious. An aged general of the Revolution, he had never been a Radical, but a staunch aristocrat who favored strong central government. His address was almost wholly inconsistent with his entire life, the final outburst of a man frustrated by his own impotence and inability to adapt to a changing society. But if the delegates to the convention marveled at St. Clair's address, they did not heed his demands. They quickly drafted a liberal state constitution while St. Clair's enemies rushed copies of his address to the President. Jefferson could hardly ignore the governor's statements or let them pass with only a reprimand, and although he was reluctant to set such a precedent, he fired St. Clair.[23]

23. The quote is from G. L. Wilson, "St. Clair," 355. See also *ibid.*, 355–63; Carter, *Territorial Papers*, III:212–14, 231; Smith, *St. Clair Papers*, I:241–43; Downes, *Frontier Ohio*, 226–33; Bond, *Foundations*, 474–75; Bond, *Old Northwest*,

St. Clair was not the only governor to oppose statehood, but no other went so far, even if he genuinely felt that his territory was not ready for statehood. In Colorado, for example, anti-statehood men were governors from 1863 to 1873, and the first two governors of the period helped to squelch a statehood movement. In 1864, three years after organizing the territory, Congress passed an Enabling Act but, with the active assistance of Governor John Evans, the opponents of statehood were able to convince the voters to reject the state constitution the following year. Undaunted, the statehood proponents proceeded to hold elections for state offices under the state constitution and petitioned Congress to admit Colorado to the Union. When Congress refused to admit the state their movement waned, and then they attributed their lack of success in part to the new governor, Alexander Cummings, who had certified the anti-statehood candidate as territorial delegate after an election of questionable legitimacy. In the end, the first Colorado statehood struggle involved conflicts between Cummings, who was a Johnson appointee, and the Radical Republicans, as well as between Golden and Denver, but the governors and the "Golden Crowd" based their opposition to statehood on the argument that there were not enough people in the territory to support a state government. Perhaps, like St. Clair, Evans and Cummings really thought statehood would bring "misery and ruin" to an unprepared populace. Whatever the rationale, once the movement was defeated, Cummings and his successors apparently had to do nothing except fail to encourage statehood sentiment in order to discourage it, and the movement languished until 1873, when Samuel H. Elbert became governor and revived it.

During the late 1880s, Governor Thomas Moonlight, who was interested in promoting agricultural settlement, sought to prevent statehood for Wyoming, which he considered tantamount to turning

---

115–18; Burnet, *Notes*, 379–80; Sears, "Philosophy of St. Clair," 54–56. Sears (*ibid.*, 56) feels that it is not a stretch of the imagination to see St. Clair's speech as a call to arms and forcible resistance to the federal government if necessary, and contends that this is precisely what the governor intended to propose. Sears concludes that St. Clair was reckless, either from despair or from liquor, or both, and cites an entry in Worthington's diary for July 26, 1802, that St. Clair passed through town and "as usual got very drunk." Worthington, of course, was no friend of the governor's.

the territory permanently over to the Stock Growers' Association, with the result that progressive agrarian reforms would never be realized. By and large, however, governors did not overtly oppose statehood movements, especially if the movements clearly were supported by a majority of the people. On the other hand, in the numerous instances where the thrust toward statehood was the work of a minority and the forces for and against statehood were rather equally divided, the governor's attitude could be crucial to the success or failure of a movement. He might influence the course of events simply by staying out of the conflict, or by lending subtle aid to one side or the other. But perhaps most frequently, governors actively supported burgeoning statehood movements, often hoping to secure for themselves an important office in state government.[24]

If most governors supported statehood, few went to the lengths of promoting it that William Blount did in the Southwest. Blount's leadership of the Tennessee statehood movement in the mid-1790s stands as the polar opposite of St. Clair's position half a dozen years later, and the relationships of all other governors to statehood movements in subsequent territories can be said to have fallen between those of the first two.

Immediately after the second stage began in the Southwest, Blount realized that he was still caught in the crossfire between the federal peace policy toward the Indians and the popular clamor for an aggressive Indian policy. Moreover, as the legislature demanded greater participation in government, the governor saw his dominance and popularity begin to wane. Sevier, whose popularity remained high, also wanted the governorship badly, and Blount, now determined to extricate himself from his problems by moving the territory into statehood, made a deal with him. Blount would help "Nollachucky Jack" Sevier obtain the state governorship in exchange for Sevier's aid in assuring that Blount got a United States Senate seat. But even before the first General Assembly met in the autumn of 1794, Blount began a personal campaign advocating statehood as the only means of achieving protection against the Indians. When it did meet, the legislature

24. Neil, "Territorial Governors," 108–10, 134–35, 136; Bond, *Foundations*, 471; Carter, *Territorial Papers*, VIII:380; XII:475, 984; Lamar, *Dakota Territory*, 209, 229–30, 247–67, 281; Lamar, *Far Southwest*, 185–86, 191, and *passim*.

promptly passed a resolution supported, and perhaps drafted, by the governor, calling for a new census and a poll on the question of statehood. Blount fully anticipated the population of the territory to reach 60,000 by October 1795, and it proved to be well in excess of that figure. More importantly 6,504 voters favored statehood whereas only 2,562 opposed.[25]

On receiving the results of the census and referendum, Blount apportioned the Southwest and set dates for the election of a constitutional convention. In contrast to St. Clair, Blount skillfully and successfully promoted the election of his allies while running for a seat himself. Blount led the Knox County delegation to the convention, and when it met in Knoxville on January 11, 1796, the governor was elected its president. The governor's forces formed almost half of the convention membership and were able to control the entire writing of the constitution by making relatively few concessions to the other delegates, whose party affiliations were rather fluid on most issues. Blount's group was able to protect its members' property interests against unfavorable taxation and prevent the establishment of a unicameral system. In order to head off a drive to grant the franchise to every male who was subject to militia service, however, they had to accept the virtual abolition of property qualifications for voting.

Blount apparently did not take an open part in the convention. His name appears only on the roll calls. Nevertheless, it is clear that he wrote or influenced the wording of a number of sections in the constitution, which provided for a strong executive. This contrasts completely with the Ohio constitution wherein the authors, reacting to St. Clair, stripped the governor of a veto and drastically limited his powers in other respects.[26]

The Tennessee convention, completing its work at breakneck speed, did not bother to provide for popular ratification of the state constitution. It simply sent a copy to Secretary of State Pickering and instructed the governor to issue writs for the election of state officials. Blount also acted swiftly: the first state legislature met on

25. Masterson, *Blount*, 266, 282–85.

26. *Ibid.*, 285–91; Bond, *Old Northwest*, 130; Sears, "Philosophy of St. Clair," 50. According to Masterson (*Blount*, 291), the Tennessee governorship was to be stronger than that of North Carolina, after which it was patterned.

March 28, 1796—just two and a half months after the convention began drafting a constitution. On March 30, the legislature elected Blount to the United States Senate without opposition, and by mid-April he was on his way to Philadelphia to take part in the battle for admission.[27]

Throughout the period of the statehood campaign, Blount maintained constant pressure to hurry things along, and though he came close to losing the initiative in Philadelphia, he never did. There was strong opposition to statehood in the Southwest, and in this way the governor was able to prevent its becoming effectively organized before the state government was in operation. The numerous complaints against Blount's tactics were brought before Congress when the statehood bill was introduced. The opponents of statehood argued that Blount's emphasis on speed, which the governor urged as necessary in order to bring Tennessee statehood before Congress before it adjourned, had been deliberately aimed at thwarting the will of a majority of the people. They contended that the census and referendum had been conducted improperly—by taking advantage of all travelers on the roads to swell the totals, for example—and that Blount had held the elections for delegates to the convention too soon and for too short a time to get an honest sampling of the voters' sentiments. Finally, they implored Congress to delay statehood for at least two years so the people would have an opportunity to reconsider their actions thoroughly.

At home, opponents of Tennessee statehood leaned heavily on an argument which would be repeated endlessly by statehood opponents, including St. Clair of course, in the other territories: statehood would require higher taxes as a result of the loss of federal subsidies and offered no compensating advantages. This and similar arguments could not have been more valid in Tennessee than they were in the territories west of the Mississippi River, where federal support of territorial governments was much greater. Though federal subsidies were prominent because they were often bound up in controversy, they probably covered no more than a tenth of territorial and local expenditures even in the later territories.[28]

27. Masterson, *Blount*, 291–94.

28. *Ibid.*, 284, 291–92, 294; Neil, "Territorial Governors," 172–73; Pomeroy,

Blount's enemies in Tennessee gave Congressional opponents of statehood valuable ammunition, but the debates in Philadelphia centered on the legality of the state government and national party needs. When, on April 8, 1796, President Washington sent the Tennessee constitution to Congress without comment, the westerners' probable vote in the upcoming national election was apparent both to the Federalist-dominated Senate and the Republican-controlled House. Thus the House quickly voted to approve admission, despite a delay caused by the debates over the Jay Treaty, while the Senate procrastinated. All the arguments against statehood were trotted out in the Senate. In addition, the committee in charge of the admission bill found the state constitution to be imperfect and in conflict with the federal Constitution, yet its recommendation, which the Senate finally adopted, was only that statehood be withheld pending a Congressionally-supervised census of the territory.

Since the Senate's action was incompatible with that of the House, the question of statehood had to be sent to a conference committee. By chance, two of its Senate members who opposed statehood resigned, and Aaron Burr, a man susceptible to manipulation by Blount, became one of the replacements. Exerting all his charm, and pointing to the risk that Tennessee might declare its independence if Congress did not admit it to the Union, Blount was able to bring Burr around to his position. Burr in turn used his influence to obtain a favorable recommendation from the committee, and on May 31 the Senate capitulated, but only after forcing a reduction in Tennessee's representation in the House to one representative and requiring the reelection of the senators and representative, none of whom had been seated during the debates. The reelection of Tennessee's Congressional delegation was a mere formality.[29]

It was natural enough for Congress to raise questions regarding the legality of the Tennessee statehood process, since it was the first

---

Territories, 1861–1890, 99. See also G. L. Wilson, "St. Clair," 367–69; Bond, *Old Northwest,* 117; Bond, *Foundations,* 433–38, 471–72; Carter, *Territorial Papers,* III:212–14; XIV:252–56.

29. Masterson, *Blount,* 294–98. Blount lost his slight remaining loyalty to the Federalist party during the debates, and turned to the opposition for support after hearing his administration and himself roughly handled by Federalists.

United States territory to be admitted to the Union, but it is surprising that the federal government did not fully resolve them during either the First or Second Empire. Rather, the government vacillated between the two positions enunciated with respect to the Tennessee statehood process. According to the Senate committee in 1796, Blount's actions had been illegal because he had not received prior authorization from Congress to initiate the change to statehood. This was diametrically opposed to the apparent attitude of the House, if not the whole Congress, during the previous year. At the beginning of his move toward statehood, Blount had urged the territorial delegate to introduce a bill in Congress specifically authorizing statehood after a favorable referendum. In March 1795, however, the delegate informed the governor that Congress would not act. It was his opinion that Congress expected the governor to take the initiative—to hold a referendum, call a constitutional convention and put a state government in operation before petitioning for admission. Blount, of course, followed this advice, there being no contrary law or theory to suggest a more exact legal procedure for obtaining statehood. The only precedent was the irregular procedure followed by Kentucky.[30] When the questions of federal recognition of the state and its admission to the Union arose in the Tennessee constitutional convention one delegate, Alexander Outlaw, reverted to his old State of Franklin position. If Congress refused to admit the state, he said, it should declare independence—an idea not dissimilar to St. Clair's in 1802, but one not seriously considered in Tennessee or subsequent territories.[31]

Between Tennessee statehood and the admission of Arkansas (1836) and Michigan (1837) it was customary for territories to make the transition to statehood according to the prescriptions of Congressional Enabling Acts. This began in the Northwest largely because the governor refused to initiate a change he opposed, but Tennessee's difficulties must also have been fresh in mind. In any case, Ohio set a general pattern of petitioning Congress for authorization to organize a state government. In seven succeeding territories—Ohio, Indiana, Illinois, Louisiana, Missouri, Mississippi, and Alabama—Congress ap-

30. *Ibid.*, 283, 294.
31. *Ibid.*, 290.

portioned the territories, laid down rules for the election of convention delegates, and set the dates both for the election and for the convention of delegates. In each case Congress required the delegates to poll themselves on the desirability of statehood before drafting a constitution. The governors simply issued the writs of election, then certified the results of the elections and the convention in accordance with the Enabling Acts. This precluded the kind of control exercised by Blount, but did not mean that governors could not take an active part in statehood movements and conventions.[32]

For fifteen years after Missouri's admission, no new states entered the Union. Then, between 1836 and 1848, as "Manifest Destiny" blossomed, the admission of five territories—Arkansas, Michigan, Iowa, Florida, and Wisconsin—brought the First Empire to an end. The liquidation of the Empire was casual, rather than planned, in that Congress failed to pass Enabling Acts for all but the Wisconsin Territory, and it was apparently intended mainly to aid the statehood movement. Instead, Congress let the people, or leaders, in each of the territories take the initiative, choose their own means of organizing a state government, and apply for admission whenever they were ready. It was logical for Congress to shift the primary responsibility for statehood to the territorial inhabitants in this way during the 1830s and 1840s, even if it did so by default, since it had previously made major changes in the territorial system which extended home rule. Nonetheless, the laissez-faire attitude of Congress in this period not only broke with the tradition of the preceding forty years but ignored official opinion. Just as Arkansas began to make the transition to statehood, the Attorney General ruled that a Congressional Enabling Act was required before a territory could hold a constitutional convention and establish a state government. Inasmuch as the territories were not sovereign, they could not do these things on their own, so any territorial laws designed to bring about the organization of a state government were invalid.[33]

32. See the acts in Thorpe, *Constitutions,* 92–94, 967–72, 1053–57, 1376–80, 2029–32, 2145–50, 2897–2900. See also Valentine, "Territorial Governor," 117–18.

33. Valentine, "Territorial Governor," 117; Thorpe, *Constitutions,* 264–65, 662–64, 1118–22, 1926–30, 4071–74. Michigan's right to form a state government to enter the Union without prior consent of Congress was tested in *Scott v.*

When Wisconsin became a state at the end of May 1848, the First Empire ended, but Congress' laissez-faire attitude toward statehood carried over into the Second Empire. For at least twenty years, both Congress and the territories continued to ignore the Attorney General's ruling. Between 1848 and 1868, California, Oregon, and Kansas organized state governments without Enabling Acts; Minnesota and Nebraska obtained Congressional authorization before setting up state governments; and Congress passed an Enabling Act for Nevada during the period of transition to statehood. Neither Congress nor the inhabitants (even of the last three territories), however, seemed to consider the Enabling Act to be a prerequisite to the formation of a state government.[34]

In contrast, the governors and citizens of most of the remaining

---

Detroit Young Men's Society Lessee. (See Carter, *Territorial Papers*, II:49n; 1 Douglas, 119; 5 Howard, 344–82.)

Beginning in 1838, several bills were introduced in Congress to permit the organization of states in Wisconsin and Iowa. Apparently none of them received much consideration, and in January 1846 the Wisconsin legislature instructed Governor Dodge to begin the transition to statehood, by polling the voters, without an enabling act. A majority of the voters wanted to enter the Union, so the governor apportioned the territory and issued writs for election on August 1, five days before Congress passed the Enabling Act and the President signed it. In this case, then, the Enabling Act did nothing but add federal sanction to the change already in progress, and assure admission of the state. (See Milo M. Quaife, ed., *The Movement for Statehood, 1845–46* [Madison, 1918]; and *NA*, H–779, 25 Cong., May 11, 1838; *NA*, H–1068, 25 Cong., May 23, 1839; *NA*, H–133, 26 Cong., May 5, 1840; *NA*, H–298, 28 Cong., Apr. 2, 1844.)

In Florida the thrust toward statehood began early, but it lost much of its impetus when, in July 1838, Congress enlarged the legislative council and made it a bicameral body. Late in the year, the diehards nevertheless met and drafted a constitution. They proclaimed it early in 1839, but did not immediately organize a state government, and Congress did not admit Florida until 1845, along with Iowa. (See Thorpe, *Constitutions*, 662–82, for the admission act and constitution; Carter, *Territorial Papers*, XXIII:619n; XXV:532; and 5 *Statutes*, 263–64.)

34. Thorpe, *Constitutions*, 390, 1176–78, 1988–91, 2343–48, 2397–2400, 2996–97. In addition to the acts, the range of Congressional attitudes regarding the proper nature of the statehood process is well illustrated by the following bills. *Oregon: NA*, H–332, 33 Cong., Aug. 18, 1854; *NA*, H–7, 34 Cong., Feb. 18, 1856; *NA*, H–642, 34 Cong., Jan. 16, 1857; *NA*, S–239, Apr. 5, 1858. *Kansas: NA*, S–172, 34 Cong., Mar. 17, 1856; *NA*, H–411, 34 Cong., May 29, 1856; *NA*, S–356, 34 Cong., June 30, 1856; *NA*, S–15, 35 Cong., Dec. 18, 1857; *NA*, S–161, 35 Cong., Feb. 18, 1858. *Nebraska: NA*, H–628, 37 Cong., Dec. 22, 1862; *NA*, S–522, 37 Cong., Dec. 12, 1863; *NA*, S–447, 39 Cong., July 23, 1866; *NA*, S–456, 39 Cong., Dec. 5, 1866.

continental territories of the Second Empire apparently assumed that they could not act on their own and that if Congress did not initiate the change to statehood it was because it wanted to keep their territory out of the Union. The Colorado statehood movement waned after the voters defeated the 1865 constitution, in part because its leaders, having once failed under the 1864 Enabling Act, seemed to think that they could not reconvene or call a new convention to write another constitution unless Congress provided a new law. Until the early 1870s, they lacked strength and the support of the governor, but when Governor Elbert backed statehood and the statehood proponents petitioned for a new Enabling Act, Congress responded quickly. Undoubtedly, the Colorado statehood leaders, like those in Nevada, Nebraska, and Minnesota, wanted an Enabling Act to bolster their movement even though it was probably strong enough to succeed without one. Such was not the case, however, in Dakota, Washington, Montana, Idaho, and Wyoming before the late 1880s, for, despite arguments that Enabling Acts were not prerequisites, the people were either apathetic or thought that Congress had to act first. The governors evidently did not encourage them to think differently, and statehood had to wait for a small group of proponents to build up sufficient pressure to

---

Minnesota: NA, S–86, 35 Cong., Jan. 26, 1858. *Montana: NA,* H–808, 40 Cong., Feb. 25, 1868.

In Minnesota, the object of obtaining an Enabling Act before beginning the change was to head off the opponents of statehood and fix the state's boundaries to forestall a secession movement in the southern part of the territory. (See Theodore C. Blegan, *Minnesota. A History of the State* [Minneapolis, 1963], 220–21.)

Enabling Acts were sought by statehood proponents in both Nevada and Nebraska to add impetus to their movements, after previous constitutions had failed of ratification. For Nebraska this meant a second Enabling Act. The Nevadans, on the other hand, had drafted one constitution in 1863 without an Enabling Act. When it was turned down at the polls, following a party and secessionist conflict, the statehood advocates decided that they could renew their position if they had a Congressional Enabling Act. (See Effie Mona Mack, *Nevada. A History of the State From the Earliest Times Through the Civil War* [Glendale, California, 1936], 247–67, hereafter cited as Mack, *Nevada.*)

Only state histories of exceptional merit are cited here and elsewhere as almost any state history will adequately illustrate the relationship between the Enabling Act and statehood movement.

overcome the lethargy of national political parties and the opposition of large corporate interests.[35]

Finally, in February 1889, Congress provided enabling acts for the territories of Washington, Montana, and Dakota, the last of which was to be divided into two states, and before the end of the year the four "Omnibus States" entered the Union. Idaho and Wyoming were left out, and this slight was probably far more important in spurring their citizens on to organize state governments without prior authorization from Congress than was the Attorney General's declaration of the same year that the territorial legislatures had the power to enact all laws necessary for the purpose. Regardless of the prime motivating force, Congress promptly admitted both states in 1890. Statehood for Arizona and New Mexico, on the other hand, was delayed for some years after Congress passed an enabling act in 1906, which also applied to Oklahoma, because the Arizonans and New Mexicans would not join together in the formation of a single state as provided by the law. When they established separate state governments in contravention of the law, however, Congress nevertheless acceded.[36]

The strength of vested interests opposed to statehood, the rapidly declining relative importance of the territories in national politics, and the failure of territorial citizens to take the initiative would seem to have been the basic factors that accounted for the prolongation of territorial status, or delay in the attainment of statehood, during the post-Civil War period of the Second Empire. A comparison of the populations of states with those of territories at the time of their admission and an analysis of other characteristics, however, indicates

35. See, for example, Lamar, *Dakota Territory*, 222–34, 244. The Washington Territory legislature wrote a state constitution in 1878, but nothing ever came of it. In 1889, Congress refused to acknowledge the constitution's validity and required that a special convention draft a new one. Mary W. Avery, *History and Government of the State of Washington* (Seattle, 1961), 314. Sectional factionalism and apathy in Idaho were apparently insuperable until the territory found itself left out of the Omnibus Act. The enabling and admission acts are in Thorpe, *Constitutions*, 913–18, 2289–2300, 1852–53, 3355–57, 3971–73, 4111–17.

36. See Thorpe, *Constitutions*, 2960–81; Valentine, "Territorial Governor," 117. See also Gruening, *Alaska, passim*; John D. Hicks, *The Constitutions of the Northwest States* (Lincoln, 1924), 21–23, hereafter cited as Hicks, *Constitutions;* Dora Ann Stewart, *The Government and Development of Oklahoma Territory* (n.p. [Norman], 1933), 327–86.

that population growth and territorial initiative were the most fundamental factors behind the timing of statehood.

After Congress divided the Northwest Territory in 1800 and admitted Ohio, it dropped the 60,000 population requirement of the Ordinance of 1787 and adopted the policy that territories could petition for statehood whenever they desired. Since, under the Ordinance, Congress had reserved the right to admit states with fewer than 60,000 people, the deletion of the requirement in fact served no purpose and did nothing to alter the course of admissions. Only three territories—Illinois, California, and Nevada—clearly had fewer than 60,000 people at the time they entered the Union. The average population for all territories through 1912, excluding Oklahoma as exceptional, was 133,000. The average of the thirteen territories of the First Empire was 97,000 inhabitants, and that of the thirteen territories admitted during the main period of the Second, 1850 through 1890, was 137,200. The average population for the three territories admitted between 1890 and 1912, again excluding Oklahoma, was 269,300. By comparison, the mean population of Delaware increased from 78,000 (average 1800–1850) to 130,000 (average 1850–1890) and finally 185,400 (average 1890–1910). Concurrently, the total population of the United States rose from 5,297,000, in 1800, to 23,261,000, in 1850, to 63,-056,000 in 1890, and 92,407,000, in 1910.[37]

As the above figures illustrate, the population of territories at the time they became states rapidly decreased, relative to that of the whole United States, but the territorial average for each of the three periods was somewhat larger than Delaware's mean population in each period, and Delaware consistently had the smallest population of the original thirteen states. The last set of features would lead one to conclude that the statehood provision of Jefferson's Ordinance of 1784 in fact prevailed, albeit unconsciously, were it not that individual

37. *Historical Statistics*, 7 (Series A 1–3). The United States data are for the continental area only. An alternative periodization for the bulk of the Second Empire (1850–1896) would raise the average territorial population at the time of statehood to 145,300. The average for the period after 1896 would simply be the average of Arizona and New Mexico, 278,800, if Oklahoma were excluded, but 651,600 if the Oklahoma data were included. The average for the four states admitted in the period from 1890 to 1912, including the Oklahoma data, would be 552,600.

TABLE 2. POPULATIONS AND GROWTH RATES AT THE TIME OF STATEHOOD

Date[1]	*Territory (State)*	*Rate of Growth*[2]	*Terr. Pop. Density*[1]	*Territorial Population*[1]	*Delaware*[3]	*Smallest State*[4]	*Federal Apport. Ratio*[5]
1796	TSRO (Tennessee)	187 [35.1]	1.8	77,640	62,220		33 [1]
1802 [03]	TNRO (Ohio)	408 [36.4]	2.0	82,480	65,980		[1]
1812	Orleans (Louisiana)	100 [33.1]	1.9	91,960	72,700		35 [1]
1816	Indiana	500	2.7	98,120	72,700		[1]
1817	Mississippi	140	1.3	62,170	72,700		[1]
1818	Illinois	350	.83	46,620	72,735		[1]
1819	Alabama	1322	2.2	116,010	72,740	50,910[a]	[1]
1820 [21]	Louisiana (Mo.)	236	.96	66,586	72,749	55,211[a]	40 [1]
1836	Arkansas	220 [32.7]	1.3	70,720	77,540		48 [1]
1836 [37]	Michigan	575	2.4	140,020	77,540	70,720[b]	[1]
1845	Florida	60 [35.9]	1.2	70,950	84,800		71 [1]
1845 [46]	Iowa	345	2.1	117,650	84,800	70,950[c]	[2]
1847 [48]	Wisconsin	890	4.0	223,050	87,480	77,530[c]	[2]
1850	California	—	.58	92,597	91,532	87,445[c]	93 [2]
1858	Minnesota	182 [35.6]	1.8	149,800	108,060		[2]
1859	Oregon	333	.50	48,460	110,130		[1]
1861	Kansas	240 [22.6]	1.6	132,920	113,480	56,240[d]	127 [1]
1864	Nevada[f]	515[f]	.25	21,140[f]	117,320	67,460[d]	[1]
1867	Nebraska	313	1.2	94,740	121,160	31,820[e]	[1]
			[0.5]	[1861 = 38,220]			
1876	Colorado	387 [30.1]	1.3	132,540	137,960	54,380[e]	131 [1]
			[.34]	[1864 = 36,540]			
1889	North Dakota	417 [25.5]	2.5	175,590	166,310	48,890[e]	152 [1]
	South Dakota	255	4.2	323,570			[2]
	Washington	375	4.8	328,990			[1]
	Montana	265	0.9	132,530			[1]
1890	Idaho	172	1.1	88,548	168,493	47,355[e]	174 [1]
	Wyoming	200	.64	62,555			[1]

TABLE 2.—Continued

Date[1]	*Territory (State)*	*Rate of Growth*[2]	*Terr. Pop. Density*[1]	*Territorial Population*[1]	*Delaware*[3]	*Smallest State*[4]	*Federal Apport. Ratio*[5]
1896	Utah	31 [20.7]	2.95	250,340	178,220	44,340[e]	[1]
1907	Oklahoma	110[g] [21.0]	20.	1,397,160	197,020	70,020[e]	194 [5]
1910 [12]	New Mexico	67	2.7	327,301	202,322	81,875[e]	211 [1]
1912	Arizona	63 [14.9]	2.0	230,360	206,440	81,000[e]	[1]
1959	Hawaii	27 [12.0]		619,500	433,480	272,780[e]	345 [1]
	Alaska	76		216,440			[1]

[1] Dates are for the year of the data given, and for statehood of all but six states; these admission dates are in brackets. Bracketed dates with populations in the column "Territorial Population" for Colorado and Nebraska indicate populations at the time of abortive statehood movements whose constitutions were rejected by the voters. They afford useful comparisons with the Nevada data. Territorial population density is the number of people per square mile at the time of admission based on present state areas.

[2] Percentage growth rate during the decade of statehood or, for dates coinciding with the decennial censuses, during the decade immediately preceding statehood. The bracketed figures are the United States growth rates during the same periods.

[3] Delaware was consistently the smallest of the original thirteen states. [4] These are population figures for the smallest state in the Union at each date when it was other than Delaware. They are identified in the text. [5] The first figure is the apportionment ratio in thousands of persons per representative in the House of Representatives. The bracketed figures indicate the number of representatives given each territory at the time it entered the Union.

[a] Illinois was the smallest state in the Union. [b] Arkansas. [c] Florida. [d] Oregon. [e] Nevada. See note *f*.

[f] Straight line interpolation is inadequate to describe Nevada's population during the 1860s, both as to the population at the time it entered the Union and in 1867 as the smallest state in the Union. The 1861 census improves both. There were 16,374 people on the first of July and an estimated 20,000 at the beginning of October. This jump from 6,900 in one year was to be expected during a mining rush. (See Mack, *Nevada*, 227.) Using the 1861 figures and interpolating over a nine-year period, the Nevada population in 1864 would be between 27,500 and 30,000. The 1867 population would be about 35,000. This growth pattern is more in line with that from 1870–1880. The 1861–1870 Nevada growth was 112%.

[g] Oklahoma's growth between 1890 and 1900 was 205%. This percentage and the one in the Table include the white and Indian populations in the parts of Indian Territory that were incorporated in the state.

SOURCES: *Historical Statistics*, 12–13, 693; *Historical Statistics of the United States: Continuation to 1962 and Revisions* (Washington, 1965), 1, 2, 95.

state populations ranged widely from that of Delaware at the time of their admission. Excluding Nevada and Oklahoma because of their extreme variance, the population of new states ranged from as little as 37 percent of Delaware's population (Wyoming) to 2.56 times Delaware's population (Wisconsin).[38] During the First Empire, five territories—Mississippi, Illinois, Missouri, Arkansas, and Florida—entered the Union with populations smaller than Delaware's, while the other eight had considerably more people. Between 1848 and 1890, on the other hand, seven of the thirteen territories became states with fewer people than Delaware had at the time of their admission. Thus, both in relative and in absolute terms, Delaware's population exceeded that of more territories entering the Union during the Second Empire than during the First.

As one would anticipate, the rate of population growth in every territory during the decade in which it became a state was well above the national average. In only two cases, Florida and Utah, was the territorial rate less than twice the current United States rate. The average growth rate around the time of statehood for the territories of the First Empire was 410 percent, which was 12 times the national average. That of the territories in the Second Empire was 305 percent, 11 times the average for the United States.[39] Thus the relationship between average territorial and national growth rates changed only slightly, by a factor of one, which is probably not significant, from the First to the end of the Second Empire. The territorial average for the aftermath of the Second Empire, between 1890 and 1912, however, was less than three and a half times the national average for the same period.

During the 1850s, at least, Stephen A. Douglas among others

38. The range of variation on each side of Delaware's population was comparable: Delaware's population in 1890 was 2.69 times that of Wyoming. Nevada's population was less than one-fifth of Delaware's when Nevada was admitted, while Oklahoma had seven times as many people as Delaware in 1907. In all cases, the population estimates were derived by linear interpolation between federal censuses.

39. California was omitted from the calculations for the Second Empire since its growth rate could not be determined. When the Second Empire is broken down into two periods—1850–1876 and 1889–1890, which had average territorial growth rates of 328 and 281 percent, respectively—the territorial rate works out to eleven times that of the United States during each of the periods.

sought to make statehood contingent on the federal apportionment ratio. He wanted Congress to require that each territory have a population equal to the federal ratio prevailing at the time it organized as a state and petitioned for admission.[40] Nothing came of his proposals, and as a comparison of territorial populations with the federal ratios shows, the latter had little if any relevance to the timing of statehood. Congress evidently paid little attention to the populations of territories on the threshold of statehood. In all but a few cases, it apportioned Congressional representation to new states on the basis of the Constitutional minimum and each territory's population at the time of the decennial census preceding statehood. On the latter basis, only Louisiana, Missouri, and Oklahoma qualified for more than one representative when they entered the Union. Nevertheless, Congress allowed the first two states only one representative each. On the other hand, it provided Oklahoma with five representatives although the census of 1900 indicated that it was entitled to no more than four. Similarly, when Congress gave Iowa, Wisconsin, and Minnesota two representatives apiece, it must have based its decisions on estimates of their populations at the time of statehood. Congress admitted California with two representatives while the census of 1850 was in progress. That census showed California's population to be smaller than the federal ratio, consequently it should have received only one representative. Similar incongruities can be found in the representation granted to the Omnibus States, none of which had a population as large as the federal ratio if the census of 1880 were used for a guide. By 1889, however, the populations of Washington and South Dakota were nearly the same size, yet Congress gave Washington, like North Dakota and Montana, one representative and South Dakota two. By and large, then, the common practice seems to have been for Congress to pay little attention to the populations of territories when admitting them as states, except between 1840 and 1860, and to allow each new state no more than the minimum representation.

40. See, for example, *NA*, S-555, 35 Cong., Feb. 4, 1859 and Feb. 23, 1859. This was a bill for the organization of Arizona and Dakota (renamed Jefferson) territories, to which Douglas offered an amendment that would have applied to all existing territories except Utah. In it a "sufficient population to constitute a State" was defined as a population equal to the apportionment ratio.

Population densities at the end of the territorial period ranged from lows of 0.25 in Nevada and 0.34 in Colorado to a high of 20.0 in Oklahoma. As in Oklahoma, where statehood was delayed because of difficulties regarding the disposition of the rump Indian Territory, Congress made no effort to withhold statehood from Wisconsin, which had a population density of 4.0 in 1847. The high ratios for both territories resulted from avalanches of settlement just prior to their admission. Utah was the only territory deliberately kept out of the Union for a significant period of time, yet its density ratio when admitted was substantially lower than those of Washington and South Dakota. Thus in general, the statistical measures indicate that statehood coincided rather closely with territorial settlement. In addition, they suggest that differences from territory to territory in the total population and in population density at the time of statehood reflected the nature of settlement in each territory, the size of territories, and the varying intensity of desires for statehood.[41]

It is difficult to assess the governor's influence on the statehood movement in some of the territories, except by repeating that it fell within the range of variation already delineated. The Enabling Acts of the Second Empire gave the governors no greater power during the critical period of transition than did that of Ohio.[42] Depending on how he conceived his role during transition, a governor might take an active part in writing the state constitution and organizing the state government, but he usually also had a good deal of other work to do with respect to the mechanics of transition.

The transfer of authority to the new state government was almost

41. See Pomeroy, *Territories, 1861–1890*, 95.

42. The only provision in subsequent Enabling Acts that differed basically from that of the Ohio Act is to be found in the acts for Nevada, the Omnibus States, Oklahoma, Arizona, and New Mexico. In these acts, Congress authorized the governor to help apportion the delegates for the constitutional convention. Beginning in the Civil War period, two territorial officials, one of whom might be the governor, were to carry out the apportionment. In Nevada and Oklahoma, the governor, district attorney, and chief justice, or any two of them, were to conduct the apportionment. Under the Omnibus Act, the governor, secretary, and chief justice, or any two of them, were to do the job. This device effectively destroyed the territorial delegate's influence over the apportionment of a territory prescribed by Congress, and probably made for no less equitable an apportionment. Compare the acts in Thorpe, *Constitutions*.

always accompanied by some confusion, which often involved the timing of the change. The federal government used at least three means of establishing the date of admission and the one to apply to a given territory was not always specified in the Enabling Act. In some cases, more than one method was used. A state might be admitted when Congress seated its delegation or on a date when either Congress or the President issued a formal declaration. At times, however, governors in effect preempted the power to admit states by proclaiming that the transfer of authority had been completed. A governor might do this simply through a proclamation or concurrently with the convening of the first state legislature. Then, too, the first state governor might begin state government before the formal date of admission, not only by assuming the normal executive duties but by ordering the state legislature to convene. Finally, the first state legislature might convene on its own authority, according to provisions of the state constitution, before the territorial government expired. Consequently, as many as five dates may be given for the beginning of statehood in Ohio and some other territories.

After Montana officially became a state in 1889, the territorial legislature for a time refused to surrender equipment used during the territorial period to either federal officials or to the state government. The United States marshal and attorney were finally moved to telegraph the Secretary of the Interior for authority "to immediately take charge of this property of the United States." In 1836 and 1837, the Michigan state government began operating before the territory officially became a state, and the territorial legislature continued to pass laws after statehood. This caused some confusion and led to the initiation of court cases to determine the legality of laws enacted under each authority. The Minnesota and Nebraska state legislatures also met before the states were formally admitted to the Union. The state governor did not join the state legislature in either case, and the result in each instance was a temporarily mixed government. The state legislatures adopted bills and the territorial governors, acting as their executives, signed them into laws. The Nebraska mixed government arose out of problems created by Congress. Territorial Governor Alvin Saunders called the state legislature into session before statehood so that it could comply with conditions for statehood imposed by

Congress. These examples, however, illustrate the exception rather than the rule. Usually, during the transition period, the territorial government withered to no more than a small caretaker regime headed by the governor, and when the last territorial governor became the first state governor there was a minimal break in the continuity of administration. Thus, even in Michigan, the confusion over laws probably had little effect on administrative continuity, since Stevens T. Mason was simultaneously the acting territorial governor and first state governor.[43]

43. See Valentine, "Territorial Governor," 116–18; Philbrick, *Laws of Illinois*, R169n, R171n; McCarty, *Governors of the Northwest*, 141–43; George W. Irvin and Ebbert D. Weed to John W. Noble, November 25, 1889, in Interior Department Territorial Papers, Montana, 1867–89, Microcopy 192, Roll 2.

VIII

Indian Affairs

DURING the First Empire, territorial legislatures normally met every year in sessions of about thirty days, but in the first phase of the Second Empire they began with increasing frequency to meet biennially. In 1868 Congress made biennial sessions uniform throughout the Empire and limited them to forty days. Twelve years later, however, it authorized sixty-day sessions, so that in general, governors of both Empires had to face legislatures on an average of no more than one month a year. Except for the periods surrounding legislative sessions, the governors' activities relating to lawmaking were very light, and inasmuch as they often did little direct administration, it is not surprising that many governors acted as if their duties were seasonal. In some cases, they spent a considerable majority of their time doing other things, for the federal and territorial governments and for themselves. At least until the end of the First Empire, the federal government also seemed to consider the governorship a part-time job because it periodically gave the governors additional responsibilities. But as territories matured, the governors' regular executive duties tended to become more nearly continuous and in the post-Civil War period the complexity of modern administration made the governorship a good deal more than a seasonal job.[1]

1. Farrand, *Legislation for Territories*, 45–47; Pomeroy, *Territories, 1861–1890*, 39–40. In 1869 Congress made the terms of both houses of legislatures two years, and in 1878 it limited membership of the lower houses to twenty-four

Throughout territorial history the federal government found a number of odd jobs suitable for the governors' spare time, including some which threatened to take up all their time. The federal government normally financed the construction and occasionally the maintenance of buildings such as the capitol and the penitentiary. The governor handled the building funds and sometimes was asked to recommend or select the sites, draw up the plans, and oversee the construction of buildings. Similarly the federal government solicited advice from the governors regarding the location of roads and post offices, and for appointments to be made in their territories. In addition, various federal agencies asked the governors to gather and report information on a wide variety of subjects, ranging from Indians to botany.[2]

In the early period of territorial history, before the multiplication of federal agencies, governors had the most extra duties. They were expected to settle various kinds of claims against the federal government, and in those involving a cash settlement, the governor had authority to issue drafts on the federal treasury. Land claim and title problems, arising from foreign or domestic settlements that preceded the acquisition of territory and the federal surveys, were especially time-consuming for governors in the Northwest until 1807 and in Missouri, Louisiana, and Florida. Until 1800 territorial governors, or secretaries in their stead, had to attend and supervise public land auctions and received wages for this service. After 1800 they had some responsibilities for general supervision of land disposal but did not have to attend sales. Like some other governors, Ninian Edwards held a commission as Superintendent of the United States Saline. This empowered him to lease saline lands and put him in charge of the shipment and sale of the government's share of the salt. The job involved considerable correspondence and expenditures of time, as did the leasing of other types of lands that governors sometimes controlled.

---

and that of the councils to twelve. (By 1844 Florida's legislature had grown to fifty members, following an expansive tendency typical of the legislatures of Wisconsin-type territorial governments before the Congressional limitation on membership.) In 1878, when it limited sessions to forty days, Congress also raised the legislatures' per diem allowance to $4 and mileage.

2. Valentine, "Territorial Governor," 84–86; Pomeroy, *Territories, 1861–1890*, 23, 41–44; Neil, "Territorial Governors," 93–97.

Territorial executives were also supposed to prevent squatting on the public domain and keep settlers from cutting timber on public lands, by using the army if necessary. Governor Hull of Michigan protested an order to use the army to prevent illegal timber cutting, because he thought the law was oppressive, and the President finally granted him permission to issue licenses to poor settlers to cut wood on the public domain. This was only one kind of license obtainable from governors. Territorial and federal laws authorized governors to issue licenses of a number of kinds; for example, Indian trade licenses and passports to enter Indian territory could be had from the governors as superintendents of Indian affairs. Indian affairs frequently involved military action, and during the first decades of territorial history governors commonly commanded the army in their territory or region in addition to the militia, which came under their command as governor. Thus, among others, Governors St. Clair, Hull, Harrison, Wilkinson, and Claiborne concurrently held commissions as generals.

Altogether, there were few positions governors could not hold, and for which they could not receive pay, while they held the office of territorial executive. The United States Attorney General ruled that none of the above offices was incompatible with the governorship and that governors were entitled to appropriate compensation for each one held. Commissions to make treaties with Indians, for example, normally paid $6.00 to $8.00 a day and expenses, but these were usually issued to those governors who were not superintendent of Indian affairs. All elective offices, on the other hand, were held to be incompatible with the governorship and whenever a governor assumed one, his commission as governor automatically expired.[3]

The most difficult and time-consuming of the governors' extra duties were those relating to the Indians. Until 1834 each governor was also the superintendent of Indian affairs in his territory. In that year, Congress began separating the two offices and after 1873 no

3. Valentine, "Territorial Governor," 51–52, 62–64; Neil, "Territorial Governors," 89–93; McCarty, *Governors of the Northwest*, 83, 115–16; G. L. Wilson, "St. Clair," 153–56. Valentine (*ibid.*, 90) cites cases of governors' occasionally acting for judges in their absences, but such actions were assumed obligations, warranted only as expedients. Philbrick (*Laws of Indiana*, R60–95, *passim*) discusses the land claims problems in the Northwest. See also Carter, *Territorial Papers*, II:566; V:412, 417.

governor served as superintendent of Indian affairs. Whether or not they held the superintendency, however, all governors were responsible for the well-being of Indians within their jurisdiction. When a governor was also superintendent, this included Indian country; when he was not, it included only those areas within the territory in which Indian titles had been extinguished—that is, the areas of European-American settlement. For convenience, these can be called the governors' Indian-country and civil jurisdictions respectively. A survey of the former illustrates that the ineffectiveness of governors was not limited to the administration and control of territorial government, and a study of the latter highlights the weaknesses of the governor's office through the inability to assure protection and equal justice to Indians outside Indian country.[4]

Several months after adopting the Ordinance of 1787, the Confederation Congress decided to combine the offices of governor and superintendent of Indian affairs in the Northwest Territory.[5] After 1789, the federal Congress continued to unite the two through provisions of the Organic Acts for new territories, but it did not always limit the area of the superintendencies to the boundaries of the territories. As governor of the Southwest, for instance, William Blount was superintendent for all the southern tribes. His jurisdiction over Indian affairs consequently included parts of the states of Virginia, North and South Carolina, Georgia, and Kentucky as well as the Southwest Territory. Between the time Tennessee entered the Union and the organization of the Mississippi Territory, Benjamin Hawkins

4. Valentine, "Territorial Governor," 55; Pomeroy, *Territories, 1861–1890*, 16; Neil, "Territorial Governors," 64–66. The Organic Acts for all but the Kansas, Nebraska, and Oklahoma territories provided that the governor should also be superintendent of Indian affairs in his territory. Ordinarily the stipend of the superintendency equaled that of the governor's office.

5. *JCC*, XXXIII:559–601, 699–700, 711–12; G. L. Wilson, "St. Clair," 179–81. Congress combined the offices on October 3, 1787. Two days later Congress appointed St. Clair, and on October 26 it also made him high commissioner to treat with the Indians. The superintendency was to begin on August 14, 1788, or whenever St. Clair took up the duties. St. Clair arrived in the Northwest in July 1788. At that time he superseded General Butler, who was superintendent for the Northern Department under the Ordinance of 1786, by virtue of his commission as high commissioner—that is, several weeks before his commission as superintendent became effective.

was superintendent for the southern tribes. Then the duties fell to the governor of Mississippi, Winthrop Sargent.[6] In the Old Northwest, on the other hand, Congress redefined superintendencies to conform to territorial boundaries each time it created a new territory.

While all governors were superintendents before 1834, one man often controlled Indian affairs in each region and he was not necessarily a governor. After the Indians defeated St. Clair's army in 1791, leadership in the conduct of Indian affairs passed largely to General Anthony Wayne, the governor's successor as commander of the army in the Northwest. St. Clair continued to hold the office of superintendent and constantly reminded the general, his officers, and deputies of that fact, but they tended to overlook both his authority and responsibility for Indian affairs. Wayne completely ignored St. Clair. He failed to inform the governor of either the Greenville negotiations or the treaties that extinguished the Indian titles to most of the land in Ohio. St. Clair supposedly found out about these things by reading the Cincinnati *Centinel*.[7] At the beginning of the nineteenth century, Governor William Henry Harrison of Indiana assumed leadership in Indian affairs in the Old Northwest. From 1809 to the end of the War of 1812 he not only controlled them but acted as military commander for the whole Northwest. In the meantime, Governors Hull of Michigan and Edwards of Illinois played secondary roles. Hull concluded two treaties in 1807–1808 but Edwards' name appeared on none before the war.[8] Following the war, however, Edwards and Cass, the new governor of Michigan, jointly controlled Indian affairs. From 1818, when Illinois became a state, until 1836 Michigan was the only ter-

6. Francis Paul Prucha, *American Indian Policy in the Formative Years: The Indian Trade and Intercourse Acts, 1790–1834* (Cambridge, Mass., 1962), 52, hereafter cited as Prucha, *Indian Policy*.

7. Bond, *Old Northwest*, 243; F. E. Wilson, *St. Clair*, 111; Rachel Marian Jarrold, "Arthur St. Clair, Governor of the Northwest Territory" (unpublished M. A. thesis, University of Illinois, 1901), 49, hereafter cited as Jarrold, "St. Clair,"; *American State Papers, Indian Affairs*, I:231, 645, hereafter cited as *ASPIA*.

8. See *ASPIA*, I:816–23. For a description of Harrison's role in treaty making see George Dewey Harmon, *Sixty Years of Indian Affairs: Political, Economic and Diplomatic, 1789–1850* (Chapel Hill, 1941), 80–91, hereafter cited as Harmon, *Sixty Years*.

ritory in the Northwest and its governors served as superintendents over all Indians north of the Ohio River and in the upper Mississippi River Valley.[9]

Early governors like St. Clair and Harrison considered their civil responsibilities to be secondary to the administration of Indian and military affairs. They reasoned that as long as white settlement depended on Indian removal their main purpose in the territories was to wrest land from the Indians. There was, nevertheless, much more to the superintendent's job than making treaties and leading military expeditions. The scope of the governors' duties, as indicated by their instructions, might seem humorous were it not that the federal government was serious. Governors usually received instructions similar to St. Clair's of 1788. The federal government expected them to remove all causes of friction between white settlers and Indians by establishing and enforcing the boundaries of Indian country alluded to vaguely in treaties, by regulating trade with Indians and treating with them to extinguish their title to lands wanted for settlement by the United States. At the same time the governors were to make "every exertion . . . to defeat all confederations and combinations among the tribes . . . [and] use every possible endeavor to ascertain who are the real Headmen & Warriors . . . ; these Men You will attach to the United States by every means in Your power."[10] In other words, governors were expected to keep Anglo-American settlers and Indians apart and quiet, if not happy, while administering federal policies designed to undermine the power of the Indians. In the period before 1834, at least, it was nearly impossible to enforce the segregation of the two groups, each of which objected to some federal policies, and the amount of work involved in being superintendent often left governors with little time for civil administration. As a result, during much of his administration Harrison, among others, concentrated on

9. See Carter, *Territorial Papers,* XII:780–82; Valentine, "Territorial Governor," 55–56; McCarty, *Governors of the Northwest,* 109, 115, 124, 128–29, 134.

10. Carter, *Territorial Papers,* II:79; Downes, *Frontier Ohio,* 172n; Valentine, "Territorial Governor," 56; Alban W. Hoopes, *Indian Affairs and Their Administration: With Special Reference to the Far West, 1849–1860* (Philadelphia, 1932), 6–7, 74, hereafter cited as Hoopes, *Indian Affairs;* Harmon, *Sixty Years,* 27–28, 29–30.

Indian affairs to the virtual exclusion of his duties as governor, which he left to the territorial secretary.[11]

Although the federal government formally emphasized peace in its discordant medley of Indian policies, the theme of war ordinarily dominated. The Confederation Congress began by instructing St. Clair to make a treaty of amity with the Northwest Indians, but neither St. Clair nor anyone else was likely to succeed as long as the Anglo-Americans expected the Indians to do most of the accommodating by relinquishing their lands. Thus the Fort Harmar Treaty of 1789 failed to end hostilities on the frontier, and the following year President Washington, concluding that war was unavoidable, authorized St. Clair to raise an army to crush the Indians. Then Washington drafted a plan for peace to take effect after St. Clair reduced the Indians. This guaranteed justice to the Indians and called for the regulated purchase of their lands. In the meantime, Henry Knox, the first Secretary of War, assumed the stance common to his successors in the War Department, which was to control Indian affairs until 1849. Peace, he contended, rested upon the strength of the army, on its ability to respond to actual or threatened hostilities and to enforce treaties. Therefore, Knox insisted on the need to garrison the frontiers.[12]

As long as hostilities continued in the Northwest during the early 1790s, the federal government directed Governor Blount of the South-

11. Valentine, "Territorial Governor," 56; McCarty, *Governors of the Northwest*, 64, 83; Downes, *Frontier Ohio*, 127; Neil, "Territorial Governors," 65; Carter *Territorial Papers*, XXII:832. It is clear that Governors Clark of Missouri, Harrison, and Cass devoted a large proportion of their time to Indian affairs, but it is difficult to assess the real involvement of some other governors with any precision. It is common to gauge the amount of activity by the volume of correspondence. This method is clearly misleading, since most civil duties did not require the volume or kind of correspondence, particularly with the federal government and prominent individuals, that is most likely to be preserved. St. Clair provides a good illustration of another reason. As I pointed out above, Wayne superseded the governor, in practice, as superintendent of Indian affairs, in 1791. St. Clair nevertheless continued to write lengthy letters regarding Indians and this led McCarty (*Governors of the Northwest*, 64) to conclude that Indians occupied most of the governor's attention. In fact, most of the letters were unsolicited commentaries indicating more concern than action.

12. Prucha, *Indian Policy*, 40, 44, 46, 60–61; G. L. Wilson, "St. Clair," 190–91, 220–22.

west to pursue policies compatible with Washington's plan of 1791 and St. Clair's instructions of 1788. Secretary Knox ordered Blount to maintain peace at all costs, to assure the neutrality of the southern tribes if their friendship was unobtainable, until the northern tribes could be pacified so that the government's limited power would not be dissipated. Nevertheless, in settling boundary disputes with the Indians, the governor was to take advantage of every opportunity to acquire land peaceably. Instead, Blount followed a rather aggressive policy, more suited to the demands of settlers and his own designs on those Indian lands to which he held options for speculation. Squatters continued to move into disputed areas and Blount made only token efforts to make them withdraw, but he put pressure on Indian tribes to give up their claims and cede additional land. When treating with Indians the governor sought to buy their land privately, though such purchases were strictly forbidden by federal law, and at least in negotiating the Holston Treaty in 1791, to this end he deliberately made some treaty provisions ambiguous and altered others in transcription. All these things only increased friction in the Southwest and eventually, in March 1795, Blount was severely reprimanded by Timothy Pickering, Knox's successor as Secretary of War. In a letter containing a devastating critique of the governor's conduct of Indian affairs, Pickering told Blount that the government would not support war in any form, and ordered him to comply with existing treaties to the letter and to remove all white settlers on Indian lands immediately, using federal troops if necessary.[13]

Following the conclusion of the Greenville Treaty with the northern tribes in August 1795, however, the War Department adopted a more aggressive policy in the Southwest, without reducing the pressure for removal in the North. The policy reached its climax during the War of 1812 when armies in the North and South, commanded respectively by Governor Harrison and Andrew Jackson, destroyed the power of Indians east of the Mississippi River. After the war, Governors Cass of Michigan and William Clark of Missouri became the preeminent superintendents of Indian affairs in the West. Both men believed in a more limited use of the military than had

13. Masterson, *Blount,* 199–207, 211, 215–20, 270–73.

their predecessors. In their view, federal troops should be used primarily to punish extraordinary depredations by Indians and to prevent or terminate hostilities between tribes; that is, in such a way as to make the United States government the arbiter of intertribal affairs.[14]

The breakdown of the federal peace policy, however, was not simply a function of the uncontrolled desire for land. It also grew out of the faulty execution of Indian trade policies. Between 1796 and 1822 the federal government operated a chain of trading posts or factories in the West, which came under the governors' supervision. Governors had to approve and transmit factory accounts and bills for purchases. Sometimes they were asked to purchase goods for the factories, to make recommendations for improving the system, or to suggest locations for new trading posts. When the government dismantled the factory system, Governor Clark was asked to dispose of the unsold trade items.[15]

Altogether, the factory system involved governors in a considerable amount of work, but the government factories presented a minor problem compared to the private traders who also came under their supervision. The governors theoretically controlled private traders under a series of Intercourse Acts that grew out of the plan developed by the British after the French and Indian War. Like the British, the Confederation Congress, in the Ordinance of 1786, created a Northern and Southern Department for the supervision of Indian trade west of the Appalachian Mountains, using the Ohio River as the boundary between the two. Each department was to have a superintendent who would control Indian affairs primarily by limiting contacts between whites and Indians to licensed traders. The governors, of course, fell heir to the superintendents' duties when Congress organized the Northwest and Southwest Territories. In 1790, Congress superseded the Ordinance of 1786 with the first in a series of temporary Intercourse

14. Philbrick, *Laws of Indiana*, R60–64; Prucha, *Indian Policy*, 265–66.

15. Ora Brooks Peake, *A History of the United States Factory System, 1795–1822* (Denver, 1954), 22, 68–69, 95, 206, hereafter cited as Peake, *U.S. Factory System*. Both Edwards and Cass denounced the factory system. Cass urged that it be replaced by rigid federal regulation and licensing of private traders. In 1815 Governor William Clark, who also opposed the factory system, advocated its replacement by a large private company to trade with the Indians under government regulation. Harmon, *Sixty Years*, 125.

Acts, but it did not pass a permanent law for the regulation of Indian trade until 1802.[16]

In the period before 1834, all-out law enforcement was seldom possible. Besides the chronic shortage of personnel and funds, governors periodically received calls for retrenchment. As a result, Governors Clark and Hull found it necessary in 1809 to strip their services to the bone. Twenty years later the watchword was still economy, and in the early 1830s proponents used it as a primary reason for enacting the bill that was to become the Intercourse Act of 1834.[17]

Few officials in the territories were willing to take actions to insure the enforcement of the trade and segregation laws when their federal funds ran out, because they were not ordinarily empowered to commit additional government resources without specific authorization from the national administration. If a governor failed to obtain prior approval for actions not covered by existing appropriations, or if the Administration subsequently disapproved of his actions, the Treasury might refuse to honor his drafts for payment. Similarly, if he carried out federal policies using his own money, he ran the risk of not being reimbursed. This happened to St. Clair and contributed heavily to his impoverishment, but it may also help to account for the reluctance of other governors to use their money for official purposes.

By 1792 St. Clair had spent $9,000 of his own money executing War Department instructions that were not covered by Congressional appropriations. When he petitioned the Treasury Department for reimbursement, Alexander Hamilton said he could not pay the governor, though he agreed that his claims were valid, because St. Clair's vouchers were not receipted. After the governor provided receipted vouchers, however, the Treasury would not reimburse him for other reasons. St. Clair had incurred much of the debt during the Confederation period, and there was now some question as to whether he was entitled to repayment since Congress had made no provision for paying such debts. This problem was not solved before 1795, when Hamilton left the Treasury. Then, before St. Clair made any headway with Hamilton's successor, a fire in the War Department destroyed all the

16. Prucha, *Indian Policy*, 45–50, 54; *Federal Indian Law* (Washington, 1958), 94–100, 374–75, 381.

17. Prucha, *Indian Policy*, 276–77.

papers bearing on his case and brought it to an end. Some time later he applied directly to Congress for reimbursement, only to have his appeal denied because of the statute of limitations. Finally, in 1857, thirty-nine years after his death, Congress granted a settlement to St. Clair's heirs.[18]

Another obstacle to the effective administration of Indian affairs was the lack of cooperation between governors and military commanders. This was an especially common problem after the War of 1812, when few governors had the power to command detachments of the regular army in their territory. To enforce the Intercourse Acts, these governors had to rely on the cooperation of local commanders who, often resentful of civilian authorities, were slow to act. Occasionally they failed to act altogether and sometimes acted on their own, without making any attempt to coordinate their actions with those of the governors. All governors, of course, had broad powers over the militia and could theoretically use it to enforce federal policies. But unless the action was authorized in advance, the militia could not be mustered into federal service or paid out of the national treasury. Thus, inasmuch as the territorial legislatures were loath to finance federal Indian policies, which they usually disliked, and the citizens showed little enthusiasm for serving without pay, the militia had a very limited value.[19]

18. Burnet, *Notes*, 380–83; Smith, *St. Clair Papers*, I:249–52. During the embargo St. Clair saw his entire estate and nearly all his personal possessions auctioned off at a fraction of their value to satisfy unpaid debts of about $10,000. After that he lived in near destitution with his improverished widowed daughter and her family. Just before he died, both Congress and the Pennsylvania legislature voted him small pensions. Some time earlier Congress had paid some $5,000 to a creditor on St. Clair's claims, but of course, St. Clair got none of it.

During the War of 1812, when the officer in charge gave up, Governor Edwards raised a force at his own expense to defend the Illinois frontier. He apparently did so without the expectation of reimbursement and without later making a claim. Similarly, during the Civil War Governor Gilpin took it upon himself to save New Mexico for the Union by raising an expedition with his own money. When he presented drafts totaling $375,000, the Treasury at first refused to honor them but later changed its mind. Valentine, "Territorial Governor," 60–61.

19. Prucha, *Indian Policy*, 63–64; F. E. Wilson, *St. Clair*, 111; Valentine, "Territorial Governor," 77, 79–81; G. L. Wilson, "St. Clair," 181; Jarrold, "St. Clair," 49; *ASPIA*, I:231, 645; McCarty, *Governors of the Northwest*, 129.

Until 1791 St. Clair had to depend on individuals to report violations of trade laws, and on the small military detachments in the Northwest to enforce them, since there were no Indian agents to assist him. Then the federal government began appointing special agents to work alongside the governors, and two years later Congress authorized the appointment of temporary agents to live among the Indians, primarily, it seems, to promote peace and to civilize—that is, Europeanize—them. During the next two decades Congress increased the number of temporary agents and provided for the appointment of subagents whose duties were similar to those of the agents. By the end of the War of 1812 the agents and subagents became permanent members of the Indian service and their responsibilities for trade regulation were approximately the same as the governor's. In 1818, when Congress standardized their mode of appointment, there were fifteen agents and ten subagents among the Indians.[20]

The addition of agents and subagents, however, diluted the governors' control over Indian affairs and did not necessarily improve the enforcement of the trade laws. For one thing, diffusion of the power to license traders, which was a primary means of regulating trade, accompanied the multiplication of agents. Before 1790 the superintendent was the main source of trade licenses, but an act of that year empowered the President or anyone named by him to issue licenses. In this way agents began acquiring a licensing power, and by an act of 1802 Congress explicitly extended full licensing powers to all agents. Next, the federal government came to expect authorities in one Indian superintendency to honor licenses issued in another. In 1819, after they showed some reluctance to do so, Secretary of War John C. Calhoun finally ordered Governor Clark and other authorities in the Missouri superintendency to honor licenses issued in Green Bay, Chicago, and Michilimackinac.

Another factor that made the administration of Indian affairs inefficient was that the Indian agents were not wholly subordinate to the superintendents. Although they came under the governor's general supervision as superintendent, the agents were not his appointees.

20. Prucha, *Indian Policy*, 53–55. The Act of 1818 provided for the appointment of agents and subagents in the same manner as other territorial officials: Presidential nomination and Senate confirmation.

Consequently, as in their relations with military commanders, governors had to depend on the cooperation of agents for the proper enforcement of federal policies. There was little governors could do to rid themselves of corrupt or insubordinate agents besides petitioning the President or the Secretary of War for their removal. Finally, because of their special status as federal officials, the agents tended to be the governors' rivals and critics. Secretary of War Timothy Pickering, among others, took advantage of this fact when, in 1795, he sent out agents to undermine Governor Blount's control over Indian affairs in the Southwest.[21]

In order to improve the enforcement of trade laws within the limits imposed by inadequate resources and divided authority, William Blount and other governors urged the federal government to restrict Indian trade to frontier posts. The government did not adopt this idea, but in 1824, thirty years after Blount first made his proposal, Congress authorized Indian agents to designate trade sites in Indian country with the approval of the War Department. As it turned out, the use of designated sites, while improving the supervision of legal trade, did not bring an end to the illegal trade. Nor did such trade restrictions please the American Fur Company and other traders. On the contrary, they vigorously opposed a trade policy that they contended gave the British an advantage and called for return to "free" trade.[22]

The federal government considered the use of liquor in Indian trade to be a major source of conflict in the West during the period before 1834, yet it did not attempt to prohibit its use until the end of the period. In the meantime, the government's efforts to limit the traffic in liquor were largely ineffective, for reasons already suggested and because of slack policies and complicity on the part of some

21. *Federal Indian Law*, 373–75; Prucha, *Indian Policy*, 55, 60, 67, 83, 96; Valentine, "Territorial Governor," 56; Neil, "Territorial Governors," 75–76; Masterson, *Blount*, 272; Carter, *Territorial Papers*, XXIV:94–97 and *passim*. Prucha (*Indian Policy*, 81) cites a case of the secretary of the Michigan Territory assuming the power to license traders as acting governor. He issued a license to a Green Bay inhabitant on the ground that Jay's Treaty made the man a citizen and eligible for a license. The United States Attorney General revoked the license, but seems not to have questioned the secretary's right to issue it.

22. Prucha, *Indian Policy*, 68–70, 76–77, 98–101.

governors. Not until 1802, in response to a request from President Jefferson, did Congress enact a law giving the President authority to restrict the distribution of liquor to Indians. Jefferson then delegated his authority to the governors. Governor Harrison tried to curtail the flow of liquor, but after the War of 1812, when the fur trade entered its most active period, Governors Cass and Clark began using their discretionary powers extensively to permit traders to carry almost unlimited quantities of liquor into Indian country. They allegedly winked at violations of the law in order to help improve the United States traders' competitive position with respect to the British. Cass nonetheless underwent a transformation when he became Jackson's Secretary of War in 1831, for he ceased to support the premise of his former close friends, who included John Jacob Astor, that liquor was essential to the conduct of Indian trade. The following year Congress outlawed the introduction of liquor into Indian country, but although it provided for an inspection system, absolute prohibition simply inaugurated a period of wholesale liquor smuggling. The American Fur Company evaded the law by operating a still near the mouth of the Yellowstone River until its enemies reported the still's location and the army destroyed it.[23]

The liquor ban was a step in transition to the second period of Indian affairs which began with the passage of the Intercourse and Department of Indian Affairs Acts of 1834. The new laws came after years of criticism of the Indian service by governors and agents, but were primarily a product of recommendations made by Governors Cass and Clark. These two men submitted a report, in response to an official request in 1828 that they draft a set of proposals to guide Congress in writing new laws, and it was sent to the Senate in February 1829. Congress did not act on their report immediately, but when it did, it incorporated much of the joint report and another one, sub-

23. *Ibid.*, 78–81, 104–05, 110–17, 127, 135–37; 4 *Statutes*, 564; *Federal Indian Law*, 188–89, 381–84; Hiram Martin Chittenden, *The American Fur Trade of the Far West* (2 vols., New York, 1935), I:21, 26, 29; Carter, *Territorial Papers*, XXIV:94–97. See also the interesting letter in which Cass claims he never used his discretionary power to permit the sale of liquor to Indians. Cass to John Anderson, March 21, 1822, in the John Anderson Papers, Michigan Historical Collections, University of Michigan.

mitted by Cass in 1831 after he became Secretary of War, in the laws of 1834. In 1834 Congress revamped the Indian service. It replaced the informal bureau set up by John C. Calhoun a decade earlier with a separate office of Indian affairs in the War Department. Congress also strengthened the offices of superintendent and Indian agent, codified federal policies and trade regulations, and proposed to organize a new western territory for the government of Indians emigrating west of the Mississippi River. Although it created an Indian Territory, however, Congress did not pass an Organic Act for its government. Consequently, despite the continued efforts of a number of representatives and senators, primarily from Missouri and Arkansas, to push through Congress bills providing for the organization of a representative government, Indian Territory remained under the arbitrary, makeshift rule of the superintendent and agents.[24]

24. The evolution of the laws of 1834 is admirably analyzed in Prucha, *Indian Policy*. (See especially *ibid.*, 51, 57–60, 74, 96–101, 250–65. In addition, see 4 *Statutes*, 729–38; *Federal Indian Law*, 107–08.) In 1828 Clark was Superintendent of Indian Affairs in St. Louis, a position he retained when Missouri entered the Union in 1821 and his governorship ended. He served as Superintendent west of the Mississippi River until his death in 1838 (*DAB* II:144). Cass resigned the Michigan governorship to become Secretary of War in August 1831 (Woodford, *Lewis Cass*, 171–72).

Why the Missouri and Arkansas Congressional delegations were so interested in obtaining representative government for the Indian Territory in the four decades or more following the passage of the Intercourse Act of 1834 is not clear and certainly is deserving of study, but it is also peripheral to the main purpose here. So is the fact that the sponsors of those bills not introduced by Arkansas and Missouri representatives and senators, in all but a few instances, were westerners. What is clear is that these men viewed an Organic Act for the Indian Territory in the same way as Monroe and others viewed the Ordinance of 1787. Their objective was to "civilize" the Indians. It is surprising, nonetheless, that most of the bills introduced before the Civil War provided for a fully representative unicameral legislature and that those introduced after 1860 called for a standard second-stage government. Although the intent was to destroy tribal organizations, most bills guaranteed each tribe proportional representation. The bills usually prohibited white men from voting or holding office, unless the legislature passed private acts for the purpose. A bill of 1866 would have created a Territory of Lincoln in the Indian Territory, in which people of Afro-American descent alone would be eligible for homesteads, the vote, and officeholding. Another bill, introduced in 1871, would have created the Oklahoma Territory as a preserve for both Indians and Afro-Americans. A few bills, like that of 1854, which provided for the organization of three Indian territories, made the governor's office elective, but normally the governor was to be appointed in the same manner as

The laws of 1834 were supplementary to Andrew Jackson's program for the wholesale removal of eastern Indians to the land west of the frontier. As Anglo-American settlement expanded more rapidly early in the nineteenth century and Indians were pushed further west, they became relatively more concentrated and less willing to part with their lands. Nevertheless, during the decade from 1818 to 1828, governors and special commissioners maintained a steady pressure and were able to negotiate a number of treaties extinguishing Indian land titles. The pace of piecemeal removal, however, was too slow to establish, much less to maintain, the Indian segregation which was seen as the only way to end violence on the frontier. Clashes between Indians and Anglo-Americans almost invariably threatened to upset whatever precarious *détente* existed, and therefore constituted one of the governors' biggest problems. By the 1820s the magnitude of the threat and the weakness of the Indians persuaded Cass and Clark to throw their full support behind the idea of complete removal despite any misgivings they may have had regarding the motives of men like Jackson. Seeing themselves as humanitarians, they and other governors reasoned that once segregation was accomplished everyone would be safer and the Indians could be more easily "civilized." In rationalizing their position, however, Cass and Clark implicitly endorsed the idea

---

that of any other territory. In the bills of the post-Civil War period, the governor's veto was qualified, and in a few it was omitted entirely. Like most Organic Acts, most of these bills were silent on the matter of statehood, but in a number of them there was some mention of eventual membership in the Union. For a representative sample see *NA*, H–490, 23 Cong., May 20, 1834; *NA*, H–579, 30 Cong., June 27, 1848; *NA*, S–221, 33 Cong., Feb. 20, 1854; *NA*, S–483, 33 Cong., July 28, 1854; *NA*, S–274, 37 Cong., Apr. 16, 1862; *NA*, H–492, 37 Cong., June 2, 1862 and Jan. 2, 1863; *NA*, S–459, 38 Cong., Feb. 20, 1865; *NA*, H–367, 40 Cong., Jan. 6, 1868; *NA*, H–1208, 40 Cong., June 9, 1868; *NA*, H–1001, 41 Cong., Jan. 28, 1870; *NA*, S–679, 41 Cong., Mar. 17, 1870; *House Bills*, 39 Cong., H–647, June 9, 1866 and June 30, 1866; *ibid.*, 42 Cong., H–113, Mar. 13, 1871; *ibid.*, 42 Cong., H–3578, Jan. 20, 1873; *Senate Bills*, 41 Cong., S–1186, Jan. 10, 1871; *ibid.*, 41 Cong., S–1237, Jan. 20, 1871; *Congressional Globe*, 24 Cong., 1 sess., III:174; *ibid.*, 25 Cong., 2 sess., VI:269–74, 338; *ibid.*, 25 Cong., 3 sess., VII:216; *ibid.*, 42 Cong., 1 sess., XLIV:14, 78; *ibid.*, 42 Cong., 2 sess., XLV:58, 830, 2954; *ibid.*, 42 Cong., 3 sess., XLVI:83, 84, 611, 658, 717, 1522; *Congressional Record*, 43 Cong., 2 sess., 19, 72, 66. See also Roy Gittinger, *The Formation of the State of Oklahoma, 1803–1906* (Norman, 1939), 103–05; Grant Foreman, *A History of Oklahoma* (Norman, 1942), 41–53, 169–90.

that Anglo-American expansion was inevitable and that Indians could survive on the Great Plains which were not then considered suitable for white habitation.

In 1826 a bill to establish a permanent Indian Territory west of the Mississippi failed to pass in Congress, but when the vindictive Andrew Jackson entered the Presidency he promptly called on Congress to readdress itself to the matter of removal and to act immediately. Congress enacted the desired legislation in 1830 and Jackson moved swiftly to oust the Indians east of the Mississippi River. By 1834, when Congress created the new permanent Indian Territory, the humanitarian Secretary of War Cass lost patience with obdurate tribes that, in his words, did not know what was best for themselves. After trying to convince the Cherokee that he was right, Cass decided that discussion was useless and curtly told them they would have to move because the federal government was not going to change its policy.[25]

Although the establishment of a permanent Indian frontier was fundamental to a "final solution" of the Indian "problem," the federal government's approach to Indian affairs continued to change after 1834. In the first decade the military-logistic problems of removal predominated. Then the concurrent acquisition of new lands and the rapid dispersal of Anglo-American settlers across the Great Plains to the Pacific Ocean during the Mexican War period changed conditions radically. Settlers cutting through the permanent Indian Territory revived and exaggerated all the problems that had existed east of the Mississippi. The War Department was as hard pressed to cope with the new possessions and their Indian populations as with the widely scattered white settlements. By the late 1840s the War Department's Office of Indian Affairs badly needed reorganization if it was to deal effectively with its new problems. But in 1849, before the reorganization took place, Congress created the Department of the Interior and gave it extensive control over Indian affairs.

25. Prucha, *Indian Policy*, 225–47, 256–58; *Federal Indian Law*, 180–83, 191, 199; Carter, *Territorial Papers*, XXIII:385, XXIV:83, 147–48. After 1803 Jefferson concluded that Indians must cross into the land of the Louisiana Purchase and that the country east of the Mississippi should be for white men. Under his administration southern Indians began emigrating beyond the Mississippi voluntarily under federal sponsorship. Harmon, *Sixty Years*, 78–79.

The transfer of routine Indian affairs to the Interior Department at the beginning of the Second Empire, however, did not end conflict between civilian and military authorities in the field. Nor did it simplify matters for the governor who was also superintendent, because he was now responsible to an additional secretary. He had to answer to the Secretary of the Interior for the conduct of normal Indian affairs and to the Secretary of War insofar as he was involved in the military aspects of Indian policy that fell within the jurisdiction of the War Department.

Within twenty-two years of the organization of the Interior Department, the federal government reversed its Indian policies. During the first decade, the government modified its idea of a permanent Indian frontier and returned to a policy of piecemeal removal. In contrast to previous policies, under which Indians had been moved to lands beyond the frontier line, however, the government began, in 1851, increasingly to direct its efforts toward the segregation of Indians on rather clearly defined reservations within what was primarily a white man's country. Moreover, during the 1860s unilateral federal legislation rapidly replaced bilateral treaty-making in settling the future of Indian tribes, and in an act of March 3, 1871, Congress declared Indians to be wards of the United States government rather than independent nations and tribes. In adopting the new apartheid policy Congress in effect decided that the Indians were not competent either to choose their own course or to negotiate treaties with the federal government.

As these changes were occurring, a number of territorial governors were agitating for others. Basically, they urged that the administration of Indian affairs and control over policy-making be fully centralized, and called for the adaptation of policies to the conditions of the Great Plains and Rocky Mountain regions. In 1868 Congress acted in accordance with their recommendations. On July 27 it consolidated control over Indian affairs by vesting all supervisory and appellate authority in the Commissioner of Indian Affairs and the Secretary of the Interior, and completed concentrating power in the field in the hands of the Indian agents.[26]

26. *Federal Indian Law,* 24–26, 42–43, 49, 102, 110–14, 177, 210–11; Hoopes, *Indian Affairs,* 9–10, 17; Neil, "Territorial Governors," 87.

As the government's approach to Indian affairs changed, so did the governor's job as superintendent. In 1834 the governors began losing much of their control over Indian affairs to the agents, and their superintendencies started dwindling in size. Unlike the preceding period, when they were frequently much larger than the governor's civil jurisdiction, superintendencies after 1834 were smaller and more nearly coterminous with territorial boundaries. In 1834 Congress separated the governorship superintendency in Florida and Arkansas, and the governors of those territories ceased to have any control over affairs in Indian country. Similarly, of the seven territories created during the first decade of the Second Empire, the governors of five—Oregon, Minnesota, New Mexico, Utah, and Washington—lost their superintendents' commissions before the outbreak of the Civil War. The Kansas-Nebraska Act of 1854 did not provide for the governors of those two territories to hold the office of superintendent. Congress, however, did combine the two offices in the Organic Acts for the seven territories organized during the 1860s—that is, in the Colorado, Nevada, Dakota, Arizona, Idaho, Montana, and Wyoming Acts, but by 1870 they had been separated in all except Montana. In 1873 the Montana governorship and superintendency were fully divorced and from that time forward Congress maintained them as separate offices in all territories.[27]

Despite the changes made in the system, those governors who were superintendents between 1834 and 1873 faced the same basic problems as earlier superintendents. As the agents became more powerful, they attained a degree of autonomy within their domain not unlike that of the oligarchies in local government, and this made it ever more difficult for the governors to counter corruption, inefficiency, and insubordination for which they could still be held responsible.[28] Thus, as a whole, the governors' role in Indian affairs declined. Nevertheless, throughout the 1850s and 1860s some govern-

27. Carter, *Territorial Papers*, XII:780–82; 4 *Statutes*, 735; Valentine, "Territorial Governor," 55; Neil, "Territorial Governors," 64; Pomeroy, *Territories, 1861–1890*, 16–18, 95; Prucha, *Indian Policy*, 260–61; Hoopes, *Indian Affairs*, 26–27, 70–72, 76–77, 128, 155, 175–76.

28. Prucha, *Indian Policy*, 70–71; Neil, "Territorial Governors," 75–76; Hoopes, *Indian Affairs*, 130–40. *House Documents*, No. 39, 41 Cong., 2 sess. (S.N. 1464), 11–15; No. 98, 42 Cong., 2 sess. (S.N. 1578), 2–3.

ors, like William Gilpin of Colorado, Joseph Lane of Oregon, and Isaac Stevens of Washington, continued to consider Indian affairs to be their first responsibility and took an active part in treaty-making and, in a few instances, in military operations against Indians.[29]

All the governors who were superintendents handled or supervised the distribution of presents and payments to Indians and faced the same problems. Congress was often sluggish when it came to ratifying treaties and voting monies, even in emergencies, but once the Indians had signed a treaty, they did not like to wait. Thus, in the 1790s St. Clair voiced the lament echoed by governors throughout the nineteenth century, when he complained that Indians became restless and held him personally responsible if they failed to receive promised treaty gifts and payments on time. Sixty years later, in 1853, Governor David Meriwether of New Mexico was hard pressed to keep peace when annuities did not arrive and his lack of money finally made it impossible for him to feed the Indians within his superintendency. By 1867 the Nez Percé in Idaho were becoming impatient because Congress still had not ratified the treaty signed in June 1863 or voted monies in accordance with its provisions. Neither had Congress appropriated money for the Ute treaty made in Colorado in 1863, though the Senate had ratified it in 1864. When governors did receive funds for Indians, it was often in bank drafts that were heavily discounted and paid off in depreciated currency. During the 1860s, for example, Indians were getting paper worth about sixty to sixty-five cents in coin on the dollar. The Indians objected and governors repeatedly urged Congress to require that such drafts be paid in hard money.

Before the end of the eighteenth century Governor Sargent of Mississippi added another complaint. As superintendent, he was responsible for the distribution of gifts and supplies to Indians, but he had little

29. Hoopes, *Indian Affairs*, 87–97, 100–23, 173–74; Neil, "Territorial Governors," 79.Territorial secretaries also continued to act in Indian affairs during governors' absences, much as earlier secretaries had. During one of Governor Stevens' absences from the Washington Territory in 1855, Secretary C. H. Mason used his authority as acting governor to requisition troops for a punitive expedition against marauding Indians. Similarly, during Governor Meriwether's absence from New Mexico in 1854, Secretary William S. Messervy countered an Apache uprising and continued to hold councils.

real power over the military commanders who in this case actually distributed them. He insisted, to no avail, that he should either have complete control over all Indian affairs within his jurisdiction or should not be held responsible for the actions of other officials. When, in the nineteenth century, Indian agents became the primary distributors, the complaint was the same and the governors were relieved of their responsibilities only when they ceased to be superintendents.[30]

From the passage of the Intercourse Act of 1796 through much of the nineteenth century, governors had authority to arbitrate individual claims of Indians against whites and vice versa. These claims frequently involved offenses such as horse thefts. If an award were due an Anglo-American, the governor paid it out of Indian annuity funds, but if it were due an Indian and payable by the federal government the governor had to complete a report and apply to the War Department for payment. When a report was incomplete in any way, payment was delayed beyond the normal time required for processing in the cumbrous machinery of the War Department. The accounting system in itself was always fraught with problems that seemed at times to cause officials more trouble than the actual dealings with the Indians.[31]

Probably more significant and enduring than the Indian activities of governors as superintendents, however, were those of all governors in their capacity as governor. Whether superintendents or not, all governors were obligated to cope with the basic causes of unrest, to protect Indians from settlers, and to help "civilize" them. These duties were much harder to carry out because unlike the war, removal, and extermination policies, they ran counter to the basic desires and objectives of most frontier settlers.

30. There were only a few cases of governors' misusing federal Indian monies entrusted to them. Apparently all the abuses occurred in the 1860s, just before the complete separation of the offices of governor and superintendent. At the end of the Civil War Caleb Lyon of Idaho was accused of misappropriating $47,000 of Indian funds, and the government rejected his story of having been robbed. A short time later the government asked Governor Green Clay Smith of Montana to answer charges that he had spent $1,645 of such money gambling. (See Valentine, "Territorial Governor," 57–58; Neil, "Territorial Governors," 71–72; G. L. Wilson, "St. Clair," 182; 13 *Statutes* [appendix], 73–79; 14 *Statutes*, 647–54; Hoopes, *Indian Affairs*, 78, 171–72.)

31. Prucha, *Indian Policy*, 59, 207–10.

Protection of Indians fell into two basic areas: crimes committed against Indians in Indian country and crimes against Indians perpetrated elsewhere. Since Congress never saw fit to enact laws to cover violations of Indian rights outside Indian country the division can be further defined as primarily one of federal *vs.* state or territorial justice. As far as the governor was concerned, the division was also one between his office as governor and his office as superintendent. This distinction was only technically relevant when the offices of superintendent and governor were combined and the areas of jurisdiction of both commissions coincided. The distinction generally was of real importance, however, for in most cases either the governor was not also superintendent or the boundaries of the two jurisdictions were not the same. Where the governor was not also superintendent, his commission extended only to those portions of his territory free of Indian titles, meaning that he had no authority over those parts of Indian country within his territory. Nevertheless, he still had an obligation to cooperate with Indian agents in the apprehension of individuals found within his jurisdiction who had committed crimes in Indian country. Cooperation between superintendents and agents was sometimes hard to achieve and jurisdictional disputes were frequent. Such conflicts were important, since the exact location where a criminal act took place determined the court system and kind of law that pertained.[32]

Federal law covered Indian trade and crimes against Indians only in Indian country. Into the nineteenth century governors could also apply territorial laws to crimes committed in Indian country, but trade regulation and crimes against Indians in any other part of a territory or state within the superintendent's jurisdiction came entirely under territorial or state laws. In 1790 at the behest of Governor St. Clair and President Washington, Congress equated crimes committed by whites against Indians with crimes committed by whites against whites, thereby making it clear that territorial criminal codes and federal laws were to be applied in the same way to both types of cases.

In 1793 Congress gave the territorial judges, and federal judges in

32. Valentine, "Territorial Governor," 70–71; Pomeroy, *Territories, 1861–1890*, 16–18; Neil, "Territorial Governors," 69–73; Prucha, *Indian Policy*, 105; *Federal Indian Law*, 375.

the states, jurisdiction over crimes against Indians that were committed in Indian country, and three years later, federal criminal laws for Indians began developing along lines parallel to those of the territories. With the Intercourse Act of 1796 Congress assumed the power to define acts that constituted crimes whether they were committed by Indians or by whites, and provided for the prosecution of both Indians and whites under federal law. On March 17, 1817, Congress enlarged the list of crimes to include any act committed in Indian country that was punishable anywhere "under the sole and exclusive jurisdiction of the United States." Presumably this pronouncement made all criminal laws of the territories and those federal laws pertaining to the public domain, the District of Columbia, and any other federal property or installation applicable to Indians and whites in Indian country. Following nearly twenty more years of piecemeal growth, Congress clarified and codified federal Indian laws. The comprehensive code adopted June 30, 1834, was the basic federal Indian law into the twentieth century.[33]

While a number of early governors exerted some influence on the development of federal law, they were often instrumental in obtaining the enactment of special territorial laws regarding Indians. In 1790 Sargent and the Northwest judges enacted the first territorial law prohibiting the sale of "ardent spirits" to Indians and regulating trade with them. Five years later the governor and judges repealed the law, but in 1799, on St. Clair's recommendation, the first Northwest General Assembly enacted another liquor control law. Laws of this sort and others prohibiting or restricting the sale of firearms and ammunition to Indians became standard subjects for specific territorial legislation and regularly appeared among governors' recommendations to legislatures.[34]

33. *Federal Indian Law*, 24–25, 94–110; Prucha, *Indian Policy*, 189–93; 4 *Statutes*, 729–35. The quote from the 1817 Act is in 3 *Statutes*, 383, and in Prucha, *Indian Policy*, 193. Courts eventually ruled that unlicensed Indian traders operating outside Indian country were not subject to federal regulation and could not be prosecuted under federal law. Thus traders avoided prosecution for violations of federal law by trading from barges anchored in a stream bordering an Indian reservation or on private land within a reservation. (See *Federal Indian Law*, 375.)

34. Pease, *Laws of the Northwest*, A26–28, A256, A415–16. See also, for

Theft by Indians, especially of livestock, was a constant problem. Horse theft, of course, was common on the Great Plains and in other regions where Indians placed a high economic or cultural value on horses, but it also reached large proportions elsewhere. In 1801 Governor Harrison urged the government to garrison Kaskaskia in order to curtail the extensive horse stealing in that area. Earlier, in the Southwest, Governor Blount had been plagued by the same problem. In that territory the Indians stole horses primarily for sale in the Carolinas and Georgia. In 1792 Blount claimed that they had stolen about 500 horses. Such thefts generated great hostility toward Indians, but since the government rejected the governor's recommendation that it send agents into the Carolinas and Georgia to intercept Indian horse traders, all Blount could do to assist in the recovery of missing animals was to issue passports allowing individuals to enter Indian country in search of them. In some cases, early in the First Empire, it was possible to get stolen horses back by pressuring tribal chiefs. Between 1808 and 1815, Governor Clark apparently used this method successfully to obtain the return of some stolen horses from the Osages, who were notorious horse thieves in Missouri. And, as federal power increased relative to that of the Indians during the nineteenth century, the Indians became more susceptible to pressure and horse thieves were more easily apprehended.[35]

Theft, however, was not a pastime peculiar to Indians. White frontiersmen were frequently to be found marauding in Indian country. During much of St. Clair's administration, organized raiding parties from Kentucky helped to keep the Northwest in turmoil. Although such bands ostensibly started as punitive expeditions, their members often seemed to be at least equally interested in plundering Indian settlements. Moreover, white marauders tended to differentiate less between raiding for plunder and murder than did the Indians who primarily purloined goods and animals. The reasons are not hard to find. On the one hand, Indians had little personal property that white

---

example, Philbrick, *Laws of Indiana*, A40, A91, A97, A216, A452, A497–98, A590–92; Philbrick, *Laws of Illinois*, A89–90, A154–55; and Prucha, *Indian Policy*, 103–07.

35. Prucha, *Indian Policy*, 203–06. Clark's zeal and harshness in dealing with Indians are well illustrated in Carter, *Territorial Papers*, especially XIV:215, 445–46.

frontiersmen coveted. On the other, both Indian land and scalps had a potential or immediate cash value to the white.[36]

The problems of enforcing laws that pertained to crimes committed by or against Indians were similar to those that governors normally faced during the early years of a territory's history, when they dealt with offenses that involved only whites. It was apparently somewhat more difficult to apprehend white than Indian offenders, however, for in spite of the obvious inequities they suffered, Indians maintained a respectable record for turning members of their tribes over to the courts. Nevertheless, the foremost problem at all times, especially during the early years, was one of obtaining justice in the courts. In general, the higher courts tended to treat Indians more fairly and to convict whites more frequently. As the courts got closer to the people, the quality of justice deteriorated. In local courts it was virtually impossible to secure the conviction of a white man who had committed a crime against an Indian, no matter how clear the case might be, and if he were convicted, the punishment meted out was usually trivial. On the other hand, any crime allegedly committed by an Indian seemed to warrant harsh punishment. In both cases the very relevance of the laws was questionable, but the judicial system clearly broke down when the crime was murder. White frontiersmen ordinarily assumed that Indians had no rights either in or out of court, and white juries could not bring themselves to convict, much less to punish, their white peers for murdering Indians until well along in the nineteenth century.[37]

St. Clair's quest for justice in the Northwest illustrates the difficulties faced by many governors. He was plagued by roving bands of whites who killed Indians who were peacefully hunting on their own lands, and he seemed to be unable to stop the bloodshed. In 1795 a group of whites murdered two Indians who were at the time in the custody of a sheriff and militiaman. St. Clair used all his authority to

36. Carter, *Territorial Papers*, II:159; Neil, "Territorial Governors," 74; Smith, *St. Clair Papers*, II:374–75. See also the Congressional committee report of July 26, 1787 (Carter, *Territorial Papers*, II:56–57) for an early expression of dismay by the central government at the "mutual depredation & hostilities" of whites and Indians and of special concern over the "wanton and unjust attacks upon the Indian."

37. Prucha, *Indian Policy*, 139–44.

bring two of the men to trial, but despite the compelling evidence presented, he could not even obtain an indictment for manslaughter, much less for murder. During the same year he threatened to invoke martial law to stop mobs from molesting peaceful Indians who passed through Cincinnati on their way home from the Greenville negotiations. His attempt to secure the conviction of one mob's leaders failed for "lack of evidence." Both St. Clair and Sargent complained bitterly about the corrupt manner in which the local courts of the Northwest dealt with Indians, and the outright refusal of local officials to take any action to protect Indians within their jurisdiction.[38]

While numerous governors tried to end both casual and organized murder of Indians, others actively supported campaigns to wreak vengeance on Indians, if not to exterminate them. Governor Edwards, for example, approved an 1814 act of the Illinois legislature that offered bounties to people who killed "those blood thirsty monsters." More often, however, bounty schemes were aranged privately because governors refused to approve legislation of that kind. For this reason, it seems, a committee of citizens in the Miami Purchase in the Northwest issued a "Public Notice" in 1794 offering bounties for Indian scalps. Presumably each of the "many good citizens" represented by the committee contributed to the war chest. Similar associations were to be found subsidizing the murder of Indians in other territories. At the beginning of the Civil War, Governor Gilpin of Colorado was complaining about the bands of white men in his territory who were out to kill Indians for their scalps, and he lamented his lack of resources to cope with the situation. In 1866 an alarmed Governor Lyon of Idaho took steps to counter the decision of a mass meeting of citizens to outfit and maintain, full time and at public expense, a twenty-five man unit of Indian hunters. The men were to receive bounties for Indian scalps ranging from $100 for a buck to $25 for children under ten. The earnestness with which whites pursued this avocation is indicated by the fact that the number of murders soon reached alarming proportions. Despite the efforts of governors and other officials concerned with protecting the Indians, it was not until 1824 that a white jury convicted

38. Philbrick, *Laws of Indiana,* R185; Attig, "Governmental Problems," 86; Smith, *St. Clair Papers,* II:374–75, 396–97; Downes, *Frontier Ohio,* 141–42. See also succeeding note and Chapter IV above.

a white man for murdering an Indian. This precedent, however, was set in an Indiana court and was not one followed with notable enthusiasm along the frontiers.[39]

The largest number of crimes committed by whites were lesser offenses involving violations of the Intercourse Act and other trade laws. But the power of the traders and the sympathies of the Anglo-American settlers were such that it was as difficult to obtain convictions for these crimes as for major ones. Moreover, attempts to enforce the trade laws sometimes boomeranged, and the enforcing officers ended up under indictment. In the absence of strong support from the federal government, the threat of retaliation discouraged officials in the territories from vigorously enforcing the trade laws, and in some instances they gave up all efforts to enforce them.[40]

There was probably no territory in which governors did not have to deal with illegal invasions of Indian country by white settlers, but although they were responsible for preventing encroachments and

39. Philbrick, *Laws of Illinois*, A177–78; Prucha, *Indian Policy*, 194–201; Neil, "Territorial Governors," 74–75. The 1824 conviction seems to have been the first of its kind in United States history. (See Philbrick, *Laws of Indiana*, R185.)

40. Captain William R. Jouett, commandant of Fort Snelling, was involved in drawn-out law suits between 1832 and 1834, as a result of his seizure of whiskey discovered on two boats owned by the American Fur Company and Joseph Renville. The owners retained James Duane Doty, the future governor of the Wisconsin Territory, as attorney and charged Jouett with trespass, assault, and illegal imprisonment. The court eventually upheld Jouett's actions but the inconvenience and lack of strong federal support discouraged him from displaying such zeal again. During Jouett's ordeal, Indian agent Joseph M. Street apprehended Jean Brunet, a Prairie du Chien trader, logging in Indian country and took him to Fort Crawford for confinement. When the post commander, Major Stephen W. Kearney, turned Brunet over to civil authorities, they released him and he promptly brought suit against Street and Kearney for their actions. A jury found them guilty, the court fined them $1,400 for damages and costs, and they had to petition Congress for a special relief act to reimburse them. In a third case, Major Alexander Cummings, who later became the governor of Colorado Territory, simply gave up trying to enforce the Intercourse Act in Arkansas when, in November 1824, after submitting with evidence a list of people who were illegally hunting on Indian land, the district attorney refused to prosecute. The accused found out about Cummings' list and 200 of them prepared to march on his military post. Cummings thwarted their attack by seizing two of the leaders, but he could not prosecute them because the district attorney could not find sufficient evidence of insurrection. (See Prucha, *Indian Policy*, 70–74, 108–09, 126, 131–32, 170, 184–85, for elaboration and other examples.)

removing squatters on Indian lands, there was little governors could or would do that had a lasting effect. They repeatedly condemned violations of federal laws and treaties, ordered settlers to leave Indian country, and threatened to remove them forcibly. Force was generally necessary, since settlers were seldom willing to withdraw voluntarily, but governors were reluctant to use force and normally contented themselves with menacing edicts and recommendations that the federal government secure additional land cessions from the Indians. One reason for their reluctance to use force was that the governors often questioned both their authority to call out the army and the feasibility of doing so. Thus, in June 1812 Benjamin Howard took the position that he could not evict the white settlers on Indian lands in Louisiana-Missouri Territory unless he were ordered to do so by the President, because the Intercourse Act specifically gave only the Chief Executive the power to remove squatters. Rather than request authorization to remove them, Howard suggested that the government remove the Indians, pointing out that the valuable farm land occupied by the squatters had a salt spring. His successor as governor, William Clark, renewed the recommendation that the Indians be removed and the General Assembly provided a supporting resolution. Instead of waiting for the federal government to act, however, Clark reread the Osage treaty of 1808 and decided that it had extinguished all Indian titles to the land in question even though, as Clark himself admitted, the land was "claimed by the Socks and Ioways." This fact notwithstanding, the legislature promptly organized Howard County to cover the area. Similarly, in the early 1820s Governor James Miller of Arkansas called for the removal of the Choctaws from their new treaty lands, rather than the removal of white squatters, because the lands were the best in the territory, had the only salt spring, and contained about a third of the territory's white population. Miller contended that two organized counties would be depopulated if the squatters were removed, that some of the settlers had already been removed several times to no avail, and that there was nothing to be gained by repeating the process.

By the early nineteenth century, squatting on Indian lands had developed into the same sort of game as squatting on the public domain. Squatters left forbidden lands when federal troops actually arrived, and returned as soon as the army withdrew. The governors tended to empty their bag of excuses before calling out the army, not only because they knew that squatters could not be kept off those lands or because their sympathies were with them, but as a matter of political expediency. A governor who showed too great a concern over the rights of Indians or the sanctity of treaties and too great a willingness to use the sword against his own people ran the risk of precipitating campaigns for his removal.[41]

In addition to all their other duties, governors were supposed to help educate the Indians in the mysteries of Anglo-American civilization, and during much of territorial history, to encourage their assimilation. The Ordinance of 1786 and St. Clair's instructions of 1787 and 1788 did not mention the desirability of "Americanizing" the American Indians, but it seems to have been understood. In messages to the Indians in 1791, President Washington, Secretary of War Knox, Governor St. Clair and others extolled the value of "civilization" and began actively promoting European forms of agriculture and learning among the Indians. For these purposes, the federal administration sent explicit instructions to territorial officials, and in the Intercourse Act of 1793 Congress sketched in the first lines of a formal policy. Temporary agents were to be sent to live with the Indians and teach them European agriculture and "domestic arts." A decade later, in his annual address to Congress on January 13, 1803, President Jefferson elaborated the aims of the assimilation policy. He ended his address with a statement that sums up the government's official attitude thereafter: "in leading them thus to agriculture, to manufacture, and civilization; in bringing together their and our sentiments, and in preparing them ultimately to participate in the benefits of our Government, I trust and believe we are acting in their greatest good."[42]

In the meantime, territorial governors and Indian agents had been using the presents and funds for the manufacture of implements, which Congress and the War Department provided, in an effort to recast the Indians in the mold of Anglo-American farmers and craftsmen. Jefferson apparently was impressed by their achievements, and

41. Neil, "Territorial Governors," 76–77; Prucha, *Indian Policy*, 145, 149–50, 153–57, 161–62, 166–69, 171–73, 176–78, 181; Carter, *Territorial Papers*, XIV:728.

42. Prucha, *Indian Policy*, 53–54, 213, 216; *ASPIA*, I:144–66. Jefferson's address is in Richardson, *Messages*, I:353.

made a special point of noting the progress in civilizing the Indians in his first annual message on December 8, 1801. Nevertheless, early in the nineteenth century the federal government began to adopt the more rigid devices of land allotment and formal schooling as its campaign to annihilate the tribal fabric of Indian societies got up a full head of steam.

Joseph Hopkinson, the federal agent who negotiated with the Oneidas in 1798, wrote the first allotment or severalty provisions into a United States Indian treaty. Under them, the federal government promised to deed land to those individual Indians and families that wanted to stay behind as farmers after their tribe ceded its lands. No provision for allotments, however, seems to have been made in any other Indian treaty until after the War of 1812. Between September 1816 and November 1838, governors and special commissioners included allotment clauses in at least thirty treaties—that is, in about one-fifth of the treaties, conventions, and agreements negotiated during the twenty-two year period. Lewis Cass, William Clark, and Andrew Jackson were especially prominent among the men negotiating treaties that included allotment articles. In fact, it was Jackson who incorporated in the second of the thirty treaties, the Cherokee Nation Treaty of July 8, 1817, the provision that made Indians who accepted land in severalty eligible for United States citizenship. Federal guarantees of full citizenship began to appear in treaties with increasing frequency toward the middle of the century, and as their inclusion became more common the allotment provisions also began to assume a standard form. During the 1850s and 1860s, Congress enacted laws and the Senate ratified treaties that resulted in the issuance of 8,595 patents to individual Indians and 1,195 allotment certificates. In sum, throughout the first seven decades of the nineteenth century, the territorial governors were important treaty makers and they seem to have played a prominent part in the development of the allotment system that culminated in the passage of the Dawes Severalty Act on February 8, 1887.[43]

43. The Oneida Treaty is printed in *ASPIA,* I:641. See also Prucha, *Indian Policy,* 56, 71; Hoopes, *Indian Affairs,* 23–24, 36–37; Richardson, *Messages,* I:326; D. S. Otis, "History of the Allotment Policy," in H.R. 7902, 73 Cong., 2 sess.,

The governors' hands were more conspicuous in the promotion of formal education for Indians. In 1791 St. Clair began promoting the idea of teaching Indian children to read and write and the notion soon became current, but it was more than a decade before a treaty provided for formal schooling. Governor Harrison included an article in the important Kaskaskia Treaty of 1803 under which the government was to make seven annual contributions for the support of a Roman Catholic priest who would live with the Indians and teach them literature and other subjects. In 1806 an overly optimistic Indiana legislature adopted a law creating a territorial university, and Harrison seems to have been responsible for its including a section providing for Indian students to be maintained and educated at the expense of the institution. From then until the end of the treaty-making period, provisions for some sort of formal Indian education were made in virtually every treaty and occasionally in territorial laws. But Congress established the basis for most educational work of the Indian service long before it ended treaty-making with Indians in 1871. Acting on President Monroe's recommendations in 1819, Congress began making annual appropriations to support various kinds of Indian education.[44]

The average governor's attitude toward the Indians was almost always far more enlightened than that of the settlers, who generally seemed intent on exterminating them. Both before and after 1871, when their principal problem was to secure equal justice for Indians, the governors ordinarily assumed a humanitarian posture. Often, of course, they lacked the will or the power to do more than pose, but perhaps more often they used what authority they could command to safeguard Indian rights. Arthur St. Clair is, in this respect, probably representative of many governors. Despite his military experience, the cruelty of whites to Indians never ceased to amaze him. More importantly, although he thought the Indians were savages, he could not see that they were any worse than the white frontiersmen, and concluded that they should be treated the same in all respects. None-

---

pt. 9 (1934), 428; *Federal Indian Law,* 111–124, 473–76, but especially notes. Also compare *Federal Indian Law* with 7 *Statutes: Indian Treaties.*

44. Prucha, *Indian Policy,* 46, 220–22; *Federal Indian Law,* 118–19, 174–75, 270–74; *ASPIA,* I:144–46, but especially 166, 687–88; Harmon, *Sixty Years,* 157, 158, 158–59, 359; Philbrick, *Laws of Indiana,* A182, A537.

theless, at times he showed a genuine sympathy for the Indians that was not evident in his dealings with whites, and when he was in the Northwest, he seems to have worked diligently in their behalf despite the difficulties this entailed. In subscribing to a strategy of "divide and conquer," St. Clair was more interested in ending violence than in subjugating the Indians. Even governors like William Henry Harrison, who sometimes seemed to have an obsessive desire to remove Indians, had some humanitarian feelings for them and worked toward securing justice for them. It is clear that the governors as a whole, but most notably during the early period of expansion, held firmly to what they considered the most advanced humanitarian ideas of the day. Consequently, it is difficult to find more than a few governors whose official attitude toward the Indians, if not their private feelings, even approached that of the average white frontiersman. Even men like Secretary Thomas Meagher of Montana, a hotheaded ex-revolutionary from Ireland who was acting governor for over a year in the mid-1860s, had no interest in exterminating the Indians. He frankly considered Indians always to be enemies, either real or potential, yet his correspondence indicates that his primary aim in using crushing military tactics was to keep the peace by nipping violence in the bud.[45]

For those governors who were also superintendents of Indian affairs, the job of obtaining justice for Indians was doubly difficult. The combination of offices was a shortsighted, if logical, economy measure that did not necessarily result in economy. During the nineteenth century the paper work of the superintendency alone threatened to bury the governors. By the middle of the century the office involved masses of paper work. Governors were frequently asked to prepare lengthy reports and recommendations for Congress and various federal agencies. In addition they collected, reviewed, and transmitted the reports of Indian agents in their superintendencies.

45. Sears, "Philosophy of St. Clair," 46–50; G. L. Wilson, "St. Clair," 185–86, 249–52, 406; Prucha, *Indian Policy*, 200–03; Neil, "Territorial Governors," 85–87; Lamar, *Far Southwest*, 93, 97, 244–45 and *passim;* Carter, *Territorial Papers*, XIV:614–22; XVII:35–36, 442–43; XXV:123, and *passim*. See also Lamar, *Dakota Territory*, 88, 189 and *passim;* the annual reports of the governors in the House and Senate Documents; and sources cited in Chapter IX. An excellent exposition of St. Clair's attitude and that of other Federalists in the Northwest is in Burnet, *Notes*, 383–93.

But as the work of the superintendencies increased, so did that of the governor's office; as territories matured, the governors usually had to choose between the two offices. When this necessity occurred, all but the early governors and a few exceptional others saw the governorship as their first responsibility. Even governors who had a strong desire to help the Indians, and who would have preferred having only the superintendency, tended to neglect it out of necessity. Expected to look after the best interests of two conflicting groups, the governors, as white men themselves, were usually drawn to the side of the settlers when a choice was unavoidable. Nevertheless they defied the will of the white population with some frequency. When they did, however, their opponents sometimes fabricated charges of misconduct of Indian affairs and petitioned for their removal. One such campaign to discredit a governor apparently succeeded in Idaho. David W. Ballard lost his job following charges of misconduct as superintendent that, in this instance as in most others, were politically motivated and probably lacked any foundation in fact.[46]

As a whole it seems that the governors' conduct of Indian affairs conformed to the same basic pattern as their administration of territorial government. Their actions were generally those of well-intentioned yet largely impotent officials who exerted some leadership but who tended to follow the path of expediency. Often governors made a sincere effort to carry out their duties in Indian affairs and to protect the rights of Indians. When trouble was brewing, most of them were willing to make the long and arduous trips to trouble spots to try to ease tensions. And governors obtained numerous leaves of absence to handle Indian affairs in Washington and elsewhere. At times they made these trips at the request of the Indians, which indicates the extent to which some governors succeeded in befriending them. That the governors met with more failures than successes was not due so much to their attitude toward the Indians as to the weakness of their

46. See Neil, "Territorial Governors," 66–67, 76–88; Valentine, "Territorial Governor," 56, 70–71; Pomeroy, *Territories, 1861–1890*, 16–18, 95–96. Neil ("Territorial Governors," 84) could find no instances, in the territories he studied, in which bad relations between the governor and legislature induced or could be blamed for inducing governors' neglect or maladministration of their superintendent's duties out of a desire to obtain the good graces or support of the legislature.

position and the hostility of the white settlers. The governors' inability to act effectively resulted fundamentally from the federal government's unwillingness to deal fairly with the Indians, a fact that was manifested by its failure to develop a sound system that would guarantee the Indians their rights and to give its agents in the West adequate moral or material support.

IX

The Governors

ONE hundred sixty men held the office of governor in the contiguous territories of the United States between 1787 and 1912. For some of them, the governorship came at the end of a long political career or represented an isolated foray into politics, but for most it was an important episode in the establishment of a lifelong involvement in politics. The job was a difficult one, in which success might assure a bright future, and failure, oblivion. Thus, inasmuch as he symbolized a sometimes detested system of colonial government and had very limited powers, a governor's ability to adapt and succeed in the office can be measured roughly by the length of his tenure. It took an unusually capable man to be effective, either as a leader or as an administrator, especially where unpopular policies were concerned. Moreover, the governor's salary and working conditions were usually poor. Operating funds were generally inadequate and, as Thomas Moonlight of Wyoming put it, the threat of removal always hung over the governors like "the ever trembling soward [*sic*] of Damocles suspended by a single hair." Given the nature of the job, it is difficult to understand why some men sought to advance their careers through the governor's office rather than along surer routes. Nevertheless, nearly all of the governors had actively solicited appointment to the office and either considered it to be the summit of their career or an important steppingstone—whether they had sought it purely for political reasons or for its unofficial money-making potential.[1]

1. The quotation is from Neil, "Territorial Governors," 165. See also Master-

Generally, when a vacancy occurred would-be governors scrambled for the office. Candidates usually submitted formal applications, with as many recommendations as possible, to the secretary of the department in charge (it was the Department of State until 1873 and the Department of the Interior thereafter), who normally forwarded them, in a digested form, to the President. While their applications were being processed, the office-seekers drummed up additional personal support and brought as much pressure as possible to bear on the President. Strong backing from a senator, representative, or other prominent member of the President's party was invaluable, and the recommendation of the Secretary of State or Interior could be expected to carry considerable weight. But, with few exceptions, the Presidents apparently made their own appointments both in form and in fact, and they occasionally chose a man who had not solicited the office.

After selecting an appointee, the President sent his name to the Senate for confirmation. If the man were confirmed, the department in charge drew up a commission for the President's signature and sent it with an oath to be executed to the governor-designate. Almost a third of the governors, however, received their first commission and assumed office while Congress was not in session. The Senate apparently either refused or seemed unlikely to ratify about eight of

---

son, *Blount*, 178; Carter, *Territorial Papers*, IX:281; James Ripley Jacobs, *Tarnished Warrior* (New York, 1938), 215; and succeeding notes.

The territorial governors are listed by territory in Valentine, "Territorial Governor," Appendix C, 150–58. Carter (*Territorial Papers*, I:3–33) lists all governors, secretaries, and judges up to 1872, including those who declined to serve; and Pomeroy (*Territories, 1861–1890*, Appendix, 109–49) lists governors, secretaries, judges, and territorial delegates from 1861 to 1890. Valentine's is the only complete list of governors who served from 1788 to 1912, but it does not include appointees who declined to serve. All three give dates of commissions, residence of governors as listed on their commissions, and the official reasons for leaving office. The three sources agree in most respects but all are incomplete in some details. I have checked and supplemented Valentine's list, insofar as possible, and have collected biographical information on the governors, using state legislative blue books and manuals, the *Congressional Directory*, the *National Cyclopaedia of American Biography*, the *Biographical Directory of the American Congress, 1774–1961*, the *Dictionary of American Biography*, state and local histories, and miscellaneous other sources. These provided the sources of information for the otherwise undocumented discussion in this chapter.

these recess appointments and as a result the governors either resigned or were removed. In addition, in several instances, Presidents may have taken advantage of the ad interim tenure of recess appointments to remove governors who were not satisfactory.[2]

The Presidents chose the men whom they appointed as governors for a wide variety of reasons, but William Clark became governor of Missouri in a unique way. In 1813 James Madison sent a blank governor's commission to Governor Benjamin Howard with instructions that he take either that one or the military commission sent earlier. Howard was to fill in his name on the commission he wanted and give the other one to Clark. Sometimes the candidate's qualifications were not uppermost in the President's mind when he made an appointment. In 1878 Hayes made John C. Frémont, who was then sixty-five, governor of Arizona apparently to help relieve him of the chronic poverty of his later years. On the recommendation of Representative Packer of Pennsylvania, in 1854, Franklin Pierce sent Andrew Reeder, a prominent Philadelphia lawyer with no political experience, to be the first governor of Kansas Territory, and had to remove him in less than a year. Similarly, political influence was behind Andrew Johnson's appointment of Alexander Cummings in 1865, and Secretary of War Cameron was mightily embarrassed when an investigation revealed his role in obtaining the office for that controversial governor of Colorado. As a rule, however, people were discreet when recommending or promoting candidates for the governorship, and Presidents gave due consideration to their qualifications before making nominations.[3]

Very often, if not generally, Presidents chose men for the governorships because of their supposed political adroitness and familiarity with western conditions. Indeed, relatively few of the governors who

2. Valentine, "Territorial Governor," 35–36, 40–43; Pomeroy, *Territories, 1861–1890,* 6–7, 19, 62–66. On appointive policies after 1860, compare Pomeroy, *Territories, 1861–1890,* 64–78; and Valentine, "Territorial Governor," 129; with the discussion below, but especially with Tables 6 and 7.

3. Valentine, "Territorial Governor," 38, 41, 125; James H. Baker and Leroy L. Haffen, eds., *History of Colorado* (Denver, 1927), 447–48, hereafter cited as Baker, *Colorado.* The role of special interests in the selection of governors is discussed in Lamar, *Dakota Territory,* 208–09 and *passim;* and in Lamar, *Far Southwest, passim.*

were appointed could have been ignorant of the nature of the job when they accepted it. But many individuals were also appointed to execute specific policies. Problems relating to Indian affairs figured prominently in the selection of numerous governors, among them Harrison, Cass, and the Missouri executives during the First Empire. One of President Hayes's main reasons for sending Lew Wallace to New Mexico was to stop the Lincoln County war. Grant made J. Wilson Shaffer the governor of Utah in the hope that he could strengthen federal control over that territory, but Shaffer died shortly after reaching Utah. All of the Kansas governors were expected to establish order and promote harmony, and one of Robert J. Walker's paramount objectives was to make that territory into a Democratic stronghold. A number of governors received their appointments because of their unusual aptitude as peacemakers and were sent to a territory largely for the purposes of ending intraparty strife and creating a strong party organization. Presidents twice sent governors to Dakota with specific instructions to harmonize warring Republican factions; each time, the governor reestablished a working majority for the party. When Benjamin Harrison became President he replaced all the territorial governors with Republican stalwarts whose primary duties were to establish, strengthen, or maintain Republican majorities and to make sure that the territories about to enter the Union would be reliable Republican states.[4]

Whatever the other grounds for individual appointments might have been, the territorial governorship almost always went to loyal members of the President's party, and it was frequently a reward for service, but this, of course, tells nothing about the worth of the men appointed. Although Presidential appointment policies varied from an emphasis on pleasing eastern politicians during the 1870s and early 1880s to concern with gratifying westerners, the latter seem most often to have influenced the selection of federal officials for the territories. Occasionally, legislatures or parties let it be known that a particular candidate, who was not always a territorial resident, would be acceptable, and asked that he be appointed governor. The

4. See Pomeroy, *Territories, 1861–1890*, 64–80; Clifford Wheeler Patton, "Robert J. Walker, Governor of Kansas Territory," (unpublished M.A. thesis, University of Illinois, 1932), 1, 29; Valentine, "Territorial Governor," 38–41.

Arkansas General Assembly petitioned Congress, in 1831, for the right to elect the governor and secretary and in 1868 Wyoming Republicans urged upon Secretary of State William H. Seward the idea of establishing territorial nominating conventions. These and other proposals of a similar nature received a cool reception, but when it was expedient, Presidents appointed as governor men who were popular in the territories.[5]

From the date of the Arkansas petition until 1892 there was a rising din of opposition to the appointment of nonresidents, although an increasing number of governors were chosen from among the territorial residents. At times the appointment of a territorial resident as governor satisfied western demands more than administrative needs, but in 1884, after a ten-year period during which, with a single exception, all new governors were drawn from the states, the Democratic House of Representatives passed a bill making residence a requirement for the office. In refusing to enact the bill, the Republican Senate contended that by giving the President the greatest freedom of choice the traditional system assured the appointment of the most unprejudiced and impartial executives obtainable. Nevertheless, in 1885, by which time the territories of the Second Empire were fairly mature, President Cleveland inaugurated a new policy. Six of the nine governors he appointed during his first administration resided in the territory of their governorship at the time of their appointment. Only two of Benjamin Harrison's governors were not residents and the eighteen executives appointed to the contiguous territories after Cleveland reentered the Presidency in 1893 were all residents.[6]

5. Valentine, "Territorial Governor," 113; Neil, "Territorial Governors," 7; Pomeroy, *Territories, 1861–1890*, 63; Carter, *Territorial Papers*, XXI:438.

6. See Table 3 below, and Valentine, "Territorial Governor," 120–22. Pomeroy (*Territories, 1861–1890*, 72–78) erroneously credits Benjamin Harrison with making the policy change. The agitation over residence during the 1880s and the policy of the 1890s undoubtedly contributed to the requirement in the Hawaii Organic Act of 1900 that only Hawaiian citizens (hence residents) could be appointed governor, but this provision also worked to assure that the planters and their brethren would remain in power under the United States government. (Thorpe, *Constitutions*, 881, 895; Dill, *Hawaii*, 27.) The single exception in the period from 1874 to 1884 was John B. Neil's appointment as governor of Idaho in 1880. He was from Utah Territory.

While most westerners demanded that only residents be appointed governor, there was considerable opposition to the adoption of such a policy. In many cases, and especially when territories were sparsely settled, Presidents were reluctant to appoint residents because it was so difficult to find anyone who was qualified to their satisfaction. Consequently, as late as 1884, two months after the House Committee on Territories condemned nine out of every ten nonresident governors as having carpetbag motives, the corresponding Senate committee endorsed the President's policy of appointing nonresidents. It maintained that it was so difficult to find competent men to serve as governor that the President should be free to recruit from anywhere in the country. The positions of both committees were exaggerated, but nonresidents who were appointed governor not infrequently had purer motives in accepting the office and often had a more ameliorative influence on the territories, particularly on their politics, than did residents. President Grant appointed only four territorial residents to governorships during his eight years in office because by 1873 he had concluded that they were politically undesirable. Many of the Republican parties in the territories were already badly split and the appointment of a governor from any of the factions in most territories would only accentuate existing conflicts and end in grief. For essentially the same reasons, territorial leaders sometimes recommended the appointment of nonresidents as a means of allaying intraparty squabbles.[7]

Mason Brayman, who was governor of Idaho from 1876 to 1880, complained that he and the territory were at the mercy of outsiders. He contended that state politicians so completely controlled appointments to Idaho that it was "a political dependency of Oregon . . . where men unfit and unacceptable in Oregon were billeted." Brayman himself had come from Wisconsin to be governor. His allegation was manifestly untrue, but throughout much of the First and Second Empires, there was a tendency to draw appointees for some territories from a rather small group of states.[8]

7. Valentine, "Territorial Governor," 122; Neil, "Territorial Governors," 8; Pomeroy, *Territories, 1861–1890,* 62. Grant appointed two residents as governors in Colorado and two others as governors in Washington.

8. Quoted in Pomeroy, *Territories, 1861–1890,* 67–68. Pomeroy concludes that

That most governors were not territorial residents when they received their appointments had little relevance, inasmuch as most settlers preceded them in the migration from the states by only a few years. Though territorial citizens liked to rail against the appointment of nonresidents as governor, they tacitly admitted the speciousness of their complaint by reserving the informal title of "bona fide resident" for the men whom they accepted regardless of their qualifications for office and residence at the time of appointment. The real criticism was not that appointments brought most of the officials to the territories but that those who otherwise would have stayed in the East often made no effort to become "bona fide residents." For many men, however, federal appointments to territorial offices led to a permanent change of residence, and a large number of those who were territorial residents at the time they became governor had initially come to the territories with minor appointments.[9]

In some cases the actual residence of an individual when he was first appointed governor is difficult to determine. The state or territory listed on his commission could have been his legal residence although he might have been living somewhere else.[10] In addition, a number of commissions omitted the appointee's residence, so it was necessary both to supply it for these commissions and, insofar as possible, to verify or correct the others in order to compile information that

---

certain state Congressional delegates controlled appointments to some territories, but he offers no evidence. He is clearly wrong with respect to general territorial officials. His conclusion may have limited validity in the appointment of minor officials, but there were relatively few of these to be handed out by the federal government.

9. *Ibid.*, 74, 105; Valentine, "Territorial Governor," 120–21.

10. Similarly, subsequent commissions issued to the same governor often did not reflect changes in residence. When W. C. C. Claiborne became temporary governor of Orleans Territory in 1803, he was also governor of Mississippi Territory and his residence was listed as Mississippi. The following year he was governor of Orleans only, with a Tennessee residence on his new commission. His commission did not list the territory as his residence until 1806. St. Clair's residence, throughout his administration, was listed as Pennsylvania—probably accurately in this case; Hull's was Massachusetts during his governorship of Michigan, and Edwards' was Kentucky until his 1816 commission. Harrison's secretary, John Gibson, who carried out most of the civil administration of Indiana, similarly was always listed as a Pennsylvanian. Carter, *Territorial Papers*, I:3–33.

would accurately reflect the real residence of the governors at the beginning of their administrations. Since twelve of the 160 governors either held office in two territories or had two nonconsecutive administrations in the same territory, they are counted twice, bringing the total number of administrations to 172. In round terms, the governors of forty percent of these 172 administrations were residents of a territory when they entered office and four out of every five were living west of the Appalachian Mountains when appointed (see Table 3).

TABLE 3. REGIONAL ORIGINS OF THE TERRITORIAL GOVERNORS

	First Empire 1787–1848		*Second Empire 1848–1893*		*Aftermath 1893–1912*		*Total 1787–1912*	
	Governors		*Governors*		*Governors*		*Governors*	
Region[1]	*No.*	*%*	*No.*	*%*	*No.*	*%*	*No.*	*%*
Southeastern states	9	25.7	4	3.4	0	0	13	7.6
Northeastern states	7	20.0	15	12.6	0	0	22	12.8
Ky. and Public Lands states south & west of the Ohio River	6	17.1	15	12.6	0	0	21	12.2
Public Lands states north & west of the Ohio River	3	8.6	38	31.9	0	0	41	23.8
Far Western states	0	0	7	5.9	0	0	7	4.1
Territories:								
Resident of territory to which appointed	7	20.0	35	29.4	18	100.0	60	34.9
Resident of another territory	3	8.6	5	4.2	0	0	8	4.7
Total appointments from within territories	10	28.6	40	33.6	18	100.0	68	39.5
Total governors	35	100.0	119	100.0	18	100.0	172	100.0

[1] See p. 279.

As a whole, the data illustrate that the residential origins of the governors seemed to tend westward as the nation expanded its domain and organized new territories. The five-state region of the Old Northwest, however, figured most prominently as the supplier of governors. A large number of the men who became governor had lived there before going to the southern and more western territories, and about a quarter of the territorial governors were living in an Old Northwest state or territory when appointed. Thirty-one of the latter were appointed governor of one of the territories west of the Mississippi

---

Note to Table 3: Breakdown of regions by state

State	*1st Emp.*	*2d Emp.*	*Total*
S.E.:			
Ga.	2	1	3
S.C.		1	1
N.C.	3	1	4
Va.	2	1	3
Md.	2		2
	9	4	13

State	*1st Emp.*	*2d Emp.*	*Total*
S.W.:			
Ky.	4	7	11
Tenn.	1	1	2
Ala.		2	2
Miss.		1	1
La.	1		1
Ark.		1	1
Mo.		3	3
	6	15	21

State	*1st Emp.*	*2d Emp.*	*Total*
N.E.:			
N.J.	1	1	2
Pa.	3	6	9
N.Y.	1	5	6
Mass.	1	1	2
N.H.	1	1	2
Me.		1	1
	7	15	22

State	*1st Emp.*	*2d Emp.*	*Total*
N.W.:			
Ohio	3	8	11
Ind.		9	9
Ill.		8	8
Mich.		3	3
Wisc.		3	3
Iowa		4	4
Kans.		2	2
Nebr.		1	1
	3	38	41

State	*1st. Emp.*	*2d Emp.*	*Total*
Far West			
Cal.		2	2
Ore.		3	3
Nev.		2	2
		7	7

during the Second Empire. The Presidents' normal emphasis on choosing westerners for governor whenever possible, as well as the westward shift in appointments, is most evident when appointees from states adjacent to territories are added to the appointments of residents—a not-unwarranted coupling in that these nonresident appointees, with few exceptions, came from states that had recently entered the Union. Together, these two groups account for about two-thirds of the governors during the First Empire and half during the Second Empire.

The large number of officials who moved from one territory to another or from a relatively new state to a territory, particularly when a new territory was organized, strongly suggests that something like an informal colonial service existed throughout the First and Second Empires. In the First Empire, one can point to the careers of James Wilkinson, Henry Dodge, and numerous other governors. President Jefferson, for example, transferred Governor Claiborne from Mississippi to Orleans to organize that territory in 1804, four years after John Adams had appointed William Henry Harrison, the ex-secretary and current territorial delegate of the Northwest, governor of the new Indiana Territory. Lewis Cass was trained by Return Jonathan Meigs, Jr., a territorial judge in the Northwest and later governor of Ohio, and was a legislator and federal marshal in Ohio before he became governor of the Michigan Territory. James Duane Doty moved up from a judgeship in the Michigan Territory to become the delegate to Congress from the Wisconsin Territory, and then its governor. During the Civil War he became, successively, superintendent of Indian affairs and governor in Utah Territory. Many other men followed similar paths to the governorship in the Second Empire.

The territorial judges provide perhaps the clearest examples of a colonial service in operation. John Coburn of Kentucky became an Orleans territorial judge in 1805. Two years later he received an appointment to the Michigan bench, which was superseded by one to the Louisiana-Missouri Territory court. William Sprigg of Ohio held minor offices under the Northwest government and became a judge on the state Supreme Court when Ohio entered the Union in 1803. He served on that court from 1803 to 1806 and from 1808 to 1810. Between 1806 and 1808, he spent a year as territorial judge in Michigan and in Orleans Territory. After 1810 he became a territorial judge, first in Missouri, then in Illinois, and served in Illinois until it achieved statehood. Return Jonathan Meigs, Jr., who also held minor offices in the Northwest, became a territorial judge there in 1798 and kept the office until statehood, when he became an Ohio Supreme Court judge, along with Sprigg. In December 1804, however, Meigs left the Ohio bench to become the first judge on the Louisiana-Missouri territorial Supreme Court. After two years he moved to the Michigan Territory court, but in 1808 rejoined the Ohio Supreme Court. A year later he resigned to run for governor of Ohio, won, and in 1814, after he had served as governor for four years, President Madison appointed him United States Postmaster General.

Regardless of an individual's tenure in any one place, appointment and officeholding patterns like these imply the conscious transfer of well-trained, competent administrators from one spot to another for special purposes, such as organizing or reordering parts of territorial government. Whether or not the careers of most territorial governors are compatible with the idea of an informal colonial service, the governors' average tenure indicates that a large majority of them came to the job with considerable experience, adapted quickly and were able to work reasonably well in the office.

Several factors besides personal motives or shortcomings are necessary to an appreciation of the tenure of the governors individually. The governors of the First Empire received three-year commissions, but beginning with the Oregon Act of 1848 and extending throughout the Second Empire and Aftermath, the governors of the contiguous territories were appointed for four years. In all cases, however, the Presidents could replace a governor at anytime before his commission expired; Presidential attitudes and policies thus could significantly affect the governors' tenure. Until 1889, governors' commissions bore the date of Senate confirmation; subsequently they carried the date on which the President signed them. The date on a commission, however, was never the date at which service began. A commission normally became effective only when the appointee took the oath of office or actually entered into its duties, and governors usually took some time to settle their affairs before assuming office. In some cases it took them six months or more to get to their territories.[11]

11. In conjunction with this discussion see Valentine, "Territorial Governor," 36–43; Meyerholz, "Federal Supervision," 178; Pomeroy, *Territories, 1861–1890,* 27.

For purposes of analysis, I have placed each governor in one of five basic categories—eight months or less, nine months to three years, three to six years, six to eight years, and eight years or more in office—which were chosen somewhat arbitrarily to indicate the degree of clustering and the nature of the distribution of tenure (see Table 4). The governor's legal tenure was taken to be the time lapse between the date on his first commission and the approximate date on which he left office. The tenure of those individuals who took an exceptionally long time in getting to their territories was corrected, insofar as possible, to bring it within the range of error assumed to exist in the data for the other governors and in order to have it more accurately reflect their actual time in office. Executive absences, on the other hand, were ignored because in most cases they cannot be determined with any accuracy. Consequently, the data presented here represent optimal rather than maximal estimates of tenure.

Given the nature of the data, it may be assumed that an eight-month time lapse approximates no more than six months' actual service. This category was adopted to define a term in office during which a governor can be considered to have had a negligible influence. It might be equally valid to enlarge the classification to include governors with a tenure of up to one year. In addition to the seventeen governors who held office for eight months or less, twelve others were in office for between eight months and one year. Only three of the twenty-nine men, who constituted 18 percent of the governors, held office during the period of the First Empire. One of the men was suspended, eight were removed, nine resigned, five had their terms ended by statehood, and three died in office. The remaining three had recess appointments, and the Senate failed to confirm their appointments for full terms. The most important conclusion to be drawn from this group of governors is that the tensions of the Civil War era had a decisive effect on tenure in the territories. Twenty of the twenty-nine governors whose tenure was one year or less held office during the first half of the Second Empire or, more precisely, between 1850 and 1872. They constituted 27 percent of the governors appointed between 1848 and 1876, and 12.5 percent of all the territorial executives.[12]

12. Seven of the seventeen governors who held office for eight months or less were appointed within the first three months of a new President's administration

By way of contrast, approximately 78 percent of the governors of each period—the First Empire, Second Empire, and Aftermath—held office for two years or more. Almost half the territorial governors

---

and might be considered spoilsmen, but at least four of them were certainly not political hacks. Benjamin Harrison removed the governors of Dakota, Montana, and Washington as soon as he became President. He replaced them with A. C. Mellette, B. F. White and M. C. Moore, respectively, who served in the brief but important intervals before the territories achieved statehood and were responsible for assuring Republican control of the new states. President Buchanan sent Robert J. Walker to Kansas to carry out a specific policy, but when strong opposition developed against it, Buchanan decided to use Walker for a scapegoat and forced him to resign. A Pierce appointee to Oregon, John W. Davis, resigned on his own after about eight months in the territory. Grant removed James M. Ashley of Montana shortly after Ashley's enemies began circulating rumors that the governor was criticizing the President's policies. The seventh man, Governor William Jenkins of Oklahoma, obtained a recess appointment from McKinley, after serving for four years as territorial secretary, but Congress would not confirm his appointment for a full term.

The other ten governors were mid-term Presidential appointees; that is, all received their appointments after the first six months of a new President's administration. Three men resigned: Thomas Bowen, a Grant appointee to Idaho; J. S. Crosby, appointed to Montana by Arthur; and J. W. Geary, a Pierce appointee and Robert Walker's immediate predecessor in Kansas. Two governors were removed: A. H. Reeder, the first Kansas Territory governor, also appointed by Pierce; and V. H. Vaughan of Utah, another Grant appointee who fell from favor. President Arthur appointed B. P. Carpenter to the Montana governorship after Crosby resigned, but seven months later he had misgivings, suspended Carpenter, and appointed a successor without first removing him. John W. Dawson of Utah and George E. Cole of Washington held recess appointments under Lincoln and Johnson, respectively, and their appointments for full terms were not confirmed when Congress convened. Dawson may have resigned when it became clear that the Senate would not approve his appointment for a full term, and it is not clear that he ever took up the duties of the office. The remaining two governors, Francis Burt of Nebraska and J. A. Gurley of Arizona, died in office in 1854 and 1863, respectively. Burt died after only two days in office.

Four other men are not included among those who held office for eight months or less. It seems certain that George Baxter, an 1886 Cleveland appointee to Wyoming, resigned on request without serving, and he is not counted among the 160 governors. Joseph Lane of Oregon is included among the governors who served longer terms, because he held office in the territory for over fifteen months before 1850, in addition to his three days in 1853. Similarly, E. M. McCook of Colorado is not counted for a second term of seven months in 1874–1875, since his total service in Colorado was about fifty-five months, nor is S. B. Axtell who served about six months in Utah and over thirty-four months in New Mexico.

Five men are excluded from the group of governors who held office for eight to twelve months. The dates of service for three men are imprecise, but they certainly held office for a year and quite possibly served longer. Lincoln appointed

served for at least three years, and nineteen had a tenure of six or more years.[13] Lewis Cass's eighteen years as governor of Michigan far surpassed the tenure of any other governor, but he never pre-

---

William Gilpin as governor of Colorado in 1861, and removed him the following year. Secretary John P. Hoyt of Arizona held a governor's commission for a year or so in 1877–1878, and then resigned after declining the Idaho governorship, in order to become an associate justice on the Washington Territorial Court where he served from 1879 to 1887. William A. Pile, a Grant appointee in New Mexico, resigned sometime in 1870. All three of these men received their appointments during the first three months of a new President's administration. John N. Irwin resigned the Idaho governorship in 1884, after about a year in office, but six years later he became governor of Arizona and served there for nineteen months. Grover Cleveland removed Nathan O. Murphy of Arizona in 1893, at the beginning of his second Presidential administration, but McKinley reappointed him to the same territory five years later. Murphy held office for a total of about fifty-nine months.

Only three of the twelve men who are counted as having held office for eight to twelve months were governors during the period of the First Empire: John Branch and James Clarke lost their posts when Florida and Iowa, respectively, entered the Union in 1845 and 1846. James K. Polk removed Nathaniel P. Tallmadge of Wisconsin in the first three months of his Presidency in order to reappoint Henry Dodge, whom William Henry Harrison had removed four years earlier. Four other men were governors during the decade before the Civil War. Two were Kansas governors, Wilson Shannon and James W. Denver, who lost the office in the turbulent second half of the decade. Pierce was no more satisfied with Shannon than he was with his other appointees in Kansas and he, too, was removed. Denver resigned. He had been secretary before becoming governor and probably served as executive for a little over a year. William A. Richardson resigned the Nebraska governorship in 1858, after a little more than eleven months in office. In addition to all the others, Pierce removed William C. Lane of New Mexico at about the middle of 1853 to make room for a friend, but he had difficulty getting someone to take the appointment; at least one man declined it before David Meriwether was commissioned.

Three of the remaining five men resigned, one was removed, and the fifth died. J. W. Shaffer of Utah died on October 1, 1870, after about nine months in office. Grant appointed Alvan Flanders as governor of Washington in April 1869, and removed him a year later. The three governors who resigned were William H. Wallace of Idaho, late in 1863; Sidney Edgerton of Montana, in September 1865; and M. H. McCord of Arizona, in mid-1898.

It should be noted that, in addition to the three men enumerated above (Jenkins, Dawson, and Cole), Vaughan of Utah and Shannon of Kansas held recess appointments but are classified as removed.

13. The six men who served seventy-two to ninety-six months were: Richard K. Call of Florida, from 1836–1839 and 1841–1844; William Clark of Missouri, 1813–1820; William Hull of Michigan, 1805–1812; Eli H. Murray of Utah, 1880–

sided over a full-fledged second-stage government. Similarly, although St. Clair held office for fourteen and a half years, his tenure during the second stage was only about three years. If only second-stage service is considered, Benjamin F. Potts's thirteen years as governor of Montana (1870–1883), was the longest single administration. Twice as many governors had six-year or longer terms before 1848 as in the later periods, but only between 1887 and 1897 and after 1906 were there no long-term executives holding office in the contiguous territories. Outside the contiguous United States, Ernest Gruening's thirteen-year administration in Alaska (1939–1953) is noteworthy for length. In light of the generally uncertain tenure of the period when Potts was governor and of the greater complexity and political difficulties involved in being governor of a second-stage government in the second half of the nineteenth century or in the twentieth century, as opposed to administering a first-stage or unicameral government, it is clear that the length of both Potts's and Gruening's administrations was more significant than that of either Cass's or St. Clair's and implies that they were more able executives.

The average tenure of the governors varied significantly from territory to territory and from one period to another (see Table 5). The average tenure for service during the second stage within the First Empire was three and a half years—a year more than the average of all Second Empire governors, and six months more than during the Aftermath. If the governors who served eight months or less are subtracted from the totals, however, the average tenure for the Second Empire alone, for the two empires combined, and for all three periods is in each case approximately the same, about three

---

1886; John Pope of Arkansas, 1829–1835; and Alvin Saunders of Nebraska, 1861–1867. Four men held office for ninety-six months: Henry Dodge of Wisconsin, 1836–1841 and 1845–1848; Elisha P. Ferry of Washington, 1872–1880; A. P. K. Safford of Arizona, 1869–1877; and Brigham Young of Utah, 1850–1858. Nine others held office for over 100 months: W. C. C. Claiborne in Mississippi, 1801–1804, and Orleans, 1804–1812; Ninian Edwards of Illinois, 1809–1818; David Holmes of Mississippi, 1809–1817; Miguel A. Otero of New Mexico, 1897–1906; Lewis Cass of Michigan, 1813–1831; William P. Duval of Florida, 1822–1834; William H. Harrison of Indiana, 1800–1813; Benjamin F. Potts of Montana, 1870–1883; and Arthur St. Clair of the Northwest, 1788–1802. The last five men each held office for twelve years or more.

TABLE 4. DISTRIBUTION BY TIME PERIOD OF GOVERNORS' TENURES, 1788–1912

Period	No. Governors[1]	8 or fewer months: No. Govs.	8 or fewer months: %	9–35 months: No. Govs.	9–35 months: %	36–71 months: No. Govs.	36–71 months: %	72–95 months: No. Govs.	72–95 months: %	96 or more months: No. Govs.	96 or more months: %
First Empire											
1788–1848	32	0	0.0	11	34.4	9	28.1	4	12.5	8	25.0
Second Stage only[2]	25	2	8.0	8	32.0	8	32.0	3	12.0	4	16.0
Second Empire											
1848–1893	113	16	14.2	51	45.1	40	35.4	2	1.8	4	3.5
First half only[3] 1848–1876	74	12	16.2	31	41.9	26	35.1	1	1.4	4	5.4
Aftermath											
1893–1912	18	1	5.6	7	38.9	9	50.0	0	0.0	1	5.6
Totals and averages											
1788–1893	145	16	11.0	62	42.8	49	33.8	6	4.1	12	8.3
1794–1893 (Second Stage only)	138	18	13.0	59	42.8	48	34.8	5	3.6	8	5.8
1788–1912	163	17	10.4	69	42.3	58	35.6	6	3.7	13	8.0
1794–1912 (Second Stage only)	156	19	12.2	66	42.3	57	36.5	5	3.2	9	5.8

[1] Length of time in office is the total service as governor per man in each period. Individuals holding the governorship twice in one period are categorized according to the total time in office and are counted once each. In the First Empire, Call, Claiborne, and Dodge are so categorized and in the Second Empire there are six others: Axtell, Irwin, Lane, Medary, McCook, Warren. Doty, Murphy, and West are counted twice, having served separate terms in two time periods. For these reasons, the total number of governors here differs from that in Tables 3 and 5.

[2] Both district stage and unicameral governors and their terms in office are excluded. In addition, the tenure of these individuals who were governors of both a district or unicameral government and a second-stage government was reduced by the length of their non-second-stage service for this calculation.

[3] This group includes all men appointed to office during the period and their total length of time in office, even when it extended beyond 1876.

years, or the same as for the Aftermath alone. Thus, three years may be considered a solid figure for the tenure of the average territorial governor.

There are several reasons why the average tenure was lower for the Second Empire and Aftermath than for the First Empire. The tenure for the Second Empire is, foremost, indicative of the deterioration of conditions in the territories that accompanied the sectional crisis, most notably in Kansas, and the period of the Civil War and Radical Reconstruction. It also reflects changed attitudes of the federal government by the middle of the nineteenth century and the emergence of a high degree of territorial autonomy. The average tenures, therefore, cannot be used prima facie as evidence to show a decline in the quality of the governors. On the contrary, it is reasonably clear that unsatisfactory executives could hold office longer before 1848 than after, since the federal government was less responsive to maladministration before the full development of territorial autonomy. By the beginning of the Second Empire, even if the territorial citizens were no more critical, the Presidents at least were more willing to remove those governors who had difficulty adapting to the office or who did not reach an accommodation with the territorial legislature. As this change occurred, the territorial governorship definitely became harder to hold than a state governorship. Thus the territorial governors of the First Empire had a longer average tenure than the governors of the same areas after they had achieved statehood, and the governors of the territories created in the Second Empire held office for about a year less than the state governors.[14]

The average tenure of territorial governors, however, is surprisingly similar to that of all the state governors in the three different periods. Not only is the overall average of state governors for the period

14. Pomeroy (*Territories, 1861–1890,* 62) contends that, within the period of his study, "The typical territorial officer was inexperienced at the outset, and *did not retain office long enough to become experienced.*" (Italics mine.) If the average governor's tenure of 2.5 years, in the Second Empire, was not "long enough," what is one to conclude about the typical secretaries of the Interior, Treasury, or War, or the typical Attorney General or Postmaster General? The average tenure for each of these departments between 1861 and 1890 ranged from about 2.1 years in the Department of the Interior to about 1.7 years in the Department of War.

TABLE 5. ANALYSIS OF TENURE OF TERRITORIAL AND STATE GOVERNORS, 1788–1965

	Entire Territorial Period			*Territorial Period—Second Stage Only*[4]			*State Governors Average Tenure*[2]	
Territory/State	*Number of Years*[1]	*Number of Governors*[1]	*Average Tenure in Years*	*Number of Years*	*Number of Governors*[1]	*Average Tenure in Years*	*Statehood to the Civil War*	*Civil War or Statehood to Present*
FIRST EMPIRE:								
TNRO (Ohio)	14.4	1	14.42	3.25	1	3.25	2.48	2.86
Indiana	16.5	2	8.25	11.9	2	5.95	3.54	3.71
Michigan	28.1	3	9.36	—	—	—	2.10	3.40
Illinois	9.6	1	9.58	6.2	1	6.17	3.68	4.55
Wisconsin	12.3	4	3.06	12.3	4	3.06	2.00	3.55
Iowa	8.4	3	2.81	8.4	3	2.81	3.50	3.32
TSRO (Tennessee)	5.8	1	5.75	1.6	1	1.58	3.67	3.48
Orleans (Louisiana)	7.5	1	7.50	6.8	1	6.75	3.00	3.06
Mississippi	18.8	4	4.71	16.4	4	4.10	1.95	3.47
Louisiana (Missouri)	14.7	4	3.37	7.6	2	3.79	2.74	3.47
Alabama	2.2	1	2.17	2.2	1	2.17	2.80	3.40
Arkansas	16.9	4	4.23	16.2	4	4.04	4.00	3.19
Florida	22.3	6	3.72	5.75	4	1.44	4.00	3.58
Subtotals and Averages (1788–1848)	177.5	35	5.07	98.6	28	3.52	3.04	3.46
SECOND EMPIRE:								
Oregon	9.5	5	1.90	same	same	same		3.57
Minnesota	9.1	3	3.03					3.50
Kansas	5.5	6	0.92					2.94
Nebraska	11.7	5	2.33					2.85
Nevada	3.6	1	3.58					4.27
Colorado	15.5	8	1.94					2.48
Washington	35.3	13	2.72					5.07
Montana	23.4	9	2.60					4.87

Dakota	27.8	10	2.78				(North)	2.88
							(South)	3.46
Idaho	25.8	12	2.15					2.83
Wyoming	21.1	7	3.01					2.92
Utah	42.8	14	3.06					6.90
Oklahoma	2.67	2	1.33					3.30
New Mexico	40.5	13	3.12					2.55
Arizona	27.8	11	2.52					3.53
Subtotals and Averages (1848–93)	302.1	119	2.53	302.1	119	2.53		3.62
AFTERMATH:								
Utah	2.75	1	2.75	same	same	same		6.90
Oklahoma	14.5	5	2.90					3.30
New Mexico	19.3	5	3.85					2.55
Arizona	18.8	7	2.69					3.53
Subtotals and Averages (1893–1912)	55.4	18	3.08	55.4	18	3.08		3.62
GRAND TOTALS:								
1788–1893	479.6	154	3.11	400.7	147	2.73		
1788–1912	535.0	172	3.11	456.1	165	2.76		3.55
Excluding Govs. in Office 8 mo. or less[3]								
1788–1893	467.6	136	3.44	386.7	126	3.07		
1788–1912	522.3	153	3.41	441.4	143	3.09		3.55

[1] Number of Years is the number of years governors held office, not the total length of the territorial period. Number of Governors is the number of administrations. Governors who served more than one term, in one or two territories, are counted once for each term. Similarly, the men who were transferred without interruption from one territory to another are counted in each for their period of service in each.

[2] Dates for the Civil War are 1860, 1861, or 1862, depending on the data; those for the present are 1962, 1963, 1964, or 1965.

[3] Excluded from the First Empire data are 3 governors from Second Stage Only and 2 years; Second Empire: 18 governors and 12 years; Aftermath: 1 governor and 0.7 year. See footnote 12 and Table 4, note 1.

[4] See Table 4, note 2.

SOURCES: See note 2. Data for state tenure provided by David P. Henige.

TABLE 6. DISTRIBUTION BY PRESIDENTIAL ADMINISTRATIONS OF APPOINTMENTS, REMOVALS, AND RESIGNATIONS OF TERRITORIAL GOVERNORS

President	Yrs. in Off.	#T	#G	*Appointments*[1]			*Removals*				*Resignations*		
				Total	*1st 3 mo.*	*Last 3 mo.*	*Total*	*1st 3 mo.*	*Last 3 mo.*	*RBP*	*Total*	*1st 3 mo.*	*Last 3 mo.*
Jefferson	8	2-5	9	5[a]	1		2			1	1		1
Madison	8	6-4	10	6	2						2		
Monroe	8	6-3	6	3							1		1
J. Q. Adams	4	3	3	1	1								
Jackson	8	3-2	8	6	1						2		
Van Buren	4	2-3	4	2			2		1 (?)	1			
W. H. Harrison	1 mo.	3	3	2	2		2	2					
Tyler	4	3	5	3	1								
Polk	4	2-0-1	5	3	1		2	1					
Taylor	1½	2	3	2	1						1		
Fillmore	2½	2-4	5	3	1								
*Pierce	4	5-7	12	11	4		5	3		2	2		
Buchanan	4	7-5	16	9[a]	3		1		1	1	7	1	2
Lincoln	4	7-10-9	17	16	5		2	1 (?)		1	6		
Johnson	4	9-8-9	18	10			3				4		1
Grant	8	9-8	29	25[a]	7		7	3		4	9	1	
Hayes	4	8	16	9	1						3		
Garfield	½	8	8	1	1						1	1	
Arthur	3½	8	15	9		2	1				3	1	
Cleveland, 1	4	8	18	9	1		2				6		
†B. Harrison	4	8-4	19	12	8		4	4			6	3	
†Cleveland, 2	4	4-3	9	5	4		4	3		1			
*McKinley	4½	3	8	5	1		1				3	2	
T. Roosevelt	7½	3-2	9	6	1		1	1			4		
Taft	4	2-0	5	2	1						1		
TOTALS				165	48	2	39	18	2	11	62	9	5

Table 6.—Continued

Notes to Table 6.

There were no appointments, removals, or resignations during the second to last three months of any administration.
#T—Number of contiguous territories in existence during the administration.
#G—Number of governors holding office sometime during the administration.
RBP—indicates the number of governors removed by the President who appointed them.
[1] Only first appointments of governors are included, and only those of governors who held office.
† Presidents who replaced all governors in office within the first three months of their administration.
* Presidents who replaced all governors within the first six months of their administration.
[a] One transfer appointment by each of these Presidents is not counted; only the first appointment is included.

1787–1912 almost identical to that of the territorial governors; the trends within each period were the same. From 1787 to 1820 the average tenure of state executives was 3.26 years; from 1820 to 1865 it was 2.42 years; and from the end of the Civil War to 1912 it was 2.98 years. Although the periodizations of data for the two sets of governors differ, one may argue that they are comparable and may conclude that the turnover of second-stage territorial governors approximated the turnover of state governors at any given time. This conclusion suggests in turn that the territorial governors, as a whole, were somewhat more adept than the state governors whose jobs were decidedly more secure, at least between elections.

An analysis of the timing of appointments and removals shows that Presidents did not often distribute governorships as the spoils of election. Altogether, there were 172 first appointments as governor given to 160 men between 1787 and 1912. Excluding the appointments of St. Clair, Sargent, Blount, and Harrison as nonpartisan, there were 168 appointments from 1801 to 1912. Three men who held office in two territories were transferred without a break in federal service, and their second appointments should be excluded as nonpartisan: Jefferson moved W. C. C. Claiborne from Mississippi to Orleans Territory in 1804; Grant transferred Samuel B. Axtell from Utah to New Mexico in 1875; and, a few months after Minnesota entered the Union Buchanan sent Samuel Medary, who had, meanwhile, been postmaster in Columbus, Ohio, to Kansas. Medary was the only Kansas governor to serve for more than a year. As he had in Minnesota, he brought Kansas to statehood, then resigned and returned to Columbus to edit *The Crisis*. There remain, then, 153 men who were given 162 first appointments between 1801 and 1912. The nine men who are counted twice served nonconsecutive terms in either one or two territories.[15]

15. As used in this discussion, appointment refers only to the first appointment received by a governor, at the beginning of his administration. Succeeding or renewal appointments are not counted. The nine men counted twice are: Richard K. Call, who held the Florida governorship 1836–1839 and 1841–1844; Henry Dodge, governor of Wisconsin, 1836–1841 and 1845–1848; Joseph Lane, governor of Oregon, 1848–1850 and for three days in 1853; Edward M. McCook who held the Colorado governorship 1869–1873 and 1874–1875; Francis W. Warren, governor of Wyoming 1885–1886 and 1889–1890; N. O. Murphy, governor of Arizona 1892–1893 and 1898–1902; and Caleb W. West, who served as governor of Utah

Forty-eight men obtained their appointments during the first three months of a new President's administration and another eight received appointments in the second three months. Of the latter eight, three entered office after governors resigned, one replaced a governor who had died, and two succeeded governors whose commissions had expired. The seventh governor replaced a man who left the office for reasons unknown. Only the last, Myron H. McCord, definitely received his appointment after the President had removed his predecessor: McKinley apparently removed Benjamin J. Franklin of Arizona in 1897, but it is not clear that he was politically motivated in doing so. Seven of the forty-eight governors appointed by new Presidents held office for eight months or less and another four served for about one year each. Nevertheless, the remaining thirty-seven stayed in office for at least a year and a half, and the average tenure for all forty-eight appointees was well over three and a half years—that is, approximately a year more than the average for the 160 governors.[16]

Relatively few of the vacancies these forty-eight men filled seem to have resulted from the inspired machinations of a new President in search of patronage. George Izard of Arkansas, for example, created a vacancy when he died during the interval between Jackson's election and his inauguration, and President Adams left the office vacant. Six Presidents had to fill offices in new territories during their first three months as President. In five instances, outgoing Presidents bequeathed to their successors new territories that lacked officials. Thus Jefferson left the organization of Illinois to Madison, Polk presented Taylor with an unorganized Minnesota Territory, and Fillmore let Pierce appoint the first set of officials for Washington. James Buchanan left office without appointing officials for the newly-created territories of Colorado, Nevada, and Dakota. Though Congress had provided for the organization of Wyoming in mid-1868, President Andrew Johnson was unable to obtain Senate confirmation for the appointment of any general territorial officials, and the offices remained vacant

1886–1889 and 1893–1896. James Duane Doty was governor of Wisconsin 1841–1844 and of Utah 1863–1865; John N. Irwin was governor in Idaho and Arizona, 1883–1884 and 1890–1892, respectively.

16. The short-term governors are cited in note 12 above.

until Grant became President. In addition, Congress passed Organic Acts for Utah and New Mexico in September 1850, two months after Tyler became President. He promptly appointed Brigham Young as governor of Utah, but did not find a civilian governor for New Mexico until January 1851.

Eight of the forty-eight men who received appointments within the first three months of a new President's administration replaced governors whose terms had expired (see Table 6).[17] Thirteen others succeeded governors who had resigned. Four governors resigned during the last three months of a Presidential administration and their offices were left vacant for the incoming President to fill.[18] The remaining nine resignations occurred within the first three months of a new President's inauguration.[19] In addition, new Presidents definitely created seventeen vacancies by removing incumbents. These removals ended just over ten percent of the gubernatorial administrations. James Buchanan's removal of the governor of Nebraska, a week before Lincoln's inauguration, is not included among the seventeen, but two uncertain cases may be included to raise the total number of governors

17. The new governors were: W. C. C. Claiborne, appointed governor of Mississippi in 1801; Samuel Medary of Minnesota and Fayette McMullen of Washington, both appointed in 1857; John P. Hoyt of Arizona, appointed in 1877; Edmund G. Ross, appointed in 1885, L. Bradford Prince, appointed in 1889, and William T. Thornton, appointed in 1893—all governors of New Mexico; and Richard E. Sloan of Arizona, appointed in 1909.

18. As Table 6 indicates, there were actually five resignations. The fifth man was Samuel Medary. He resigned in December 1860, a month before Kansas became a state, and is not counted here because his resignation did not create a position for Lincoln to fill when he became President. The four vacancies passed down to new Presidents were as follows: Jefferson left the Mississippi governorship vacant for Madison to fill in 1809; Monroe passed the vacant Arkansas governorship to John Quincy Adams; Richard D. Gholson of Washington resigned effective March 4, 1861, rather than serve under a Republican (Valentine, "Territorial Governor," 129); and Johnson left the Arizona governorship for Grant to fill in 1869.

19. The nine who resigned are: John W. Geary of Kansas, 1857, after eight months; Robert B. Mitchell of New Mexico, 1869, after three years; Lew Wallace of New Mexico and John C. Frémont of Arizona, both in 1881 after about three years in office; Caleb W. West of Utah, Louis K. Church of Dakota, and Preston H. Leslie of Montana, all in 1889 after about two years' service; and William C. Renfrow of Oklahoma and W. T. Thornton of New Mexico, both in 1897, after four years in office.

removed to nineteen.[20] Besides Tyler's inability to fill the New Mexico governorship within his first three months as President, President Pierce could not commission a successor to the governor of Oregon until September 1853, and President McKinley did not fill the vacancy in New Mexico until June 1897. Thus, although there were fifty-one vacancies, new Presidents were able to commission only forty-eight governors within their first three months in office.

The singular feature of the general pattern implicit in the data for appointments, however, is that a very high proportion of the governors entered office within the very brief span of time—5.25 years—represented by the sum of three-month periods during which the appointments were made.[21] Nonetheless, it is not possible to determine satisfactorily how often new Presidents removed governors, elicited resignations, or simply took advantage of the vacancies that existed or occurred at the outset of their administrations, primarily in order to pay off political debts. The seventeen vacancies created by removal are most suspect, but most of the men who filled them do not seem to conform to the negative stereotype of spoilsmen. The same generalization applies equally well to the other governors who, if

20. James Buchanan may have removed Abraham Rencher of New Mexico just before leaving the Presidency, and Martin Van Buren may have removed Robert R. Reid, leaving the Florida governorship vacant for William Henry Harrison to fill, but it is more likely that Harrison removed Reid. The seventeen men removed and the dates of removal are: Robert Lucas of Iowa and Henry Dodge of Wisconsin in 1841; Nathaniel P. Tallmadge of Wisconsin in 1845; Alexander Ramsey of Minnesota, John P. Gaines of Oregon, and William Carr Lane of New Mexico in 1853; Marshall F. Moore of Washington, Alexander C. Hunt of Colorado and Andrew J. Faulk of Dakota in 1869; Eugene Semple of Washington, C. Meyer Zulick of Arizona, Edward A. Stevenson of Idaho, and Thomas Moonlight of Wyoming in 1889; Nathan O. Murphy of Arizona, Abraham J. Seay of Oklahoma and Arthur L. Thomas of Utah in 1893 (in the last case to reappoint Caleb West); and William M. Jenkins of Oklahoma in 1901.

21. The degree of clustering is most vividly illustrated by percentages and ratios: 29.1 percent of the governors $\left(\frac{48 \times 100}{165}\right)$ were appointed within only 4.73 percent of the time period from 1801 to 1911 $\left(\frac{5.25 \times 100}{111}\right)$; or, alternately, for the period from 1801 to 1912 an average of 1.49 governors were appointed per year $\left(\frac{165}{111}\right)$, but the ratio for the appointments made by new Presidents within their first three months in office was 9.15 governors per year $\left(\frac{48}{5.25}\right)$.

they were spoilsmen in the broad sense, certainly were not completely lacking in competence. In other words, even if both the governors and the Presidents can be classified as spoilsmen, it does not necessarily follow that political appointments meant bad governors. On the contrary, there was no reason for Presidents not to take advantage of vacancies to appoint worthy men from their own party or to remove governors from the opposition party in order to appoint new men who could be relied upon to implement new policies.

In general, the Presidents seem to have been careful to appoint qualified men and seldom hesitated to replace their own appointees when they decided they were not working out well in the governor's office. In an indeterminate number of cases governors were asked to resign, but in eleven cases Presidents removed their own appointees (see Table 6). These eleven amount to over a quarter of the governors removed. Fewer than half of the thirty-nine governors removed were fired simply because they belonged to the opposition party, and only two Presidents—Benjamin Harrison and Grover Cleveland, in his second administration—made a clean sweep immediately after they entered office. Pierce and McKinley replaced all the governors in their territories within six months, and William Henry Harrison probably removed all of the governors in his territories within his one month in office.

The only way to determine accurately the extent to which spoils politics entered into the appointment of governors and how many governors were spoilsmen or were poorly qualified for the office is through an analysis of the careers of the 160 men. Since sufficient information is not obtainable for all of the men, other measures and approximations must be used. Tenure in itself is obviously an inadequate index, since a number of highly qualified individuals were governor for a short time. Five of Benjamin Harrison's appointees, for example, were short-tenured governors, given a job that could not be entrusted to mediocre politicians—assuring that territories about to enter the Union would be loyal Republican states. Nevertheless, if it can be assumed that, as a whole, incompetent governors or ones who did not adapt were rather quickly weeded out, then tenure may be used as an indicator of their quality.[22] The rate of turnover

22. Any measure of tenure is, of course, inadequate, since it is not possible to include or exclude tenures of secretaries acting as governors. Only secretaries

during each Presidential administration provides a rough, composite measure of at least three integrants of territorial government: the adaptability and tenacity of the governors in each period, the general level of territorial autonomy insofar as it affected Presidential policies and the governors' tenure, and the extent to which spoils politics played a part in each Presidential administration (see Table 7).

The rate of turnover can also be used to determine the average prospective tenure of a governor during each President's term in office. For example, assume for a moment that all the governors appointed by a President replaced other governors; if the President replaced twenty percent, or one-fifth of the governors for each year of territorial existence, a new governor could anticipate staying in office for five years, since it would take that long for the process to run full cycle. Thus, under James Monroe a governor's prospective tenure was over eight years, under Lincoln it was over two years and nine months, using a rate of 36.1 (see Table 7), and under Roosevelt it was three and a half years.

The first governor of each territory was not a replacement, however, and the turnover resulting from appointments to vacancies existing when a President entered office do not necessarily reflect the new President's appointive policies. Nor do the appointments, made immediately after a new President was inaugurated, to fill nine vacancies that followed the resignations of governors. For these reasons, three alternative series are offered in Table 7. These series represent the sequential omission from the total data of fourteen vacancies in the first case, twenty-nine appointments in the second, and forty-five in the third. The most striking feature of the different series is the apparent increase in the rate of turnover that occurred

---

with special commissions as acting governor are included in the list of governors. A number of secretaries, most prominently Winthrop Sargent, did not hold such commissions and are not counted as governors (in Sargent's case, while he was in the Northwest) though they were, in fact, sometimes acting governors for long periods of time. Between January 1867 and October 1871, and between August 1878 and July 1880, the secretaries of Idaho acted as governor nearly continuously. At the beginning of each period a governor was suspended. During the two periods there were a total of eight attempts to appoint a new governor. One man died without taking office, three or four did not get Senate confirmation, one declined the appointment, and one immediately resigned. (See Pomeroy, *Territories, 1861–1890*, 65–66.)

during the third and fourth phases of the First Empire, which coincides with the emergence of territorial autonomy and, traditionally,

TABLE 7. RATE OF TURNOVER OF TERRITORIAL GOVERNORS DURING THE SEVERAL PRESIDENTIAL ADMINISTRATIONS

		Percentage rate of turnover: n/years × 100			
President	*Years*[1]	$n = x$	$n = y$	$n = z$	$n = t$
Jefferson*	29.8	16.8%	16.8%	13.4%	3.4%
Madison	42.9	14.0	9.3	9.3	7.0
Monroe	24.6	12.2	12.2	12.2	0.0
J. Q. Adams	12.0	8.3	8.3	0.0	0.0
Jackson	23.8	25.2	25.2	25.2	21.0
Van Buren	10.7	18.8	18.8	18.8	9.4
W. H. Harrison	0.25	80.0	40.0	40.0	40.0
Tyler	11.7	25.6	17.0	17.0	17.0
Polk	5.5	54.5	54.5	54.5	36.4
Taylor	2.7	75.1	37.6	37.6	37.6
Fillmore	10.3	29.1	29.1	29.1	9.7
Pierce	27.5	40.0	36.4	36.4	29.1
Buchanan*	22.9	39.3	39.3	26.2	26.2
Lincoln	33.2	48.2	33.1	36.1	24.1
Johnson	33.2	30.2	30.2	30.2	30.2
Grant*	71.4	35.0	32.2	29.5	29.5
Hayes	32.0	28.1	28.1	25.0	25.0
Garfield	4.0	25.0	25.0	0.0	0.0
Arthur	28.0	32.1	32.1	32.1	32.1
Cleveland, 1	32.0	28.1	28.1	25.0	25.0
B. Harrison	19.5	61.5	61.5	41.0	35.9
Cleveland, 2	14.8	33.7	33.7	27.0	27.0
McKinley	13.5	37.0	37.0	29.6	29.6
T. Roosevelt	21.2	28.4	28.4	28.4	28.4
Taft	5.8	34.8	34.8	34.8	34.8

* Transfer appointments not counted. Claiborne, Medary, and Axtell are counted only once.

x = total number of appointments accepted during each administration (from Table 6).

$y = x$ − all vacancies existing when the President entered office (total of 14).

$z = x$ − all appointments made by Presidents within their first three months in office except those resulting from removal of governors in the same period (total of 29. Lincoln couldn't fill one).

$t = x - z$ − all first appointments to new territories during each administration (total of 16).

[1] The total number of years territories existed during each administration.

with the rise of spoils politics. Secondly, after choosing the most relevant rate for each President, it is evident that the rate of turnover was unusually high under only three Presidents—Polk, Taylor, and Benjamin Harrison. William Henry Harrison's rate, for only one month in office, cannot be taken as indicative unless it is combined with Tyler's. Thirdly, the average tenure of governors under the other Presidents, again using the data selectively, was approximately three years or more.

Finally, perhaps the most significant point to be made regarding tenure is that the average governor who was sent to the territories from a state held office for at least as long a time as the territorial resident who was appointed. This suggests that, however influential considerations of state patronage may have been in determining their selection, the nonresidents gave as good a performance as governor as those individuals who were territorial residents when appointed. Between 1861 and 1873, for example, Presidents Lincoln, Johnson, and Grant gave governor's appointments to twelve territorial residents and to thirty nonresidents. Five of the former and sixteen of the latter held office for over two and a half years, but only three of the residents were governor for three years or more, as opposed to fourteen of the nonresidents. Similarly, from 1873 to 1885, Presidents Grant, Hayes, Garfield, and Arthur appointed six territorial residents to the governorship and twenty-two nonresidents. As in the preceding period, about half of each group served as governor for at least two and a half years—the numbers are three and twelve, respectively, but only one of the resident appointees held office for three years or more, in contrast to eleven of the nonresidents. These figures clearly indicate that Presidents could depend more on nonresident than on resident appointees to stay on the job, and tend to substantiate Grant's contention that it was unwise to choose governors from among territorial residents.

The myriad and divided responsibilities of the governors and the hazards of office make the overall average tenure of three years rather impressive, regardless of the fact that there was no limit on the number of terms a governor could hold the office. The governor's first responsibility in law was to the federal government he represented, but it was ill-defined and divided among numerous agencies.

Throughout the First Empire the Department of State was the principal policy-making and administrative organ. Between 1849 and 1873, State and Interior occupied this field of authority jointly, and then the latter assumed primary control over territorial affairs. The Secretaries of State and Interior, however, were normally indifferent to territorial affairs and viewed them as peripheral to their main functions. Consequently, they never challenged the right of various divisions of the War, Post Office, and what in 1870 formally became the Justice Department to formulate and administer their territorial policies independently. In those areas where jurisdictional claims overlapped, incompatible policies could have been in effect simultaneously. This situation created headaches for the governors who, on any given matter, might receive contradictory instructions or advice from different departmental secretaries and from the President. In addition, Congress got involved in policy-making and administration through legislation and through its committees—often committees other than those that dealt with territorial affairs. Finally, Congress and the executive departments occasionally sent special agents to the territories, armed with extraordinary powers, to investigate the activities of governors and other officials or to see to the execution of specific policies.

On the other hand, although the federal supervisory structure seemed formidable, it was usually more exasperating than menacing. In spite of the numbers concerned, Washington officials rarely intervened directly in territorial affairs after the beginning of the nineteenth century. As territorial home rule developed, the federal government increasingly limited itself to general supervision and left strictly internal affairs to the territorial governments, except when their actions constituted an extreme misuse of power or threatened some vital national policy. From the governor's viewpoint these developments were often unsatisfactory since, when extending territorial autonomy, the federal government did not absolve him of responsibility for what happened in his territory.

Insofar as the governors were concerned, the worst aspect of the territorial system was that they were seldom adequately apprised of federal policies or of their duties with respect to them. At times, chary Washington officials acted as if they were unwilling to divulge federal policies to the governors. As a result, when dealing with sensitive problems, governors often could not obtain advice and had to make major decisions without knowing whether the federal government would support them. These problems were less critical for the early governors, but they grew and festered as time passed. Until the late 1860s, when a governor was also superintendent of Indian affairs, he occasionally received instructions and a good deal of advice regarding the conduct of Indian affairs from the Presidents and department heads. Directions relating to other matters, however, became much more difficult to obtain as the nineteenth century progressed. When governors did receive instructions they usually dealt with the execution of limited policies. The English practice of supplying governors with detailed instructions was only partially followed during the early years in the United States, and never at the beginning of a new Presidential or gubernatorial administration.

Equally important, what instructions the governors did receive were seldom meant to be binding. They were intended to provide general guidelines, rather than rules, to help governors make their own decisions. Repeatedly, governors pleaded for precise instructions or clearly-defined policy statements, only to be told in reply to reread the Organic Act for their territory. In effect, this was a polite way to say what Secretary of State Hamilton Fish told one governor outright in 1872—that the Department did not furnish governors with instructions as to the nature of their duties. This was indeed a remarkable statement for the head of the United States version of a Colonial Office to make. Conditions did not change significantly in this respect under the Department of the Interior, but after 1874 governors were normally told to read the *Revised Statutes of the United States* in addition to the Organic Acts. Thus, throughout the period of continental expansion, most department secretaries refrained from interfering with the governors as long as they stayed within the ill-defined statutory limits of their powers and did nothing to affect adversely basic federal interests. Although their office obviously had a sizable stake in federal law and, of necessity, in territorial law, the Attorneys General, for example, usually contended that territorial affairs were beyond their purview and it was all but impossible to obtain opinions from them. Between 1861 and 1890 they provided territorial officials with only seven opinions, and all of these apparently dealt with the validity of specific territorial laws.

In addition to being responsible for the execution of vague federal policies, territorial governors were often expected to implement these policies without funds or assistance. The State Department's lack of funds to meet extraordinary territorial needs was notorious, and the War Department occasionally found itself financially embarrassed and unable to supply the wherewithal when military emergencies arose. In such cases, the territorial governors were expected to overcome their problems as best they could by using local resources, even when vital federal policies were involved. In short, the federal government expected governors, bare-handed, to massage knotty problems out of existence.[23]

To a certain extent the territories, rather than the federal government, defined federal-territorial relations, because of the looseness of federal controls. Although the governor's first responsibility in law was to the federal government, he also had to please the territorial inhabitants enough to insure the smooth operation of the colonial system. In this respect, the governor was the kingpin that held the system together. The federal government did not wish to be troubled by territorial affairs, and expected the governor to see that things were handled smoothly. If one governor could not establish and maintain tranquility in a territory, he could always be replaced.

When the citizenry became incensed over anything that could be related to government, which was often, they tended to focus their ire on the governor, as the symbol of the offending colonial system. A standard ploy, in such an occurrence, was to compare the governor to George III and the United States system to that of the pre-Revolutionary British Empire. Such rhetorical flourishes appeared in the first issue of the first newspaper published west of the Appalachians, the Cincinnati *Centinel of the North-Western Territory*, in November 1793. They were the common stock-in-trade of the dis-

23. The whole system of territorial-federal relations is thoroughly discussed in *ibid.*, 4–35, 90–106; Valentine, "Territorial Governor," 38–40, 64–66; Meyerholz, "Federal Supervision," 203–14. See also Philbrick, *Laws of Illinois*, R42–45, R463–64; Neil, "Territorial Governors," 41–42, 131–32, 193; Carter, *Territorial Papers*, XIII:116.

contented, at least until the end of the nineteenth century. Nevertheless, while settlers invariably condemned the system of government whenever it fell short of their expectations, by the 1830s the territorial system had become popular enough to be included among the standard demands made by settlers in unorganized areas. Moreover, they frequently opposed ending the system in their territory by voting against statehood.[24]

Given the attitude of the federal government and the fickleness of the territorial citizens, a strong governor could seldom feel absolutely secure in his actions or hope to avoid conflict. Nearly any act of consequence might precipitate a campaign for his removal. Although they were sometimes organized by private individuals, such campaigns were most often the products of local political machines or of a legislature desirous of ridding a territory of a particular governor. No matter how strong his constitutional grounds (for example, whenever a governor vetoed a bill—particularly a pork barrel bill—dear to the people's hearts), the citizenry were likely to respond with a spate of petitions demanding his dismissal. Similarly, attempts to force county officials to pay their counties' share of taxes were never popular. Territorial officials usually encountered resistance, and their actions often led to the drafting of removal petitions.

Intraparty clashes were especially menacing to the governor's security. Political parties and groups were commonly more factious in the territories than in the states, and no opposition was potentially so dangerous to a governor as that which came from within his own party. If a governor sided with one faction of his party, the others were almost certain to oppose him, yet if he was unable to muster sufficient support from within his party, he was bound to fail. As a matter of expediency governors often refused to become involved in political disputes and avoided direct confrontations with local bosses by ignoring issues and corruption within their party. Governor Brayman of Idaho, among others, was suspended from office primarily because of the strong resentment he engendered within his own party. Brayman's undoing seems to have come about as a result of his waging

24. Pomeroy, *Territories, 1861–1890*, 85, 104; Bond, *Foundations*, 411, 431; Bond, *Old Northwest*, 86–88.

a campaign against the corruption of local bosses who were raiding the public till.[25]

At times, party factionalism drew territorial officials together, but it also tended to arouse latent animosities within the federal cadre. When these enmities were stirred, the secretaries and judges, who liked to see themselves as the governor's equal, could be expected to join groups antagonistic to the executive, often without regard for their party affiliations. Whether these groups benefited from federal leadership or not, the rhetoric of opposition was the same. The two staples of all formal and informal charges were that the governors were drunkards and enemies of democracy, the latter including allegations of executive tyranny and the like. As the norms of moral propriety changed in the post-Civil War period, however, a long list of vile charges were added; among the more respectable was the accusation that governors publicly cavorted with "the worst prostitutes." The most effective postwar innovation for mobilizing opposition to a governor, particularly a nonresident appointee, was the superbly vague claim that he was a carpetbagger.[26]

Ordinarily, the governors' adversaries showed little regard for the facts and often frankly admitted in the territories that the charges in their petitions were without foundation. Consequently, in simply filing them, the Secretaries of State and Interior gave the bulk of the petitions about as much attention as they deserved. At times, however, they asked governors to answer specific charges and, as a whole, the removal petitions apparently received somewhat more attention in the Interior Department than they had in the State Department. In a few instances, the secretaries also sent their own investigators to the territories to look into charges. Moreover, during the Second Empire, the Presidents seemed to be more inclined to assume that where there was smoke there was fire, but though they occasionally acquiesced in the removal of governors, they seldom removed governors solely because of charges made against them. Perhaps more often than not, Presidents removed governors simply by appointing successors—that is, without

25. Neil, "Territorial Governors," 113–15, 122, 126–28, 136–40, 156–67; Valentine, "Territorial Governor," 86, 109–10.

26. Valentine, "Territorial Governor," 99–100, 128; Neil, "Territorial Governors," 138, 150–54, 167–68.

first removing the incumbents. This was a tidy way to deal with difficult situations, inasmuch as the President's prerogatives included the right to appoint new governors at any time without offering any explanations. Some governors were asked to resign, but most often they resigned without being asked when they perceived the specter of removal on the horizon. A few governors fled from territories in which there were especially violent quarrels.[27]

In all, about two-thirds of the governors who did not hold office for the full term of their commission resigned.[28] Although the opposition they experienced in the territories undoubtedly convinced a number of governors that it would be wise to resign, a majority of them pointed to the insufficiency of their salary as the main reason for leaving office. Some resigned to concentrate on their private business affairs, and quite a few were drawn off by the more lucrative pursuits surrounding them in the territories, in mining, railroading, and commerce. Numerous governors simply did not like the job, a few left office because of poor health, and at least one man, Green Clay Smith of Montana, resigned in 1869 to devote himself to the ministry. But a sizable number of men resigned the governorship to assume other public offices. Those who became territorial delegate were among the most prominent. A few individuals, like William H. Wallace, apparently accepted the governorship primarily with a view to getting into Congress. Wallace became governor of Idaho six days after his term as delegate from Washington expired, ordered the election of a delegate from Idaho as soon as he entered that territory, declared himself a candidate, and won. The first set of officials sent to the Arizona Territory "quarreled all the way across the plains about who should be the first delegate to Congress from a Territory they had never seen," but a man already on the spot won the first election.[29]

27. Neil, "Territorial Governors," 102–07, 146–47, 166–68; Valentine, "Territorial Governor," 45–47, 86; Meyerholz, "Federal Supervision," 220; Pomeroy, *Territories, 1861–1890*, 8–19.

28. The men who died in office or who had short terms because of the achievement of statehood are not included in this calculation.

29. Pomeroy, *Territories, 1861–1890*, 38; Valentine, "Territorial Governor," 44, 130–31; Neil, "Territorial Governors," 111–12. The quotation is in Pomeroy, 87–88. Green Clay Smith fought in the Mexican War and became a general during the Civil War.

Implicit in the above discussion is the conclusion that the 160 territorial governors accepted their appointments for a variety of reasons that radiated outward from the ideal of public service to the extremes of opportunism in the pursuit of power, status, and wealth. Thus, William Blount wanted the job principally for its value to his speculative ventures, Arthur St. Clair took it because he saw it as a pinnacle of power and prestige second only to the Presidency, and John Branch accepted it as a public responsibility. Branch's governorship in Florida came unsolicited, at the end of a long and distinguished public career in which he had been a state governor, Congressman, Senator, judge, and Secretary of the Navy. Nevertheless, while the interests of prospective governors covered the gamut from a desire to go to Arizona for health reasons, to fostering the growth of a strong, loyal party in the territories, the charges made in Congress that most appointees were simply young men out of work and broken-down politicians were unfair. Certainly, they should not be faulted for having been relatively young men. On the contrary, the fact that over half of the governors were between forty and fifty-two years of age, and that the median age of all 160 was forty-six, indicates that for most of them the governorship came at a critical juncture during their careers.[30]

Regardless of their reasons for accepting the appointment and its relationship to the advancement of their careers, which will be considered below, the governors were seldom inexperienced when they came to office. By the standards of the times, they were reasonably well educated. Over a quarter had earned a college or university degree, a half dozen or more were West Point graduates, and most of the others had completed their secondary or academy training. In addition, more than half of the governors had had some military experience, largely in wartime armies. Nearly all of them had been commissioned officers,

30. In conjunction with this discussion see Valentine, "Territorial Governor," 123–43; Neil, "Territorial Governors," 2–9, 41–43, 83, 102–37, 196–97; and compare with Pomeroy, *Territories, 1861–1890*, 62–63; Lamar, *Dakota Territory*, 95–97, 112–13, 130–33, 202–04, 214–21, 236–38 and *passim;* and Lamar, *Far Southwest*, 298, 483 and *passim*. See also Masterson, *Blount*, 174–77, 349. A comparative study of the period 1869–1890 suggests that the state governors' median age was only about two and a half years older than that of the territorial governors (Jack E. Eblen, "Status, Mobility, and Empire: The Territorial Governors, 1869–1890," *Pacific Northwest Quarterly*, forthcoming in 1969).

and approximately forty had acquired at least a brevet rank of brigadier general. Nevertheless, only a few could be classified as professional soldiers. Several governors had begun their careers in medicine and a number of others had been in business or journalism, but more than half had studied law and started out as lawyers.

Probably all of the governors had been actively involved in territorial, state, or national politics before their appointment as governor and perhaps three-quarters or more had previously held a public office of some importance. Roughly a quarter of the governors had held judicial or other appointive posts, and a small number had been state governors, but about half had served in a legislature or in Congress, or both. Approximately a quarter had been elected to Congress and some went directly from Congress to the governorship, either after losing an election or after having resigned.

On the basis of all the information gathered, it seems that ten percent or fewer of the governors were poorly prepared for the office or were otherwise unfit and unable to adapt to it. Furthermore, taken as a whole, the calibre of the territorial governors was probably at least as high as that of the state governors at any given time, particularly in the states adjacent to the territories. Consequently, an important feature of the territorial system is not that there were a few incompetent governors but that there were so many who were well qualified. Thus, again, it seems that even the worst of the spoilsmen kept the requirements of the office in mind when selecting governors.[31]

As governors, most of the men took an active interest in administration and in the promotion of territorial growth. Aside from supporting appropriate legislation, they commonly used propaganda and their own money to encourage development—although not always for altruistic reasons. William Blount began the practice of publishing favorable reports about the land, climate, and promise of the territories in eastern newspapers, and regardless of his personal motives, everyone

31. On this and the following discussion see, in addition to the sources cited in the previous note, Valentine, "Territorial Governor," 23–26, 88–89, 97, 118–20; Neil, "Territorial Governors," 23–39, 53, 93–98, 132–33; McCarty, *Governors of the Northwest*, 116–17, 131–32; Pomeroy, *Territories, 1861–1890*, 23 ff; William Henry Powell, *List of Officers of the Army of the United States from 1779 to 1900* . . . (New York, 1900), *passim.*

shared his desire to further settlement and economic development. By the early nineteenth century most governors accepted territorial promotion as one of their foremost responsibilities, and governors like Lewis Cass went to great lengths, and sometimes personal expense, to counter bad publicity, build up the image of the territory, and encourage immigration. Often during the first stage and occasionally during the second, governors either took advantage of eastern trips or made special journeys to lobby for the territory in Congress and to advertise its virtues in a variety of ways. In addition, their correspondence with the federal government is filled with requests for subsidies, improved land laws, more rapid land surveys, and other enhancements for territorial development.

In the post-Civil War period the governors' annual reports to the Department of the Interior became key instruments for publicizing the territories. They reached their fullest development, however, when in 1878 Secretary Carl Schurz asked the governors to include statements on a wide range of topics that would be useful to immigrants, and the government started publishing them. Prospective settlers quickly adopted the annual reports as guidebooks and before long the governors started writing other, often more elaborate tracts for publication by the territorial legislature or by private groups.

The governors also encouraged legislatures to enact laws specifically designed to attract capital and settlers. Early in the nineteenth century, territorial legislatures established immigration bureaus for these purposes, first in the East and later overseas, and most, if not all of the territories of the Second Empire organized such bureaus at one time or another. The governors usually took part in setting them up, and Governor Ashley of Montana appointed an immigration agent in New York before he left for the territory and before the legislature had appropriated money for an agency. In the early 1880s, Governor Nehemiah G. Ordway created a bureau on wheels. After convincing the legislature to equip a special railway car with agricultural exhibits, he took it on a tour through his native New England to advertise the territory.

Most governors followed Lewis Cass's example in pressing for the development of transportation to and within the territories as a means of accelerating settlement and economic growth. A few, like Thomas

"Granger" Moonlight of Wyoming, encountered fierce opposition to their promotion of agricultural settlement, land reforms, and conservation, but ordinarily no specific agricultural recommendations were necessary. People generally assumed that agriculture was such an essential part of economic development that everyone would do his utmost to advance it without encouragement.

Numerous governors invested their own money or used their contacts with the eastern money markets in such a way as to draw capital to the territories. Much of this investment was, of course, highly speculative, but though it was frequently exploitative in character, it usually had some positive influence on development. William Blount and Ninian Edwards, who developed processing and service industries, were more representative of the governor as entrepreneur than was Governor William A. Howard of Dakota, who built with his own money an insane asylum that the territory eventually bought. Blount owned a number of stores in the Southwest that he supplied through his brothers in the East and operated in a manner that provided him with double profits. Edwards ran stores in eight or ten towns in Illinois and Missouri and made trips to the East almost every year to buy merchandise for them. He also established a number of saw and grist mills in Illinois. Blount was at least a part owner of similar businesses and an iron foundry in his territory. In addition, Edwards obtained the title of benefactor of Illinois by importing prime breeding stock and various plants.[32]

For the most part, people considered speculation to be developmental when the speculator was a resident and did not charge exorbitant prices, or in the case of land, when he did not hold it off the market for too long. Under such an elastic definition it was possible for a number of governors who were large-scale land and railroad speculators to gain acceptance as "developers" and "bona fide residents" despite the questionable nature of their activities. Some of the joint executive-legislative adventures in corporate collusion have been men-

32. Pomeroy, *Territories, 1861–1890,* 36; Masterson, *Blount,* 212–13, 220–21, 278–81; McCarty, *Governors of the Northwest,* 96; Ninian Wirt Edwards, *History of Illinois from 1778 to 1883; and Life and Times of Ninian Edwards* (Springfield, Illinois, 1870), 241–42; Lamar, *Dakota Territory,* 101–02 and *passim;* Lamar, *Far Southwest, passim.*

tioned, but no governor approached William Blount's level of operation as a land speculator. By the end of his governorship he seems to have owned or held options on more than two million acres, and at one point during his reign he was kept busy trying to round up about three million acres of land to fulfill a single foreign sales contract. Like Blount and numerous later governors, James Wilkinson of Louisiana-Missouri was charged with improperly and illegally speculating in land, but only a few seem to have been formally reprimanded and it is doubtful that any were removed for that reason alone.

The average governor usually disapproved of speculation (as did Arthur St. Clair and William Henry Harrison, who contended that it was immoral and below the dignity of their office), and ran his own land operations as a small business. St. Clair and Harrison, of course, were not exactly typical governors; besides, St. Clair proved to be an inept speculator when he tried his hand at it, and Harrison was charged with misusing his office for speculative purposes. Ninian Edwards, however, is probably representative of most governors who bought and sold land. He dealt in small parcels of land and in town lots that never totalled more than four thousand acres at any given time. His average land holding was around two thousand acres or less. During the last years of his governorship there was scarcely an issue of the Kaskaskia *Intelligencier* in which he did not advertise land for sale. A rather large amount of capital must have been necessary to sustain his various operations and Edwards seems to have operated within rather narrow margins. In 1813, for example, he wrote to an agent in Illinois from Kentucky, asking him to try to collect some debts and pointed out that he was hard pressed for money "Altho I have sold land to the amount of about ten thousand dollars." At other times he had to borrow money in order to retain his lands. In short, since cash customers were hard to find and he could not afford to extend much credit, Edwards was unable to charge excessive prices, so his profits from land sales were apparently not very large, whatever the volume of sales.[33]

33. The quotation is from Edwards to ——, August 1813, in the Edwards Miscellaneous Papers, Illinois Historical Library, Folder 1. See also Masterson, *Blount, passim,* but especially 199–200, 208, 212–13, 220–21, 249–50, 254–55, 260–61, 276, 298; Solon Justus Buck, *Illinois in 1818* (Springfield, Illinois, 1917), 153; Valentine, "Territorial Governor," 144; McCarty, *Governors of the Northwest,*

Only a few governors were very wealthy either before they came to office or during their governorship, and among them two of Colorado's governors—John Evans, a prominent railroad promoter and benefactor of Northwestern University, in whose honor Evanston, Illinois, was named, and E. M. McCook, one of the largest landowners and taxpayers in the territory—were exceptional. Probably a sizable majority of the governors depended on their salary and outside jobs in the territories to provide an adequate income and could not afford extensive investments. Their salary from the federal government certainly did not provide them with speculative capital. Except in Orleans Territory, where Claiborne received $5,000, the governors in the period before 1822 were paid $2,000 a year, half of which was for their service as superintendent of Indian affairs. From 1822 to 1872, their salary was $2,500, except in Oregon, Washington, and Wyoming. In those three territories it was $3,000. After 1872 the governors' salaries were $3,500 a year in all but Oklahoma Territory where it was only $2,600. Out of this and a contingency fund, which usually ranged from $350 to $500 before 1872, when it was stabilized at the higher figure, the governors were expected to support themselves and meet all the normal operating expenses of their office. These included the purchase of equipment and supplies, office rent, and the cost of a private secretary, if the governor wanted one. In addition, until 1880, the governors had to pay the postage for all their official correspondence, and this was not always a small matter.[34]

At first, St. Clair was impressed with his salary, but within two years of the time he became governor he was complaining that it was inadequate, and this complaint was echoed by nearly all subsequent governors. Indeed, the salary was too small to meet the high costs of

---

96, 124, 130–31; Hoopes, *Indian Affairs*, 228–33; G. L. Wilson, "St. Clair," 99–103; Smith, *St. Clair Papers*, I:194; Downes, *Frontier Ohio*, 133–34; Philbrick, *Laws of Indiana*, R26, R47, R199–200; Lamar, *Dakota Territory*, 203, 242 and *passim;* Lamar, *Far Southwest*, 176, 186, 258, 266, 273–74, 286–87, 443–58, 487 and *passim;* and note 30 above. In conjuction with Harrison, see also Carter, *Territorial Papers*, VII:548, for charges that he used his position as superintendent of land sales "not only [to] found a combination to speculate in sales . . . but publicly avowed his right to carry this combination to any length he pleased. . . ."

34. Pomeroy, *Territories, 1861–1890*, 39; Valentine, "Territorial Governor," 48, 64, 145.

living in the West and cover the basic expenses of office, much less the costs of travel to and within the territories. Consequently, when their salary and contingency funds ran out, the governors were reluctant to make even necessary official trips within their territory because they could not count on being reimbursed if they paid for them with their own money. The federal government exacerbated all the above problems in several ways, besides paying low salaries. The government never paid the moving expenses of new governors, which sometimes cost a year and a half's salary or more. Moreover, a new governor's salary did not begin until he actually entered office, and the Treasury Department's policy of not making advances did not help him get started. In the few cases when the Treasury did make advances on salaries, they were only for a quarter. Finally, the federal government was splendidly lax when it came to paying salaries. In some years Congressional appropriations for salaries were deficient by twenty-five or thirty percent while in others no appropriations were madc. The first Montana officials received no pay for two years after the territory was organized.[35]

Federal salaries were so low in relation to living costs and incomes from other occupations that in mining territories, for example, the mere acceptance of a judgeship raised serious questions about a lawyer's honesty and competence. Governors frequently complained that their salary was publicly ridiculed and that they were not treated with the respect they felt their office deserved, but more importantly, the high costs in combination with Congressional niggardliness in effect discriminated against the nonresident appointee, for he had to bear the costs of moving and making a new start. Resident appointees, on the other hand, were presumably already established and had other sources of income on which they could rely.

In addition to their outside jobs and subsidies from territorial legislatures, the governors were able to supplement their federal salary by

35. For this and the following see Valentine, "Territorial Governor," 49–54, 87, 102, 113–14; Pomeroy, *Territories, 1861–1890*, 35–38, 41; Neil, "Territorial Governors," 159–65; Bond, *Old Northwest*, 80–81, 94; Carter, *Territorial Papers*, II:124, 248. See also Gruening, *Alaska*, 50–52: the Alaska Government Act of 1884 did not provide travel pay for officials going to the territory or on official trips within it, though it was one-fifth the size of the rest of the United States and had some 30,000 people scattered about the settlements.

charging fees for various official services. In January 1873, however, Congress outlawed all fees for executive services that were not specifically authorized by federal law, and by so doing abolished a major source of income for many governors. In the Northwest, St. Clair had charged $4.00 for every tavern and marriage license, as well as a fee for every civil commission he issued. Winthrop Sargent doubled all these fees when he went to Mississippi. When territories entered the second stage, the legislatures limited the governor's licensing powers but continued to allow them to charge a variety of fees. A few governors abused this privilege and the Congressional prohibition did not stop them. In 1889, for instance, Governor Louis K. Church vetoed a bill to repeal the $5.00 fee for every notary public commission he issued; this fee alone had supposedly provided him with $3,018 in supplementary income during his two years in office.

A number of governors made their financial condition sound pathetic and attributed it to their salary, but few were as impoverished as Thomas Moonlight or John C. Frémont would have one believe. In the late 1880s Governor Moonlight claimed that he could not afford to keep a horse for transportation in Wyoming because of the cost of hay —which, according to the annual report to the Secretary of the Interior in 1889, was between nine and fifteen dollars a ton in towns. He bitterly complained that he received less from his office than any other official in the territory and that everyone laughed at his salary, if not at his condition. While Frémont was governor of Arizona at the end of the 1870s, he similarly contended that his salary was too small to permit him to own a horse. Moreover, he asserted, he could not even afford to rent one; nor could he hire a housekeeper or a cook. Consequently, he had to go everywhere on foot, eat the coarsest foods, and rely on the charity of the citizens.[36]

Because of the relative flexibility of the governorship and its comparatively light duties throughout much of territorial history, the poorer governors could pursue a variety of sidelines. The most attractive, and probably the most common among those governors who could not afford to run a business or speculate in land, was to open a private law practice, but this invited the charge of impropriety. Gov-

36. Neil, "Territorial Governors," 165; Valentine, "Territorial Governor," 145; *House Executive Documents*, vol. 1, pt. 5, 51 Cong., 1 sess. (S.N. 2726), 593.

of Oregon, at least, ran for the Vice Presidency while a number of others must have tried to be nominated for that office.[40]

When the territorial governors are viewed as a unit, one must conclude that they were capable politicians. This is not to say that most of them were not also opportunists of one sort or another, who saw the governorship as an important stepping-stone to wealth and power. Indeed, for a number of them, the office provided an *entrée* into the circles of big business, although initially, most were probably interested primarily in using it to advance their political career. Next to being elected to state and federal offices, these men seem to have been intent on worming their way into the diplomatic corps or other centers of power that were controlled by old, established eastern families. But whatever their motives, their success in both business and politics makes it clear that the territorial governorship was a fundamental avenue of rapid mobility for aspiring young politicians. Moreover, inasmuch as the average territorial governor seems to have had rather humble origins, the office gave talented and ambitious westerners access to high positions in government and business that might otherwise have been denied to them altogether.

40. Valentine, "Territorial Governor," 140–43; Baker, *Colorado*, V:447–48.

Epilogue

THE general interpretation that emerges from this study can be stated briefly. The Ordinance of 1787 provided for a fully centralized, nondemocratic form of colonial government, modeled after the pre-Revolutionary British system, which remained centralized in law throughout the period of continental expansion, but which acquired a façade of democracy during the course of the First Empire. Within a half-century of its enactment, Congress abandoned the first stage of the Ordinance and dramatically reduced the officeholding and suffrage requirements of the second stage. As a whole, the modifications of the territorial system paralleled similar developments in eastern state government and, like the Ordinance itself, demonstrate that Congress was not innovative. The same was largely true of western settlers for, as in the East, the legal extension of democracy in the territories did not lead to democratic government, any more than the statutory centralization of the empire was accompanied by thorough-going federal control over the territories.[1]

On the contrary, the two overriding characteristics of territorial government both before and after the people began performing the rituals of democracy were all-pervasive oligarchic control and local autonomy. Both developed early, under the autocratically structured district stage in the Old Northwest, and persisted throughout terri-

1. For a contrasting interpretation see Lamar's Introduction in *Dakota Territory*.

torial history at all levels of government, primarily because of the inability, if not the unwillingness of the governors, in the absence of strong federal support, to control the development of the territories sufficiently or in such a manner as to produce effective democracy and insure the protection of individual rights. In this respect, the administratively weak United States colonial system would seem to have been a failure, yet the fundamental goals of empire were fulfilled.

The basic explanation for this apparent paradox is to be found in the nature of the Anglo-American conquest of the continent. The native-born white Anglo-Saxon Protestants, who constituted the overwhelming majority of the migrants to the territories, carried with them the political institutions and attitudes of the East, which shaped territorial government. Consequently, the political system that emerged conformed to and eventually fulfilled the federal design of empire, not because of federal action but because experimentation was rigidly circumscribed by the narrow middle-class norms of the Anglo-American settlers who exterminated or segregated those people who would not or could not adapt and assimilate. That the federal government and its officials in the territories—if not the whole of white American society—generally approved of this course of events is indicated by their duplicity in dealing with the Indians and their complicity in the widespread acts of racism and genocide, as well as in the use of federal power, however ineffectively, against the Mormons and other groups. Thus, in very broad terms, one may conclude that, in operation, the significance of the United States colonial system lies in its internal oligarchic character rather than in its legal structure and the mechanics of federal-territorial relations.

The broad implications of this study for future research are equally clear. Aside from the obvious need for a book-length study of the Ordinance of 1787, historians studying individual territories or groups of territories should look more closely at the real role of the average people and seek to determine more precisely the class structure and power relationships at all levels of government and the political processes of absorbing or manipulating the voters. In addition, if the operation and significance of territorial government is to be understood fully, much greater attention will have to be given to the day-to-day operation of the territorial system. Previously, historians have concentrated almost exclusively on government at the territorial level and then have dealt in depth only with the more stormy and colorful periods of territorial politics which, as this study suggests, were periods of rapid executive turnover that may well have been the least important or representative of the nature of territorial government.[2]

The tendency to treat territorial government on the continent as a thing apart should be overcome, not only to improve our perspective on United States colonialism but on the entire political system. From this study it appears that, in any given period, the political complexion and nature of partisan politics in territorial and state governments was very similar, except for the special role of the territorial governors and the somewhat greater fluidity of territorial oligarchies and parties. For example, as a whole the territorial governors seem to have been reasonably good or well-behaved executives. Perhaps the reason was that they had little real power and no viable alternative, especially if they hoped to advance in federal service or in territorial or state politics, but their activities in other offices, both before and after their territorial governorship—that is, their career profiles—suggest that they would have acted in much the same way had they had the full powers of state governors. Yet, aside from the weak and unstable tenure of the territorial governors as opposed to that of state executives, and the previously assumed differences between the two groups' overall motives, character, and qualifications for office, they also invite comparison because the average career profiles of the state and territorial executives seem to have been very similar.

A second kind of comparative research could be done on different colonial periods or empires. The United States Empires should be compared more thoroughly with both the Old and New British Empires, but perhaps the most immediate need is for a comparative analysis of the continental and overseas imperialism of the United States. The

2. The extent to which long periods of relative tranquility have been overlooked is evident in the choice of governors considered and the extensiveness with which their administrations are treated in such studies as Lamar, *Dakota Territory;* Lamar, *Far Southwest;* McCarty, *Governors of the Northwest;* Neil, "Territorial Governors"; and Kenneth Nelson Owens, "Frontier Governors: A Study of the Territorial Executives in the History of Washington, Idaho, Montana, Wyoming, and Dakota Territories" (unpublished Ph.D. dissertation, University of Minnesota, 1959).

forms of government for the first two United States Empires, for example, underwent a drastic change in meaning when they were applied to the Third. The analysis of colonial government during the first two empires, however, indicates that the manner in which the territories of the Oceanic Empire were governed was not related to any structural or functional deficiencies of the continental system. Rather, the new use of old forms of government seems to have resulted primarily from changes in objectives and in attitudes toward colonial administration and colonial peoples, a shift that should be thoroughly examined.

Selected Bibliography

The sources listed below are intended to indicate the range of materials available. Biographical information on the governors was obtained from a large number of sources that cannot be enumerated in full. They include the *Dictionary of American Biography*, the *National Cyclopaedia of American Biography*, and state and local histories. The state legislative manuals, yearbooks, blue books, and registers were somewhat less useful. A sampling of the more important scholarly state histories are included, but none of the frequently valuable subscription histories are cited.

Manuscript collections were used primarily for the study of the First Empire. I have consulted the Ninian Edwards papers in the Illinois State Historical Library and the Chicago Historical Society Library, the Lewis Cass papers and other relevant collections in the W. L. Clements Library and other depositories in the Detroit-Ann Arbor area, and the extensive holdings of the Wisconsin State Historical Society Library, including the James Duane Doty papers and the Henry Dodge papers. The Library has manuscripts and microfilm copies of the American Fur Company papers which provided a valuable perspective on the territorial governors' role in Indian affairs. Nevertheless I have relied foremost on the published papers of the governors and other important individuals and of governmental agencies. In studying the development of the territories, the primary sources in the various state historical *Collections* and *Publications* were especially useful, and the most important ones are listed below. Some of the newspapers published in the territories of the First Empire were also occasionally helpful.

In addition to the federal publications cited below, the standard sources have been used extensively. These include the *Annals of Congress*, *Congressional Debates*, *Congressional Globe* and *Congressional Record*. The *House Documents* and *Senate Documents* were extremely valuable to the study of both territorial government and Indian affairs, particularly in the period after about 1850, while the *American State Papers* were useful for studying Indian affairs in the early national period. Finally, for the territories whose papers have yet to be edited and published in *The Territorial Papers of the United States* the author has used the microfilmed Territorial Papers of the State and Interior Department collections in the National Archives.

For any analysis of the evolution of the territorial system, David W. Parker's *Calendar of Papers in Washington Archives Relating to the Territories of the United States (to 1873)*, published by the Carnegie Institute in 1911, is an indispensable guide. In studying the legal development of the system at the federal level, the manuscript House and Senate bills in the National Archives were used whenever possible. The published *House Bills* and *Senate Bills* in the Library of Congress were used as necessary, as were the official proceedings of Congress mentioned above. The *United States Statutes at Large* were, of course, utilized thoroughly.

PRIMARY SOURCES:

FEDERAL PUBLICATIONS

Biographical Directory of the American Congress, 1774–1961. Washington, 1961.

The Territorial Papers of the United States. Carter, Clarence E., ed., 26 vols., Washington, 1934–1962.

Horne, Frank B., and Hurley, Margaret F., *Federal Indian Law.* Washington, 1958.

Historical Statistics of the United States, Colonial Times to 1957. Washington, 1960.

Historical Statistics of the United States: Continuation to 1962 and Revisions. Washington, 1965.

Journals of the Continental Congress, 1774–1789. 34 vols., Washington, 1904–1937.

Indian Land Cessions in the United States. Royce, Charles C., comp., Washington, 1900.

Territorial Expansion of the United States. Washington, 1900.

The Organic Acts of the Territories of the United States. Washington, 1900. Sen. Doc. 148, 56 Cong., 1 sess.

The Federal and State Constitutions, Colonial Charters, and Other Organic Laws of the States, Territories, and Colonies Now or Heretofore Forming the United States of America. Thorpe, Francis Newton, comp., 7 vols., Washington, 1909.

TERRITORIAL LAWS

Fragments of the Mississippi Session Laws Passed at the First Session of the Second General Assembly of Mississippi Territory, December, 1802 to March, 1803. Chicago, Illinois, 1939.

Laws of the Mississippi Territory [September 1799 to May 1800]. Beauvoir Community, Mississippi, 1948.

Laws of the Territory of Michigan. 4 vols., Lansing, Michigan, 1871–1884.

Sargent's Code: A Collection of the Original Laws of the Mississippi Territory Enacted 1799–1800 by Governor Winthrop Sargent and the Territorial Judges. Jackson, Mississippi, 1939.

Statutes at Large of Pennsylvania, 1682–1801. Philadelphia, Pennsylvania, 1898.

Statutes at Large . . . of Virginia . . . 1619–1792. W. W. Hening, comp., 13 vols., Richmond, Virginia, 1819–1823.

The Laws of Indiana Territory, 1801–1809. Philbrick, Francis S., ed., *Collections of the Illinois State Historical Library*, XXI, Law Series II. Springfield, Illinois, 1930.

The Laws of Indiana Territory, 1809–1816. Ewbank, Louis B., and Riker, Dorothy, eds., *Indiana Historical Collections,* XX. Indianapolis, Indiana, 1934.

The Laws of Illinois Territory, 1809–1818. Philbrick, Francis S., ed., *Collections of the Illinois State Historical Library*, XXV, Law Series, V. Springfield, Illinois, 1950.

The Laws of the Northwest Territory, 1788–1800. Pease, Theodore C., ed., *Collections of the Illinois State Historical Library*, XVII, Law Series, I. Springfield, Illinois, 1925.

The Mississippi Territorial Session Laws of May 2, 1802. Chicago, Illinois, 1938.

The Statutes of Ohio and the Northwestern Territory. . . . Chase, Salmon P., ed., Cincinnati, Ohio, 1833.

OTHER PUBLISHED PRIMARY SOURCES

Alaska Statehood Commission for the Alaska Constitutional Convention, *Constitutional Studies.* 3 vols., [Juneau], 1955.

Benton, Thomas Hart, ed., *Abridgment of the Debates of Congress, From 1789 to 1856.* 16 vols., New York, New York, 1856–1861.

Blount, William, *The Blount Journal, 1790–1796. The Proceedings of Government over the Territory of the United States South of the River Ohio, William Blount, Esquire, in his Executive Department as Governor.* Facsimile, Nashville, Tennessee, 1955.

Boyd, Julian P., ed., *The Papers of Thomas Jefferson.* Princeton, New Jersey, 1950.

Burnet, Jacob, *Notes on the Early Settlement of the North-Western Territory*. Cincinnati, Ohio, 1847.

Burnett, Edmund C., ed., *Letters of Members of the Continental Congress*. 8 vols., Washington, 1921–1935.

Cass, Lewis, "Indians of North America," in *North American Review*, XXII n.s. (January, 1826), 53–119, and XXIV n.s. (April, 1827), 365–442.

——, *Considerations on the Present State of the Indians and Their Removal West of the Mississipi*. Boston, Mass., 1828, and in *North American Review*, XXX n.s. (January, 1830).

Colorado Territorial Officers and Members and Officers of the Legislative Assemblies Under Territorial Government. n.p., 1959.

Dillon, John B., *A History of Indiana . . . to 1856*. Indianapolis, Indiana, 1859.

Esarey, Logan, ed., [Indiana Territory] *Governors Messages and Letters*. [William Henry Harrison, Acting Governor John Gibson, and Thomas Posey.] 2 vols., Indianapolis, Indiana, 1922.

Fitzpatrick, John C., ed., *The Writings of George Washington from the Original Manuscript Sources, 1745–1799*. 39 vols., Washington, 1931–1944.

Ford, Paul L., ed., *The Works of Thomas Jefferson*. 12 vols., New York, New York, 1904–1905.

Hamilton, Stanislaus M., ed., *The Writings of James Monroe*. 7 vols., New York, New York, 1898–1903.

Harrison, William Henry, "A Discourse on the Aborigines of the Ohio Valley. . . ," in the Ohio Historical and Philosophical Society *Transactions*, I (1839), 217–67. Also published privately under the same title, Boston, Mass., 1840.

Hulbert, Archer Butler, ed., *The Records of the Original Proceedings of the Ohio Company*. 2 vols., Marietta, Ohio, 1917–1918.

Journals of the General Assembly of Indiana Territory, 1805–1815. Thornbrough, Gayle, and Riker, Dorothy, eds. *Indiana Historical Collections*, XXXII. Indianapolis, Indiana, 1950.

King, Charles R., ed., *The Life and Correspondence of Rufus King, Comprising His Letters, Private and Official, His Public Documents and His Speeches*. 2 vols., New York, New York, 1894.

Otero, Miguel Antonio, *My Nine Years as Governor of the Territory of New Mexico, 1897–1906*. Albuquerque, New Mexico, 1940.

Quaife, Milo M., ed., *The Movement for Statehood, 1845–46*. Vol. XXVI Wisconsin State Historical Society *Collections*. Madison, Wisconsin, 1918.

——, *The Convention of 1846*. Vol. XXVII, *ibid*., Madison, Wisconsin, 1919.

——, *The Struggle over Ratification, 1846–47*. Vol. XXVIII, *ibid*., Madison, Wisconsin, 1920.

———, *The Attainment of Statehood.* Vol. XXIX, *ibid.*, Madison, Wisconsin, 1928.

Rantaul, Robert S., comp., "The Part Taken by Essex County in the Organization and Settlement of the Northwest Territory," in *Essex Institute Historical Collections,* XXV (1888), 165–243.

Richardson, James D., ed., *A Compilation of the Messages and Papers of the Presidents, 1789–1897.* 20 vols., Washington, 1917–1920.

Smith, William Henry, ed., *The St. Clair Papers. The Life and Public Services of Arthur St. Clair . . . with His Correspondence and Other Papers.* 2 vols., Cincinnati, Ohio, 1882.

Staples, William R., ed., *Rhode Island in the Continental Congress, with the Journal of the Convention that Adopted the Constitution, 1765–1790.* Providence, R. I., 1870.

The Mississippi Archives, 1798–1803. Executive Journals of Governor Winthrop Sargent and Governor William Charles Cole Claiborne. Nashville, Tennessee, 1905.

Washburne, E. B., ed., *The Edwards Papers; Being a Portion of the Collection of . . . Ninian Edwards, . . Presented to the Chicago Historical Society . . . by his Son. . . .* Chicago, Illinois, 1884.

SECONDARY SOURCES:

BOOKS

Abernethy, Thomas P., *From Frontier to Plantation in Tennessee: A Study in Frontier Democracy.* Chapel Hill, North Carolina, 1932.

———, *The Formative Period in Alabama, 1815–1828.* Montgomery, Alabama, 1922.

———, *The South in the New Nation, 1789–1819.* Baton Rouge, Louisiana, 1961.

Alderman, L. A., *The Identification of the Society of the Cincinnati with the First Authorized Settlement of the Northwest Territory at Marietta, Ohio, April Seventh, 1787.* Marietta, Ohio, 1888.

Alvord, Clarence W., *The Illinois Country, 1673–1818.* Springfield, Illinois, 1920.

Atherton, Lewis, *Main Street on the Middle Border.* Bloomington, Indiana, 1954.

Austin, Oscar P., *Steps in the Expansion of Our Territory.* New York, New York, 1903.

Avery, Mary W., *History and Government of the State of Washington.* Seattle, Washington, 1961.

Bakeless, John, *Lewis and Clark, Partners in Discovery.* New York, New York, 1947.

Baker, James H., and LeRoy L. Haffen, *History of Colorado.* 5 vols., Denver, Colorado, 1927.

Bancroft, H. H., *History of the Pacific States of North America.* 17 vols., San Francisco, Calif., 1886–1897.

Barnhart, John D., *Valley of Democracy. The Frontier Versus the Plantation in the Ohio Valley, 1775–1818.* Bloomington, Indiana, 1953.

Barrett, Jay Amos, *Evolution of the Ordinance of 1787, with an Account of the Earlier Plans for the Government of the Northwest Territory.* New York, New York, 1891.

Blegan, Theodore C., *Minnesota, A History of the State.* Minneapolis, Minn., 1963.

Blume, W. W., and Brown, E. G., *Digests and Lists Pertaining to the Development of Law, 1787–1912.* 6 vols., n.p. [Ann Arbor, Michigan, University Microfilm, Xerox], 1955.

Bond, Beverley W., Jr., *The Civilization of the Old Northwest, A Study of Political, Social, and Economic Development. 1788–1812.* New York, New York, 1934.

———, *The Foundations of Ohio.* Columbus, Ohio, 1941.

Buck, Solon Justus, *Illinois in 1818.* Springfield, Illinois, 1917.

Buley, R. Caryle, *The Old Northwest: Pioneer Period, 1815–1840.* 2 vols., Indianapolis, Indiana, 1950.

Burnett, Edmund Cody, *The Continental Congress.* New York, New York, 1941.

Carr, Lucien, *Missouri, A Bone of Contention.* New York, New York, [1888] 1894.

Caruso, John Anthony, *The Great Lakes Frontier.* Indianapolis, Indiana, 1960.

Chittenden, Hiram Martin, *The American Fur Trade of the Far West.* 2 vols., New York, New York, 1935.

Coles, Edward, *History of the Ordinance of 1787.* Philadelphia, Pennsylvania, 1856.

Comford, Benjamin F., *Lewis Cass and the Indian Treaties. A Monograph on the Indian Relations of the Northwest Territory from 1813 to 1831.* Detroit, Michigan, 1923.

Corey, Lewis, *The Decline of American Capitalism.* New York, New York, 1935.

Corwin, Edward S., *American Constitutional History.* New York, New York, 1964.

Cutler, William P., *The Ordinance of July 13, 1787, for the Government of the Territory Northwest of the River Ohio.* Marietta, Ohio, 1887.

Dill, William C., *Statehood for Hawaii.* Philadelphia, Pennsylvania, 1949.

Donaldson, Thomas, *The Public Domain.* Washington, 1884.

Downes, Randolph C., *Frontier Ohio, 1788–1803.* Columbus, Ohio, 1935.

Edwards, Ninian Wirt, *History of Illinois, from 1778 to 1833; and Life and Times of Ninian Edwards.* Springfield, Illinois, 1870.

Esarey, Logan, *A History of Indiana.* 2 vols., Indianapolis, Indiana, 1915–1918.

———, *et al., Courts and Lawyers of Indiana.* 3 vols., Indianapolis, Indiana, 1916.

Farrand, Max, *The Legislation of Congress for the Government of the Organized Territories of the United States, 1789–1895.* Newark, New Jersey, 1896.

Foreman, Grant, *Advancing the Frontier, 1830–1860.* Norman, Oklahoma, 1933.

———, *A History of Oklahoma.* Norman, Oklahoma, 1942.

———, *Indian Removal. The Emigration of the Five Civilized Tribes of Indians.* Norman, Oklahoma, 1932.

Fritz, Henry E., *The Movement for Indian Assimilation, 1860–1890.* Philadelphia, Pennsylvania, 1963.

Gayarre, Charles Etienne Arthur, *History of Louisiana.* 4 vols., New York, New York, 1854–1866.

Gittinger, Roy, *The Formation of the State of Oklahoma (1803–1906).* Berkeley, Calif., 1917. Norman, Oklahoma, 1939.

Greene, Jack P., *The Quest for Power. The Lower Houses of Assembly in the Southern Royal Colonies, 1689–1776.* Chapel Hill, N. C., 1963.

Harmon, George Dewey, *Sixty Years of Indian Affairs. Political, Economic, and Diplomatic, 1789–1850.* Chapel Hill, N. C., 1941.

Havighurst, Walter, *Wilderness for Sale; The Story of the First Western Land Rush.* New York, New York, 1956.

Hicks, John D., *The Constitutions of the Northwest States.* Lincoln, Nebraska, 1924.

Hinsdale, B. A., *The Old Northwest with a View of the Thirteen Colonies as Constituted by the Royal Charters.* New York, New York, 1888.

———, *The Ordinance of 1787; Origins, Features, and Results.* Akron, Ohio, 1887.

Hoopes, Alban, W., *Indian Affairs and Their Administration with Special Reference to the Far West, 1849–1860.* Philadelphia, Pennsylvania, 1932

Horn, Calvin, *New Mexico's Troubled Years: The Story of the Early Territorial Governors.* Albuquerque, New Mexico, 1963.

Houck, Louis, *A History of Missouri from the Earliest Explorations . . . Until the Admission of the State into the Union.* 3 vols., Chicago, Illinois, 1908.

Hulbert, Archer Butler, *Ohio in the Time of the Confederation.* Marietta, Ohio, 1918.

Jacobs, James Ripley, *Tarnished Warrior, Major-General James Wilkinson.* New York, New York, 1938.

Jensen, Merrill, *The New Nation. A History of the United States During the Confederation, 1781–1789*. New York, New York, 1950, 1958.
———, *The Articles of Confederation. An Interpretation of the Social-Constitutional History of the American Revolution, 1774–1781*. Madison, Wisconsin, 1940, 1962.
Lamar, Howard R., *Dakota Territory, 1861–1889, A Study of Frontier Politics*. New Haven, Conn., 1956, 1966.
———, *The Far Southwest, 1846–1912. A Territorial History*. New Haven, Conn., 1966.
McCarty, Dwight G., *Territorial Governors of the Old Northwest*. Iowa City, Iowa, 1910.
McLaughlin, Andrew C., *Lewis Cass*. New York, New York, 1891, 1899.
McLaughlin, Constance Green, *Washington, Volume I, Village and Capital 1800–1878. Washington, Volume II, Capital City 1879–1950*. Princeton, New Jersey, 1962, 1963.
McMaster, John Bach, *A History of the People of the United States, From the Revolution to the Civil War*. 8 vols., New York, New York, 1883, 1911, 1914.
McReynolds, Edwin C., *Oklahoma: A History of the Sooner State*. Norman, Oklahoma, 1954.
Mack, Effie Mona, *Nevada. A History of the State from the Earliest Times Through the Civil War*. Glendale, Calif., 1936.
Malin, James, *Indian Policy and Westward Expansion*. Lawrence, Kansas, 1921.
Masterson, William H., *William Blount*. Baton Rouge. La., 1954.
Merrian, John M., *The Legislative History of the Ordinance of 1787*. Worcester, Mass., 1888.
Peake, Ora Brooks, *A History of the United States Indian Factory System, 1795–1822*. Denver, Colorado, 1954.
Pease, Theodore Calvin, *The Laws of the Northwest Territory, 1788–1800*. Springfield, Illinois, 1925.
Philbrick, Francis S., *The Laws of Indiana Territory, 1801–1809*. Springfield, Illinois, 1930.
———, *The Laws of Illinois Territory, 1809–1818*. Springfield, Illinois, 1950.
———, *The Rise of the West, 1754–1830*. New York, New York, 1965.
Pomeroy, Earl S., *The Territories and the United States, 1861–1890. Studies in Colonial Administration*. Philadelphia, Pennsylvania, 1947.
Poole, William Frederick, *The Ordinance of 1787, and Dr. Manasseh Cutler as an Agent in its Formation*. Cambridge, Mass., 1876
Porter, Kenneth Wiggins, *John Jacob Astor: Business Man*. 2 vols., Cambridge, Mass., 1931.
Porter, Kirk H., *A History of Suffrage in the United States*. Chicago, Illinois, 1918.

Pound, Merritt B., *Benjamin Hawkins—Indian Agent.* Athens, Georgia, 1951.

Powell, William Henry, *List of Officers of the Army of the United States from 1779 to 1900. . . .* New York, New York, 1900.

Priest, Loring B., *Uncle Sam's Step Children: The Reformation of United States Indian Policy, 1865–1887.* New Brunswick, New Jersey, 1942.

Prucha, Francis Paul, *American Indian Policy in the Formative Years: The Indian Trade and Intercourse Acts, 1790–1834.* Cambridge, Mass., 1962.

Sacks, A., *Be It Enacted: The Creation of the Territory of Arizona.* Phoenix, Arizona, 1964.

Samonte, Vedasto Jose, *The American System of Colonial Administration.* Manila, The Philippines, [1925].

Schumpeter, Joseph A., *Imperialism and Social Classes.* New York, New York, 1951.

Smith, Alice Elizabeth, *James Duane Doty, Frontier Promoter.* Madison, Wisconsin, 1954.

Smith, Joseph H., *Appeals to the Privy Council from the American Plantations.* New York, New York, 1950.

Smith, William L. G., *Fifty Years of Public Life. The Life and Times of Lewis Cass.* New York, New York, 1856.

Snow, Alpheus H., *The Administration of Dependencies. A Study of the Evolution of the Federal Empire, with Special Reference to American Colonial Problems.* New York, New York, 1902.

———, *The Question of Aborigines in the Law and Practice of Nations.* New York, New York, 1921.

Sosin, Jack M., *The Revolutionary Frontier, 1763–1783.* New York, New York, 1967.

Stewart, Dora Ann, *The Government and Development of Oklahoma Territory.* n.p. [Norman, Oklahoma], 1933.

Strong, Moses M., *History of the Territory of Wisconsin From 1836 to 1848.* Madison, Wisconsin, 1885.

Thomas, David Yancey, *A History of Military Government in Newly Acquired Territories.* New York, New York, 1904.

Thomas, William Sturgis, *Members of the Society of the Cincinnati, Original, Hereditary and Honorary.* New York, New York, 1929.

Thornton, A. P., *Doctrines of Imperialism.* New York, New York, 1965.

Van Alstyne, R. W., *The Rising American Empire.* Oxford, England, 1960.

White, Leonard D., *The Federalists, A Study in Administrative History, 1789–1801.* New York, New York, 1948.

———, *The Jacksonians, A Study in Administrative History, 1829–1861.* New York, New York, 1954.

———, *The Jeffersonians, A Study in Administrative History, 1801–1829.* New York, New York, 1951.

———, *The Republican Era, A Study in Administrative History, 1861–1901*. New York, New York, 1958.

White, Lonnie J., *Politics on the Southwestern Frontier: Arkansas, 1819–1836*. Memphis, Tennessee, 1964.

Williams, William Appleman, *The Contours of American History*. Cleveland, Ohio, 1961. Chicago, Illinois, 1966.

Williams, Mary Floyd, *History of the San Francisco Committee of Vigilance of 1851. A Study of Social Control on the California Frontier in the Days of the Gold Rush*. Berkeley, Calif., 1921.

Williamson, Chilton, *American Suffrage. From Property to Democracy*. Princeton, New Jersey, 1960.

Willoughby, William F., *Territories and Dependencies of the United States, Their Government and Administration*. New York, New York, 1905.

Wilson, Frazer Ells, *Arthur St. Clair, Rugged Ruler of the Old Northwest: an Epic of the American Frontier*. Richmond, Virginia, 1944.

Woodford, Frank B., *Lewis Cass. The Last Jeffersonian*. New Brunswick, New Jersey, 1950.

Wright, Marcus J., *Some Account of the Life and Services of William Blount. . . .* Washington, 1884.

Young, William T., *The Life of Lewis Cass*. Detroit, Michigan, 1852.

ARTICLES

Attig, Chester J., "Some Governmental Problems in the Northwest Territory, 1787–1803." *Transactions of the Illinois State Historical Society for the Year 1921* (1922), 75–86.

Bailyn, Bernard, "The Origins of American Politics." *Perspectives in American History*, I (1967), 7–120.

Beals, Ellis, "Arthur St. Clair, Western Pennsylvania's Leading Citizen, 1764–1818." *Western Pennsylvania Historical Magazine*, XXII (1929), 75–96, 175–96.

Bond, Beverley W., Jr., "An American Experiment in Colonial Government." *Mississippi Valley Historical Review*, XV (September, 1928), 221–35.

Carter, Clarence E., "Apprenticeship for Statehood." Department of State *Bulletin*, XII (June, 1945), 1109–14.

———, "Colonialism in Continental United States." *South Atlantic Quarterly*, XLVII (January, 1948), 17–28.

Doherty, Herbert J., Jr., "The Governorship of Andrew Jackson." *The Florida Historical Quarterly*, XXXIII (July, 1954), 3–31.

Downes, Randolph C., "The Statehood Contest in Ohio." *Mississippi Valley Historical Review*, XVIII (September, 1931), 155–71.

———, "Thomas Jefferson and the Removal of Governor Arthur St. Clair in 1802." *Ohio Archaeological and Historical Publications*, XXXVI (1927), 62–77.

Dunn, W. Ross, "Education in Territorial Ohio." *Ohio Archaeological and Historical Publications*, XXXV (1926), 322–79.

Dyer, Albion Morris, "First Ownership of Ohio Lands." *The New England Historical and Genealogical Register*, 64 (1910), 167–80, 263–82, 256–69; 65 (1911), 51–62, 139–50, 220–31.

Graham, A. A., "Legislation in the Northwest Territory." *Ohio State Archaeological and Historical Society Quarterly* (1888), 303–18.

Greenbaum, Fred, "Capitalism and the American Frontier." *New Politics*, IV (Fall, 1965), 56–60.

Hoffnagle, Warren Miles, "The Road to Fame: William Henry Harrison and National Policy in the Northwest From Tippecanoe to River Rasin." *Papers on the War of 1812 in the Northwest* (1959).

Horsman, Reginald, "American Indian Policy in the Old Northwest, 1783–1812." *The William and Mary Quarterly*, XVIII (January, 1961), 35–53.

Jenks, William L., "Territorial Legislation by Governor and Judges." *Mississippi Valley Historical Review*, V (June, 1918), 36–50.

Johansen, Dorothy, "A Tentative Appraisal of Territorial Government in Oregon." *Pacific Historical Review*, XVIII (November, 1949), 485–99.

Langhorst, Windred B., "The Puritanic Influence in the Northwest Territory, 1788–1803." *Ohio Archaeological and Historical Publications*, XLII (1933), 409–45.

Laning, J. F., "The Evolution of Ohio Counties." *Ohio Archaeological and Historical Publications*, V (1897), 326–50.

Lynd, Staughton, "The Compromise of 1787." *Political Science Quarterly*, LXXXI (June, 1966), 225–50.

McLaughlin, A. C., "The Influence of Governor Cass on the Development of the Northwest." *Papers of the American Historical Association*, III (1889), 67–83.

Meyerholz, Charles, "Federal Supervision over the Territories of the United States." *Beitrage zur Kultur- und Universalgeschichte*, VI (Leipzig, 1908), 83–246.

Otis, D. S., "History of the Allotment Policy." H.R. 7902, pt. 9, 73 Cong., 2 sess. (1934), 428–89.

Painter, Harry M., "The Birth of a State." *Building a State: Washington, 1889–1939*. Edited by O. B. Sperlin, *et al.* Tacoma, Washington, 1940, 44–60.

Pease, Theodore C., "The Ordinance of 1787." *Mississippi Valley Historical Review*, XXV (September, 1938), 167–80.

Prescott, Frank W., "The Executive Veto in American States." *Western Political Quarterly*, II (March, 1950), 88–112.

———, "The Executive Veto in the Southern States." *Journal of Politics*, IX (November, 1948), 659–75.

Sears, Alfred B., "The Political Philosophy of Arthur St. Clair." *Ohio State Archaeological and Historical Quarterly*, XLIX (1940), 41–57.

Spence, Clark C., "The Territorial Officers of Montana, 1864–89." *Pacific Historical Review*, XXX (May, 1961), 123–36.

Still, Bayrd, "An Interpretation of the Statehood Process, 1800 to 1850." *Mississippi Valley Historical Review*, XXIII (September, 1936), 189–204.

Webster, Homer J., "William Henry Harrison's Administration of Indiana Territory." *Indiana Historical Society Publications*, IV (1907), 177–297.

Wells, Merle W., "Territorial Government in the Inland Empire." *Pacific Northwest Quarterly*, XLIV (April, 1953), 8–87.

Whitfield, James B., "All Governors of Territorial Florida Had Been Members of Congress." *Florida Historical Quarterly*, XXV (1947), 277–78.

Williams, William A., "The Vicious Cycle of American Imperialism." *New Politics*, IV (Fall, 1965), 48–55.

UNPUBLISHED THESES

Barber, William D., "The West in National Politics, 1784–1804." Ph.D. dissertation. University of Wisconsin, 1961.

Boyd, William M., "The Administration of Territories and Island Possessions by the United States." Ph.D. dissertation. University of Michigan, 1944.

Hall, John D., "The Administration of United States Territories and Island Possessions." Ph.D. dissertation. Syracuse University, 1948.

Hutchinson, William Thomas, "The Bounty Lands of the American Revolution in Ohio." Ph.D. dissertation. University of Chicago, 1927.

Jarrold, Rachel Marian, "Arthur St. Clair, Governor of the Northwest Territory." M.A. thesis, History. University of Illinois, 1901.

Neil, William MacFarlane, "The Territorial Governor in the Rocky Mountain West, 1861–89." Ph.D. dissertation. University of Chicago, 1952.

Owens, Kenneth Nelson, "Frontier Governors: A Study of the Territorial Executives in the History of Washington, Idaho, Montana, Wyoming and Dakota Territories." Ph.D. dissertation. University of Minnesota, 1959.

Patton, Clifford Wheeler, "Robert J. Walker, Governor of Kansas Territory." M.A. thesis, History. University of Illinois, 1932.

Robbins, David Earl, "Government in New Mexico, 1846–1852." M.A. thesis, History. University of Illinois, 1952.

Smurr, John Welling, "Territorial Constitutions; A Legal History of the Frontier Governments Erected by Congress in the American West, 1787–1900." Ph.D. dissertation. University of Indiana, 1960.

Valentine, Elvin L., "The American Territorial Governor." Ph.D. dissertation. University of Wisconsin, 1928.

Wilson, Gordon L., "Arthur St. Clair and the Administration of the Old Northwest Territory, 1788–1802." Ph.D. dissertation. University of Southern California, 1957.

Wright, Sidney Walter, "A Study of the Executives in the Early State Constitutions." M.A. thesis, History. University of Illinois, 1910.

INDEX

Index